the Unofficial Guide® to

London

3rd Edition

the Unofficial Guide® to London

3rd Edition

Lesley Logan

Wiley Publishing, Inc.

To Tom and Nora

Please note that prices fluctuate in the course of time, and travel information changes under the impact of many factors that influence the travel industry. We therefore suggest that you write or call ahead for confirmation when making your travel plans. Every effort has been made to ensure the accuracy of information throughout this book, and the contents of this publication are believed correct at the time of printing. Nevertheless, the publishers cannot accept responsibility for errors or omissions or for changes in details given in this guide or for the consequences of any reliance on the information provided by the same. Assessments of attractions and so forth are based upon the author's own experience, and therefore, descriptions given in this guide necessarily contain an element of subjective opinion, which may not reflect the publisher's opinion or dictate a reader's own experience on another occasion. Readers are invited to write the publisher with ideas, comments, and suggestions for future editions.

Published by:

John Wiley & Sons, Inc.

111 River Street

Hoboken, NJ 07030

Produced by Menasha Ridge Press
Cover design by Michael J. Freeland
Interior design by Michele Laseau

For information on our other products and services or to obtain technical support, please contact our Customer Care Department within the U.S. at (800) 762-2974, outside the U.S. at (317) 572-3993, or fax (317) 572-4002.

John Wiley & Sons, Inc. also publishes its books in a variety of electronic formats. Some content that appears in print may not be available in electronic formats.

ISBN 0-7645-4065-3

ISSN 1521-4907

Manufactured in the United States of America

5   4   3   2   1

Contents

About the Authors and Contributors

Lesley Logan is a freelance writer who has worked in publishing over the years as a nonfiction ghostwriter, publicity copywriter, and editor. Originally from New York, she has lived in London for many years.

Richard Ehrlich, who wrote the chapter on dining, has been writing about food and drink in major United Kingdom magazines and newspapers since 1988. His work appears regularly in *The Independent* on Sunday, *The Guardian,* and *Time Out.* An American, Richard has lived in London since 1974.

Acknowledgments

First and foremost I want to thank Tom and Nora Logan without whom nothing, least of all this book, would be possible.

And to Bob Sehlinger and Molly Merkle of Menasha Ridge Press, thanks for a wonderful assignment. I want to also thank Gabriela Oates and Mopsy Gascon for all their work in this third edition.

Many heartfelt thanks to the legions of anonymous curators, cab drivers, London Transport people, London Tourist Board employees, shopkeepers, waiters, concierges, hotel managers, bellhops, B&B owners, and people on the street, who generously gave me tips, information, guided tours, and unfailingly pointed me in the right direction.

I am grateful to all the family and friends who stayed at our house and regaled me with tales from the tourist trail, as well as forced me out onto it. They are too numerous to mention, but they know who they are, and they know they are welcome back anytime.

Thanks to all those who helped with the book: Andy Craft, Tony Heiberg, Emma Littlewood, Tracy Thompkins, Ben Feldman, and, of course, Richard Ehrlich, who has written the restaurant section for these three editions.

I also appreciated the letters and evaluations I received from so many readers, the kind and the critical. Your suggestions and your generosity in taking the time to write made me grateful to update the book, to make right some wrongs, and to learn from your own London experiences.

—Lesley Logan

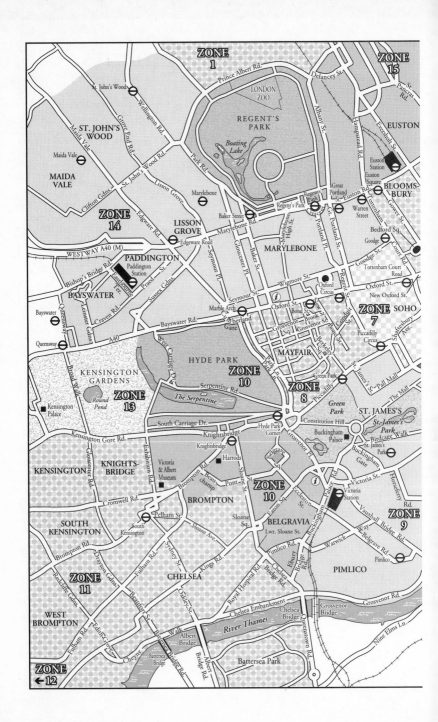

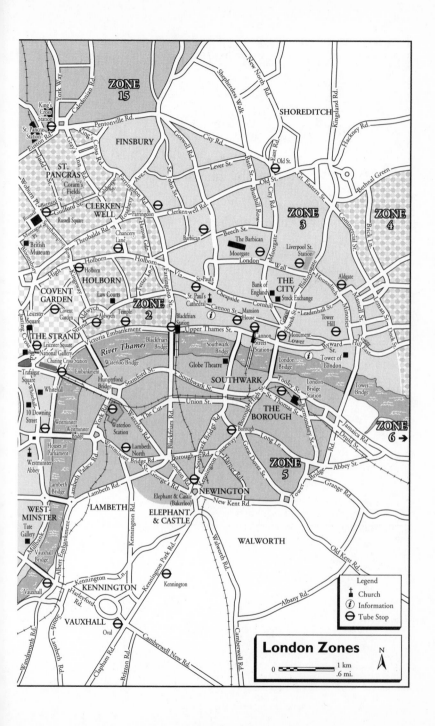

ZONE 15

King's Cross Station

St. Pancras Station

FINSBURY

SHOREDITCH

ST. PANCRAS
Coram's Fields

CLERKEN WELL

British Museum

ZONE 3

ZONE 4

HOLBORN

COVENT GARDEN

ZONE 2

THE CITY

Barbican

The Barbican

Moorgate London

Bank of England
Stock Exchange

St. Paul's Cathedral

Law Courts

Blackfriars Station

River Thames

Blackfriars Bridge

Southwark Bridge

Globe Theatre

Cannon Street Station

Monument

Tower Hill

Tower of London

Tower Bridge

THE STRAND

National Gallery

Charing Cross Station

Waterloo Bridge

Hungerford Bridge

SOUTHWARK

London Bridge

London Bridge Station

10 Downing Street

Whitehall

Waterloo Station

THE BOROUGH

ZONE 6 →

Westminster Bridge

Houses of Parliament

Westminster Abbey

ZONE 5

Lambeth Bridge

NEWINGTON

Elephant & Castle (Bakerloo)

WEST MINSTER

Tate Gallery

Vauxhall Bridge

LAMBETH

ELEPHANT & CASTLE

WALWORTH

Vauxhall

KENNINGTON

Kennington

Legend

† Church
ⓘ Information
⊖ Tube Stop

VAUXHALL

Oval

London Zones

N

0 — 1 km
.6 mi.

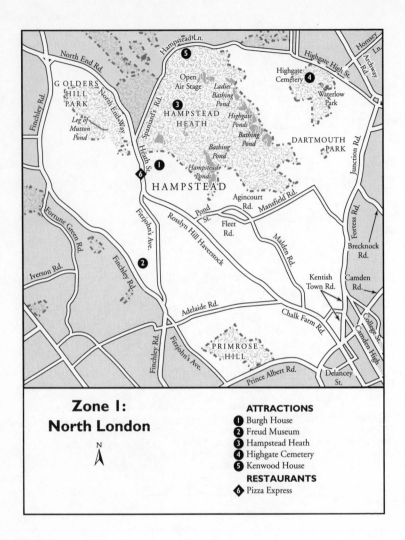

Zone 1:
North London

N

ATTRACTIONS
1 Burgh House
2 Freud Museum
3 Hampstead Heath
4 Highgate Cemetery
5 Kenwood House
RESTAURANTS
6 Pizza Express

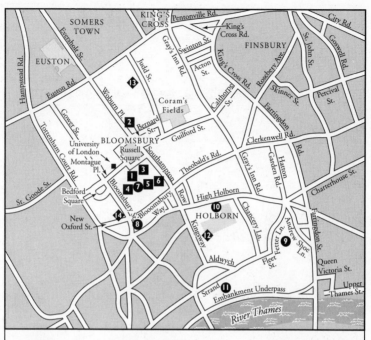

Zone 2: Bloomsbury and Holborn

N

ACCOMMODATIONS
1. Grange White Hall Hotel
2. Meridien Russell
3. The Montague on the Gardens
4. Morgan Hotel
5. Ruskin Hotel
6. St. Margaret's Hotel

ATTRACTIONS
7. British Museum
8. Dickens House

ATTRACTIONS
9. Dr. Johnson's House
10. Sir John Soane's Museum
11. Somerset House

RESTAURANTS
12. Bank
13. North Sea Fish Restaurant
14. Wagamama

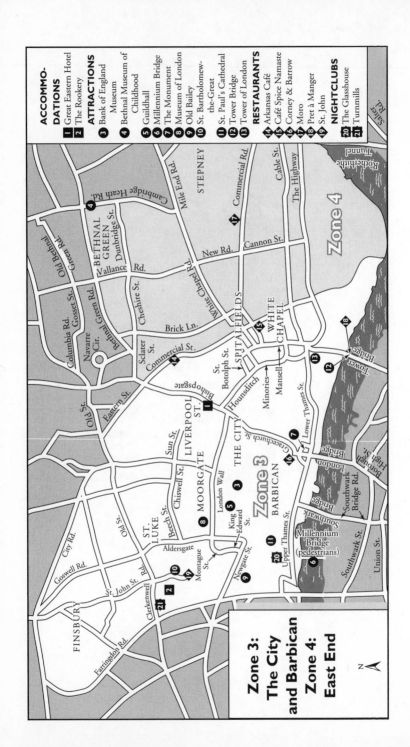

ACCOMMO-DATIONS
1 Great Eastern Hotel
2 The Rookery

ATTRACTIONS
3 Bank of England Museum
4 Bethnal Museum of Childhood
5 Guildhall
6 Millennium Bridge
7 The Monument
8 Museum of London
9 Old Bailey
10 St. Bartholomew-the-Great
11 St. Paul's Cathedral
12 Tower Bridge
13 Tower of London

RESTAURANTS
14 Arkansas Café
15 Café Spice Namaste
16 Corney & Barrow
17 Moro
18 Pret à Manger
19 St. John

NIGHTCLUBS
20 The Glasshouse
21 Turnmills

Zone 3:
The City
and Barbican
Zone 4:
East End

N

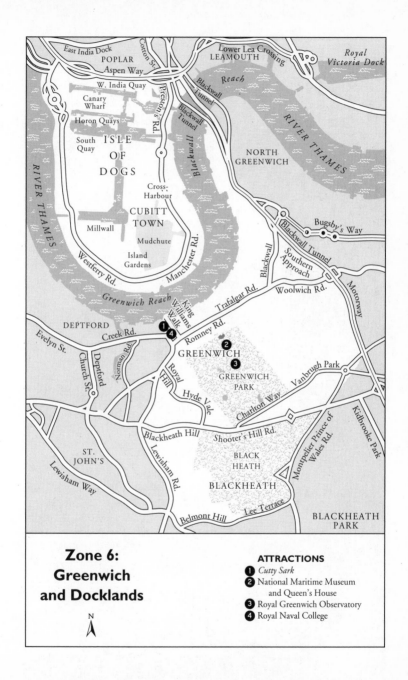

Zone 6:
Greenwich
and Docklands

N

ATTRACTIONS

1. *Cutty Sark*
2. National Maritime Museum and Queen's House
3. Royal Greenwich Observatory
4. Royal Naval College

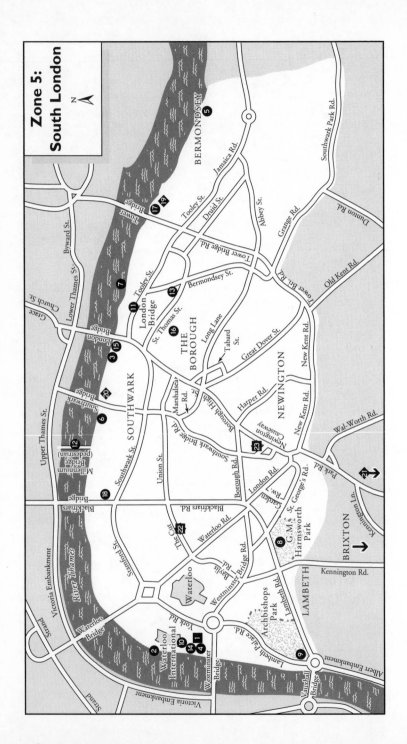

Zone 5:
South London

ACCOMMODATIONS
1 London Marriott Hotel
County Hall

ATTRACTIONS
2 The British Airways London Eye
3 Clink Exhibition
4 Dali Universe
5 Design Museum
6 The Globe Theatre
7 HMS *Belfast*
8 Imperial War Museum
9 Lambeth Palace
10 London Aquarium
11 London Dungeon
12 Millennium Bridge

ATTRACTIONS
13 Old Operating Theatre,
Museum, and Herb Garrett
14 Saatchi Gallery
15 Southwark Cathedral
16 Tate Modern
17 Tower Bridge

RESTAURANTS
18 Baltic
19 Blue Print Café
20 Cantina Vinopolis
21 Livebait

NIGHTCLUBS
22 The Fridge Bar
23 Ministry of Sound

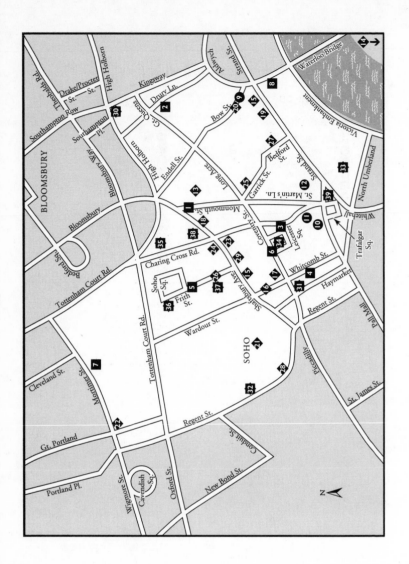

Zone 7:
Soho and the West End

ACCOMMODATIONS

1 The Charlotte Street Hotel
2 Covent Garden Hotel
3 The Fielding Hotel
4 Hazlitt's
5 The Radisson Edwardian Hampshire
6 The Radisson Edwardian Pastoria
7 Sanderson
8 The Savoy

ATTRACTIONS

9 London Transport Museum
10 National Gallery
11 National Portrait Gallery
12 St. Martin-in-the-Fields

RESTAURANTS

13 Belgo
14 fish!
15 Caffé Carluccio's
16 Chez Gérard
17 Chuen Cheng Ku
18 The Ivy
19 Joe Allen

RESTAURANTS

20 Livebait
21 Masala Zone
22 Mash
23 Mr. Kong
24 Pollo
25 Prospect Grill
26 Richard Corrigan at Lindsay House
27 Rules
28 Veeraswamy
29 Wagamama

NIGHTCLUBS

30 Browns
31 Café de Paris
32 Emporium
33 Heaven
34 Hippodrome
35 Metro Club
36 Pizza Express
37 Ronnie Scott's
38 Salsa!
39 Zoo Bar

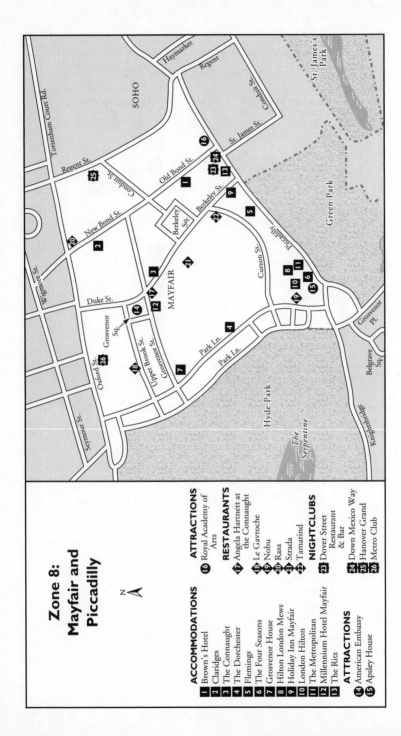

Zone 8:
Mayfair and Piccadilly

N

ACCOMMODATIONS
1. Brown's Hotel
2. Claridges
3. The Connaught
4. The Dorchester
5. Flemings
6. The Four Seasons
7. Grosvenor House
8. Hilton London Mews
9. Holiday Inn Mayfair
10. London Hilton
11. The Metropolitan
12. Millennium Hotel Mayfair
13. The Ritz

ATTRACTIONS
14. American Embassy
15. Apsley House

ATTRACTIONS
16. Royal Academy of Arts

RESTAURANTS
17. Angela Hartnett at the Connaught
18. Le Gavroche
19. Nobu
20. Rasa
21. Strada
22. Tamarind

NIGHTCLUBS
23. Dover Street Restaurant & Bar
24. Down Mexico Way
25. Hanover Grand
26. Metro Club

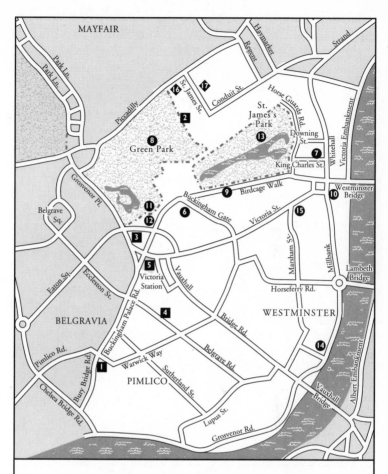

Zone 9: Victoria and Westminster

N

ACCOMMODATIONS
1 The Cherry Court Hotel
2 Dukes Hotel
3 Goring Hotel
4 Quality Hotel
5 Thistle Hotel Victoria

ATTRACTIONS
6 Buckingham Palace
7 The Cabinet War Rooms
8 Green Park
9 Guards Museum

ATTRACTIONS
10 Houses of Parliament and Big Ben
11 Queen's Gallery
12 Royal Mews
13 St. James's Park
14 Tate Britain
15 Westminster Abbey

RESTAURANTS
16 Le Caprice
17 Matsuri

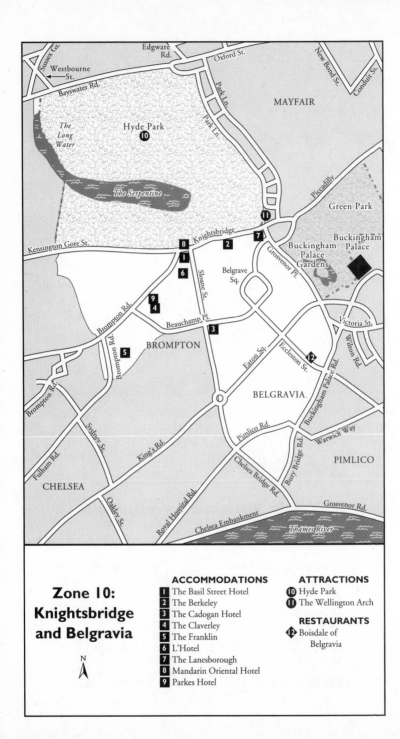

Zone 10:
Knightsbridge
and Belgravia

N
⋀

ACCOMMODATIONS
1 The Basil Street Hotel
2 The Berkeley
3 The Cadogan Hotel
4 The Claverley
5 The Franklin
6 L'Hotel
7 The Lanesborough
8 Mandarin Oriental Hotel
9 Parkes Hotel

ATTRACTIONS
10 Hyde Park
11 The Wellington Arch

RESTAURANTS
12 Boisdale of
Belgravia

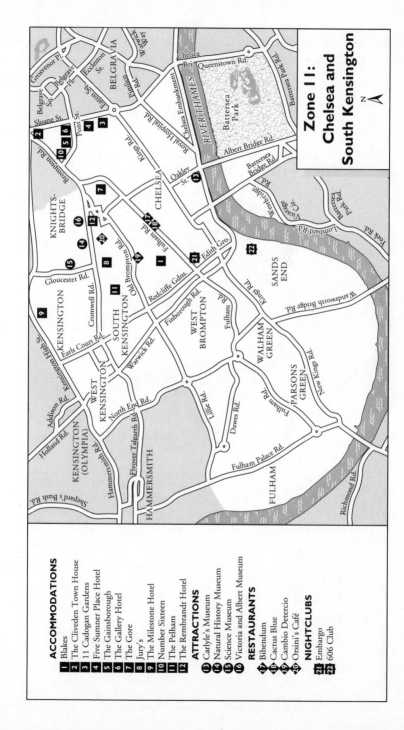

Zone 11:
Chelsea and
South Kensington

N

ACCOMMODATIONS

1 Blakes
2 The Cliveden Town House
3 11 Cadogan Gardens
4 Five Sumner Place Hotel
5 The Gainsborough
6 The Gallery Hotel
7 The Gore
8 Jury's
9 The Milestone Hotel
10 Number Sixteen
11 The Pelham
12 The Rembrandt Hotel

ATTRACTIONS

13 Carlyle's Museum
14 Natural History Museum
15 Science Museum
16 Victoria and Albert Museum

RESTAURANTS

17 Bibendum
18 Cactus Blue
19 Cambio Detercio
20 Orsini's Café

NIGHTCLUBS

21 Embargo
22 606 Club

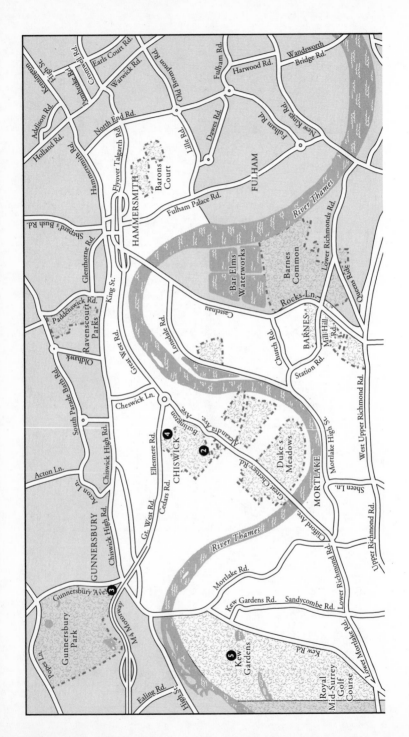

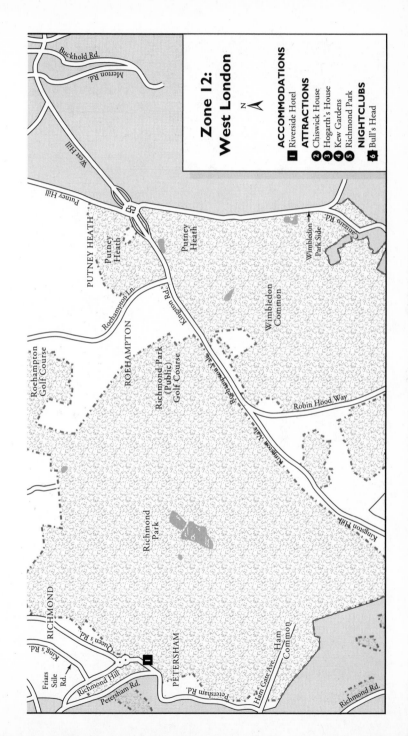

Zone 12:
West London

N

ACCOMMODATIONS
1 Riverside Hotel

ATTRACTIONS
2 Chiswick House
3 Hogarth's House
4 Kew Gardens
5 Richmond Park

NIGHTCLUBS
6 Bull's Head

Buckhold Rd.

Merton Rd.

West Hill

Putney Hill

PUTNEY HEATH

Putney Heath

Putney Heath

Roehampton Ln.

ROEHAMPTON

Kingston Rd.

Roehampton Golf Course

Roehampton Vale

Richmond Park (Public) Golf Course

Kingston Vale

Wimbledon Common

Wimbledon Park Side

Tibbet's Rd.

Robin Hood Way

Kingston Hill

Richmond Park

RICHMOND

King's Rd.

Queen's Rd.

Friars Stile Rd.

Richmond Hill

Petersham Rd.

PETERSHAM

Petersham Rd.

Ham Gate Ave.

Ham Common

Richmond Rd.

XXV

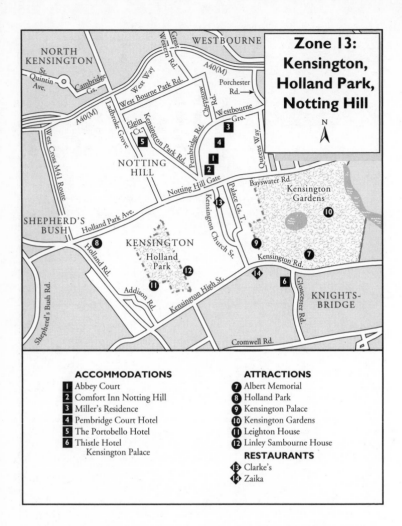

Zone 13: Kensington, Holland Park, Notting Hill

N

ACCOMMODATIONS
1 Abbey Court
2 Comfort Inn Notting Hill
3 Miller's Residence
4 Pembridge Court Hotel
5 The Portobello Hotel
6 Thistle Hotel
   Kensington Palace

ATTRACTIONS
7 Albert Memorial
8 Holland Park
9 Kensington Palace
10 Kensington Gardens
11 Leighton House
12 Linley Sambourne House

RESTAURANTS
13 Clarke's
14 Zaika

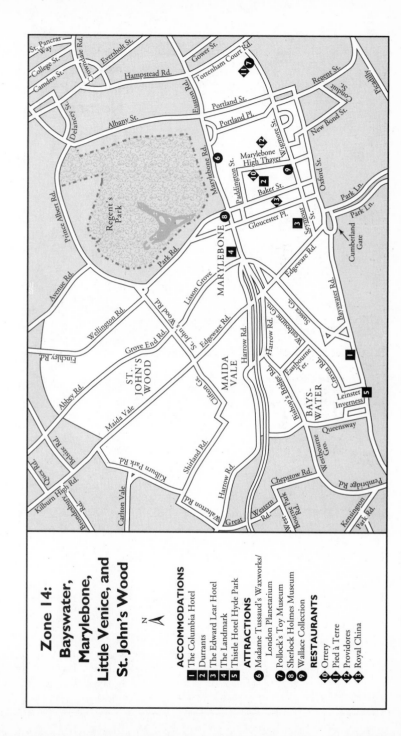

Zone 14:
Bayswater, Marylebone, Little Venice, and St. John's Wood

ACCOMMODATIONS
1 The Columbia Hotel
2 Durrants
3 The Edward Lear Hotel
4 The Landmark
5 Thistle Hotel Hyde Park

ATTRACTIONS
6 Madame Tussaud's Waxworks/ London Planetarium
7 Pollock's Toy Museum
8 Sherlock Holmes Museum
9 Wallace Collection

RESTAURANTS
10 Orrery
11 Pied à Terre
12 Providores
13 Royal China

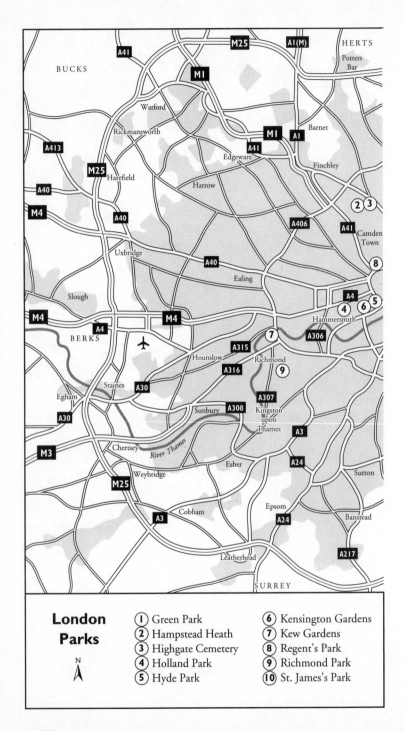

London Parks

N

① Green Park
② Hampstead Heath
③ Highgate Cemetery
④ Holland Park
⑤ Hyde Park
⑥ Kensington Gardens
⑦ Kew Gardens
⑧ Regent's Park
⑨ Richmond Park
⑩ St. James's Park

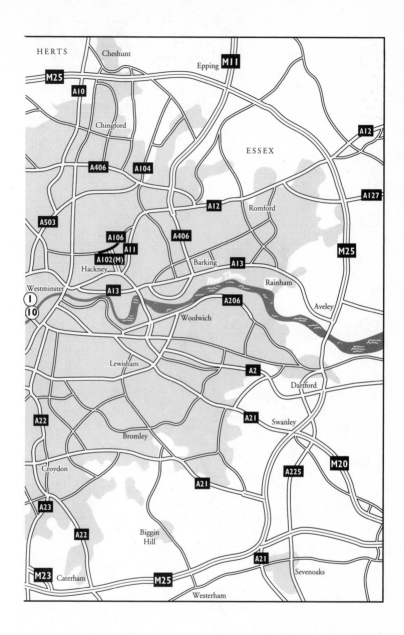

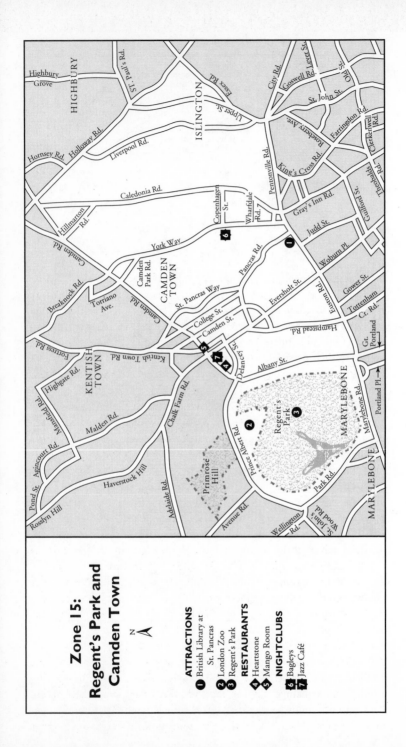

Zone 15:
Regent's Park and Camden Town

N

ATTRACTIONS
1 British Library at St. Pancras
2 London Zoo
3 Regent's Park

RESTAURANTS
4 Heartstone
5 Mango Room

NIGHTCLUBS
6 Bagleys
7 Jazz Café

Introduction

London Calling

Let's just get it out of the way, shall we? Dr. Samuel Johnson's quote about his beloved city is as famous as Big Ben: "When a man is tired of London, he is tired of Life, for there is in London all that Life can afford." Only in London could the words of an eighteenth-century writer be put to such persistent, modern public-relations use; it is exactly this easy—some might say surreal—conversation between past and present that makes London so appealing to its visitors and residents alike.

London is a historical free-for-all where, against the gorgeous Georgian facade of the Royal Academy, you'll find a series of seriously modern sculptures; where horse-drawn carriages and soldiers on horseback in full regalia barely merit a passing glance from Londoners in their cars; where the Liberty department store on the eighteenth-century Nash-designed Regent Street is housed in a Tudor building straight out of a fairy tale. This wonderful palimpsest of centuries—the layering of post–World War II London over Edwardian elegance, on top of Victorian glory, over eighteenth-century exuberance, under which the medieval and even the Roman city can be appreciated—is, especially to the American eye, a miracle of conservation and civic pride. But if London was only the sum of its past, it might not be the contemporary scene of a constantly evolving culture of theater, arts, and music, not to mention the birthplace of cutting-edge clothing designers, rock and rollers, and nightclubbers.

In 1978, Bette Midler said, "When it's three o'clock in New York, it's still 1938 in London." Today, this remark might be received with some puzzlement, except perhaps by those who expect all stores to be open on Sunday and remain open past six and who believe that the London Underground trains (the subway system in London we commonly refer to as the tube or, more formally, the underground) ought to run after

1

midnight. Despite its high prices, London attracts over 25 million visitors a year, swelling its permanent population of 7 million. This is not to say it's a nirvana for visitors—London is no quaint theme park. This city takes a bit of work, and visitors may struggle to reconcile the picture of London carried in their minds against the sometimes dirty, indifferent, and confusing modern reality of the place. But the payoff for a little footwork is huge.

London can be many cities to many people. Contrast Dr. Johnson's hymns of worship ("The happiness of London is not to be conceived but by those who have been in it") with Percy Bysshe Shelley's assessment of early-nineteenth-century London: "Hell is a city much like London—a populous and smoky city." People may have a wide range of feelings about London, but indifference is usually not one of them. It's rare for an English speaker to come here without a mental trunk full of preconceptions. Those of us of a certain age had an intimate acquaintance with the bells of St. Clements, London Bridge, and the Drury Lane home of the muffin man before we could even read. When we could read, we absorbed the London of Charles Dickens, who captured the nineteenth-century city in all its degradation and beauty, who spent hours each night exploring his city on foot, and who left his unforgettable impressions on the pages of his novels and in the psyches of his readers. London has appeared as a character in so much English literature and so many films that it is a place we carry in our collective consciousness like a dream.

Waking up to London is another story. To arrive here for the first time is to suddenly confront the fantasy with the fact. The most outstanding fact about London is its sprawling geography—there is nothing so neat as a "downtown" of London. It isn't so much one big city as a series of interconnected villages on a human-size scale, liberally dotted with breathing spaces of greenery. London can take a lifetime to explore fully, and a tourist with only a week to cover the major sights will find it impossible to take it all in. The best approach to London is to decide where your interests lie; you will soon discover that there are few interests known to humanity that London cannot entertain.

We want you to make the best of this best-of-all-possible cities. We want you not to waste one minute getting lost on the tube or taking a taxi if walking would be quicker. We don't want you to get such a bad case of museum legs that you can't make it to the theater that night, and we definitely don't want you to spend your hard-earned money buying anything that's cheaper back home. London is a great place for visitors—tourism is its second largest industry—and we love the fact that we Anglophones can, for the most part, communicate with the locals without needing a course from Berlitz. We hope to identify and address any difficulties you might have in visiting London, so that you can pursue whatever course of entertainment you desire, efficiently and happily. And there's so much to be done. . . .

London has the best museums in the world, the famous as well as some lesser-known ones. There are miles of parks, offering some of the most beautiful natural scenery to be found in any metropolis. Part of London's charm lies in the sudden deluges from leaden skies that will just as quickly be sliced open with swords of sunlight. There are also the people of London, who speak in a rich concoction of accents, in over 200 languages, and represent multiple classes, nationalities, and political views. No matter what moves you—theater, architecture, sports, antiques, markets, designer clothing, contemporary art and old masters, heart-stopping cathedrals, Internet cafés, palaces, poetry readings, elegant casinos, lunatic nightclubs, pubs, bungee jumping, horticulture, witchcraft, fencing, boating—there truly is, as the good doctor pointed out almost three centuries ago, "in London all that Life can afford."

About This Guide

Why *Unofficial?*

Most London travel guides follow the usual tracks of the typical tourist, automatically sending everyone to the well-known sights without offering any information about how to do this painlessly; recommending restaurants and hotels indiscriminately; and failing to recognize the limits of human endurance in sight-seeing. This guide is different: We understand that in a huge city like London it is essential for one to discriminate, make plans, whittle the town down to size, and be just a little bit flexible when hours-long lines appear out of nowhere or when the clouds burst and you've forgotten your umbrella.

We'll tell you what we think of certain tourist traps, what the real story is on the famous restaurants and hotels, what the options are if you want to stay off the beaten track, or how to spend a little less money on one thing so you can spend more on another. We'll complain about rip-offs, we'll advise you on bargains. We also hope to give you the kind of information that will make you love London all the more—some of the endearing eccentricities that make you realize you're definitely not in Kansas anymore.

London is such a complex and sprawling city, so full of fantastic anecdote and incident, that it's hard to edit out the trivia—it's all great stuff, and the more tales you hear, the more you want to know. London is all about history—every building and monument, every alley and lane has a story. The longer you stay here, the larger London becomes in some ways. Each door that opens reveals ten windows through which to gaze. In the old days a visit to London was a rite of passage for the upper classes of North America, and they used to spend six months at it. You probably haven't got that luxury (unless you're here as an exchange student), so you have to be very efficient and organized if you want to make the most of your time. The majority of overseas visitors stay only for about five to ten days. How much can you squeeze into that time? How much do you want to see? What are your priorities, and how can they best be served? Like any worthwhile undertaking, some preparation and strategy are needed to make London reveal its charms to you. We have done the footwork: We've checked out the hotels to find the best deals and the most interesting buildings; Richard Ehrlich, who has been reviewing restaurants for years, will give you the benefit of his experience; and we've got the lowdown on the nightlife from those who have crawled through their fair share of clubs. If a museum is dull, or there's a two-hour wait for an attraction that just isn't worth it, we'll tell you why—and we hope in the process to make your visit more fun, efficient, and economical.

We've tried in this book to anticipate the special needs of older people, families with young children, families with teenagers, solo travelers, and people with physical challenges.

London has hundreds of attractions, and we've tried to sort them based upon which are first rate, which are intended for those with special interests, and which are hype jobs. Obviously, even if you visit London dozens of times, you won't be able to see all that we describe to you, and by then you'll have discovered some of your own favorite haunts. But we want you to always have the options of exploring more and more of this endlessly interesting city, and we want to give you the best tips for doing so. We take things easy, the way we think you'll want to, but we don't forgive exploitation or stupidity. If it isn't fun, if it isn't informative, if it isn't a reasonable deal, if there's a better alternative, we want you to know. We hope to keep the quality of your visit high and the irritation quotient low.

We cover attractions in these various ways because we want to make sure you can pick out the ones you'd enjoy most. For those of you who don't wish to do it all yourselves, we've listed a number of good commercial and customized tours on pages 155–158 in Part Six, "Sight-Seeing and Tours."

Even keeping in mind that your time will be filled, we have included a list of opportunities for exercise. Travel can be pretty hard on the body— airplane stiffness, walking around galleries and streets—and it's wise to get some endorphins going at some point in your visit. Also, London has so many great restaurants and opportunities to try new foods that you may well need a little calorie-corrective run or swim, unless you want to take home more than photos and souvenirs (try a few days of cream teas and you'll see what we mean).

Please do remember that prices and admission hours change constantly; we have listed the most up-to-date information we can get, but it never hurts to double-check times in particular (if prices of attractions change, it is generally not by much). Remember, this is one of the busiest tourist towns in the world, so make your reservations early and reconfirm.

About Unofficial Guides

Readers care about authors' opinions. The authors, after all, are supposed to know what they are talking about. This, coupled with the fact that the traveler wants quick answers (as opposed to endless alternatives), dictates that travel authors should be explicit, prescriptive, and above all, direct. The authors of the *Unofficial Guide* try to do just that. We spell out alternatives and recommend specific courses of action. We simplify complicated destinations and attractions to allow the traveler to feel in control in the most unfamiliar environments. Our objective is not to give the most information or all the information, but the most accessible, useful information. Of course, in a city like London, there are many hotels, restaurants, and attractions that are so closely woven into the fabric of the city that to omit them from our guide because we can't recommend them would be a disservice to our readers. We have included all the famous haunts, giving our opinion and experience of them, in the hopes that you will approach (or avoid) these institutions armed with the necessary intelligence.

An *Unofficial Guide* is a critical reference work; we focus on a travel destination that appears to be especially complex. Our authors and researchers are completely independent from the attractions, restaurants, and hotels we describe. The *Unofficial Guide to London* is designed for individuals and families traveling for fun as well as for business, and it will be especially helpful to those hopping "across the pond" for the first time. The guide is directed at value-conscious, consumer-oriented adults who seek a cost-effective but not spartan travel style.

SPECIAL FEATURES

- Vital information about traveling abroad.
- Friendly introductions to London's "villages."
- Listings that are keyed to your interests, so you can pick and choose.
- Advice to sightseers on how to avoid the worst crowds; advice to business travelers on how to avoid traffic and excessive costs.
- Recommendations for lesser-known sights that are off the well-beaten tourist path but no less worthwhile.
- A zone system and maps to make it easy to find places you want to go and to avoid other places.
- A hotel section that helps you narrow down your choices quickly, according to your needs and preferences.
- A table of contents and detailed index to help you find things fast.

- Long, useless lists where everything looks the same.
- Information that gets you to your destination at the worst possible time.
- Information without advice on how to use it.

How This Guide Was Researched and Written

In preparing this work, we took nothing for granted. Each hotel, restaurant, shop, and attraction was visited by trained observers who conducted detailed evaluations and rated each according to formal criteria. Team members conducted interviews with tourists of all ages to determine what they enjoyed most and least during their London visit.

Though our observers are independent and impartial, they are otherwise "ordinary" travelers. Like you, they visited London as tourists or business travelers, noting their satisfaction or dissatisfaction.

The primary difference between the average tourist and the trained evaluator is the evaluator's skills in organization, preparation, and observation. A trained evaluator is responsible for more than just observing and cataloging. Observer teams use detailed checklists to analyze hotel rooms, restaurants, nightclubs, and attractions. Finally, evaluator ratings and observations are integrated with tourist reactions and the opinions of patrons for a comprehensive quality profile of each feature and service.

In compiling this guide, we recognize that a tourist's age, background, and interests will strongly influence his or her taste in London's wide array of attractions and will account for a preference for one sight or museum over another. Our sole objective is to provide the reader with sufficient description, critical evaluation, and pertinent data to make knowledgeable decisions according to individual tastes.

Letters, Comments, and Questions from Readers

We expect to learn from our mistakes, as well as from the input of our readers, and to improve with each new book and edition. Many of those who use the *Unofficial Guides* write to us asking questions, making comments, or sharing their own discoveries and lessons learned in London. We appreciate all such input, both positive and critical, and encourage our readers to continue writing. Readers' comments and observations will be frequently incorporated in revised editions of the *Unofficial Guide* and will contribute immeasurably to its improvement.

How to Write the Author

Lesley Logan
The Unofficial Guide to London
P.O. Box 43673
Birmingham, AL 35243
UnofficialGuides@menasharidge.com

When you write, be sure to put your return address on your letter as well as on the envelope—sometimes envelopes and letters get separated. Remember, our work takes us out of the office for long periods of time, so forgive us if our response is delayed.

How Information Is Organized: By Subject and by Geographic Zones

To give you fast access to information about the best of London, we've organized material in several formats.

Hotels

There are many hotels in London that are small, quirky, and unique. Even the world-class, well-known, and very expensive hotels can vary dramatically in room size and amenities, and a hotel priced somewhere in the middle of the price range can have under one charming roof and at a similar price both closet-size attic rooms and magnificent salons with French windows. We have tried to stick to the hotels that are more reliable and consistent in their accommodations, and we have attempted to summarize this somewhat unwieldy and problematic subject in ratings and rankings that allow you to quickly focus your decision-making process. We concentrate on the specific variables that differentiate one hotel from another: location, size, room quality, services, amenities, and cost.

Entertainment and Nightlife

Visitors frequently try several different clubs or nightspots during their stay in London. Since clubs, like restaurants, are usually selected rather spontaneously after arriving, we believe that detailed descriptions are warranted. The best nightspots in London are profiled in Part Nine, "Entertainment and Nightlife." Be warned, though, that the popularity and character of clubs can change, even disappear, overnight. We've tried to select places that have withstood the tests of time and fluctuations of fashion.

Restaurants

We provide plenty of detail when it comes to restaurants. You will probably eat a dozen or more restaurant meals during your stay, and not even you can predict what you might be in the mood for on Saturday night. You can browse through our detailed profiles of the best restaurants in London before dining out.

Once you've decided where you're going, getting there becomes the issue. To help you do that, we have divided London into geographic zones, which we briefly describe below to give you an idea of what they're about. These zones are unrelated to and should not be confused with the zones laid out by the London's public transportation system for purposes of assigning traveling cost—the London Transport zones 1 and 2 are probably the ones you will be traveling in, and they are the minimum price of a bus or tube ticket.

The post codes that appear at the end of an address are for the purpose of delivering mail and are known to the citizens as shorthand for a certain area. Everyone knows that SW1 is part of the royal borough of Westminster and includes the neighborhoods of Victoria, Pimlico, and parts of Knightsbridge and Belgravia. Chelsea and Kensington are in the SW3 and SW7 codes. Neighborhoods to the north are known by their "N" prefix followed by a number. They represent compass directions (N, S, W, E) that radiate generally from central London (C), with the lowest numbers being in the center of town, roughly to the east of Hyde Park. The higher the number, the farther from the center you will be.

But, to get back to the zones as determined by this guide: we have made what seemed to us to be natural divisions between areas or neighborhoods, and have numbered them to make it easier for you to get a handle on the far-flung environs of London. These divisions are germane only to this book, and again, have nothing to do with the London Transport zones.

All profiles of hotels, restaurants, attractions, and nightspots include zone numbers. If you are staying in Knightsbridge, for example, and are interested in a place to eat within walking distance, look at the profiles for restaurants in zone 10.

Zone 1: North London—Hampstead, Highgate

This is an almost suburban area, which can seem to be in the heart of the country when you're standing in Hampstead Heath looking out at a castlelike mansion on a hill, surrounded by old trees and wild grass. Hampstead Heath is approximately 800 acres of natural beauty, with a bucolic bounty not often found within miles of a large city. Hampstead has always been a salubrious place: during the Black Death of the early 1200s and again during the Great Plague of 1665–66, people fled to Hampstead. By the eighteenth century, Hampstead had become a fashionable resort for Londoners seeking fresh air and healthy springwater. The nineteenth century saw an influx of artists, writers, and intellectuals, a community still found here. There are views from Highgate and Hampstead across the whole of London which, along with the charm of the high street, make this a satisfying destination for the discerning tourist. Kenwood House is a stately home on the heath that is well worth a visit.

Zone 2: Bloomsbury and Holborn

Bloomsbury is dominated by the British Museum, as well as by many hospitals and institutes of learning. In Holborn, one finds many traces of old London: Dickens's House, Coram's Fields, Dr. Johnson's House, the Silver Vaults, and more. There are a number of reasonably priced lodgings here, within walking distance of the West End—a good thing for the club crawlers, as many buses and all trains stop running shortly after midnight. There's also a lot of literary history here: the famous Blooms-bury Group of the early 1900s—a tightly related gang of writers and artists that included Virginia Woolf and Lytton Strachey—will always be associated with this area, and this is reflected in the content of numerous blue plaques on various buildings.

Zone 3: The City, Clerkenwell, Barbican

This is the oldest part of London, where you will find the magnificent St. Paul's Cathedral, the occasional whispers of a medieval past, and some remnants of the town the occupying ancient Romans called Londinium—things that managed to survive the devastating Great Fire of 1666 and the Blitz of World War II. This is also where most of the financial business of London is conducted. The area pretty much dies at night and on week-ends, but during the day you'll find many good restaurants here. The Bank of England Museum and the Lloyd's of London building by Richard Rogers are two other attractions. There are some amusing architectural visions here, such as the grasshopper on the top of the Stock Exchange and the new high rise known as "the gherkin" for its shape. The old markets—Smithfield's, Billingsgate, and Leadenhall—are fun to check out.

Zone 4: East End—Spitalfields, White Chapel, Bethnal Green

Besides the Tower of London, zone 4 offers markets, Victorian architec-ture, art galleries and churches, and cockney English. The once-thriving Jewish center of London used to be here, and you can still go to the schwitzes, the old-style men's steam baths, or get a great piece of smoked fish and latkes from the oldest Jewish deli in London. The East End is, like so much of this crushingly expensive city, experiencing a bit of gen-trification, as the prices of real estate in central London push people ever further afield. New luxury apartments, artsy nightspots, galleries, and even the Prince of Wales's School of Architecture now share the streets where Jack the Ripper stalked his prey and Sweeney Todd made mince-meat of his customers. Here, too, you can get boats to Greenwich, see some of the old Roman wall around London, and visit Tower Bridge.

Zone 5: South London—South Bank, Lambeth, Brixton

Zone 5 encompasses the great renaissance of the South Bank—the Lon-don Aquarium, the Marriott Hotel, the National Theatre, the Hayward Gallery, the magnificent British Airways London Eye Ferris wheel—as well as the ancient palace of Lambeth, where the archbishop of Canter-bury lives; Waterloo Station, from which the Eurostar leaves; and the Old Vic Theatre. There's great nightlife in Brixton, with lots of reggae venues, thanks to its large Caribbean contingent. From the South Bank you get the very best views of the halls of Westminster and Big Ben, and in the summer along the promenade you will find outdoor cafés where you can lounge and watch the river run.

Zone 6: Greenwich and Docklands

Greenwich, where the time of the day is calculated as Greenwich Mean Time, has a lot for the scientifically as well as historically inclined visitor. There is the Old Royal Observatory, the National Maritime Museum, the Royal Naval College, Indigo Jones Queen's House, and two old tea clippers. One of every visitor's favorite photo ops in Greenwich is the spot from which the world's longitude, known as the Prime Meridien, is measured. The great thing about Greenwich is that all its attractions are within walking distance of each other, including the street market that's open on the weekend. You could easily spend a full day seeing Greenwich. The Docklands are less appealing, featuring mainly Canary Wharf, a high-rise office complex, and the currently empty shell of the Millennium Dome, which may become a sports arena.

Zone 7: Soho and the West End

This is where the nightlife and the theater district are located. Charing Cross bookshops, St. Martin-in-the-Fields, Trafalgar Square, rowdy Leicester Square, Chinatown, the National Gallery, and pubs, pubs, pubs are in this zone. Carnaby Street and Neal's Yard are the alternative lifestyle, clothing, and health-therapies areas, and Covent Garden has absolutely everything for everybody. There's also the London Transport Museum, the Trocadero, the Rock Circus, and the Theatre Museum. You might want to stay in a hotel around here, but it can get loud at night, with drunks roaring up and down side streets and tourists as far as the eye can see. Of course, that may be part of the appeal.

Zone 8: Mayfair and Piccadilly

This is a very high-class area, in which you can find the most expensive shops in the world—from the designers on New and Old Bond Streets, to the bespoke trade in St. James, to the White House linen shop, where you can spend thousands on bedclothes. There is every imaginable hotel here, except for inexpensive ones—the Atheneum, Park Lane, Ritz, Brown's, Dorchester, Metropolitan, Claridges . . . the list is impressive. Hatchard's, the oldest bookstore in London, is on Piccadilly, as are Fortnum and Mason's, the Burlington Arcade, and the wonderful Royal Academy, whose exhibits are always top-notch. Here is Shepherds' Market, which in the 1600s was the site of the riotous saturnalia known as the May Fair and a place for the entertainers of the day—jugglers, fire eaters, boxers, prostitutes—to parade their talents. Today, Shepherds' Market is a mere shadow of its former self, but interesting nonetheless.

Zone 9: Victoria and Westminster

This zone encompasses the halls of government and power in London: Whitehall, Westminster Abbey, Parliament, and Buckingham Palace. There are plenty of hotels to go along with the preponderance of tourist attractions. Due to the heavy concentration of World War II bombing in this area, there are patches of ugliness here and there where rebuilding went on without much attention to architectural coherence. Much of Westminster simply closes down on the weekend—not the attractions but the eateries, which cater mainly to the business crowd. Pimlico, to the south, has lots of cheap hotels and bedsits, but may not be the greatest place to be late at night. This zone runs from the seedy to the sublime. There is the most magnificent vista here—the fairy-tale view from Buckingham Palace across St. James's Park toward Westminster Abbey will have you reaching for your camera.

Zone 10: Knightsbridge and Belgravia

This zone is the stronghold of the very wealthy—expatriate entrepreneurs, British aristocrats, movie stars, rock-and-roll gods, and sultans coexist peacefully in the splendor of Georgian town houses or in deceptively simple mews houses within walking distance of Hyde Park, Harrods, and Harvey Nichols. Knightsbridge is mainly about shopping: Sloane Street, Walton Street, and Beauchamp Place have all the trendiest designer shops; the auction house Bonhams is in Knightsbridge Village, as is an assortment of secondhand designer-clothes shops. Knightsbridge is famous for having the most consonants in a row in any English word. Belgravia has less to talk about, as it is an enclave of ambassadors and billionaires, with enormous attached mansions, some of which are five houses strung together as one, as in the humble home of the sultan of Brunei. The zone is a very convenient to stay, if you can afford it. You can walk to Oxford Street; the Victoria and Albert Museum; the Natural History Museum; Hyde, Green, and St. James's Parks; and Piccadilly. Also, from Hyde Park Corner there are buses that go everywhere.

Zone 11: Chelsea and South Kensington

South Kensington was known as Albertopolis and Museumland because of the many cultural institutions Prince Albert founded here, including the Victoria and Albert and the Natural History Museums, Royal Albert Hall, the Royal Art College, Imperial College, and numerous other learned societies. You can now see the Albert Memorial in all its restored glory; its gold magnificence was covered in black for close to a century.

South Kensington is also known as Little France, thanks to the Lycee Français and the Institute Français in the middle of town. There are lots of great patisseries, a few good restaurants, and plenty of fine hotels. Chelsea is to the south and boasts the famous King's Road—the once-swinging high street for to 1960s hipsters, 1970s punks, 1980s yuppies, and 1990s just-plain-rich folk. In the neighborhoods off King's Road, there are a multitude of blue plaques identifying the many writers and artists who once called Chelsea home: Oscar Wilde, George Eliot, Thomas Carlyle, Dante Gabriel Rossetti, James Whistler . . . the list goes on. Chelsea is very beautiful and a very smart area in which to live—and the property prices reflect this.

Zone 12: West London—Hammersmith, Chiswick, Richmond, Kew

These are primarily residential areas outside of central London, with only a couple of tourist attractions. Chiswick has Hogarth's House, Chiswick House, and a few good restaurants; Richmond has the huge Park and Wimbledon Common; Hammersmith has its beautiful old bridge that one can walk across, a theater, Olympia Arena, some old pubs, and new strip clubs. Kew is, of course, the home of the gorgeous and world-famous Kew Gardens, and nearby is historic Syon House on whose grounds will be found the London Butterfly House and an aquatic feature. Hampton Court, the great Tudor palace on the Thames, is in this zone, too.

Zone 13: Kensington, Holland Park, Notting Hill

As a result of King William and Queen Mary moving their royal residence to the then far-flung country village of Kensington in 1689, lots of grand houses were built in this area. As rich attracts rich, the neighborhoods to the west and north, especially in Holland Park, developed into very exclusive places to live. Kensington High Street is a big bustling shopping street, with a huge range of clothing for young and old alike, and Kensington Church Street is lined with interesting, although expensive, antiques shops. Notting Hill used to be a big Jamaican enclave, but was soon attracting the idle trust-fund kids who were dubbed "trustafarians." It is a very happening place as its ever-increasing rents attest. This is where the famous Portobello Market is, which is worth a look on Saturday as long as you're not prone to agoraphobia. Attractions: Kensington Palace and Gardens, Leighton House, Holland Park, and the Kensington Church Street antiques-store mecca.

Zone 14: Bayswater, Marylebone, Little Venice, St. John's Wood

At the north border of Hyde Park, Bayswater and Marylebone have an enormous Arab population and a lot of great Middle Eastern restaurants. Here you'll find the Wallace Collection, Whiteley's Shopping Mall, skating rink and bowling alley, Regent's Canal Waterbus, Sherlock Holmes Museum, Madame Tussaud's, and two horseback-riding stables that take customers for trots around Hyde Park. There are tons of cheap hotels here, some downright dismal, some of relatively good value. Paddington Station is the terminus for the train from Heathrow, as well as for trains that serve the West Country and South Wales. There's a bit of a sleaze factor, with hooker hotels in the vicinity. Farther north is Little Venice, which has a canal running through it with boats that can be taken on Regent's Canal and the Grand Union Canal. St. John's Wood is the home of the American School, where a lot of the expats send their kids. The main attraction is the Abbey Road zebra crossing, where tourists annoy the locals by taking pictures of themselves re-creating the Beatles's famous album cover.

Zone 15: Regent's Park and Camden Town

Regent's Park houses the London Zoo, the London Central Mosque, Regent's Open Air Theatre, and it affords some of the most beautiful eighteenth-century vistas in London. Designed in concert with King George IV, who was regent at the time, this area is the crowning achievement of architect John Nash. Camden Town, to the northwest, is a bustling market town, and rivals Portobello Road for good buys and cool stuff. There's a great antiques market and lots of hip clothing and knick-knacks, plus plenty of body piercing and tattoos on display. It's a must-go for teenagers. Primrose Hill is another sylvan glade in this zone and is one of the best places to watch the Guy Fawkes Day fireworks.

Part One

An Overview of London

London offers something for every mood, desire, and interest, and there are so many ways to appreciate it. Music, sports, architecture, theater, fashion, antiques, gardens, nightlife . . . London is an amazing place today, but it takes on even more interesting dimensions when you know what it was yesterday. A bit of the history of this town on the Thames is just as useful for the discerning visitor as a street map. So, here we go.

The Long Life of an Ancient City

London's history, perhaps because the city is situated on the banks of a wide river cutting through a large island, is initially one of invasion and conquest. Because of England's system of monarchy, her later history is one of bloody factionalism and revolving persecutions. As the empire began to take shape, the blood was shed on foreign soil, as England's sovereignty was propped up by the exploitation of foreign continents and by the labor of the impoverished workers in London. But throughout all of it, the history of the city of London has been the history of commerce: This port city has beckoned to artisans and sailors, farmers, prostitutes, and wheelers and dealers of all shades of corruption for two millennia. London shows no signs of flagging in its appeal in the third millennium.

Some of the highlights from London's past can be found in the Museum of London, where you can wander from the prehistoric banks of the Thames all the way through to the Millennium Dome, seeing the everyday sights of London's long life that you won't find anywhere else, such as the underground heating system of Roman Londinium, or an Anderson shelter from the days of the Blitz. The museum's overall style is nostalgic and cheerful, although you do get to look into a cell of Newgate Gaol. It's a great experience for the young and the old, the well-informed and the merely curious.

When Rome Ruled Londinium

Julius Caesar's famous remark about how Britons were simply not good slave material was sour grapes: in 55 B.C.and 56 B.C., he tried to subdue England twice and failed. In A.D. 43, the Romans again sent an army to conquer the island. This time they built a bridge over the Thames at the narrowest crossing, near the present London Bridge. Soon, this Roman fort called Londinium grew into a thriving port of commerce, as luxury goods from all over the Roman Empire arrived and were exchanged for corn, iron, and—Julius Caesar, notwithstanding—slaves. Roman historian Tacitus wrote that Londinium was "famed for commerce and crowded with merchants," a description that would remain accurate for the next 2,000 years (and will doubtless continue to do so). Roadways, the most ubiquitous and long-lasting feature of Roman rule, soon headed in every direction from this trading post and were well traveled by Romans and Britons in search of adventure and wealth. After a period of Pax Romana (peace imposed by ancient Rome on its dominions), the Roman rule became increasingly unbearable to the local tribes. Queen Boudicca of the Iceni tribe led a violent revolt, invading Londinium, massacring everyone in sight, and burning the camp to the ground. The revolution was short lived, however; Londinium was rebuilt with a huge wall around it, encompassing what is presently the City and Barbican area. A piece of the wall is preserved near the Museum of London.

In 410, the sun was setting on the Roman Empire. The troops were withdrawn, leaving the sprouts of the newly adopted Christian faith behind. London then went into a decline; when new invaders arrived, they superstitiously stayed away from the Roman ruins, which were soon buried, not to be rediscovered until after the Blitz of World War II.

The Saxon's Lundenwic

After the Saxons came over the North Sea in about 450 to settle in southeast England, London slowly began its rise from Roman ashes to again become a trading post, called Lundenwic. After presiding over a pagan society, King Ethelbert became a Christian convert, and the first cathedral of St. Paul was built. The Saxon kings spent most of the next five centuries fighting Viking invaders and fortifying their kingdom and its capital at Winchester. London has King Alfred to thank for rebuilding it after Danish invaders left it in ruins, as well as for lighting a few other candles in those dark ages. The tenth century saw a new prosperity as neighborhoods and parishes were formed on the banks of the Thames River. In the eleventh century, the Danes finally won the day, and England was forced to accept the Danish King Canute as its leader. He put London on the map as the capital of the kingdom, and by 1042, when Edward the Confessor took the scepter, London was poised on the brink of a great architectural leap forward. Westminster Abbey and the Palace at Westminster gave the raucous commercial port a dignity that was soon complemented by the construction of the White Tower, the tallest building at the Tower of London.

William the Conqueror

In 1066, at the Battle of Hastings, a Norman army led by William conquered the Saxon armies, and with that victory spelled a new dawn for London. William decided to have his coronation in Westminster Abbey, a tradition since that time. He saw that London was perfectly placed to be a rich capital and located the impressive stronghold of the White Tower on the Thames to show the inhabitants of this headstrong city just who was in charge. However, he was also a smart politician and granted freedoms to the Saxon-dominated church and the local governors that ensured a pleasant and profitable back-scratching for all concerned. London grew rich under the watchful eye of the monarchs, who knew the key to their power lay in the wealth and acquiescence of London's merchants and churchmen. In 1180, William Fitzstephen, in the preface to his *Life of Thomas à Becket,* sang high praises of London: "It is blessed by a wholesome climate . . . in the strength of its fortifications, in the nature of its site, the repute of its citizens, the honour of its matrons; happy in its sports, prolific in noble men. . . . I can think of no other city with customs more admirable. . . . The only plagues of London are the immoderate drinking of fools and the frequency of fires." He forgot that other plague of London: the plague.

A Vibrant Medieval Port

Medieval London was a crazy conglomeration of streets, alleys, markets, outdoor brothels, bear-baiting pits, pubs, and theaters. The vibrancy of the streets was matched in energy by the jostling for power among the court, the burgesses, and the church. In 1215, the Magna Carta, which attempted to limit the excesses and power of the king and establish personal rights and political freedom for the nobility, was signed by King John, who was forced to do so by rebellious barons and the newly created lord mayor of London. Soon Parliament and the House of Commons were created, and England became a place of liberty and justice for at least a few more than before. Though the Magna Carta was designed to free the aristocracy from the despotism of a monarch, it contained the fateful word *freemen* and so signaled at least theoretical rights for the common people.

The port was thriving with houses and warehouses lining the river banks, and the power of the guilds and merchants grew apace. The position of London as a window on the world, crowded with thousands of people living in appalling sanitary conditions, led to the first outbreak of plague. The Black Death of 1348 came across from the European continent, which was reeling from the disease. Nearly half of London's population succumbed to the plague, which was carried by rats that multiplied in the filthy streets and fetid sewers. The general unrest and loss of labor led to the ill-advised poll tax imposed in 1381 by a financially strapped court—a shilling a person, regardless of income or situation. The Peasant's Revolt, led by Jack Straw and Wat Tyler, put every future monarch on notice that Londoners had a breaking point that should be avoided. After a riotous spree of looting, burning, and murder, the rebels were overcome, and a young King Richard II restored order, but the point was taken—and the poll tax was quietly dropped.

A new intellectual age dawned around this time. In the 1390s, Geoffrey Chaucer wrote *The Canterbury Tales,* and in 1476 William Caxton set up his printing press at Westminster. The numerous and wealthy monasteries became centers for teaching and learning, and literacy began creeping into the merchant and upper classes, setting the scene for the Renaissance culture of the Tudor era.

Tudor London

The War of the Roses between the fractious factions of the House of Plantagenet—York and Lancaster—provided William Shakespeare with superabundant material for his tragedies.

The bloody dynastic feud for the throne had relatively little effect on the daily lives of Londoners scrambling for a living, but when Richard III allegedly smothered the two young princes, the rightful heirs to the throne, in the Tower of London, the citizenry grew restless; few regretted the end of Richard's reign. Next came the Tudor dynasty, whose heirs were at least as ruthless when it came to insulting relatives as any of the previous Plantagenets had been.

Henry VIII married his brother's widow, Catherine of Aragon, to keep the peace with Spain. After 20 years of marriage and one daughter, Mary, Henry fell in love with Anne Boleyn and decided he had to marry again in order to have a male heir. He cast off his wife, alienating the Catholic Church in Rome, which refused to grant him an annulment. Not one to take no for an answer, and a man who willingly threw out baby *and* bath with the bathwater, Henry reformed the church in England, styling himself as its supreme ruler. Then he went on a serial marital spree that left in its wake a total of six wives; as the nursery rhyme goes, "two beheaded, two divorced, one died, and one survived." The most radical expression of this religious overhaul was in the dissolution of the monasteries, in which Henry took for the Crown all the property of the Catholic cathedrals, churches, priories, convents, and monasteries in England. He destroyed huge numbers of beautiful gothic and medieval buildings, redistributing the land among the new, loyal-to-Henry aristocracy, creating new streets, houses, and courtyards where there had once been wealthy Catholic establishments. Resistant nuns and clergy were hung, drawn, and quartered; the army of crippled, diseased, and homeless who had been supported by the charity of the churches were thrown upon their own resources, and the streets of London resounded with the cries of their misery.

After Henry VIII died, syphilitic and obese, the six-year reign of the child-king Edward didn't amount to much more than further religious persecutions and a vicious power struggle among his courtiers. When Bloody Mary, Henry's first daughter, became queen after Edward's early death, she put her half-sister, Elizabeth, in the Tower of London, and it was the Protestants' turn to have their property seized and be hung or burnt alive. The daily spectacle of burning heretics at the marketplace of Smithfields finally disgusted even the Londoners accustomed to gruesome public punishments. In another turn of the dynasty, Elizabeth returned England to its Protestant base, forestalling any Catholic overthrow by having her cousin, Mary Queen of Scots, executed at the Tower. (The Tower of London is probably as haunted a place as you can find in ghost-ridden London. Heads rolled like billiard balls there, innocent souls were racked and tortured regularly, and their tormented specters are well known to the people who remain there past nightfall, such as the governor of the Tower and his family and others who work and live on the property.)

The Elizabethan Flowering of London

What were the good citizens of London doing while all the royal kinkilling kerfuffle and musical thrones were being played out? Well, while the aristocrats built over-the-top estates from the remains of the monasteries, and Hyde Park became a happy hunting ground for King Henry, the ordinary Londoner was going about the usual: earning and eating, fornicating and frolicking, marrying and burying. In 1586, William Shakespeare arrived in London, joining Ben Jonson, Christopher Marlowe, John Donne, and others of the day's glitterati in the boom years of English letters, helping record the uproar that was London. The city now had a population of 200,000 people, up from 50,000 in the 1300s, and more arrived every day. The great era of exploration was under way as the English plied the oceans in search of riches, returning with sugar, spice, coffee, and tobacco. Sir Thomas Gresham started the Royal Exchange from its humble beginnings as a coffeehouse and made London the world's most important financial center, a position it maintained into the early twentieth century.

Although Queen Elizabeth could be as dangerous a friend (and cousin) as she was a foe, she was devoted to the welfare of her kingdom and understood that her greatest power lay in the love her subjects had for her—she had an instinctive gift for public relations. Perhaps the greatest gift she gave the nation was her much vaunted virginity: By not marrying a foreign prince, she kept England solidly English for 45 prosperous years. By the end of her long reign, the memories of those ugly battles of succession had faded.

Roundheads and Restoration

The Gunpowder Plot, in which a group of Catholic conspirators, including Guy Fawkes, were thwarted in their plan to blow up King James, his ministers, and Parliament at the Palace of Westminster, rather appropriately opened London's apocalyptic seventeenth century. King James died in 1625, leaving on the throne a somewhat backward son, Charles I.

Although at this time London was the wealthiest city in the world, Charles I simply could not leave well enough alone. Insisting on the divine right of kings, a philosophy that was anathema to the Parliament and businessmen of London, he started a civil war. The monarchist Cavaliers were defeated by the Puritan Roundheads, and Charles I was beheaded outside his beloved Banqueting Hall, designed by Inigo Jones. (The king's last walk is still commemorated on the last Sunday in January.) Although the majority of London had been on the side of the Commonwealth, 18 years of dour Puritan reign under Oliver Cromwell's rule, during which all fun was canceled, left the city gasping for a breath of fresh air. The diarist John Evelyn wrote at Cromwell's death that "it was the joyfullest funeral I ever saw, for there were none that cried but dogs." In 1661, London warmly welcomed the exiled Charles II back from France, "shouting with inexpressible joy" and watching undismayed when Charles ordered the exhumation of the three-year-old corpses of Cromwell and two cronies for the dubious purpose of hanging and beheading them publicly for the murder of his father. Perhaps the citizens thought it fitting punishment for closing the theaters, brothels, and gambling houses.

1660s: Plague and Fire

Charles II barely had time to adjust his crown when disaster struck. In early 1665, the first cases of a second major round of the bubonic plague were seen in London. Samuel Pepys, the great diarist, first heard of the outbreak in April, writing, "Great fear of the sickness here in the city, it being said that two or three houses are already shut up. God preserve us." The hot summer saw the outbreak burst into an epidemic, with affected houses painted with red crosses and shut up with a guard outside— people trapped inside died either of the plague or starvation. By September, red crosses bloomed everywhere, and the rattle of the death cart was heard in the streets with its mournful accompaniment, "Bring out your dead!" a wretched parody of the cries of the apple or mussel sellers that had been silenced by the calamity. On September 7, John Evelyn wrote, "I went all along the city and suburbs from Kent Street to St. James's, a dismal passage and dangerous, to see so many coffins exposed in the streets thin of people, the shops shut up and all mournful silence, as not knowing whose turn might be next."

It was not humanity's finest hour: The stricken were prevented from leaving their homes, or if they had escaped London, from traveling on roads. They were often pelted with rocks and dung at the outskirts of villages. Con artists and quacks sold phony cures, and the rich and powerful jumped ship like the rats who were carrying the plague. The problem was that no one had figured out that it was the rats'—or, more accurately, the fleas' on the rats—fault. Mistaking the disease as airborne, someone decided that the very cats and dogs who could have helped control the rats had to be destroyed and, in killing 60,000 animals, certainly added to the disaster. The horror and pain of the disease was unspeakable, dispatching an estimated 100,000 by the time this epidemic began to abate, around Christmas 1665. In February, the king returned to London to survey—in safety, he thought—the melancholy scene of a decimated London still smelling of rotted flesh. But the rough hand of fate hadn't finished with London yet.

On September 2, 1666, a baker's oven in Pudding Lane was left unbanked. Its sparks, teased out of the chimney by a stiff wind, fired like tinder the dry wood of summer-baked houses and ignited the city in a matter of hours. Pepys was called at three in the morning by a servant to look at the fire, and being used to little local fires in the cramped wooden alleys and byways of London, he "thought it to be on the back side of Mark Lane at the furthest . . . I thought it far enough off, and so went back to bed."

The lord mayor also brushed the fire off, saying "a woman might piss it out," and no measures were taken to control the conflagration until it was too late. Amazingly, only a handful of people lost their lives, one of them a servant in the house of the baker where the fire had started. John Evelyn describes a ghastly picture of the event two days after it started: "The burning still rages, and it was now gotten as far as the Inner Temple; all Fleet Street, the Old Bailey, Ludgate Hill, Warwick Lane, Newgate, Paul's Chain, Watling Street, now flaming, and most of it reduced to ashes; the stones of St. Paul's flew like grenados, the melting lead running down the streets in a stream, and the very pavements glowing with fiery redness, so as no horse nor man was able to tread on them, and the demolition had stopped all the passages, so that no help could be applied."

King Charles finally stepped in and did what the lord mayor should have done sooner: His navy blew up the houses in the way of the fire, creating a break in its path. After four grim days, the driving wind died down and the fire finally ended. In its wake lay an unrecognizable London, suffering untold losses in its architecture, treasures, books, and art. In all, 436 acres of London had been consumed by the fire: 13,200 houses, 87 parish houses and many of their churches, 44 merchants' halls, the Royal Exchange, the magnificent medieval Guildhall, and St.

Paul's Cathedral. It was, if nothing else, an opportunity to rebuild the city along straight and reasonable lines, obliterating the medieval maze of streets that had contributed to the tragedy.

But this was not to be. Although both John Evelyn and the young Christopher Wren submitted designs for a new London with wide thoroughfares and sensible squares and circuses, the urgent need for housing and the legal problems of ownership of land assured that the rebuilding followed the original "plan" of medieval London somewhat faithfully. The main differences were that the lanes were widened to a mandatory 14 feet, and the buildings were made of stone. This was Wren's great opportunity, as he rebuilt 51 of the ruined churches, including St. Paul's Cathedral. Despite the loss of many of those edifices during World War II, Wren's name will forever be associated with the glory of that age, as London rose like a phoenix from the ashes of the fire into the magnificence of the eighteenth century.

Georgian London

To most London connoisseurs, the 1700s remain the very apex of the city's greatness: In architecture, literature, theater, painting, sculpture, in the building of stately homes and parks, in philosophy and sciences, there can be no other century to rival the verve and creativity of the eighteenth. The names of the artists, thinkers, and artisans of the day have come to define their disciplines: William Hogarth, Sir Joshua Reynolds, Thomas Gainsborough (painting); Jonathan Swift, Henry Fielding, Oliver Goldsmith (literature); David Garrick (theater); Alexander Pope (poetry); John Nash, Robert Adams (architecture); Edward Gibbon (history); John Gay (opera); David Hume (philosophy); Capt. James Cook (exploration); Adam Smith (economics); James Watt (technology); and the naturalized British subject, composer George Frederic Handel. Of course, you can hardly mention London and the eighteenth century in the same breath without a bow to the looming figure of the formidable writer and lexicographer Dr. Samuel Johnson and his biographer and friend, James Boswell. There are countless other figures who made major breakthroughs in technology, medicine, and science in this robust century. There was something in the air it would seem, and not just the stench of the tanneries, slaughterhouses, and privies. In the 100-year span of this period, London grew from 650,000 souls to close to a million. The small villages north and west of the city were embraced by London's expansion. Near the bucolic hamlet of Knightsbridge, a country house was bought and grandly rebuilt by the duke of Buckingham, later to go to King George III as a private royal residence.

The 12-year reign of Queen Anne left her name to a wildflower and a style of furniture. In 1714 came the Hanover succession from Germany. Georges I through IV presided over the acquisition of imperial lands from

Canada to Australia and the ignominious loss of the wealthy American colonies to the war of independence. They saw the rise of a new technology that revolutionized the cotton and wool trades of England. They watched as the Bastille was stormed, igniting the French Revolution, and managed to keep their crowns on while across the channel others were losing their heads. They continued to prefer the German language while ruling an English-speaking kingdom. Due to this oddity, the position of prime minister came to be; thanks to the madness of King George and the dissolute lifestyle of the prince regent, the policy-making powers of the monarch were carefully whittled away by an increasingly powerful Parliament.

The expansion and progress of London were attended by an increase in crime, corruption, drinking, and poverty. Dr. Johnson, famed for his remark that "when a man is tired of London, he's tired of life," wrote a poem about London that exposes this dark underbelly:

Here malice, rapine, accident, conspire,
And now a rabble rages, now a fire;
Their ambush here relentless ruffians lay,
And here the fell attorney prowls for prey;
Here falling houses thunder on your head,
And here a female atheist talks you dead....
Prepare for death if here at night you roam,
And sign your will before you sup from home....

There was an increasing polarization—due to the incipient Industrial Revolution—of London's society into owners and workers, rich and poor. The coarseness and insensitivity to the less fortunate on the part of the wealthy was truly shocking. Their entertainment included outings to the insane asylums for a laugh and attendance at public executions. There was one law for the rich and one for the poor; the criminals who weren't executed for the slightest offense were made to endure a grueling and often fatal passage to the new penal colony in Australia. It was only by the most repressive of measures that the revolution in France did not spread to London's gates, especially after the Gordon Riots of 1780, in which the Newgate Gaol was stormed and 300 were left dead. There were a few reformers and progressive thinkers, most memorably Jonathan Swift who, with his "Modest Proposal" of solving the problem of the Irish poor by feeding their babies to the rich, refined a tradition of savage English satire and social commentary that found many talented exponents in the Victorian century.

Victorian London

Queen Victoria's reign started in 1837, after the unlamented last gasp of Georgian rule by the grotesque George IV. He may have been the patron of John Nash, who developed Regent's Park and filled the city with white stucco-covered houses, but other than that, George IV didn't do much for London, although the extravagances and vices of his court certainly helped fill the coffers of moneylenders, gambling dens, and whorehouses. Princess Victoria was a woman of only 18 years when she became queen and gave her name to an age of change and reaction, reform and wretchedness, empire and exploitation.

There is another name so completely identified with nineteenth-century London that it has become an adjective describing it: Charles Dickens. He is never far from the hearts and minds of the London dweller; his face appears—appropriately for one who wrote so much about money's awful power—on the £10 note. It is the London of Dickens we tend to think of when we envision the nineteenth century: poor Bob Cratchit freezing in Scrooge's office; the convict Magwitch and Pip fleeing on the Thames under cover of a pea-soup fog; Oliver Twist asking for more food in the orphanage. Dickens was an insomniac who walked the streets of London for hours every night, and in his travels he picked up the sounds and secrets of the city. He is as much the voice of nineteenth-century London as Pepys and John Evelyn were of the seventeenth. Through his deeply compassionate reporting and fiction, Dickens opened up the eyes of the middle class to the misery of the poor. He helped steer England toward a more humane course as reformers worked to abolish the slave trade, put limits on child labor, allow women to keep their own property, extend voting rights, and open the first state schools.

The Industrial Revolution didn't so much flower as detonate in the nineteenth century; its effects were not entirely salutary. The gulf widened between rich and poor, the landscape and atmosphere were degraded, and as people in the country lost their self-sustainability, they trickled into a city already bursting at the seams with immigrants from the far reaches of the empire. But with all that cheap labor available, London grew at an amazing rate. New houses were built in every direction, with formerly quiet outlying villages becoming part of London's urban scene. The first underground trains began operation, sewers were built, transatlantic cable laid, the first police force was established, train tracks originating in London crisscrossed the country, omnibuses were pulled through the streets by huge workhorses, streets were gaslit, and roads were laid all over the city. Museums, monuments, learned societies, and public libraries flourished. The Great Exhibition of 1851, organized by Victoria's husband, Prince Albert, showed the world that London was a city of cosmopolitan suaveness and culture, firmly looking to the future.

That Karl Marx wrote *Das Capital* while living in this two-faced city, has a certain poetic logic. The terrible contrast between the shiny new city, with its shops and theaters, hotels and town houses, and the unmitigated squalor of the East End slums in many ways defined the Victorian Age. It's interesting to see how rosy with nostalgia that era has come to be: Look at the industry that has sprung up around all things Victorian in the last 20 years. It couldn't have been all that much fun to be alive then: The sexual hypocrisy, claustrophobic class system, sexism, racism, xenophobia, and social Darwinism must have been about as easy to deal with as a night out with Jack the Ripper. Yet it was a time in which enormous changes took place, a time in which terrible injustices were at last redressed, and a time of unforgettable literature and indelible heroes. After all, any age that could produce Florence Nightingale, Oscar Wilde,and Lewis Carroll can't be all bad.

World War I

Queen Victoria made a perfect exit in January 1901, keeping her era clearly defined by century. And now the twentieth century dawned with poor old Bertie, prince of Wales, at last out from under his mother's long shadow to lend his own name of King Edward to a new age. It was a short reign—only a decade, a mere fraction of his mother's 64 years on the throne—but it was distinctive enough to earn the title of the Edwardian Age—England's last era to be described in terms of the monarch. It was a clear cusp between the centuries, a time of accelerated progress. Motorcars became common, corsets came off, women demonstrated for the vote and smoked in public, and people started to challenge a number of tired Victorian verities. As a well-known sensualist of the time, King Edward helped usher in a more permissive era in which free love, divorce, and bohemian living arrangements were practiced without the terror of ostracism from an uptight moral majority. The famous freethinking Bloomsbury Group formed around this time, during which artists and writers who lived in the then shabby-genteel neighborhood of the British Museum redefined not only their artistic disciplines but also their relationships. Virginia Woolf's famous quote, "In or about December 1910, human character changed," underscores the leap made in thought and behavior by this new generation.

In 1914, London and the British empire enjoyed the zenith of their world power. The British pound sterling was as safe as gold and was the currency of international commerce all over the globe. There was peace and prosperity. Social activists were kept busy working to get the vote for women, get children out of the factory and into a classroom, and force legislation that would make the government responsible for its neediest citizens. But the shadow of the German zeppelins loomed above London. Despite the efforts of pacifists like George Bernard Shaw, England was plunged into the ghastly war fought across the English Channel that came close to wiping out an entire generation of young Englishmen. When it was over in 1918, the whole social order changed. It was a completely different London, filled with emancipated working women and powered by electricity.

The Long Weekend: 1918–1939

There is a sense that this period between the two World Wars was a last gasp of glamour for London. There is something to that, despite the ugly rumblings from the black-shirted British fascists led by Nazi-sympathizer Sir Oswald Mosley; despite the economic depression that left millions unemployed; and despite the terrible losses of life, limb, and hope during World War I. It may be that we view this interlude with an acute awareness of how much was soon to be buried under the Blitz, which makes the frivolity of that time seem all the more poignant.

People embraced the work of humorist P. G. Wodehouse, which helped them shake off the blues of the war and depression. To this day, the country still loves Wodehouse's version of London between the wars: gin-soaked parties with bright young things, dim Right Honorables, creaking lords and terrifying aunts, the Drones Club, and of course the unflappable Jeeves and his young master Bertie Wooster. They inhabit a hilarious fictional world that reveals what made London laugh between cataclysms. Noël Coward, Cecil Beaton, Virginia Woolf, George Orwell, Nancy Mitford, W. H. Auden, and T. S. Eliot are a few of the artists whose work also captures the feeling of the time.

London gave Hollywood a run for its money, making movies with such luminaries as Sir Laurence Olivier, Peggy Ashcroft, Charles Laughton, and Alfred Hitchcock. Agatha Christie and Dorothy Sayers fed the increasing demand for murder mysteries. The West End was alive with plays, from melodramas to social realism. But nothing cooked up in the imagination could even come close to the real-life drama of 1936: the abdication of King Edward VIII for the woman he loved, the American divorcée Mrs. Wallis Simpson. Although the event was billed as a grave constitutional crisis, it was clear that the monarch of England was becoming increasingly irrelevant to the citizenry, except as gossip and newsreel fodder. The citizens were mainly concerned with their own lives as they joined trade unions, built suburban communities, and tried to figure out the map of the underground. In 1931, this tangled web was simplified into the sleek art deco design we know and love, and the population of eight million began using the tube to escape the brown-fogged city to ever-more distant reaches of residential London.

Meanwhile, across the English Channel, Europe was increasingly threatened by Adolf Hitler, dismissed in the early days by most intelligent Londoners as a twisted clown and admired by a shameful number of hate-filled fascists and dim-witted minor nobility known as Right Honourables. They would all come to despise his name, as his Luftwaffe rained destruction on London, and Europe's fleeing Jews came to town with stories of concentration camps and genocide.

The Blitz: "Our Finest Hour"

World War I, the "war to end all wars," couldn't live up to that promise for long; only two decades after the armistice was signed, London was once again anxiously watching the skies over Whitehall. Though this time it wasn't the lumbering zeppelins, but the significantly more deadly Messerschmitts, Stukas, and the unpiloted "doodlebugs" that spelled disaster. The attack started in earnest on a sunny day on September 7, 1940, when hundreds of fighter planes and bombers buzzed up the Thames and destroyed docks, gasworks, and power stations. The Luftwaffe went on to bomb London nightly for 76 consecutive nights, dropping over 27,000 high explosives and thousands more incendiaries. The Blitz was on. Children were hurriedly sent to the countryside or to America, but the royal family made a point of staying in town, even after nine bombs dropped on Buckingham Palace. People sheltered in the tube stations in staggeringly large numbers, sleeping on the ground or in bunk beds placed on the tracks and platforms. Above ground, civilians coped with bombed-out streets, nightly fires, disrupted railways, power and water failures, the destruction of their homes, and, most terribly, the deaths of their friends, neighbors, and families. Novelist Nancy Mitford described the scene vividly in a letter to a friend:

> I find my nerves are standing up to the thing better now—I don't tremble quite all the time as I did. . . . NOBODY can have the slightest idea of what it is like until they've experienced it. As for the screaming bombs, they simply make your flesh creep but the whole thing is so fearful that they are actually only a slight added horror. The great fires everywhere, the awful din which never stops, and wave after wave after wave of aeroplanes, ambulances tearing up the street and the horrible unnatural blaze of lights from search-lights, etc.—all has to be experienced to be understood. Then in the morning the damage—people ring one another up to tell one how their houses are completely non-existent. . . . People are beyond praise, everyone is red eyed and exhausted but you never hear a word of complaint or down-heartedness. It is most reassuring.
>
> (Selina Hastings, Nancy Mitford
> [London: Hamish Hamilton, 1985], p. 134.)

The bombardment put to the test the famous English stiff upper lip, and London's amazing rise to the challenge earned the admiration of the rest of the country and the world. Prime Minister Winston Churchill was the voice of the people during those dark days, author of such unforgettable war cries as "we shall defend our island, whatever the cost may be, we shall fight on the beaches, we shall fight on the landing grounds, we shall fight in the fields and in the streets, we shall fight in the hills; we shall never surrender," and "Let us therefore brace ourselves to our duties, and so bear ourselves that, if the British Empire and its Commonwealth last for a thousand years, men will still say, 'This was their finest hour.'"

And so it was. Despite the thousands killed, the millions wounded and made homeless, the destruction of hundreds of thousands of dwelling places and buildings, and the nearly total destruction of the city and the East End, London carried on. The people lived in corrugated steel caves called Anderson shelters (to be replaced later by the heavier Morrison shelters) buried three feet underground. The homeless were sheltered by hotels—when the East End was first bombed, a huge crowd marched to the Savoy and demanded to be admitted, which they were—as well as by the not completely invulnerable tube stations. Brigades of men and women pulled all-night duties to put fires out in likely targets such as Westminster Abbey and St. Paul's Cathedral, saving some of the precious treasures of London's past. When the war finally ended, it could be well said of the Blitzed Londoners that, again in the words of Churchill, "their will was resolute and remorseless, and as it proved, unconquerable."

Sunset of the Empire

In 1948, England lost the jewel of her colonial crown when India became independent, and over the next decade it continued to lose colonies around the world, as well as much of the shipping and manufacturing business that made her rich. The 1950s were spent cleaning up the wreckage of the Blitz and continuing to live under strict food rationing. There was a grayness in the city; grim gaps of bomb sites yawned among the old Victorian buildings that were still black with coal grime and sagging under the weight of the years. People abandoned the city for the suburbs, whose spread was contained by the public lands of the Green Belt on the outer perimeters of London. Yet London was buoyant; the welfare state of the Labour government helped people rebuild their lives and gave them a sense of security unknown up to that time. In 1946, Heathrow Airport was opened, followed by Gatwick Airport three years later; the city was quickly rebuilt with modern glass-and-steel towers (Samuel Johnson and Charles Dickens would weep with confusion if they time-traveled to their old haunts); and domestic laborsaving devices were new, plentiful, and affordable.

The most influential of these was certainly the television, on which people watched the colorful coronation of Queen Elizabeth II in 1953 from the comfort of their own armchairs. The prime minister, Harold Macmillan, said in 1959, "Most of our people never had it so good."

The Festival of Britain celebrated the centennial of Prince Albert's Great Exhibition, and it was on that site the South Bank Arts Centre came to be. The fog lifted, thanks to antipollution measures, and the future looked as bright as the sky on a clear day. A new age was indeed coming, and it was a doozy. After the war, a quarter of the map of the world had been colored with pink empire; by the mid-1960s, England had lost almost all of her colonial possessions.

The Swinging Sixties and Punk Seventies

Whatever England may have lost in her empire, London certainly tried to overcome by becoming ground zero of the 1960s "youth quake." The quintessential 1960s figures of the Beatles and James Bond joined the thinner ones of Twiggy and Julie Christie in making all things British very hip. England was swinging like a pendulum, and London, as always, was the epicenter of the groove. Movies such as *A Hard Day's Night, Blowup, To Sir with Love,* and *A Man for All Seasons* were worldwide hits. The comedy of Spike Milligan gave way to Monty Python. Michael Caine, Vanessa and Lynn Redgrave, Oliver Reed, and Terrence Stamp were among the many English stars who could pull off a Hollywood blockbuster as well as do Pinter in the West End. Peter Sellers's Inspector Clouseau made him a superstar—a word and concept born in the bright light of the 1960s. Fashion designers of Carnaby Street and the King's Road started the miniskirt and bell-bottom trends, and fashion photographers like David Bailey became as famous as their subjects. The Rolling Stones, The Kinks, Cream, The Yardbirds, Led Zeppelin, The Who . . . London's bands in the 1960s were a veritable Debrett's Peerage of rock and roll. Twentysomething rock stars and their birds got their clothes at Granny Takes a Trip and Biba, drove around in Bentleys, and bought stately old piles in the country from hard-up toffs. *Hair* was performed in the West End; the Rolling Stones put on a free concert in Hyde Park, home to political demonstrations and love-ins. Drugs, sex, and rock and roll became a way of life for many of the new generation.

No one did sex, drugs, and rock and roll better than the glam rockers and punks of the 1970s. Green Mohawk hairdos, safety pins piercing cheeks, very high platform shoes, and in-your-face attitudes were the usual for the King's Road, where designer Vivian Westwood and Malcolm McLaren (later manager of The Sex Pistols) had a punk-rock clothing shop—still there with the fast backward-moving clock outside—under a series of interesting names ("Sex" was one, and "Too Fast to Live, Too Young to Die" another). Feminism had many local, brilliant exponents, with Angela Carter writing in south London and Aussie expat Germaine Greer lecturing around the city. The literature of the day was pretty dark; Martin Amis's *Dead Babies* was a savage and chilling portrait of young people in 1970s London that opened the door to many imitators. *A Clockwork Orange,* filmed by Stanley Kubrick in 1972 from the novel by Anthony Burgess, was a surreal prediction of a London gone viciously mad in the not-too-distant future. Squatters took over entire buildings that were earmarked for renovation; value-added tax was introduced; and a Women's Year Rally coincided with the election of Margaret Thatcher as leader of the Conservative Party. By the time Sid Vicious of The Sex Pistols had stabbed his girlfriend and then overdosed in New York City, people were exhausted and disillusioned with the 1970s. It seemed time to get on to more upbeat pastimes—like making money, that old-time London passion.

The Thatcher Years

When Margaret Thatcher was made prime minister in 1979, she announced the somewhat astonishing goal of returning to Victorian values. She axed 40,000 civil-service jobs, wrested control of London Transport away from the Greater London Council (GLC), and sold it to private investors. The gap between rich and poor became wider, as a very Victorian economic and social Darwinism—the survival of the fittest and fattest cats—took shape. After fighting constantly with the Labour-based GLC over social services and privatization, she abolished the GLC altogether in 1986. People in the city were suddenly making piles of dough (as they were on Wall Street across the pond), property prices were sky-high, and the materialistic yuppie came to define the era in both England and the United States.

London in the 1980s also saw race riots in Brixton, the first cases of AIDS, strikes by tube- and steelworkers, and a ban on smoking on the London Underground after a fire at King's Cross killed 31 people. Homelessness rose most disturbingly, as Thatcher dismantled the socialist safety net, and the real-estate boom took its toll on government housing. In 1989, Thatcher closed out her decade nicely by resigning, and John Major took over as another Conservative prime minister.

Cool Britannia: The 1990s

The 1990s started with the historical joining of the French and English sides of the new tunnel beneath the English Channel, linking Paris and London with a three-hour train ride. The local fear that hordes of foreigners would breach London by rail never quite materialized, although the train surely had a part to play in the huge upsurge of tourism in the 1990s.

In 1992, the queen suffered her famous *annus horribilis* (you've got to love a queen who thinks everyone still understands Latin). A fire at Windsor Castle caused extensive damage, two of her sons were going through horrendously public marital scandals, and she started paying taxes for the first time in her life. Not one to leave books unbalanced—this is a woman who lived through the Blitz and food rationing—the queen decided to pay for the repair of Windsor Castle by opening Buckingham Palace to the public for two months a year. They're now raking in so much money that there was enough left over to upgrade the Queen's Gallery, where we can now see even more of the royal treasures.

The 1990s saw *Big Issue* launched, the magazine that helps the homeless earn money and tries to keep a conscience alive in the city. The 1990s also saw the premiere of the runaway television hit *Absolutely Fabulous* which neatly and hilariously skewered the hypocrisies of the day. The two royal divorces, between Charles and Diana and Andy and Sarah (Fergie), as well as the mad-cow disease that rocked the British beef industry, helped to keep the media eye on London. By the time the Brit-pop explosion signaled the start of "Cool Britannia," everyone in the world knew that London was again the place to be. The Spice Girls, Oasis, All Saints, and Robbie Williams put British music back at the top of the charts. London Fashion Week became one of the hottest tickets in Europe, rivaling even Milan and Paris as the event in which to showcase new collections.

In May 1997, Tony Blair of the Labour Party was voted in as prime minister, signaling an end to the Conservative Party's 18-year run. Blair ran on a platform of finding the "third way" between the policies of Tory and Labour, and he has succeeded in annoying both parties. The same year also saw the tragedy of Princess Diana's death in a car crash in Paris, and the resulting week of completely un-British mourning. It was a spasm of national grief that had Buckingham Palace doing back flips to appease the people who found fault with how the royal family was responding. People stood in line for days to sign the condolence book at St. James's Palace, while a sea of flowers numbering in the millions was left at the gates of Kensington Palace. It was a London no one had ever seen before and will likely never see again.

Next up for London was the opening of the Millennium Dome, the much maligned and hyped exhibition to celebrate the turning of the century and the next millennium. To the bitter delight of its critics, the exhibition failed to draw the crowds anticipated, and plans on what to do with the hulking thing are still up in the air, but it's possible that it will become an arena for sports and entertainment.

Another millennium damp squib was the Sir Charles Foster–designed footbridge over the Thames, connecting the Globe Theater and St. Paul's Cathedral. While it beautifully fulfilled its design as a "blade of light" across the Thames, on the opening day it shook so dangerously that it had to be closed for a rethink, with everyone involved blaming each other for the humiliating foul-up. Now the bridge is fully operational and vies with the nearby Hungerford Bridge as the best walk across the Thames.

An unmitigated success, however, is the British Airways London Eye, the elegant Ferris wheel that now looms over the Thames with surprising grace, adding to the grandeur of views of Parliament Square and beyond. It was originally intended to be temporary with a five-year lease, but that's been extended to 20 years, and it is most likely that your great-grandchildren will be queuing up to take that stately ride.

A more mixed blessing to London was the election of its first mayor, one with actual power, unlike the honorary Lord Mayor. Former Greater London Council–head Ken Livingstone has been trying, with varying degrees of success, to make London a better place to live, with his first priority being to make the public transport system more efficient. Not an easy assignment.

A New World: After September 11

The terrorist bombing of the Pentagon in Washington, D.C., and the World Trade Center in New York City threw the world into a state of panic, and the hardest hit business was the travel trade, from airlines to souvenir shops. London, an equally significant symbol of Western capitalism and culture as New York, went into the same high alert as the United States. Of course, London, having coped with the years of IRA terrorism, went quietly into action without much ado: permanently closing the street in front of the American Embassy, arresting suspected Al Qaeda members, and stepping up security in the Parliament and other high-profile institutions, such as the museums and cathedrals. The number of visitors to London dropped dramatically in the months following the attack, and the buoyant financial outlook of the 1990s gave way to a nervous slide in the stock market, real estate, and consumer goods. With the war in Iraq, tourism took an even greater hit as England and Prime Minister Tony Blair became partners with the United States in the coalition forces in the Middle East. At the time of publication, the state of the tourist industry in London is pretty dire, but if there is anything that the history of London teaches us, it's that you can't keep a good city down.

The year 2002 was the Queen's Golden (50th) Jubilee, which turned out to be a total love-fest for Lizzie. The House of Windsor was royally entertained by a lineup of rock and roll's own royalty. Queen's Brian May kicked off a great concert in the garden at Buck House, playing "God Save the Queen" on his electric guitar on the palace roof, and Prince of Darkness Ozzy Osbourne managed to perform without swearing. The Queen certainly needed the cheering up, as she had recently lost her sister, Princess Margaret, and her mother, the Queen Mum Elizabeth, who was over 101 years of age when she died.

Ken Livingstone, the beleaguered mayor of London, has presided over the abolition of the traditional pigeon-feeding from Trafalgar Square, as well as the closing of its northern end to traffic, creating a pigeon-free, automobile-free pedestrian area. No less controversially, he introduced a congestion charge for traffic going into the central part of London in February 2003. The world is watching to see how it goes, as street traffic is one of the greatest banes of city living all over the world. The scheme is designed to cut down traffic to the West End of London by requiring a payment of five pounds per day to pass through a perimeter that roughly outlines the high-commerce area of London. It uses cameras and pre-payments, and not surprisingly, in the first week almost 10,000 people were falsely accused of not paying. So far, the main difference is that the tube, already groaning under its commuter weight, is being pressured even further: The tube saw an increase of 17,000 trips a day just a month after the congestion charge was introduced. The buses move a bit more freely in some areas, but actually have added time to their trip in other places. Retailers in the congestion areas have seen a distressing drop in business. The money raised by the congestion charge is supposed to be used to improve public transportation and quality of life in London, but at the time of publication, the city is still unwieldy and difficult for the citizen. Tube strikes bring the city to a standstill regularly, automobile traffic is still bad, roadwork is constantly causing traffic jams, and the streets after midnight are rife with the shouts of drunken louts and the assault of the occasional mugger. Livingstone has plans to increase the police force to 35,000 by 2006, which should sort out the crime problems considerably. It's a big city with big problems, along with its huge delights. But no matter what the century, London will *always* remain a fascinating, fast-paced, infuriating, and fun-filled destination of choice.

British Culture:
Queues, the Weather, and a Stiff Upper Lip

A Foreign Tribe

The most wonderful thing about coming to London is the opportunity for English-speaking transatlantics to learn more about a foreign culture than could be possible in any European city with a language barrier. That is not to say that there won't be communication problems, but at least you'll know the words, if not the meaning behind them. The great misunderstandings are not in language but in nuance. This is a society based on the oblique and the tacit, with an intrinsic orderliness based on the old class system. You'll never understand it in the course of a visit, so just be polite and go along with the program. They're not going to change a hair for you.

George Bernard Shaw said that it is impossible for one Englishman to open his mouth without inviting the disdain of another. These days some people would very much like to believe that this is no longer true; whether it is still reality is open to argument. It is certain, however, that as a foreigner, you will never have to go through the process of having your class and social status sized up, judgments made, and conclusions drawn. You will likely be treated as an unknown, perhaps a novelty, and if you are American, with a curious combination of admiring amusement and contempt.

The primary exposure most Brits have to Americans is via Hollywood, and the Brits may check you out to see if the stereotype matches up with the real thing. You, of course, are free to do likewise. But you will probably not find Mary Poppins, Bertie Wooster, Jeeves, James Bond, Miss Marple, or Austin Powers. You will find that they are not amused by any attempts to claim some kind of special kinship with them—this is essentially an island culture, insulated for centuries against all comers, and still in some ways quite impenetrable by outsiders. This gives Brits their strength, eccentricity, and quiet assumption of superiority. The wonderful thing about us transatlantics is how we buy into this assumption in an automatic, reflexive way. Americans, it has been observed, can go weak before an English accent—and it doesn't even have to be a "posh" accent, which we wouldn't necessarily recognize, because we've somehow trained ourselves to think of the English as indeed superior in intelligence and experience. It could be thought of as the *Masterpiece Theatre* complex, except that it existed long before television. Don't fall into that trap—we're just different, like apples and oranges, or, as the British say, chalk and cheese.

Get in Line: The English Art of Queuing

All the rumors are true: the British queue for everything. Even soccer hooligans queue for tickets and beer. To jump the queue is the height of bad manners, and to do so is to invite certain tut-tutting, muttered comments, and possibly even an open challenge. In fact, it is such a violent breach of etiquette that it is about the only time the British will break another taboo, the one that prohibits raising one's voice in public (markets, pubs, and soccer stadiums notwithstanding). Raising one's voice attracts attention and may possibly give someone the *wrong idea,* whatever that is. However you may be tempted, *do not* jump the queue.

Also, always stand to the right when riding on escalators—the locals, even if they have no intention of passing you, hate it when tourists stand two abreast and clog up the path.

Weather Reports

The old saw about how everyone talks about the weather but no one does anything about it is not entirely true in London. The passion that the British have for talking about the weather amounts nearly to an interactive hobby. They will even go so far as to discuss it vigorously with complete strangers. Part of the reason may be the basically mild but changeable weather. London often goes through four seasons in one day (except in the winter, when cold, dark, and damp are the standards). The casting of aspersions on the abilities of the forecasters is a tried-and-true icebreaker and will pave the way for inquiries from the Brits about the extreme and interesting weather (tornadoes, blizzards, hurricanes, monsoons, sandstorms, and so on) of former colonial continents. As everyone must know by now, the famous London fogs of the past were a result of the coal burned in London, and a bona fide "pea-souper" hasn't been sighted since the early 1960s, after the Clean Air Act of 1956 put a stop to industrial pollution. The idea that it does rain constantly in London is also a myth, although there isn't one Londoner who doesn't own at least one umbrella (called a brolly), nor will you find too many visitors who haven't been forced to buy a rain poncho or umbrella on short notice.

At Your Service, Sort Of

A recent study concluded that the British complain more about poor service than the residents of any other country. However, it also concluded that this is because they have more to complain about. They have only recently realized that it's OK to enjoy good food; the deprivations and sacrifices of the postwar years have cast a long shadow. There's good food all over London now, and extra-virgin olive oil is no longer considered a foreign delicacy. However, they will not put iced water and a basket of bread on the table as a matter of course (worse, they may charge you a pound). They will not rush to take your order or bring you your bill. They will not take kindly to complaint—it's not so much that the customer is always wrong, but that the customer overestimates his or her importance. Don't take it personally: It's a British thing.

The Great British Reserve

This is alive and well, stiffening the upper lip and continuing to define "Englishness." You will see it manifested in the advertising, where wit and wordplay take precedence over volume, sloganeering, and repetition (although this may come to be a relic of the past, as vulgarity and briefly clad people in sexist ads grow apace on the sides of buses and billboards). It is apparent in the weather forecasts ("Today will be rather damp, with a possibility of patchy fog and maybe a spot of drizzle in between clear intervals") and on the tube at rush hour, where instead of mouthing off at an annoying commuter who refuses to move down in the carriage, passengers will mutter "excuse me's," issue irritated coughs, and initiate great flappings of newspapers. All pass for expressions of anger and frustration. This quietude can be almost soothing to an American accustomed to the chattering hordes of compatriots asking personal questions and offering the usual too much information, but it can take a bit of getting used to at first and might leave the visitor feeling a little out in the cold.

However, this reserve is not to be taken for granted. Road rage is a big problem in traffic-choked London, but luckily the gun laws are stringent enough that it results in shouting matches and fisticuffs rather than more serious consequences. There is nothing quite so terrifying as standing on the terraces at a soccer game, trapped among 10,000 grown men singing with one voice, "You're shite and you know you are!" Not for them the cozy familiarity of the seventh-inning stretches and the lilting tones of "Take Me Out to the Ballgame."

A similar contradiction to the stereotype is found during the prime minister's question period in the House of Commons. Barely veiled or even naked insults are hurled by members of Parliament at one another,

DIVIDED BY A COMMON LANGUAGE:

Thanks to the broadcasting of television shows and films (in London, films are viewed at the cinema, as opposed to movies or flicks viewed at the theater), the British are more hip to our lingo than they may let on. But if your exposure to Brit-speak has been limited to watching some shows on PBS or A&E, you may need a bit of a leg up. We have provided a short glossary of some words you may not have caught on *Prime Suspect* or *Pride and Prejudice*. With the globalization of culture, it is almost quaint to assume that we English speakers might misunderstand each other, but just in case, here goes:

AMERICAN	ENGLISH
At the airport	
cart	trolley
bill	bank note
wallet	billfold/purse
telephone booth	telephone box/kiosk
On the road	
baby carriage/stroller	pram/buggy
dead-end road	cul-de-sac
delivery truck	van
divided highway	dual carriageway
detour	diversion
gas	petrol
highway exit	motorway junction
hood (car)	bonnet
license plate	number plate
minivans	people carriers
sedan car	saloon car
subway	underground or tube
overpass	flyover
one-way ticket	single journey
pull-off	lay-by
round-trip ticket	return ticket
station wagon	estate car
truck	lorry
trunk	boot
underpass (pedestrian, under streets)	subway
At the hotel	
antenna	aerial
apartment hotel	service flats
apartment building	block of flats, mansion flats
baby crib	cot

A BRITISH/ENGLISH GLOSSARY

AMERICAN	ENGLISH
At the hotel (continued)	
baggage room	left-luggage office
bathe (verb)	bath (bathing—short "a" sound)
bathrobe	dressing gown
cot	extra bed or camp bed
call collect	reverse charges
closet	cupboard/wardrobe
comforter/quilt	eiderdown/duvet
elevator	lift
first floor	ground floor
second floor	first floor
long-distance call	trunk call
milk in coffee/tea or not	white or black
outlet/socket	power point
rent	let
vacuum	Hoover
washcloth	face flannel
In a restaurant or food store	
buffet	sideboard
can (of food)	tin
candy	sweets
check	bill
cookie	biscuit
cotton candy	candy floss
cracker	savoury biscuit
dessert	pudding
diaper	nappy
downtown	town center/high street
druggist/drugstore	chemist/chemist's shop
eggplant	aubergine
eraser	rubber
French fries	chips
hamburger meat	mince
hardware store	ironmonger
lima bean	broad bean
molasses	black treacle
potato chips	crisps
pit	stone
Popsicle	ice lolly
raisin	sultana
smoked herring	kipper
zucchini	courgette

DIVIDED BY A COMMON LANGUAGE:

AMERICAN	ENGLISH
At the theater	
aisle	gangway
balcony	gallery/upper circle
intermission	interval
mezzanine/loge	dress circle
movie theater	cinema
In the markets and on the high street	
liquor store	off license
newsstand	newsagent
notions	haberdashery
panties	knickers
panty hose	tights
raincoat	macintosh (or mac)/kagool
rest room	public convenience/loo/w.c./lavatory

while howls of derision and guffaws of braying laughter render the institution more like a high-school classroom when the teacher has stepped out than a hallowed hall of government. There is something rather invigorating about this cacophony, and it gives you an idea of the healthy self-regard in which the English hold themselves. The great paradox is that they yield to no one, except for the monarch.

To Do or Not to Do: That Is the Culture

There was an article in *The Spectator* magazine a few years ago in which the staff gave the worst possible advice to put in a tourist guide to London. They came up with, among others, "Introduce yourself and shake hands all around in your train compartment," and, "Try out the famous echo in the British Library Reading Room." As funny as we find this concept, we will resist temptation and will give you the following dos and don'ts guaranteed to be 100% valid.

Don't call older people by their first names unless expressly asked to do so—it is considered normal not to use any names at all when addressing people.

Don't expect people to introduce you to others. One can spend an entire evening with a group of people who introduce neither themselves nor their friends to you.

Don't try to intervene in soccer arguments—it's a very serious subject, one no outsider can comprehend properly. Remember at games that the hooligans mean business.

A BRITISH/ENGLISH GLOSSARY *(continued)*

AMERICAN	ENGLISH

In the markets and on the high street (continued)

sneakers	trainers or plimsolls
Scotch tape	cellotape
shorts (underwear)	pants
sweater	jumper
undershirt	vest
vest	waistcoat

In sickness and in health

acetaminophen (Tylenol)	paracetamol
emergency room	casualty
Band-Aids	plasters
pimples	spots
rubbing alcohol	surgical spirit

Don't take it personally when people act as if you're not there, correct your pronunciation, look at you as if you're daft when asking directions to "Lye-cester Square," act slightly exasperated by your inability to read a complex map of London, or try to run you down in the street. You'll get a lot of this—get used to it.

Don't brag about how much sunlight you get at home; this will not endear you to anyone.

Don't tell anyone that their accent is "cute." It is you who has the accent, and it is not considered remotely cute by the British.

Don't gloat about the American Revolution or the sunset on the British Empire. Again, not cute.

Do watch out for queues and take your place in them.

Do be courteous; be very courteous—it's much more appreciated than friendliness.

Do remember that this is a country of rules, rules, rules—and they aren't just making them up as they go along, though it sometimes seems that they are.

Do be patient in restaurants and stores; use your vacation as an opportunity to slow down and practice your manners.

Do learn to enjoy being called "love" and "darling" and "sweetheart" by certain strangers.

Do prepare for your visit by reading as much as you can about London; try to listen more than you speak. This is a very interesting place, and the people are fascinating. Make the most of your visit.

Part Two

Planning Your Visit to London

Airline Deals

British Airways (call (800) AIRWAYS, **www.britishairways.com**) and Virgin Atlantic Airways (call (800) 862-8621, **www.virgin.com**) are the two largest transatlantic carriers in and out of London and are certainly the ones to check with first to get a baseline on a fare. They often engage in price wars, which means the other airlines will lower their prices too, or at least match the lowest rate.

Obviously, if you are collecting frequent flier miles with a particular carrier, that's the airline to use because you will accumulate a tidy sum of miles with a round-trip. With the recent difficulties in the airline industry, there is no predicting which airlines will have the best deals or the largest selection of flights to London, so you will need to call or surf around. Some of the United States–based, transatlantic airlines are American (call (800) 433-7300, **www.aa.com**); Delta (call (800) 241-4141, **www.delta.com**); Northwest (call (800) 447-4747, **www.nwa.com**); and United (call (800) 241-6522, **www.united.com**). They all fly into either Heathrow or Gatwick.

Flight consolidators are a good way to shop for the best deal, but be sure that the one you use books foreign travel. Consolidators buy up blocks of unsold seats from airlines and resell them to you. Some consolidators deal primarily with domestic tickets, and while they may get you a ticket to London, it might be the same price as the published fare from an airline, and more restrictions may apply. The Internet has made it so easy to shop for fares, but in these days of crumbling dot-com companies, you want to be aware of the here-today-gone-tomorrow qualities of the Web. So far, the following discount and flight consolidator businesses are doing well, but we are including several to increase your options. Some of the so-called discount websites are actually owned by various airlines and offer no discount at all, and some are merely agencies to sell tickets.

Before you start searching the Internet, call a couple of the big airlines to get an idea of what prices are available directly from them.

www.airdiscounters.com	Airfares from the U.S. to most major cities worldwide
www.bestfares.com	Big database; lots of vacation options (cars, hotel rooms, packages)
www.blueskytravelinc.com	An airfare consolidator with discounted tickets to Europe
www.cheapflights.com	Discounted flights from travel agents in the U.K.
www.cheaptickets.com	Finds cheapest Web fares available
www.discountairbrokers.com	International travel discounts
www.1800airfare.com	Airfares for American, Delta, United, Northwest, and Continental
www.expedia.com	Well-established website; always check prices against the airlines' websites before booking
www.flightdiscount.com	Discounted airfares for any destination
www.flights4less.co.uk	U.K.-based cheap flights
www.goodfare.com	International travel discounts, including consolidator fares
www.orbitz.com	Good place to browse (thousands of fares); not always best prices (owned by airlines)
www.ticketplanet.com	International travel discounts
www.travelocity.com	Full-service everything; may not have the best prices, but will have the most info

If you prefer to telephone, call (800) FLY-4-LESS or (800) FLY-CHEAP; or contact Council Travel at (800) 226-8624 (**www.counciltravel.com**). You will also see ads for flight consolidators in the travel section of most Sunday-newspaper editions.

Winter is London's off-season, and that's when some hotels offer impressive air-and-land packages. For information about finding and negoatiting hotel deals, see page 64 in Part Three, "Hotels."

Quick Check

Travel Insurance   Your own insurance company may offer travel insurance, so check first with them before buying any additional coverage. You can purchase insurance for canceled travel, lost luggage, and medical emergencies through Travel Guard International at (800) 826-1300, **www.travelguard.com;** or Travel International, Inc. at (800) 243-3174, **www.travelinsured.com.** While we're on the subject of emergencies, here's a website for worriers: **www.travelriskcenter.com.** With links to the U.S. State Department and the British Foreign and Commonwealth Office, it will apprise you of any health, political, or terrorist risks current in any location, and it has special reports on safety and security.

Luggage   Every airline has different rules, so call ahead to find out number of bags that can be checked, maximum weight, and size and weight of carry-ons. Virgin is very strict about carry-on luggage and will make you check even a backpack if it is too heavy. This also depends on the class in which you are traveling—if it's economy, don't try to bring all your luggage on board with you; it may not get by check-in, and if the flight is full, you will be depriving others of their fair share of space.

With the more stringent security enforced for carry-on luggage, you must be careful to put the following items in your check-in luggage: scissors, nail files, nail clippers, penknives, razors or razor blades, knitting needles, or any other sharp object that could conceivably be used as a weapon. Also try to limit the electronic equipment you carry on board—cellular phones, CD players, laptops, handheld games. Screening these devices creates delays at check-in. The same goes for bottles of liquid.

Valuables   Be sure to bring valuables, such as cameras, jewelry, money, and anything particularly fragile or precious, including medication, on the plane with you. They may be able to send a man to the moon, but they can't always match up the luggage with the flight.

Medications   You may want to bring an extra supply of any medicine you are taking, as well as a spare pair of eyeglasses. If you do lose your medication, it will help to know its generic name in order to get a new prescription. Prescriptions from a foreign doctor will usually be honored in England, so you might ask your doctor for a backup before you go. Wear a Medic Alert tag if you have a serious health condition.

Personal Electronics   Your laptop probably has a built-in electrical transformer, and all you'll need to do is buy a plug adapter. In London, the most common electrical plug is the three-prong type, which is not the same as in the rest of Europe (where two round pins are used). RadioShack or Brookstone has foreign-plug adapter packages that cover pretty much any type of plug. Forget about hair dryers, electric toothbrushes, and other personal electronics; you will blow them up if you plug a 110-volt into the British 220-volt system without running it through a currency converter. Your cell phone, unless it is one of the expensive tri-band world-wide-use models, will not work in England. Many hotels have cell phones to rent, and you can pick up a pay-as-you-go U.K. cell phone for about $100.

Car Rental   It's not a bad idea to reserve a rental car before you go to London; you can often get a better price from your country of origin. You should call your hotel and ask if there is a nearby rental place, so you don't have to cross the entire city to pick the car up and drop it off.

BritRail   If you are going to travel around rural England by train, you can purchase a BritRail Pass before you leave and save a bundle. Call

(888) BRITRAIL in the United States or (800) 555-BRIT in Canada, or order the pass through **www.raileurope.com.** You can also order Travel Cards for the tubes and buses at that website, but there's no financial incentive, only convenience. You can buy Travel Cards when you get to London at any tube station or London Tourist Office.

Money   There are ATMs with Cirrus, MAC, and credit-card account systems all over London. This is your best bet for getting the best rate. Remember, you can't access your credit-card funds from an ATM without a PIN number, so make sure you have one before you go. If you don't have a credit card or ATM card, be sure to ask for traveler's checks in pounds only.

The Weather

London measures its mild weather in degrees Celsius (centigrade) rather than Fahrenheit, so you might want to memorize a few conversions. You can check out the weather from the United States before you go. Call (900) WEATHER and dial the first four letters of your destination city (LOND), and you'll get a recording of current temperatures, current weather conditions, and the forecast for the next few days. Go online to the Weather Channel website at **www.weather.com** or check CNN weather at **www.cnn.com.** You can also access local newspapers at **www.sunday-times.co.uk, www.guardian.co.uk,** or **www.telegraph. co.uk** for weather info.

Convert temperatures (approximately) from Celsius to Fahrenheit by doubling Celsius and adding 30. Here are some more exact numbers:

$-3°C = 26.7°F$	$1°C = 33.8°F$	$15°C = 59°F$	$30°C = 86°F$
$-1°C = 30.2°F$	$5°C = 41°F$	$20°C = 68°F$	$37°C = 98.6°F$
$0°C = 32°F$	$10°C = 50°F$	$25°C = 77°F$	(normal human
(freezing)			body temperature)

AVERAGE DAYTIME TEMPERATURES AND RAINFALL IN LONDON		
Month	**Temperature (°F / C)**	**Rainfall (inches)**
January	40° / 4	2.1"
February	40° / 4	1.6"
March	44° / 7	1.5"
April	49° / 9	1.5"
May	55° / 13	1.8"
June	61° / 16	1.8"
July	64° / 18	2.2"
August	64° / 18	2.3"

	AVERAGE DAYTIME TEMPERATURES AND RAINFALL IN LONDON *(continued)*	
Month	Temperature (°F / C)	Rainfall (inches)
September	59° / 15	1.9"
October	52° / 11	2.2"
November	46° / 8	2.5"
December	42° / 6	1.9"

What to Bring

What to bring on your trip to London depends on the weather, which we've mapped out seasonally, but there are a few things that you might appreciate having handy at all times of the year:

- this book

- small map of central London and a portable street atlas, a small pocket-size book that has exhaustive maps on all of London, which even the natives can't do without; *London A to Z, Collins,* or *Nicholsons London Street Atlas* are all equally good

- £50 to £100, to be on the safe side, you might bring some cash for transportation from the airport in case the ATM machine at the airport is on the frit, although you can also have a taxi driver stop at a money machine (do try to avoid paying money-changing commissions).

- money belt

- good backpack or shoulder bag

- small, collapsible umbrella

- folding rain poncho

- currency converter

- portable electrical transformer if you can find a small one and want to bring your own hair dryer or electric toothbrush (check amps to make sure it can handle your appliances—hair dryers are notorious for blowing out transformers) input from the wall outlet will be British 220 volts, which will be transformed into 110 volts for American electronics

- camera and lots of extra film (like everything else, film is expensive here)

- sugar substitute (it's not as readily available in restaurants as it is in the United States)

- favorite snacks (American snacks and candy are not always easy to find and often can't be found anywhere)

- books on London that relate to your interests

- comfortable walking shoes

- passport-size photos for travel card (you can also get these done here easily)

Clothing

London is a city where people still dress with a certain degree of decorum—women of all ages still wear skirts occasionally, and women of a certain age wear only skirts on the streets of central London. This neatness may have to do with the fact that the majority of schools require uniforms. If you happen to come across a wedding, you'll see how seriously Londoners take their clothing—formal suits and amazing hats are de rigueur at most British nuptials, even at civil ceremonies at town hall. Harrods, which has a ridiculously high opinion of itself, actually has a dress code, as does the Ritz Hotel (no blue or black jeans at the Ritz; at Harrods it's completely and mysteriously up to their discretion). Generally speaking, globalization has ensured that the Western countries of the world all dress pretty much the same way, and except for very fancy and/or uptight places, there is no need to change the way you dress normally. Theaters no longer require dressing up, thank goodness. We would urge you to dress in layers as it can get quite warm in the middle of a sold-out play.

Bring one or two good comfortable outfits for stepping out to restaurants; smart casual is always safe. This is not Paris, where urban chic is the style on the street and the average human being can feel hopelessly dowdy. London is more about being presentable than being fashionable, but there is no snobbery about it, and as a nation of grand old eccentrics, they are mostly unflappable when it comes to other people's personal styles. If you do end up at a restaurant with a tie-and-jacket code, they will likely be able to lend you one.

When to Go

The best time to go to London is whenever it's possible for you. If you want more than anything to see this remarkable city but can't afford the high-season airfare, then by all means go in the winter, when the fares drop by as much as 75%—if you book sufficiently in advance and look around for the good deals. Other considerations might include the special events you're eager to see—perhaps Wimbledon or the Chelsea Flower Show—or the attractions in which you're most interested. Some of your choices—stately homes, for example—are usually closed for the winter. Although the winter is dark and dreary, it's free of the swarms of tourists that you find in the summer. Let's take it season by season:

Summer For many of us, summer is the *only* option because of our children's summer vacation and the slowdown in our work lives. Summer in London, though unpredictable, is often quite gorgeous. Henry James was probably thinking of England, his adopted home, when he declared the two most beautiful words in the English language to be "summer afternoon." One thing these summer afternoons can't promise, though, is heat—three consecutive days of 75° and sun is considered a heat wave. However, the global-warming trend is upsetting London's traditional brisk summer, and the past few years have seen record-breaking heat that upset many tourists, as air-conditioning is relatively rare in shops, restaurants, and many hotels. The worst is that it's nonexistent in buses and trains, where the heat can get dangerously high—you'd be arrested for transporting animals in conditions similar to the tube in an August heat wave. But don't take the warming trend as a given—the summer of 2000 was wet and chilly, confounding the meteorologists, although the summer of 2003 broke all existing heat records with a high of 101°F during a long heat wave. At night the temperature of even a very hot day will drop, and, generally speaking, a fan will suffice to cool a hotel room.

During each season in London, you should plan your clothing in layers, as the weather can change dramatically in one day. *Don't* pack only shorts and T-shirts, which you may not even get a chance to wear. Be sure to bring socks, a sweater, trousers ("pants" here are underpants, also known as knickers), a light jacket, and a rain poncho. The most crucial piece of clothing is a good pair of walking shoes, whichever shoes you personally find most comfortable, be they sneakers or sandals.

In the summer you can count on all the museums and attractions being crowded. Busloads of tourists are constantly bearing down on the most popular attractions, and the decent hotels are often completely booked by April or May. Unless the global economy goes completely into the toilet (or the "loo," as it's called here), a summer visit to London can require nerves of steel and the planning capabilities of Winston Churchill.

On the plus side, summer in London means that the parks are at their most fragrant and riotously floral and that all the stately homes and palaces are open (many have an April–October season). Buskers (street performers) are everywhere on the streets; there are carnivals, street fairs, and more outdoor dining than makes sense in a country with such variable weather. Private garden squares are open to the public on one Sunday in June. The Royal Parks have green-and-white-striped lawn chairs ready for hire, and stables lay on extra horses for rides in the parks. The locals take off on holiday, so the streets are relatively free to accommodate the stampede of tourists.

Fall   We much prefer the autumn to the summer in London for many reasons, the most important being that the crowds simmer down. Also, there is something wonderfully atmospheric about London in the fall, with leaves starting to turn brown, and winds twisting them off the branches and twirling them along the street. Because of London's mild climate, many flowers in the parks last all the way into November, and to see their radiance blending with the hues of the changing leaves is wonderful. The sunny days are mood lifting and the brisk air invigorating. The main thing to remember is that most of the stately homes and palaces close October 30, so come before then if these sights are on the top of your list. (Buckingham Palace closes at the end of September or in the first week of October.) November can get as cold as 45°F, but not much below that. Bring gloves and a hat for the windy days. The days get shorter and shorter.

Winter   There is a beautiful old English folk song heard at Christmas called "In the Bleak Midwinter" ("ground as hard as iron, water like a stone"), which plays in many Londoners' minds as they wake up to the darkness that returns around 4 p.m. The ancient trees in the parks have shed their leaves, standing like skeletons against a leaden sky. We personally don't mind the bleakness much, as it doesn't include temperatures below freezing very often and as the museums are so warm and inviting in the winter. The airline deals are fantastic, the hotels are cheaper, there aren't many tourists (just busloads of uniformed schoolchildren flooding the museums), and your choice of plays at the half-price ticket booths expands considerably. All in all, it's an economical time to make a cultural holiday. No one does Christmas quite like the English. They aren't constrained by Thanksgiving a month earlier and start their decorating and selling in the first couple of weeks of November. There are the Oxford Street and Regent Street Christmas lighting ceremonies, and there's a Santa Parade when Santa arrives at Harrods the first week of November. The decorations of Oxford and Regent Streets are getting tackier and more commercial every year—go to Marylebone High Street, Bond Street, or St. Christopher's Place for more appealing Christmas lights. There are scores of wonderful Christmas concerts at churches and cathedrals—check *Time Out* or *What's On* for where and when. What you won't find much of is snow, which may be a relief for some of you. But there is plenty of rain, and it's the cold kind. The best news is that after December 21, the days start getting longer.

Spring   Spring starts early in London. Carpets of crocus cover Hyde Park as early as February, with daffodils not far behind. It's a fine time to visit; the stately homes reopen at the end of March or beginning of April, and the parks and gardens come into bloom. Early May is a time when Londoners fall in love all over again with their city, despite the pummeling from the pollen and the flying fluff from the flowering trees (the allergy-prone should pack plenty of meds). Lovely as it is, early May can also be downright nippy, even though the cafés start putting tables on the street long before then. London starts coming back to its outdoor life, with the London Marathon, boat races on the Thames, and the Chelsea Flower Show. The weather can be fantastic with not as much rain as in winter, but it's the foolish optimist who ventures outside without an umbrella.

Gathering Information

Lucky for you, the British Tourist Authority is ready to help with your vacation. They have the following offices in the United States and a central toll-free number for information: (800) GO TO BRITAIN. (In London the number is (0208) 846-9000.) They have brochures, maps, and a booklet that they will be happy to give you. Make a point of calling, writing, or going in for these goodies.

In Chicago   No phone calls; write or walk in at 625 N. Michigan Avenue, Suite 1510, Chicago, IL 60611.

In New York   (212) 986-2200 or (800) 462-2748; 555 5th Avenue, 7th Floor, New York, NY 10176. There is a bookstore next door to the office, which has many London-related items of interest.

In Australia   (02) 267-4555 or fax (02) 267-4442; University Centre, 8th Floor, 210 Clarence Street, Sydney NSW 2000.

In Canada   (800) 847-4885; 111 Avenue Road, Suite 450, Toronto, Ontario M5R 3J8.

In New Zealand   (09) 303-1446 or fax (09) 377-6965; Dilworth Building, Suite 305, Queen and Customs Streets, Auckland 1.

Websites

There are so many websites about London, it's hard to keep up with them. They are always being improved, or sometimes removed, and the addresses may change, but the following websites should provide you with enough links to keep you glued to your computer for weeks:

www.londontown.com	This is the London tourist board's website with up-to-the-minute info on events, hotels, restaurants, sight-seeing, exhibits, and more
www.livesights.com	Real-time views of the Thames' various vistas, via Thames Cam!, plus weather
www.royal.gov.uk	Info on royal palaces, castles, and museums, other links
www.westminster.gov.uk	Links to London sites
www.cityoflondon.gov.uk	City government site
www.london.gov.uk	Another government site
www.24hourmuseum.org.uk	Info on museums, plus many London- and art-related links
www.timeout.com	*Time Out* magazine, the city's best source for events, online
www.londonnet.co.uk	Magazine guide to events, plus articles
www.guardianunlimited.co.uk	*The Guardian* and *The Observer* newspapers online
www.thisislondon.co.uk	Event-listings and local news from the *Evening Standard*

Special Considerations

Passport, Visas, and Customs

If you're American, Canadian, or from New Zealand, all you need to enter England is a valid passport. If you have one, be sure to check the expiration date at least a month before going. Americans can find passport information, including downloadable forms, at the Department of State Bureau of Consular Affairs website, **www.travel.state.gov-passport_services.html.** Alternatively, call the National Passport Information Center at (900) 225-5674. You don't need a visa for a vacation; you will be allowed in for up to 90 days. Make two copies of the information page of your passport and give one to someone at home to keep. Put the other in your luggage to expedite replacement in case your passport gets lost or stolen.

What You May and May Not Bring into the United Kingdom

You can bring in, duty-free, a carton of cigarettes, a few bottles of wine, perfume, toilet water, and other items, up to a value of £136 (about $225). You may not bring in controlled drugs (any medication you take should be in its original bottle with your name on it), firearms and/or ammunition, plants and vegetables, fresh meats, or any kind of animals.

Electricity

The electricity supply is 220 volts AC, which will blow out any American 110-volt appliance you may have. Electric lamps are the only items that don't require a transformer. Check to be sure your laptop computer has a built-in transformer; it's a standard feature. Razors, hair dryers, boom boxes, cell-phone rechargers—all will need to be plugged into a transformer. Leave them at home is our advice. Since the British outlets are made for large three-prong plugs, you will also need to get an adapter, available at any ironmonger (hardware store), chemists (drugstore), supermarket, or gadget store. *Don't plug anything in until you've checked the voltage on the transformer!* It should be set to "Input AC 220 volt, output AC 110 volt." You'll know by the pop, flash, and smoke if you got it wrong.

Pounds, Pence, and Traveler's Checks

The British are going slowly into this European Union business, taking a wait-and-see attitude toward the Euro Unit. At this writing, they are still using pounds (£), and the pound converts to about $1.60. Check any major newspaper's business section for current exchange rates, or go to **www.travlang.com** or **www.x-rates.com.** The pound is a unit divided into 100 pence, abbreviated "p." One p is called a penny. Gone are the days of the shilling, the tuppence, and the farthing; what we lose in quaintness we make up for in manageability.

There are no longer any £1 notes. There are red 50s, purple 20s, brown 10s, and green 5s. Coins are divided into £2, £1, 50p, 20p, 10p, 5p, 2p, and 1p. It's a worrisome sign of inflation that the government intends to introduce a £5 coin soon, which will no doubt add to the already considerable weight of a pocketful of British change. Coins cannot be changed into foreign cash, so spend them while you're in London. Better still, donate them on your way home to the brilliant UNICEF Change Collection scheme that most airlines sponsor.

Go to your bank before you leave and buy about £100 worth of British pound sterling notes so you will have plenty on hand to pay for transportation from the airport and maybe even that first meal. Request 20s, as 50s can sometimes be hard to break.

See Part Four, "Arriving and Getting Oriented," for details on ATMs, changing money, and using your credit cards.

Value-Added Tax (VAT)

VAT is one of the great frustrations of shopping in London. It is a 17.5% tax slapped on everything from hotel rooms to lipstick; the only exceptions are food, children's clothing, and books, yet these are still very expensive. There are ways to get this tax refunded, which we'll tell you about in Part Ten, "Shopping in London." Almost everything has the VAT added into the sticker price, except for merchandise sold in some small shops, as well as various services. Check before you book a hotel as to whether the quoted price includes VAT. It can make a huge difference in your bill, obviously.

Embassies and High Commissions

United States

The American Embassy is housed in Mayfair at 24 Grosvenor Square, London, W1A1AE; (0207) 499-9000 (zone 8; tube: Bond Street). This is where you will go if your passport gets lost or stolen or if you have some emergency. The embassy's website is **www.usembassy.org.uk.** The hours are 8:30 a.m.–5:30 p.m. Passports are handled Monday through Friday, 8:30–11 a.m.; and Monday, Wednesday, and Friday, 2–4 p.m. The Passport Office is on 55 Upper Brook Street, around the corner from the main entrance (tube: Marble Arch or Bond Street).

Canada

The high commission is at MacDonald House, 38 Grosvenor Square, W1; (0207) 258-6600 (zone 8; tube: Bond Street). It is open Monday through Friday, 8–11 a.m.

Australia

The High Commission is at Australia House, Strand, WC2; (0207) 379-4334 (zone 7; tube: Charing Cross) and is open Monday through Friday, 10 a.m.–4 p.m.

New Zealand

The High Commission is at New Zealand House, 80 Haymarket at Pall Mall, SW1; (0207) 930-8422 (zone 7; tube: Charing Cross). It's open Monday through Friday, 9 a.m.–5 p.m.

Ireland

The Irish Embassy is at 17 Grosvenor Place, SW1; (0207) 235-2171 (zone 10; tube: Hyde Park Corner). Hours are Monday through Friday, 10 a.m.–4 p.m.

Traveling with Children

In planning your vacation, remember that children get jet lag, too, and plan your first day so you all can recover from it. We have a rating system in our attraction profiles that attempts to gauge suitability for children and adults of various ages, but bear in mind that all children have different interests and differing levels of tolerance for museums and attractions. See Part Seven, "Children's London."

Disabled Access in London

London may be more wheelchair- and disabled-access ready than many cities in Europe, but it still has some insurmountable problems in many of its attractions. In America one can count on wheelchair access and disabled rest rooms in public buildings; in London you need to call ahead or use any of the following excellent references:

Access in London is the best book on the subject, researched by disabled people and updated regularly. It is published by the Access Project and is available at various bookstores and in the London Museum Giftshop; you can also call or write to order it: Access Project, 39 Bradley Gardens, London, W13 8HE; (0208) 858-2375; **www.artsline.org.uk.** You can also try **www.amazon.com** or another online bookstore.

Access to the Underground is a brochure published by London Transport, and is available at tube stations or by writing the London Transport Unit for Disabled Visitors, 172 Buckingham Palace Road, London, SW1 9TN.

Information for Wheelchair Users Visiting London is a pamphlet that you can find in any tourist office in London.

Holiday Care Service offers advice on disabled-friendly lodging; call (0129) 377-4535 or visit **www.holidaycare.org.uk.**

Tripscope gives advice and information on transport for the elderly and disabled throughout the United Kingdom and London. Call (0208) 994-9294 or visit **www.justmobility.co.uk/tripscope.**

Can Be Done is a tour operator specializing in London holidays and tours for disabled people; call (0208) 907-2400 or visit **www.canbedone.co.uk.**

Easing Jet Lag

Jet lag is a very real problem as any long-distance traveler can tell you. The number of time zones passed through is directly proportional to how much jet lag you'll suffer; visitors from Los Angeles will feel worse than New Yorkers. The common wisdom is that you will have roughly one day of symptoms for each hour of time difference. Though some people don't experience jet lag at all (or so they say), most of us do to varying degrees. The symptoms include fatigue, muscle aches and headaches, changes in appetite, sleep disturbances, irritability, forgetfulness, confusion, and dizziness. Of course, these symptoms could also describe middle age, but jet lag is much more pronounced. There are a number of confusing remedies—eating a certain kind and amount of food on either end of your trip, taking homeopathic remedies every hour on the plane, digesting a number of vitamins, and so on. For me, and I learned this through many painful flights between Hong Kong and New York, the best remedy is to try to reset your internal clock as soon as possible. The main thing to remember on the plane is to drink lots and lots of water, but *no* alcohol, and eat sparingly. Sleeping on the plane is not always an option, but do try. When you arrive, change your watch immediately and try to forget what time it is "for you." Your time is the time of wherever you are, and you've got to get on it as soon as possible. The best way to reset your clock is to get as much sunlight as possible when you arrive—not always easy in London. I advise my friends to use their first day to take an open-top bus tour, not just for the great introductory overview of the city but also for the generous helping of sunlight you (might) get. Exercise is also advised; a walk in the park helps stretch muscles that are achy from hours of immobilization on a plane.

Lately, I have been hearing about the great benefits of massage in helping jet lag, which is not only a natural way to deal with it, but also so very pleasant. I know of a couple from Los Angeles who book a two-hour massage the minute they arrive at their hotel, and swear by it. Look at **www.bodytissue.com** for a reputable and convenient mobile massage therapy service. They work 20 hours, seven days a week, and will come to your hotel room. Their prices will be better than any you would book through the hotel. I can personally vouch for the great professionalism and healing gifts of Justine, whom I have known for years. She assures me that all her colleagues at Body Tissue Service (BTS) are excellent.

A CALENDAR OF FESTIVALS AND EVENTS

London has a huge number of traditional and modern events each month, so many that we had to try to narrow them down to the most interesting and important. When you arrive in London, pick up a *Time Out* magazine for the full selection, dates, and times, or if you're the kind of person who likes to plan ahead, go to **www.timeout.com, www.visitbritain.com,** or to the London Tourist Board's website at **www.london town.com.**

January

London Parade *January 1.* A big, brash spectacle with giant balloons, marching bands, clowns, vintage cars, and more, much in the style of the big Fifth Avenue parades in the United States. Starting at Parliament Square at noon, the parade follows Whitehall, Trafalgar Square, Lower Regent, and Piccadilly, ending up at Berkeley Square at 3 p.m. Lots of spillover fun can be had in Hyde Park later that day. (tube: for start of parade, Westminster, zone 9; for middle, Charing Cross, zone 7; for end, Green Park, zone 8)

Charles I Commemoration *Last Sunday of January.* The English Civil War Society, dressed in authentic seventeenth-century uniforms complete with arms, follows the route King Charles I took on January 30, 1649, before he lost his head. They march from St. James's Park at 11:30 a.m., down the mall, through the Horse Guards, to the Banqueting House. It's an amazing sight. (zone 9; tube: St. James's Park)

London International Boat Show The biggest boat show in all of Europe, it takes place in mid-January and lasts about ten days. A must for even the most casual water bug. For information, call (0178) 447-222. (zone 11; tube: Earl's Court)

February

Chinese New Year Celebrations Chinese New Year changes every year, but is always in either late January or early February. The celebration is usually on the first Sunday after the first day of the new year. London's Chinatown is located in Soho, around Garrard Street. It comes alive with bright decorations, red streamers, and the Lion Dance. Great food is everywhere. Call the Hong Kong government office at (0207) 499-9821. (zone 7; tube: Piccadilly Circus)

Great Spitalfields Pancake Race *Shrove Tuesday* (changes yearly; check calendar—it can also fall in early March). Starts at noon at the Old Spitalfields Market. Here's fun: teams of people running around Spitalfields flipping pancakes as they go. If you want to join in, call a few days before—(0207) 375-0441. (zone 3; tube: Liverpool Street)

March

Ideal Home Exhibition *Mid-March through April, Earl's Court Exhibition Centre 5.* Enormous display of every possible gadget, knickknack, or consumer item one could attach to or use in a home. Call (0207) 244-0371. (zone 11; tube: Earl's Court)

Head of the River Boat Race *End of March* (usually the Saturday before the Oxford vs. Cambridge Boat Race). Starting at Mortlake and ending at Putney, this is a smaller affair than the mighty Oxford and Cambridge race, but no less interesting to observe from the banks of the Thames. The Surrey Bank above Chiswick Bridge is a good viewing station, or you can park yourself in any of the riverside pubs along the way. Call (0193) 222-0401 for date and starting time. (west of zone 12; BritRail: Mortlake for start; tube: Hammersmith for midpoint, Putney Bridge for finish).

Oxford vs. Cambridge Boat Race   This takes place on a Saturday in late March or early April and is considered the big magilla, held since 1829. Teams of eight battle the current, rowing 6.8 kilometers upriver from Putney to Mortlake. Be prepared for crowds on the bridges, on banks, and in riverside pubs. Call (0207) 379-3234 for information. (west of zone 12; BritRail: Mortlake for finish; tube: Putney Bridge for start, Hammersmith for mid-point;)

April

Gun Salute to Mark the Queen's Birthday   *April 21* Fatures a 41-gun Royal Salute to Queen Elizabeth II, fired at noon by the King's Troop Royal House Artillery in Hyde Park, opposite Dorchester Hotel, then a 62-gun fiesta at the Tower of London at 1 p.m. Take your pick or enjoy both. Bring earplugs. If the date falls on a Sunday, the event will take place on the Monday that follows. (zones 10 and 3; tube: Marble Arch for Hyde Park, Tower Hill for Tower of London)

London Harness Horse Parade   *Easter Monday, Battersea Park.* This competition of magnificent "working" horses drawing carriages and carts makes the parade a treat unlike any. Battersea Park is a beautiful place in which to enjoy it. For information, phone (0173) 323-4451 or visit **www.eastofengland.org.uk.** (zone 11; tube: Sloane Square, then bus to Battersea)

London Marathon   Occurs on a Sunday in mid-April, starting at Greenwich Park and ending at Buckingham Palace. On average, 35,000 competitors participate, so if you want in, you'd better apply early. Entries close in October. Call (0207) 620-4117 or check **www.londonmarathon.co.uk.** (zones 7 and 6; BritRail: Blackheath or Greenwich for start; tube: Charing Cross for finish)

May

Chelsea Flower Show   Runs for two weeks in May at the Chelsea Royal Hospital. This is the *ne plus ultra* of London's spring affairs, so you'd better get tickets in advance and prepare to be jostled. Go early in the morning to see the amazing flora and garden accoutrements, the great passion of even the city-dwelling English. Call Ticketmaster at (0207) 344-4343; for more information, call (0207) 630-7422. (zone 11; tube: Sloane Square)

May Fair and Puppet Festival   *Second Sunday at St. Paul's Church Garden and Covent Garden.* A procession, a service at St. Paul's, and then hours of Punch-and-Judy shows amount to family fun. Call Alternative Arts at (0207) 375-0441 for information. (zone 7; tube: Covent Garden)

Royal Windsor Horse Show   *Mid-May, Home Park, Windsor Castle.* A wonderful day out for everyone, equestrian or not. Besides the jumping and showing competitions, there are amazing Pony Club games, booths galore, and a few carnival rides, all conducted under the impressive, hulking shadow of Windsor Castle. For information, call (0207) 341-9341 or visit **www.olympia-show-jumping.co.uk.** (outside zones; BritRail: Windsor)

A CALENDAR OF FESTIVALS AND EVENTS *(continued)*

June

Beating Retreat Household Division *Early June, Buckingham Palace.* This is a floodlit nighttime spectacle of all the queen's horses and all the queen's men. Tickets available from March; book early. Call the Household Division at (0207) 839-5323.

Trooping the Colour *Early June, Horse Guards Parade, Whitehall.* Yes, the lucky queen gets two birthdays: one in April when she was actually born, and an official one in June, when the weather is better for her to inspect her troops, who parade before her. There is a procession to Buckingham Palace, where the air force flies overhead and a gun salute is fired. Tickets are awarded by ballot; call (0207) 414-2479 for details. Check in Hyde Park during the preceding Saturdays—you may catch a rehearsal. (zone 9; tube: Westminster)

Kenwood Lakeside Concerts These are held at the beautiful Kenwood House grounds, every Saturday night until September in Hampstead Heath. A 50-year-old tradition, these open-air classical concerts also feature laser shows, fireworks displays, and the Heath at sundown—enchanting. For info call (0208) 233-5892. (zone 1; tube: Archway, Golders Green, or Highgate, then bus 210)

Royal Academy Summer Exhibition *From early June to mid-August, the Royal Academy in Piccadilly.* For over 200 years, the Royal Academy of Art has been showing the work of contemporary artists in its summer exhibitions, many of which have caused scandals in their day. You can browse or buy. Call (0207) 300-8000. (zone 8; tube: Green Park or Piccadilly Circus)

Royal Ascot *Mid-June, Ascot Racecourse, Berkshire.* Made famous to Americans by the scene in the movie *My Fair Lady*, Ascot brings out all of social London. It's almost more entertaining to dish the outfits and hats than to watch the races. For information call (0134) 462-2211. (outside zones; BritRail: Ascot)

Wimbledon Lawn Tennis Championships *Late June to early July,* Wimbledon, Southwest London. This is where all true tennis fans want to be, and everyone else loves the strawberries and cream. Tickets are hard to come by, so make plans in advance, if possible. Tickets for Centre and Number One Courts are awarded by ballot. Call (0208) 946-2244 for information. (zone 12; tube: Wimbledon)

July

BBC Henry Wood Promenade Concerts (the Proms) *Mid-July through September, Royal Albert Hall, Kensington Gore.* Known affectionately as the "Proms," these eight weeks of a variety of orchestral concerts, from classical to contemporary, can be seen for a small fee (standing) or for significantly more (sitting). The last night is the big extravaganza. Call (0191) 222-0381 to get a copy of the BBC Proms Guide. For more information, call (0207) 765-5575. (zone 13; tube: South Kensington or Gloucester Road)

August

Opening of Buckingham Palace *Early August through October.* While the queen's away, the tourists will play. Lines and lines of camera-laden hoi polloi wait to take the grand tour through Queen Elizabeth's town house while she summers in Scotland. Tickets can be ordered in advance by calling (0207) 321-2233 or bought at the ticket booth in Green Park. For recorded info, call (0207) 799-2331, or visit **www.royal residences.com.** (zone 9; tube: Green Park or St. James)

Notting Hill Carnival   *End of August, Ladbroke Grove and Portobello Road.* It's the biggest street fair in all of Europe, held on a rather slim street, so be ready to stand shoulder to shoulder to enjoy the Caribbean flavor of steel bands and wild partying. Call (0208) 964-0544 for exact date. (zone 13; tube: Notting Hill)

September

Great River Race   *Mid-September, starting on the Thames at Richmond.* You have never seen such a collection of boats. Over 200 traditional crafts—including such diverse specimens as whalers, Viking longboats, Chinese dragon boats, and canoes—race from Ham House in Richmond at 10:30 a.m., finishing at Island Gardens, across from Greenwich Pier about three hours later. Call (0208) 398-9057. (zones 12 and 5; tube: Richmond for start; Docklands Light Rail: Island Gardens for finish)

Horse of the Year Show   *End of September, Wembley Arena, Wembley.* In a country that takes its horses seriously, this event features the finest creatures and most gifted riders. It doesn't get any better than this. Get your tickets early from the Wembley Arena Box Office at (0208) 900-1234. (outside zones; tube: Wembley Park)

Open House London   *Mid-September.* Finally, a chance to get in to look (for free!) inside more than 500 amazing houses and buildings usually off-limits to the likes of us commoners. Call (0900) 160-0061 for information or visit **www.londonopenhouse.org.**

October

Costermongers Pearly Harvest Festival   *First Sunday in October, St. Martin-in-the Fields, Trafalgar Square.* An old cockney tradition celebrating the apple (coster) harvest that starts with a service at the church and displays a Pearly King or Queen decked out in a costume bombarded with white buttons. Musical merrymakers are everywhere. Service starts at 3 p.m. Call (0207) 930-0089 for details. (zone 7; tube: Charing Cross)

Trafalgar Day Parade   *Third Sunday in October, Trafalgar Square.* Big traditional, military-style parade commemorating Lord Nelson's sea victory at the Battle of Trafalgar in 1805. Marching bands, Sea Cadets. Call (0207) 928-8978. (zone 7; tube: Charing Cross)

November

Bonfire Night and Guy Fawkes Day Firework Displays   *November 5, all over London.* Guy Fawkes was the Catholic conspirator who gave his name to history to commemorate the narrowly averted Gunpowder Plot to blow up King James I and Parliament. To find out the best displays and the best places to see them, consult *Time Out,* call the London Tourist Board at (0207) 971-0026, or check their website at **www.londontown.com.**

London to Brighton Veteran Car Run   *First Sunday of November.* Come to Hyde Park to see the array of vintage cars that will drive to Brighton. Call (0175) 368-1736 for time and exact place. (zone 10; tube: Hyde Park Corner)

A CALENDAR OF FESTIVALS AND EVENTS *(continued)*

November (continued)

Lord Mayor's Show   *Mid-November.* This is an event that goes back 700 years, old even by England's standards. The lord mayor rides through the city in a let-them-eat-cake-type gilded carriage (which can be seen at the Museum of London during the rest of the year), followed by a retinue of floats, bands, and military marchers. Call for details at (0207) 606-3030. (zone 3; tube: Mansion House)

Remembrance Day   *November 11.* At the 11th hour on the 11th day of the 11th month, all of England falls silent in remembrance of those who died in the two World Wars. Red poppies are bought and worn by an enormous number of Londoners to show respect for the soldiers who gave their lives for England. On the nearest Sunday to the 11th, there is a service for the war dead at the Cenotaph in Whitehall. (zone 9; tube: Whitehall)

Another jet-lag treatment is the hormone melatonin. It is a controversial supplement, and the strict scientific rules for its use are so complicated that only a trip of 12 time zones could really merit trying to follow them. Melatonin cannot be bought in England, but it is easily found in the United States in health-food stores, vitamin shops, and pharmacies. It is often used as a sleep aid, which can be helpful in the first few days of your trip, when your body clock tells you it's 7 p.m. but it's really after midnight and you have a full day of sight-seeing planned for the next day. Take two to three milligrams for sleep—more than that will leave you groggy in the morning, and it can have a depressant effect. As with any drug, check with your physician before taking it.

Health

You may want to take out medical insurance before you leave—you won't be covered by the National Health Service, unless you're an EU citizen. You may be eligible for free emergency care, but anything else, including follow-up or specialist services, will be paid for out of your pocket. Check your existing policies to see if they cover medical services abroad. If they don't, call Mutual of Omaha at (800) 228-9792 or Healthcare Abroad at (800) 237-6615. Both companies offer good coverage at a good price.

Pharmacies are open 24 hours and on Sundays on a rotating basis. Call your front desk or the local police station for a list. Zafash Pharmacy, 233-235 Old Brompton Road, SW5 (zone 11; tube: Earl's Court) is open 24 hours every day; phone (0207) 373-2798. Bliss Chemist, 5 Marble Arch, W1 (zone 1; tube: Marble Arch) is open from 9 a.m. until midnight every day; phone (0207) 723-6116.

December

Christmas Lights and Tree   *Late November and December, central London.* Various Christmas lighting ceremonies take place on Regent, Oxford, Bond, and Jermyn Streets, among others. These often involve some flavor-of-the-month celebs. Check *Time Out.* The real fun is the tree-lighting ceremony in Trafalgar Square, which is followed by caroling around the tree each evening, between 4 and 10 p.m. Consult the London Tourist Board at **www.londontown.com** or try **www.timeout.com.**

Olympia International Show Jumping Champions   *Mid-December, Grand Hall, Olympia.* This is a fun-filled exhibition, rivaling even the Wembley Show for sheer excitement. Lots of trade booths provide plenty of Christmas-shopping opportunities for horse lovers. Call the box office for tickets at (0207) 373-3113. (zone 13; tube: Olympia)

Dentists   For dental problems, call the Dental Emergency Care Service 24 hours a day at (0207) 937-3951. They will give you the name of the nearest dental clinic.

Doctors   The better hotels will have their own doctor on call. If not, contact Doctor's Call at (0700) 037-2255. There's a private clinic in the famous Harley Street (number 117A) (zone 14; tube: Baker Street) where you can seek medical help; call Medical Express at (0207) 499-1991. It's open 9 a.m.–6 p.m. Monday through Friday, 9:30 a.m.–2:30 p.m. on Saturday, and closed Sunday.

In England the emergency room is called the Casualty Department. Call 999 or 112 for an ambulance. You'll be taken to the nearest hospital, or, if your symptoms are not life threatening, you'll be advised which is the closest hospital to you.

We really don't think you'll get sick—London has good water and food. But you had better watch out for the cars. Americans and Europeans will automatically look in the wrong direction when crossing the street, which is why you'll see directions ("Look Left") written on the street. Also keep a beady eye out for bicyclists and motorcyclists; they also drive like maniacs here.

Self-Help

If you're looking for 12-step meetings, there are plenty in London. Call for times and places.

Alcoholics Anonymous   (0207) 833-0022;
www.alcoholics-anonymous.org.uk

Narcotics Anonymous   (0207) 730-0009; www.ukna.org

Overeaters Anonymous   (0142) 698-4674

Part Three

Hotels

Selecting Accommodations

Your accommodations can really make or break a vacation or business trip. Traveling is stressful, touring around London is certainly tiring, and nothing takes the edge off like sinking into a warm, comfortable, hospitable room—that doesn't cost an arm and a leg—after a long day.

London hotels, like everything else here, are expensive. The standards for hotels are different than those for hotels in the United States: When you're paying enough, you can safely assume a variety of goods and services, such as bellhops, concierge, 24-hour room service, a health club, king-size beds, air-conditioning, full business facilities, minibar, cable TV, and so on. Because many hotels in America are part of a chain, they tend to have standardized properties with predictable amenities. Not so in London. You can go from crash pads to castles in one neighborhood, even on the same street, maybe even in the same hotel. In a typical town house–conversion hotel, you can have a room on the first floor with a balcony and French windows looking onto a garden square, and for the same price get a room on the top floor with small windows, a slanted ceiling, and a view of the brown-bricked backs of white-fronted houses. Even the chains that do operate here can have wildly varying properties with unvarying prices.

The aftermath of the terrorist strikes of September 11, the war in Iraq, and the occasional travel advisories from various state departments, not to mention the inconvenient security measures at airports worldwide, have all conspired to put a serious dent in London's tourist trade. This is not to say that the British Museum's halls have tumbleweed rolling through them. Indeed, the attractions seem to be as crowded as ever, but the hotels are certainly hurting from the missing tourists. They are ready to make a deal (except in June, when Wimbledon is on). They will do upgrades, discounts, and saver-rates without too much pushing, so don't neglect to do some homework. Some of the bigger hotels who offer package tours may be filled, but the smaller boutique hotels will have empty rooms that they are most willing to fill, and will put whatever discounts they give as the cost of developing devoted customers—which they do indeed develop. The very charming Franklin Hotel or the atmospheric Hazlitt's, to name just two, count heavily on the loyal custom of return visitors. London will no doubt rebound one day, but as long as the tourist trade is in the doldrums, make a point of asking for the best rate. Although the prices given here are rack rate, don't let that scare you off: Talk to the manager.

What to Expect

Here are some important facts to remember and resign yourself to regarding London hotels:

1. Expect small rooms. A single room usually means a very small room, with a single full-size bed.

2. Certain amenities are not a given. Air-conditioning is not always available. Neither are minibars, safes, cable TV, health facilities, or even private bathrooms. We have listed some of the amenities, but call or check websites to be sure of what is offered.

3. If the price is really low, say £30 a night, the likelihood is high that the hotel is going to be pretty funky, and you'll be sharing a bathroom. Budget hotels can be abysmal. I have included a couple of places costing £50 that have proven to be clean and reasonably bearable.

4. When you're looking for a discount, you're better off calling a hotel directly and making a deal with the reservations manager than booking through a travel agent.

5. Take advantage of the weekend break rates at the five-star hotels, and spend the weekdays at a moderately priced one.

6. Don't expect the level of service you would get in a moderate-to-expensive hotel in the United States in comparable London hotels. It's pretty much only the five-star hotels here that have the customer-is-always-right-what-can-I-do-for-you-right-away-sir-yes-ma'am kind of service.

7. Always check to see if breakfast is included in your price. Also, it's very important to know if service and the 17.5% value-added tax (VAT) are included in the price. These two add-ons can amount to a considerable addition to your bill.

Best of Britain

The hotels listed here are those that we think are very English, with the best kind of British atmosphere and charm. To us (and with all due respect to lovers of modern minimalism) it seems a shame to come to London and miss out on traditional English style. We've included a few plain, chainlike, moderate hotels, as well as a couple of nice minimalist places, but we have concentrated on the ones that provide a sense of historical England. There are so many hotels in London with pleasing sitting rooms that have gas fires, antiques, and deep sofas, and that serve an authentic cream tea and massive English breakfast—they simply must be experienced to get the full flavor of a certain ideal of London. Of course, some of the standard chain hotels might well have features that make the most sense for you, such as wheelchair access, fitness club, frequent-flier-mile tie-ins, good incentive packages, and the price and location you prefer. We have our own preferences as to neighborhoods, but they may not be yours.

Neighborhoods for Hotels

There are a number of excellent neighborhoods in which to stay. Here are our favorites:

Zone 11 South Kensington: an easy walk to Hyde Park and Kensington Gardens, three museums, Harrods, Albert Hall, Christies' Auction House, and Chelsea; three tube lines, many buses; French bakeries, restaurants for every budget; and a small-town feeling in the big city. Downside: a bit expensive for smallish quarters (although that could be said of most hotels in London).

Zone 8 Mayfair and Piccadilly, where you'll find Hyde Park, Green Park, St. James's Park, Bond Street shopping, art galleries everywhere, the Royal Academy, an easy walk to the West End, and good transportation. Charming neighborhoods. Downside: extravagantly expensive—look for deals at the (few) moderately priced choices.

Zone 7 Soho and the West End: theaters, restaurants, National Gallery, Covent Garden, bookstores on Charing Cross, better people-watching and nightlife than anywhere else. Downside: noise and fumes, and a bit dicey at night. When the bars close, the drunks and louts come out.

Zone 2 Bloomsbury: convenient to the British Museum, bookstores, the West End and Soho as well as Lincoln's Inn and the City. Downside: a little desolate here and there at night.

Zone 1 Hampstead: enjoy fresh air, the heath, the feeling of country. Downside: need to commute to everything on the Northern line.

Cheap but Not Always Cheerful Hotel Neighborhoods

Bayswater, Earl's Court, and Victoria This is not to say that these neighborhoods don't have any wonderful hotels; it's just that they have a surprising number of fleabags, so beware of low-priced hotels in these neighborhoods—you won't be able to know just how sleazy a place is by looking on the Internet.

Out There

There's something to be said for staying well out of central London, but not all of it is good. The public transportation can be dreadful and downright unapproachable at rush hours. Many of the outer areas of London do not offer a wide choice of amenities like restaurants, convenience stores, and entertainment. There are also parts of outer London that are aesthetically unpleasing, downright grotty, or dully suburban. Whatever hotels you may find may be less expensive, but will rarely offer the standard of service that the central London hotels will.

Having said that, there *are* good bed-and-breakfast deals in areas that are far from the sound and fury and pollution of London and are served by tube and rail services, which can get you into the middle of town in 30–40 minutes or less. People can get more house for their money out there, and so you may find a bed-and-breakfast with a garden, your own private entrance, perhaps a basement apartment or your own floor, cleanish air, and blessed quiet. The innkeepers probably will leave you quite alone, as personal reserve is still one of the great British traditions.

Call for Deals

As stated above, almost every hotel in London, except for the already cut-rate ones, will have some kind of saver scheme, be it a weekend reduction, a package that includes breakfast and a free night, price reductions during the seasonal (January and August) sales held in London's big shops, a summer season, a low season, a Christmas season, a corporate rate, a half-price scheme, a desperate-for-business rate, a no-reason lowered rate, and so on. They want you to come to London, and they want you to stay in their hotel. There is also the possibility of a last-minute room, in which a hotel with an empty room will agree to a huge reduction just to fill it. This requires flexibility but it can spell big savings.

Rule number one in making any of these deals is to talk to the reception manager—she or he is the only person who can agree to make deals. Chat with the manager and see what can be arranged—service is their business, and they do aim to please. But remember that some hotels don't need to make deals; check out the listings and see how many rooms a hotel has. Chances are that the more rooms there are, the more rooms will be empty. Often, the rooms that remain empty are the junior, executive, or superior suites. To get one of those for the price of a standard double is a worthy coup, and you will be very happy in such a room, especially in the grand hotels.

Bed-and-Breakfasts

Bed-and-breakfasts are big in Britain, and in London there are some drop-dead gorgeous homes that are open to you through agencies. The price with a few exceptions includes breakfast and is per person per night. There is often a minimum stay required. You may be asked to pay a booking fee and to place a deposit in sterling or credit card.

Some Excellent Companies

The Bulldog Club   (phone (0207) 371-3202; fax (0207) 371-2015; www.bulldogclub.com. In the United States, call (877) 727-3004; in Australia, call (612) 9960-5812.) Only the crème de la crème of houses are included in this exclusive group. There are about 30 properties available. The criteria are that the guests have a reasonably separate area from the host family's quarters, the rooms are within a five-minute walk to public transportation, there are amenities such as bathrobes and tea and coffee-making facilities, and that the inn be in a very fine and beautifully decorated house. Prices range from £85 for a single to £105 for two people and include breakfast. You pay a fee of £25 to join the "club" for a three-year membership, which is the best money you'll spend in London.

Uptown Reservations   (phone (0207) 351-3445; fax (0207) 351-9383; www.uptownres.co.uk) This is another very high-tone agency, with fine houses of high standard in good central neighborhoods as well as in outer London's leafy zones. Singles are £72 a night, double or twin is £95, triple is £125, and a room for four is £135.

London Homestead Services   (phone (0207) 286-5115; www.lhs london.com) This service has about 200 homes in the London area, many of which are pretty far out of central London, where you can get a double room for as little as £20. Naturally, rooms cost more in central London.

London First Choice Apartments   (phone (0208) 990-9033; fax (0208) 754-1200; www.lfca.co.uk) LFCA has a large assortment of hotels, serviced and nonserviced apartments, and bed-and-breakfasts. See the website for more information. Prices vary according to neighborhood and type of accommodation, from £89 for a studio in Earl's Court, to £3,310 per week for a three-bedroom apartment in Mayfair.

Serviced and Self-Serviced Apartments

A serviced apartment can be a good alternative to a hotel room, with commensurate prices and much more room—to be able to close a door on your traveling companion(s) once in a while can be a great luxury. The best ones will offer everything a hotel does; some even provide meals. You may get a 24-hour concierge, cable TV, laundry, and daily maid service; you may even get a washer/dryer in the apartment, secretarial services, membership to a health club, a fully equipped kitchen, and more. When you factor in the costs of eating all your meals in restaurants, a hotel costs considerably more than its nightly rate. An apartment can save you wads of dosh, as they say here, by allowing you to make some of your meals yourself.

Manors & Co.   (phone (800) 454-4385 in the United States or (0207) 486-5982 in London; fax (0207) 486-6770; www.manors.co.uk.) Manors & Co. offers a selection of high-end apartments in good neighborhoods, from studios to five-bedroom pads. Luxurious one-bedrooms start at £140; three-bedrooms/two-bathrooms at £310 per night.

Home From Home   (phone (0207) 233-8111; fax (0207) 233-9101; www.homefromhome.co.uk.) With over 200 properties in London, Home From Home can be dialed from America toll free at (800) 748-9783 for a brochure, but its website suffices to show you what gorgeous houses and decent prices they offer: a one bedroom starts at £575 per week.

London's Luxury Hotels

The various star ratings given by Michelin have placed the five-star hotel firmly at the top of the heap. In the *Unofficial Guide to London,* we have our own star-rating system, ranging from five to one, five being the best. When we give a hotel a five-star rating, it is only in the relative context of the hotels covered in this book, and doesn't reflect the standard five-star rating of hugely expensive, world-class luxury hotels that we have listed below.

The reason these luxury hotels are listed separately is that some of them are classic London establishments, such as the Ritz or Claridges, and no book on London would be complete without them. But if you can afford the $500 plus a night that these hotels charge, you really don't need guidance from us. You will know that an expensive luxury hotel in London will have all the amenities and services found in the great hotels all around the world.

However, a word of caution about the following hotels: The styles vary to a large degree, from the stark minimalism of the Hempel to the Georgian excesses of the Lanesborough or the art deco insouciance of Claridges. They will also vary in size. Views are never a given, even when you're paying $600 a night; and business amenities are not always part of the package. So buyer, beware: If you are splurging on a luxury hotel, question the reservations clerk closely as to what is offered, and make a point of requesting a good view, a spacious room, and a good location on your floor. In the converted–town house variety of hotel, the first-floor (first above the ground floor, that is) rooms in the front will have the balconies and the French windows, and the top floors may have tiny windows and angled ceilings.

The majority of the following hotels are in the Mayfair and Piccadilly areas of zone 8. In the hotel-profile listing, you will find somewhat more moderately priced establishments in this zone (except for the extended profile on Brown's), but the fact is that this is a very expensive hotel neighborhood, frequented by movie stars on studio tabs, assorted millionaires, and corporate bigwigs with expense accounts.

You can, however, call any of the following hotels and look into a discount. There are a number of possibilities: low-season rates, applicable in January and February; summer discounts; weekend break rates; upgrading to a bigger room; paying for your room in advance in dollars; executive discounts; and frequent-flier tie-ins. Call directly and talk to the reservations manager to work out a deal—many of the good hotels have toll-free numbers in the United States. A few of these luxury hotels are owned by chain groups, such as Savoy, Forte, Intercontinental, and Hilton. Chains may offer any number of promotional deals, from holiday discounts to packages that include meals. Some of these otherwise astronomically priced hotels have single rooms at surprisingly good rates—the room may be small, but you'll have the best of comfort and service you can imagine. Many will upgrade you to a junior suite if there's one available. Remember that no hotel likes an empty room. All the prices quoted below are for standard double rooms and we have calculated and included the 17.5% VAT, which adds up to a sizable dollop on top of a sizable basic rack rate—the more expensive hotels just don't have the nerve to include it in quoted prices. Some think the best way to experience these hotels is to have tea or a meal in one, and save your money on a less pricey pad.

The Berkeley   Right off Knightsbridge by Hyde Park Corner, this hotel has a magnificent spa, the excellent Gordon Ramsey's Voxwood Cafe, and well-appointed, spacious rooms. There are 214 rooms, starting at £295 (zone 10, Wilton Place, SW1; phone (0207) 235-6000; fax (0207) 235-4330; www.savoy-group.com; tube: Knightsbridge).

Blakes   Completely gorgeous hotel in South Kensington, catering to rock stars, models, actors, and so on. Although less expensive than the others in this class, you can still fracture your credit card between the tariff and the very fine restaurant, also called Blakes. The rooms are exuberantly and individually decorated in styles ranging from expensive bordello to country squire to Raj's field tent. Good value for a five-star hotel, even though some of the rooms are smallish. There are 47 rooms, starting at £299 (zone 11, 33 Roland Gardens, SW7; phone (0207) 370-6701; fax (0207) 373-0442; www.blakeshotel.com; tube: South Kensington).

Brown's Hotel   Victorian gentlemen's club atmosphere and beautiful antique furnishings; there's nothing showy or over the top about this place except for its prices. Some of the rooms can be surprisingly small, although cozy. They serve an excellent afternoon tea from 2 to 6 p.m. in one of the three lovely sitting rooms. There are 118 rooms, starting at £290. See profile for more information (zone 8, 30–34 Albemarle Street, W1; phone (0207) 493-6020; fax (0207) 493-9381; www.brownshotel. com; tube: Green Park).

Claridges   Bold decor evokes Jazz Age glamour and royal luxury. People of serious substance stay here. Fantastic, albeit expensive tea in impressive surroundings, with a likely chance to see a society wedding. There are 203 rooms, quite deluxe, starting at £435; the top price is for the penthouse at £3,850 per night (zone 8; Brook Street, W1; phone (0207) 629-8860; fax (0207) 499-2210; www.savoy-group.com; tube: Bond Street).

The Connaught   Grand country house is the style here, and perfect service the watchwords. It's been around since 1897; Charles de Gaulle made it his wartime headquarters, and Cecil Beaton and David Niven called it home. It attracts so many regulars that it's almost a club; make reservations well in advance of your visit. There are 92 rooms, starting at £234 plus service charge (zone 8; 16 Carlos Place, W1; phone (0207) 499-7070; fax (0207) 495-3262; www.savoy-group.com; tube: Bond Street).

The Dorchester   One of London's grandest establishments, this hotel is right across from Hyde Park and walking distance to some of the toniest shops in London. Restaurants and the health club are of the highest standards, as are the rooms and the decor. You can see where your money is going at this hotel. There are 244 rooms, starting at £388 (zone 8; 53 Park Lane, W1; phone (0207) 629-8888; fax (0207) 409-0114; www.dorchesterhotel.com; tube: Marble Arch).

The Four Seasons   Owned by the Four Seasons Group, this hotel often offers promotional packages. The decor is opulent without being ostentatious; they provide excellent service and food. There are 220 rooms, starting at £400 (zone 8; Hamilton Place in Park Lane, W1; phone (0207) 499-0888; fax (0207) 493-6629; www.fourseasons.com; tube: Hyde Park Corner).

(Le Meridien) Grosvenor House   Old and fabulous, this hotel houses the Park Room Brasserie, among other fine eateries. It's a bit formal, but very luxurious, and is owned by the Meridien group. There are 586 rooms, starting at £458 (zone 8; Park Lane, W1; phone (0207) 499-6363; fax (0207) 493-3341; www.lemeridien-grosvenorhouse.com; tube: Hyde Park Corner).

The Landmark   The Landmark gives good value for money because it's out of the Mayfair-Piccadilly high-rent district. There's an impressive atrium in which to eat, a fitness center and pool, and good-size rooms. Modern refurbishment in an old building. All 298 rooms are double and start at £495 (zone 14; 222 Marylebone Road, NW1; phone (0207) 631-8000; fax (0207) 631-8080; www.landmarklondon.co.uk; tube: Marylebone).

The Lanesborough   You'd never guess to look at the elaborately Georgian interior that gurneys used to be rolled around these floors instead of room-service carts. This former hospital is now a formal hotel, full of charm and mahogany-paneled splendor, with an Asian theme–decor restaurant of high quality. There's a butler call button in all the rooms; need we say more? There are 95 rooms, starting at £435 for a standard double (zone 10; Hyde Park Corner, SW1; phone (0207) 259-5599; fax (0207) 259-5606; www.lanesborough.com; tube: Hyde Park Corner).

London Hilton   The place where Elizabeth Taylor reportedly spent more than one of her wedding nights, the London Hilton has success-fully made the transition from the James Bond era to today with all five stars firmly intact. It isn't a picturesque building, but it does have the greatest views of Hyde Park available and good-size rooms. If you want to enjoy the view but not pay the £268 for a room, stop in for a drink on the 28th-floor restaurant. Half of the 449 rooms overlook the park. If you want to be near the Hilton, try the Hilton Mews around back, a slightly less expensive but charming alternative. (Zone 8; 22 Park Lane, W1; phone (0207) 493-8000; fax (0207) 208-4140; www.hilton.com; tube: Green Park.)

Mandarin Oriental Hotel   A grand old hotel in a good location. There are only suites facing north on Hyde Park; the hotel also faces Knights-bridge, one of the noisiest streets in London, but a stone's throw from world-class shopping. There is a newly renovated restaurant on the first floor—much too modern for this elegant Edwardian building, but with a good view into the park. There are 200 rooms; doubles start at £440 (zone 10; 66 Knightsbridge, SW1; phone (0207) 235-2000; fax (0207) 235-2001; www.mandarinoriental.com; tube: Knightsbridge).

The Metropolitan   Not only is this home to the esteemed and expensive sushi restaurant Nobu, it also has the renowned Met Club, a private club that was at the top of the social ladder when it opened in 1997, and is still formidable. Guests at The Metropolitan can get in, a big plus for young social types. It has a state-of-the-art gym. Its sister hotels, The Halkin in Belgravia (5 Halkin Street in Belgravia; (0207) 333-1000; 41 rooms from £359) and Myhotel in Bloomsbury (11–13 Bayley Street, Bedford Square; (0207) 667-6000; 76 rooms from £359), are also shrines to cool beige, beech, and blank walls. There are 155 rooms, from £364 (zone 8; Old Park Lane, W1; phone (0207) 447-1000; fax (0207) 447-1100; www.metropolitan.co.uk; tube: Hyde Park Corner).

The Ritz   What can you say about a synonym for luxury and extrava-gance? Before you think it's just plain out of the question, call and see what kind of deals they may have. They have a lot of rooms to fill. If all you want is tea, call well in advance of your trip to make a reservation—weekends can be booked as much as a month ahead. The decor is Ver-sailles on Piccadilly, and the comfort is sumptuousness itself. The rooms facing Green Park are the best, sharing the view with such worthy man-sions as Spencer House. Individually decorated rooms, 131 in all, start at £429 and go up, up, up (zone 8; 150 Piccadilly, W1; phone (0207) 300-2308; fax (0207) 493-2687; toll free from U.S (877) 748-9536; www.theritzlondon.com; tube: Green Park).

Sanderson   This hotel, part of the Ian Schrager chain, is favored by rich, high-profile media personalities, whose personal needs may be inferred by the excessive luxury offered here: 450-thread-count cotton, three two-lined phones in each room, a yoga studio and two-story holistic bathhouse, a private fitness area in each room, the list goes on and on (I was most struck by the children's play area—most luxury hotels hope that children will stay home). The decor is quirky, dreamy, Dali-esque, with eclectic furnishings in an array of colors and periods. Swathes of white muslin shrouding mirrors, lights, and doorways add mystique. The rooms are stark, yet chic, with chrome and white furnishings. All this makes up for the fact that Sanderson is housed in a charmless 1960s block building. There are 150 rooms, ranging from £288 upwards. Its sister hotel, St. Martin's Lane, is equally chic, hip, and trendy, but unfortunately, I have run into extreme forms of rudeness and slip-shod service from its hip employees, and two people I know fled to another hotel after one night there. Your move. (zone 7; 50 Berners Street, W1; phone (0207) 300-1400; fax (0207) 300-1401; www.ianschragerhotels.com; tube: Oxford Circus or Tottenham Court.)

The Savoy   I don't think the Savoy has changed much since it was Frank Sinatra's favorite hotel in foggy London town. It is still a gorgeous place, and has done what's known as a sympathetic renovation recently: Like Claridges, it maintains the decor of its salad days, and its service is impeccable. It's located right in the thick of things, perfect for theatergoers. Rooms, 161 in all, start at £410; £1,205 will get you a one-bedroom suite. The only rooms overlooking the Thames are junior suites plus. We believe Frank took the penthouse suite. (zone 7; 1 Savoy Hill, Strand, WC2; phone (0207) 950-5492; fax (0207) 950-5482; toll-free in United States (800) 637-2869; www.savoy-group.co.uk; tube: Charing Cross.)

Hotel Ratings

Overall Ratings   We have distinguished properties according to relative quality, tastefulness, state of repair, cleanliness, and size of standard rooms, grouping them into classifications denoted by stars. Overall star ratings in this guide apply to London properties only and do not correspond to ratings awarded by the British Tourism Board, automobile clubs, or other travel critics. Overall ratings are presented to show the difference we perceive between one property and another. They are assigned without regard to location or to whether a property has restaurants, recreational facilities, entertainment, or other extras.

| ★★★★★ | Superior | Tasteful and luxurious by any standard |
| ★★★★ | Extremely Nice | Above average in appointments and design; very comfortable |

★★★	Nice	Average but quite comfortable
★★	Adequate	Plain but meets all essential needs
★	Budget	Spartan, not aesthetically pleasing, but clean

Quality Ratings   In addition to overall ratings (which delineate broad categories), we also employ quality ratings. They apply to room quality only and describe the property's standard accommodations. In addition to standard accommodations, many hotels offer luxury rooms and special suites that are not rated in this guide. Our rating scale is ★–★★★★★, with ★★★★★ as the best possible rating and ★ as the worst.

Value Ratings   We also provide a value rating to give you some sense of the quality of a room in relation to its cost. As before, the ratings are based on the quality of room for the money and do not take into account location, services, or amenities.

Our scale is as follows:

★★★★★	An exceptional bargain
★★★★	A good deal
★★★	Fairly priced (you get exactly what you pay for)
★★	Somewhat overpriced
★	Significantly overpriced

A ★★½ room at £100 may have the same value rating as a ★★★★ room at £180, but that does not mean that the rooms will be of comparable quality. Regardless of whether it's a good deal or not, a ★★½ room is still a ★★½ room.

For each hotel we also provide the London geographic zone where the property is located.

How the Hotels Compare

What follows is a table that contains the hotels we have researched and profiled organized by overall rating. To find a particular hotel listed in this table, look through the alphabetical section of profiles later in the chapter.

If you use subsequent editions of this guide, you will notice that many of the ratings and rankings change. In addition to the inclusion of new properties, these changes also reflect guest-room renovations or improved maintenance and housekeeping. A failure to properly maintain guest rooms or a lapse in housekeeping standards can negatively affect the ratings.

Finally, before you begin to shop for a hotel, take a hard look at this letter we received from a couple in Hot Springs, Arkansas:

> *We cancelled our room reservations to follow the advice in your book [and reserved a hotel room highly ranked by the Unofficial Guide]. We wanted inexpensive, but clean and cheerful. We got inexpensive, but [also] dirty, grim, and depressing. I really felt disappointed in your advice and the room.*

It was the pits. That was the one real piece of information I needed from your book!

The room spoiled the holiday for me aside from our touring.

Needless to say, this letter was as unsettling to us as the bad room was to our reader. Our integrity as travel journalists, after all, is based on the quality of the information we provide our readers. Even with the best of intentions and the most conscientious research, however, we cannot inspect every room in every hotel. What we do, in statistical terms, is take a sample: We check out several rooms selected at random in each hotel and base our ratings and rankings on those rooms. The inspections are conducted anonymously and without the knowledge of the management. Although unusual, it is certainly possible that the rooms we randomly inspect are not representative of the majority of rooms at a particular hotel. This is particularly true in the smaller London hotels that offer such a variety of room sizes and styles.

Another possibility is that the rooms we inspect in a given hotel are representative, but that by bad luck a reader is assigned a room that is inferior. When we rechecked the hotel our reader disliked, we discovered our rating was correctly representative, but that he and his wife had unfortunately been assigned to one of a small number of threadbare rooms scheduled for renovation.

The key to avoiding disappointment is to snoop around in advance. We recommend that you ask for a photo of a hotel's standard guest room before you book, or at least get a copy of the hotel's promotional brochure.

HOW THE HOTELS COMPARE				
Hotel	**Overall Quality**	**Room Quality**	**Value**	**Zone**
Dukes Hotel	★★★★★	★★★★½	★★★★	9
Goring Hotel	★★★★★	★★★★½	★★★★	9
The Cliveden Town House	★★★★★	★★★★½	★★★	11
L'Hotel	★★★★★	★★★★	★★★★★	10
Thistle Hotel Victoria	★★★★★	★★★★	★★★★	9
Brown's Hotel	★★★★★	★★★★	★★★	8
11 Cadogan Gardens	★★★★★	★★★★	★★★	11
Basil Street Hotel	★★★★½	★★★★½	★★★★★	10
London Marriot Hotel/ County Hall	★★★★½	★★★★½	★★★	5
Milestone Hotel	★★★★½	★★★★	★★★	11
The Gore	★★★★	★★★★½	★★★★	11
The Rookery	★★★★	★★★★½	★★★	3

HOW THE HOTELS COMPARE *(continued)*

Hotel	Overall Quality	Room Quality	Value	Zone
Covent Garden Hotel	★★★★	★★★★½	★★★★	7
The Pelham	★★★★	★★★★½	★★★★	11
Charlotte Street Hotel	★★★★	★★★★	★★★★	7
Great Eastern Hotel	★★★★	★★★★	★★★★	3
Hilton London Mews	★★★★	★★★★	★★★★	8
Number Sixteen	★★★★	★★★★	★★★★	11
Millennium Hotel Mayfair	★★★★	★★★★	★★★	8
Radisson Edwardian Hampshire	★★★★	★★★★	★★	7
Thistle Hotel Hyde Park	★★★★	★★★½	★★★★★	14
The Claverley	★★★½	★★★½	★★★★★	10
Franklin Hotel	★★★★	★★★½	★★★★	10
Cadogan Hotel	★★★★	★★★½	★★★	10
Montague on the Gardens	★★★★	★★★½	★★★	2
The Portobello Hotel	★★★★	★★★½	★★★	13
Parkes Hotel	★★★½	★★★★	★★★★	10
Hazlitt's Hotel	★★★½	★★★★	★★★	7
Abbey Court	★★★	★★★★	★★★★★	13
Pembridge Court Hotel	★★★	★★★★	★★★★★	13
Miller's Residence	★★★	★★★★	★★★★	13
Durrants	★★★	★★★½	★★★★★	14
Flemings	★★★	★★★½	★★★★	8
The Gallery Hotel	★★★	★★★½	★★★★	11
Grange White Hall Hotel	★★★	★★★½	★★★★	2
Rembrandt Hotel	★★★	★★★½	★★★★	11
Thistle Hotel Kensington Palace	★★★	★★★½	★★★★	13
Jury's	★★★	★★★½	★★★	11
The Gainsborough	★★★	★★★	★★★★	11
Meridien Russell	★★★	★★★	★★★★	2
The Columbia Hotel	★★	★★★½	★★★★★	14
Morgan Hotel	★★	★★★½	★★★★★	2
Quality Hotel	★★	★★★½	★★★★	9
Holiday Inn Mayfair	★★	★★★½	★★★	8
Five Sumner Place Hotel	★★	★★★	★★★★★	11
Riverside Hotel	★★	★★★	★★★★★	12
Radisson Edwardian Pastoria Hotel	★★	★★★	★★	7
Edward Lear Hotel	★	★★★½	★★★★★	14

HOW THE HOTELS COMPARE *(continued)*

Hotel	Overall Quality	Room Quality	Value	Zone
Fielding Hotel	★	★★★	★★★	7
Comfort Inn Notting Hill	★	★★½	★★★★★	13
Ruskin Hotel	★	★★½	★★★★★	2
St. Margaret's Hotel	★	★★½	★★★★★	2
Cherry Court Hotel	★	★★	★★★★	9

HOTELS BY ZONE

Zone 2: Bloomsbury and Holborn

Grange White Hall Hotel	Morgan Hotel
Meridien Russell	Ruskin Hotel
Montague on the Gardens	St. Margaret's Hotel

Zone 3: The City, Clerkenwell, Barbican

Great Eastern Hotel	The Rookery

Zone 5: South London—South Bank, Lambeth, Brixton

London Marriott Hotel, County Hall

Zone 7: Soho and the West End

Charlotte Street Hotel	Radisson Edwardian Pastoria Hotel
Covent Garden Hotel	Radisson Hampshire Edwardian
Fielding Hotel	Sanderson
Hazlitt's Hotel	The Savoy

Zone 8: Mayfair and Piccadilly

Brown's Hotel	Hilton London Mews
Claridges	Holiday Inn Mayfair
The Connaught	The Metropolitan
The Dorchester	Hilton London Mews
Flemings	Millennium Hotel Mayfair
The Four Seasons	The Ritz
Grosvenor House	

Zone 9: Victoria and Westminster

Cherry Court Hotel	Quality Hotel
Dukes Hotel	Thistle Hotel Victoria
Goring Hotel	

HOTELS BY ZONE *(continued)*

Zone 10: Knightsbridge and Belgravia

Basil Street Hotel	L'Hotel
The Berkeley	The Lanesborough
Cadogan Hotel	Mandarin Oriental Hotel
The Claverley	Parkes Hotel
Franklin Hotel	

Zone 11: Chelsea and South Kensington

Blakes	The Gore
The Cliveden Town House	Jury's
11 Cadogan Gardens	Milestone Hotel
Five Sumner Place Hotel	Number Sixteen
The Gainsborough	The Pelham
The Gallery Hotel	Rembrandt Hotel

Zone 12: West London—Hammersmith, Chiswick, Richmond, Kew

Riverside Hotel

Zone 13: Kensington, Holland Park, Notting Hill

Abbey Court	Pembridge Court Hotel
Comfort Inn Notting Hill	The Portobello Hotel
Miller's Residence	Thistle Hotel Kensington Palace

Zone 14: Bayswater, Marylebone, Little Venice, St. John's Wood

The Columbia Hotel	The Landmark
Durrants	Thistle Hotel Hyde Park
Edward Lear Hotel	

Hotel Profiles

All prices include the 17.5% value-added tax (VAT) and refer to the starting price for standard single and standard double room. Prices for deluxe, executive, triple-occupancy, family rooms, and suites and rooms with special features (such as four-poster bed, fireplace, balcony, etc.) will be significantly higher. See websites for all prices as well as promotional deals.

ABBEY COURT £105–£140

OVERALL ★★★ | QUALITY ★★★★ | VALUE ★★★★★ | ZONE 13

*20 Pembridge Gardens, W4; (0207) 221-7518; fax (0207) 792-0858;
www.abbeycourthotel.co.uk*

Abbey Court is a lovely old Victorian house in a white-stucco-front neighborhood quite close to Portobello Road. It's a real beauty, and very well priced, too. It's quite popular with antiques dealers, not only because they can walk to Kensington Church Street and all the antiques warrens along Portobello, but also because it has plenty of really fine old furniture, art, and decorations to admire. It's comfortable and homey, as well as elegant and serene—almost like visiting a rich aunt's house who has very good taste. There are plenty of good old books, some first editions, which you can (carefully) borrow to read. Downstairs there's a small conservatory where breakfast is served (continental breakfast is included), and an honor bar is set out all day. A tiny little patio off the conservatory has a small pool with goldfish. Newspapers are ordered for you free, and there are plenty of English magazines in each room. You can get a reduction for stays longer than a week. Except for the fact that there's no elevator, this is a four-star town house hotel at three-star prices.

SETTINGS & FACILITIES

Location Notting Hill Gate. **Nearest Tube Station** Notting Hill Gate. **Quietness Rating** A in back, B in front (quiet street). **Dining** Small breakfast room. **Amenities** Newspapers, bathrobes, biscuits, and bottled water; associated with nearby health club; breakfast included, honor bar. **Services** Receptionist does work of concierge; 24-hour room service, bellhop, laundry.

ACCOMMODATIONS

Rooms 22. **All Rooms** Telephone, TV, hair dryer, iron, bathrobe, heated towel racks, Jacuzzi baths. **Some Rooms** Four-poster beds. **Bed & Bath** Italian marble bathrooms with tubs that have Jacuzzi jets, shower, and heated towel racks. The beds are excellent, some old brass bedsteads. **Favorites** The four-poster rooms are the biggest and the nicest. **Comfort & Decor** The decor is quite fine, with lovely antiques and prints all around, fantastic mirrors, and nice wallpaper. It's a pleasure to see how well appointed it is, and for us, that spells comfort. However, there is no elevator for the five floors, but the stairway is beautiful.

PAYMENT, RESERVATIONS, & RESTRICTIONS

Deposit Credit card; 48-hour cancellation policy. **Credit Cards** All major. **Check-In/Out** 1 p.m./11:30 a.m. **Pets** Not allowed. **Elevator** No. **Children** Yes. **Disabled Access** No lift.

THE BASIL STREET HOTEL £170–£240

OVERALL ★★★★½ | QUALITY ★★★★½ | VALUE ★★★★★ | ZONE 10

Basil Street, Knightsbridge, SW3; (0207) 581-3311, in U.S. (800) 448-8355; fax (0207) 581-3693; www.thebasil.com

For over 85 years, The Basil Street Hotel has been attracting loyal customers with its homey comfort and elegance. It's the kind of hotel you want to hang around in; there are a few common sitting areas that are so comfortable, so pleasing to the eye, and so well appointed that you may not be tempted outside to nearby Harrods, Hyde Park, the museums of South Kensington, Harvey Nichols, or the designer boutiques of Sloane Street. This is not an ostentatious hotel by any means, but if you look at the art on the wall—check out the paintings on glass on the way to the dining room—or the furniture, the carpets, and the bric-a-brac, you know some quiet care and expense has been lavished on the decor. The country-house feeling is maintained even against all the noise and hubbub on the streets outside. There are sitting alcoves, looking out over the roofs of Knightsbridge, that have desks supplied with writing paper, evoking a gentler time before e-mail. It's a feminine place in many ways, but it is in no way frilly; compared to some of the ye-olde-English-country-house imitation decor in so many hotels in London, it's positively restrained—probably because it's the real thing. It offers some of the best value for the money you will find in this part of town.

SETTINGS & FACILITIES

Location Knightsbridge. **Nearest Tube Station** Knightsbridge. **Quietness Rating** C on lower floors, B+ on higher floors. **Dining** Dining room was given award by the British Automobile Association. It's a very lovely, traditional sort of dining room, with live classical music most nights. There's also a warm and comfy sitting room for excellent afternoon teas. **Amenities** Women's Club (The Parrot Club) into which men only can go if accompanied by a woman, and which provides office services for businesswomen; ironing rooms on each floor; parking spaces available at a reasonable charge; smoking and nonsmoking rooms. **Services** Concierge, bellhop, laundry.

ACCOMMODATIONS

Rooms 93. **All Rooms** Cable TV, hair dryer, bathtubs, writing desk, comfortable sitting chair. **Some Rooms** Air-conditioning, bay windows, glass-fronted cabinets. **Bed & Bath** Bathrooms range from irreproachable to irresistible: some simply enormous, some paneled in pine wainscoting. Beds are quite comfortable. **Favorites** Singles are among the largest in London. Beautiful bay windows in some rooms. You can't go too wrong at the Basil, whatever room you get. **Comfort & Decor** Exquisite antiques and a huge collection of mezzotints, fine carpets, superior furniture, and really good pieces of porcelain and lamps. High ceilings, good closet space. Functional and roomy layout in all rooms (by London standards, anyway).

PAYMENT, RESERVATIONS, & RESTRICTIONS

Deposit Credit card; 24-hour cancellation policy. **Credit Cards** All major. **Check-In/Out** Midday/noon. **Pets** Not allowed. **Elevator** Yes. **Children** Yes. **Disabled Access** Limited.

BROWN'S HOTEL   *£340–£376*

OVERALL ★★★★★ | QUALITY ★★★★ | VALUE ★★★ | ZONE 8

30–34 Albemarle Street, W1; (0207) 493-6020; fax (0207) 493-9381;
www.brownshotel.com

This five-star hotel has something of a reputation among Americans as *the* English hotel to stay in, and we're including it in the profiles because so many people want to stay here. It is normal to see at least one celebrity during a typical stay: I've seen Johnny Depp and Annie Leibovitz. The service is excellent and good-natured in that arch English way, and the food, though sky-high in price, is simple and good. Especially at teatime: The afternoon cream tea is excellent, and the ambience of the sitting room is great. The history of the place is interesting: Alexander Graham Bell made the first telephone call in Britain from here, Rudyard Kipling wrote from here, and Theodore Roosevelt got married while a guest at Brown's. Lord Byron's valet, James Brown, started the hotel in 1837. His wife, Sarah, and he had learned a thing or two from living in the "mad, bad, and dangerous to know" lordship's household, and the hotel was a success from the start. After the Browns sold it in 1859, the next owner made it the first hotel in London to have an elevator, telephone, and electricity. It grew from 1 town house to 11, which is why you'll find the configurations of the rooms so completely unpredictable. Brown's is all about service: With 118 rooms, it has 160 in staff. The prices are very steep, so be sure to talk to reception about deals.

SETTINGS & FACILITIES

Location Mayfair. **Nearest Tube Station** Green Park. **Quietness Rating** A. **Dining** Fine dining (and expensive, too) at award-winning 1837 Restaurant features English fare, with the greatest wine list in London. Breakfast in dining room, and afternoon teas in The Drawing Room. St. Georges' Bar for drinks and cigars. **Amenities** Fitness room, afternoon teas, business center. **Services** Concierge, 24-hour room service and valet, laundry, business support.

ACCOMMODATIONS

Rooms 118. **All Rooms** Minibars, multiline phones, voice mail, sitting area, writing desks, cable TV, air-conditioning. **Some Rooms** Sitting areas with sofa, working fireplaces, four-poster beds, French doors. **Bed & Bath** Superior. Heated towel racks, Moulton Brown toiletries, bathrobe, and slippers. Queen- or king-size beds. **Favorites** Mayfair and Royal suites. First-floor rooms are the best, with high ceilings and big windows. Avoid the rooms at the top—they are low-ceilinged, and some of the junior suites are small. **Comfort & Decor** You will find the comfort factor high, although some of the rooms are not as large as one would expect, and some are downright cramped. The decor is English country-house traditional, very comfy and unpretentious, with some fine pieces of furniture, carvings, and art here and there. Carved fireplace in the reception, paneling, cut glass, and the stained-glass windows in the stairwells and elsewhere are all exquisite.

PAYMENT, RESERVATIONS, & RESTRICTIONS

Deposit Credit card; 24-hour cancellation policy. **Credit Cards** All major. **Check-In/Out** 2 p.m./noon. **Pets** Not allowed. **Elevator** Yes. **Children** Yes. **Disabled Access** Yes, though limited.

THE CADOGAN HOTEL   £253–£329

OVERALL ★★★★ | QUALITY ★★★½ | VALUE ★★★ | ZONE 10

75 Sloane Street, SW1; (0207) 235-7141; fax (0207) 245-0994; www.cadogan.com

At press time, the rumor was that this historical hotel was up for sale, but one cannot imagine any new owner would tamper with the charming ambience of this London institution, but do check the website to see what, if any changes are afoot. This is the hotel at which Oscar Wilde was arrested; and it incorporated into its building the home of Lillie Langtry, the actress more well known these days for her long-term affair with the prince of Wales (later King Edward) than her career, which was impressive. These two artists represent a time and place in Victorian London that the Cadogan Hotel has tried to evoke in its decor and atmosphere. It is impossible not to feel some connection with that time when you walk in the door and see the leaded windows, the William Morris–style wallpaper, and the stately and elegant drawing room that sports a notice asking people to leave their mobile phones and laptop computers outside. Jackets must be worn in the restaurant. Terribly civilized. The restaurant is quite grand looking and has an excellent menu. There are tons of great restaurants within walking distance of the hotel. The rooms aren't breathtaking, but they're attractive, each individually decorated, with some enjoying a fair amount of space and views of the greenery of Cadogan Gardens across the street. Hotel guests have access to these widely coveted gardens that have a tennis court, also at guests' disposal.

SETTINGS & FACILITIES

Location Knightsbridge. **Nearest Tube Station** Knightsbridge or Sloane Square. **Quietness Rating** A in the interior, B/C on Sloane and Pont Streets side. **Dining** Restaurant has two rosettes from the Automobile Association. **Amenities** Drawing room and a bar with leaded windows, health-club affiliation, access to gardens and tennis. **Services** Concierge, 24-hour room service, bellhop, laundry.

ACCOMMODATIONS

Rooms 65. **All Rooms** Telephone, voice mail, satellite TV, air-conditioning, hair dryer, iron, writing desk. **Some Rooms** Sitting rooms, two bathrooms, view of gardens. **Bed & Bath** High standard of both. **Favorites** The large studio in the front with two bathrooms is lovely, as are some of the luxury doubles. Try the Oscar Wilde Room. **Comfort & Decor** Beautiful William Morris wallpaper and wood paneling in halls. All rooms are individually decorated, nice, and comfortable.

PAYMENT, RESERVATIONS, & RESTRICTIONS

Deposit Credit card. **Credit Cards** All major, though they prefer to not take AMEX. **Check-In/Out** Noon/noon. **Pets** Small dogs allowed. **Elevator** Yes. **Children** Yes. **Disabled Access** Yes, though there are limits on wheelchair access.

THE CHARLOTTE STREET HOTEL   £229–£259

OVERALL ★★★★ | QUALITY ★★★★ | VALUE ★★★★ | ZONE 7

Charlotte Street, W1; (0207) 806-2000; fax (0207) 806-2002;
www.charlottestreethotel.com

The Charlotte Street Hotel is a small luxurious hotel located in an area known to locals as Fitzrovia, or alternatively, North Soho. The area is the epicenter of media activity and includes production houses, TV stations, and advertising agencies and as a result is both trendy and busy, with plenty of restaurants and bars all up and down Charlotte Street. The hotel has been decorated and furnished in a fresh, modern English style, including lots of wood paneling, wooden floors, plump soft furnishings, and leather chairs. The large lobby area leads into an "Oscar" bar and restaurant that serves modern European cuisine. The bar is very popular with the local media lushes. The drawing room and library just off the restaurant area are for guest use only and are ideal spots in which to don a smoking jacket, grab a stiff brandy, and puff on a large cigar in front of the open fireplace, while pondering on the original Bloomsbury-set artwork hanging on the walls. The bedrooms are individually decorated, with traditional British features such as floral curtains and floral wallpaper that somehow manage to avoid looking hideously chintzy. The designer, Kit Kemp, is renowned for her trademark mannequin dummies that stand sentry style in every room (a quirky, superfluous detail, yet good for draping your jacket on). If it's within your budget, try staying in a loft suite; these have stairs leading to the bedroom area on a mezzanine level and are more like a doll's house than a hotel room. Although more useful for those attending a corporate event or for a local film director, another cool feature is the state-of-the-art screening room. The gym is tiny but better than nothing.

SETTINGS & FACILITIES

Location Soho (North). **Nearest Tube Station** Tottenham Court Road/Goodge Street. **Quietness Rating** All windows double glazed. **Dining** "Oscar" restaurant serving modern European food; open Monday–Saturday and Sunday for breakfast only. **Amenities** Restaurant, lounge areas, 24-hour gym, 2 meeting rooms, 1 screening room (67-seater mini cinema). **Services** Concierge, 24-hour room service, same-day laundry service, bellhop.

ACCOMMODATIONS

Rooms 52. **All Rooms** Air-conditioning, en suite bathrooms, 2-line telephone with voice mail, cable TV, VCR and DVD, mini TV in bathroom, minibar, safe, movies to rent, CD player, hair dryer, writing desk. Fax machine, mobile phone, laptops available on request. **Some Rooms** Walk-in shower and bidet. The more deluxe rooms have bigger (king-size) beds, some four-poster. **Bed & Bath** Bathrooms are in solid granite and oak, with a shower, plus a mini TV. Regular rooms have queen-size beds which can be split into twins. **Favorites** Room 108, one of the loft suites, is very popular, as are the penthouse suites, which offer good views. **Comfort & Decor** The rooms all have a homey feel and are very comfortable.

PAYMENT, RESERVATIONS, & RESTRICTIONS

Deposit Credit card; 24-hour cancellation policy. **Credit Cards** All major, except DC. **Check-In/Out** 1 p.m./11 a.m. **Pets** Not allowed. **Elevator** Yes. **Children** Yes. **Disabled Access** Good general access (two modified rooms).

THE CHERRY COURT HOTEL   £30–£48

OVERALL ★ | QUALITY ★★ | VALUE ★★★★ | ZONE 9

23 Hugh Street, SW1; (0207) 828-2840; fax (0207) 828-0393;
www.cherrycourthotel.co.uk

The Cherry Court Hotel has the cheeriest exterior of all the many budget/backpacker hotels and hostels in this neighborhood. There are flowers in the window sills, and a wooden sign has been carefully hung. The best features of the hotel (it's really more of a rooming house, minus a dining room), besides the price and the en suite toilets and showers, are the friendliness and good will of the owners, the Patels. They've been here for over 25 years and are committed to constant improvements, one of which was turning the back patio into a rose garden. The rooms are small and utilitarian, and some are a bit sad-sack, but to the traveler on a serious budget they offer a clean place to sleep and a private toilet.

SETTINGS & FACILITIES

Location Victoria. **Nearest Tube Station** Victoria. **Quietness Rating** A. **Dining** No. **Amenities** Fruit basket and cereal bar for breakfast, though that may be upgraded in the future. **Services** Helpful management, daily cleaning.

ACCOMMODATIONS

Rooms 12. **All Rooms** Telephone, five-channel TV. **Bed & Bath** Small beds and bathrooms, which are showers and toilet in a small closet, but are clean and adequate. **Favorites Rooms** In the back. **Comfort & Decor** This is a backpacker's rooming house. The rooms are small, the beds are serviceable. There are blue carpets and wallpaper in the hallways, which are fresh and clean.

PAYMENT, RESERVATIONS, & RESTRICTIONS

Deposit Credit card. **Credit Cards** All major. **Check-In/Out** 1 p.m./11 a.m. **Pets** Not allowed. **Elevator** No. **Children** Yes. **Disabled Access** Two rooms on ground floor, but you must get up the three steps from the sidewalk to the hotel.

THE CLAVERLEY   £85–£120

OVERALL ★★★½ | QUALITY ★★★½ | VALUE ★★★★★ | ZONE 10

13–14 Beaufort Gardens, SW3; (0207) 589-8541, in U.S. (800) 747-0398;
fax (0207) 584-3410; www.claverleyhotel.fsnet.co.uk

This inn is an award winner for Best Bed-and-Breakfast Hotel in Central and Greater London. It is clean, well decorated, has a charming breakfast room much larger than what most competitors offer, and has a selection of rooms that range from serviceable to lovely. The single rooms all have large three-quarter beds. Smoking is allowed only in the sitting room downstairs, not in the rooms. The breakfast (included in the price) is big and hearty, the location is perfect, and the service is friendly and unstuffy, but completely professional. Harrods is around the corner, South Kensington museums and restaurants are a four-minute walk away, and Hyde Park can be accessed in minutes. The traditional English style of decor, the sunlight in the front rooms, and the relatively reasonable price will delight the discerning tourist.

SETTINGS & FACILITIES

Location Knightsbridge. **Nearest Tube Station** Knightsbridge. **Quietness Rating** A. **Dining** Breakfast in room or in breakfast room. **Amenities** Sitting room with carved fireplace and complimentary papers and magazines; breakfast room with waiter service and full English breakfast included in price; airport transfer and taxis. **Services** Concierge, bellhop, laundry, faxing.

ACCOMMODATIONS

Rooms 29. **All Rooms** Cable TV, hair dryers. **Some Rooms** Four-poster bed, balcony, pull-out sofa, writing desk, sitting area, walk-in closet. **Bed & Bath** Beds are new. Bathtubs in 85% of rooms; the rest have shower stalls. All the bathrooms have been recently renovated and are in pristine condition. **Favorites** Number 12 is the best junior suite, with balcony, French windows, and awesome four-poster bed. Junior suite number 33 has a walk-in closet. Single number 35, in the rear of the building, is pretty good, too, with a large bed and a charm not defeated by the view of the backs of houses. **Comfort & Decor** Individually decorated, each room is attractive and clean and some are downright luxurious. The hotel has a great collection of portraits and drawings on the walls, and curtains in the magnificent English style.

PAYMENT, RESERVATIONS, & RESTRICTIONS

Deposit Credit card; 48-hour cancellation policy. **Credit Cards** All major. **Check-In/Out** 1 p.m./11:30 a.m. **Pets** Not allowed. **Elevator** Yes. **Children** Yes. **Disabled Access** No wheelchair access.

THE CLIVEDEN TOWN HOUSE   £130–£188

OVERALL ★★★★★ | QUALITY ★★★★½ | VALUE ★★★ | ZONE 11

26 Cadogan Gardens, SW3; (0207) 730-6466; in U.S. (800) 747-4942;
fax (0207) 730-0236; www.clivedentownhouse.co.uk

As you might expect from the sister town house of the world-famous Cliveden, former country house of the Astors, the Cliveden Town House is quite grand. However, it isn't pretentious and feels like a really beautiful home. The rooms are not numbered but named after theatrical legends— Laurence Olivier, Edmund Kean, Edith Evans, George and Ira Gershwin, the Redgraves, Noël Coward, and so on. The lovely drawing room has a welcoming, comfortable atmosphere and opens onto a nice-sized garden square that makes a wonderful place to sit in good weather. As you walk in the door, there are two urns on either side, each filled with apples, only the first of many appealing touches in this hotel town house. The rooms all have Cliveden teddy bears on the beds. There are gas fires in all but the single rooms. A self-service tea is set out each day at 4 p.m., and a complimentary bottle of champagne is uncorked at 6 p.m. Ask about deals; they are extremely accommodating here. The single rooms are OK, but if you can afford it, step up to a double—even the standard doubles are quite big and have a fireplace and sofa. It's a short walk from Sloane Square and Knightsbridge, but you'd swear you were in the country when you're in a room with a garden view.

SETTINGS & FACILITIES

Location Knightsbridge/Chelsea. **Nearest Tube Station** Knightsbridge or Sloane Square. **Quietness Rating** A. **Dining** Dinner on request, but no public dining room. Breakfast room is delightful and bright. **Amenities** Private dining room, drawing room, smoking room, afternoon tea, honor bar, breakfast room, garden. **Services** Concierge, complimentary chauffeur service into city each weekday, 24-hour room service, laundry, baby-sitting.

ACCOMMODATIONS

Rooms 35. **All Rooms** Telephone, voice mail, fax and modem line, air-conditioning, satellite TV, VCR, stereo CD. **Some Rooms** View onto gardens, fireplace. **Bed & Bath** Mattresses made specifically for Cliveden; baths are superior as would be expected. **Favorites** Any of the deluxe junior suites overlooking gardens; the doubles are quite fine, too. **Comfort & Decor** Highest standard of comfort; the decor is elegance itself, light but sumptuous.

PAYMENT, RESERVATIONS, & RESTRICTIONS

Deposit Credit card. **Credit Cards** All major. **Check-In/Out** 2 p.m./11 a.m. **Pets** Dogs allowed on certain conditions. **Elevator** Yes. **Children** Yes. **Disabled Access** No, too many stairs.

THE COLUMBIA HOTEL   £65–£83

OVERALL ★★ | QUALITY ★★★½ | VALUE ★★★★★ | ZONE 14

95–99 Lancaster Gate, W2; (0207) 402-0021; fax (0207) 706-4691;
www.columbiahotel.co.uk

This is probably one of the best deals in the area—there may be cheaper rooms to be had, but not with the amenities and friendliness of the Columbia. It looks out on Hyde Park and is well located for buses and the tube. The rooms are plain hotel style, but they're clean and some are fairly roomy. The hotel is comprised of five Victorian houses strung together, so as with all such buildings, there will be great disparity among the size and shape of the rooms. Unfortunately, the first floor, with its elegant high ceilings and huge windows, is mostly conference rooms, but there are many park-view rooms on the remaining floors. The only problem is that it's noisier on the park. This is a good budget hotel and one that can accommodate families, pets, and even automobiles (parking on a first-come, first-served basis). Queensway, a few minutes' walk away, has lots of great restaurants (not to mention a skating rink and bowling alley). The staff is friendly and helpful. Breakfast is included.

SETTINGS & FACILITIES

Location Lancaster Gate (Bayswater). **Nearest Tube Station** Lancaster Gate. **Quietness Rating** C in front, A in back. **Dining** Breakfast and dinner. **Amenities** Dining room, bar. **Services** 24-hour reception desk, laundry.

ACCOMMODATIONS

Rooms 100. **All Rooms** Shower and toilet, telephone, BBC TV, hair dryer. **Some Rooms** View over park, connecting rooms, four beds in one room. **Bed & Bath** Clean and satisfactory, mostly showers. **Favorites** Big rooms. **Comfort & Decor** Very plain and simple.

PAYMENT, RESERVATIONS, & RESTRICTIONS

Deposit Credit card; 24-hour cancellation policy. **Credit Cards** All major, except DC. **Check-In/Out** 2 p.m./11:30 a.m. **Pets** Allowed. **Elevator** Two. **Children** Yes. **Disabled Access** One disabled room, and a bedroom for deaf or hearing disabled.

COMFORT INN NOTTING HILL £65–£75

OVERALL ★ | QUALITY ★★½ | VALUE ★★★★★ | ZONE 13

6–14 Pembridge Gardens, Kensington, W2; (0207) 221-3433;
fax (0207) 229-4808; www.londonhotels.net

Here's a good budget hotel within a short walk of Portobello Road and Kensington Church Street—perfect for antiques hunters who want to spend all their money on treasures instead of hotels. It's also a short walk to Kensington Gardens and Hyde Park, and the tube is very near. The hotel is on a very nice street off the busy Notting Hill Gate; there's not too much noise from it. It's undistinguished aesthetically, but clean and serviceable, with a couple of nice touches, like the huge crystal chandelier. There are two video games and a chocolate vending machine in the honesty bar/lounge, which, along with the breakfast room, has piped-in pop music. Continental breakfast is included in the price. The breakfast room is a good size and pleasant enough. Good value for money here.

SETTINGS & FACILITIES

Location Notting Hill Gate. **Nearest Tube Station** Notting Hill Gate. **Quietness Rating** A in back, B in front. **Dining** Breakfast room, honor bar. **Amenities** Breakfast included, satellite TV in bar, video games. **Services** Reception acts as concierge, laundry.

ACCOMMODATIONS

Rooms 70. **All Rooms** En suite shower/tub and toilet, telephone, five-channel TV, hair dryer. **Bed & Bath** Utilitarian, clean, and serviceable. **Favorites** Take the double or twin room if you're alone, take the twin if you're with a spouse (double beds are small). **Comfort & Decor** Serviceable comfort, plain and forgettable decor. Like a college dorm.

PAYMENT, RESERVATIONS, & RESTRICTIONS

Deposit Credit card; 48-hour cancellation policy. **Credit Cards** All major. **Check-In/Out** 1 p.m./10:30 a.m. **Pets** Not allowed. **Elevator** Two. **Children** Yes. **Disabled Access** Steps outside, small lifts.

COVENT GARDEN HOTEL   £229–£288

OVERALL ★★★★ | QUALITY ★★★★½ | VALUE ★★★★ | ZONE 7

10 Monmouth Street, WC2; (0207) 806-1000; fax (0207) 806-1100;
www.firmdale.com

Another nice hotel of the Firmdale group, which also owns—among other, newer purchases—the Pelham Hotel, Charlotte Street Hotel, and the Knightsbridge Hotel. The Covent Garden is more spacious than other Firmdale Hotels, and offers more square footage, both in the size of the beds and the size of the rooms and hallways. Amenities such as cell phones and VCRs are offered. There is a fitness area, with treatment rooms for massages, facials, etc. The brasserie has been enlarged, and a 56-seat cinema offering first-run films has been installed (not quite necessary, when you're so close to the West End cinemas). But the outstanding thing about this hotel is the decor—it is just plain appealing, not trying to be traditionally English or stylishly modern. It's just a place where all the possessions and talents of the designer come together effortlessly and pleasingly. It is a superb location: Monmouth Street, on which the hotel is situated, is a relatively quiet street in Seven Dials, but is within skipping distance of Soho, Covent Garden, Bloomsbury, and the theaters of the West End.

SETTINGS & FACILITIES

Location Covent Garden. **Nearest Tube Station** Covent Garden. **Quietness Rating** A, but perhaps C on weekend nights. **Dining** Brasserie Max is a modern-style dining room with good food. **Amenities** Two drawing rooms, one very large, with working fireplaces; restaurant; honor bar with snacks; personal safe; cell phone for rent at £10 a day; workout room; 56-seat cinema. **Services** Concierge, 24-hour room service, valet, bellhop, laundry.

ACCOMMODATIONS

Rooms 50. **All Rooms** U.S.-size queen and king beds (even in singles), air-conditioning, telephones with extra line, modem with voice mail, cable TV, VCR and movies to watch,

CD player and CDs to borrow, cell phone for rent, writing desk, bathtubs, umbrella. **Some Rooms** Ornamental fireplace, four-poster bed, sofa and sitting area, roof terrace. **Bed & Bath** Bathrooms are splendid, all gray marble and perfection. The beds are huge, outfitted in 100% cotton sheets and covered with the most beautiful duvets and pillows. **Favorites** Number 304 is a deluxe double with a blue theme, gorgeous four-poster bed, and an ornamental fireplace with two big chairs in front of it. The terrace suite is preferred by the many movie stars who stay here; it has its own little patio overlooking the roofs of the West End, a library, a sofa, and a sweetly appointed queen-size bed. The walls have been painstakingly painted with a sponge effect in red. **Comfort & Decor** All of your possible needs will be accounted for. The decor is sublime—Tim and Kit Kemp are geniuses at interior decoration, neatly blending traditional antiques with their own brand of quirky taste, creating an atmosphere of delight.

PAYMENT, RESERVATIONS, & RESTRICTIONS

Deposit Credit card; 24-hour cancellation policy. **Credit Cards** All major. **Check-In/Out** 1 p.m./11 a.m. **Pets** Not allowed. **Elevator** Two. **Children** Yes. **Disabled Access** Yes, big elevators and wide hallways.

DUKES HOTEL £230–£265

OVERALL ★★★★★ | QUALITY ★★★★½ | VALUE ★★★★ | ZONE 9

35 St. James Place, SW1; (0207) 491-4840, in U.S. (800) 381-4702; fax (0207) 493-1264; www.dukeshotel.co.uk

Behind a charming courtyard, in one of the most appealing areas of central London is the extremely deluxe Dukes Hotel. Outside this Edwardian building remain gas lamps lit by hand every night. Inside, you'll find a sumptuous hotel that promises the highest standards in service and accommodation. It's expensive and caters to the kind of clientele who likes cognac to be 100 years old and doesn't flinch at outrageous prices for it. It's an intimate, clubby kind of place, but not stuffy or intimidating. The location is great: right by St. James's Park and Piccadilly; you couldn't ask for a more central yet quiet spot to enjoy London. And if you're feeling particularly flush, check out Penthouse One, with the views of all the glory that is London.

SETTINGS & FACILITIES

Location St. James. **Nearest Tube Station** Green Park. **Quietness Rating** A. **Dining** Private dining room can be booked. **Amenities** Bar with exceptional cognacs and wines; health club with massage and personal trainer available. **Services** Concierge, butler, valet, secretarial services, 16-hour room service.

ACCOMMODATIONS

Rooms 89. **All Rooms** Telephone, satellite TV, air-conditioning, private bar, writing desks. **Some Rooms** Oversize (7 feet square) "Emperor" bed; sitting rooms; views of Big Ben, Westminster Abbey, parks, and Parliament; exceptionally large (penthouse is 700 square feet). **Bed & Bath** Magnificent marble bathrooms with bathrobes and beds that you'd be proud to call your own. **Favorites** The penthouses are more like flats, absolutely huge and unimaginably luxurious, but even the standard doubles and the deluxe singles are very big for London (190 and 140 square feet, respectively). You can't go too wrong in any of the rooms here. **Comfort & Decor** Highest standards of comfort and completely pleasing decor—not overdone, just serene and elegant.

PAYMENT, RESERVATIONS, & RESTRICTIONS

Deposit Credit card. **Credit Cards** All major. **Check-In/Out** 2 p.m./noon. **Pets** Not allowed. **Elevator** Yes. **Children** No children under age five. **Disabled Access** Limited.

DURRANTS   £110–£165

OVERALL ★★★ | QUALITY ★★★½ | VALUE ★★★★★ | ZONE 14

George Street, W1; (0207) 935-8131; fax (0207) 487-3510; www.durrantshotel.co.uk

A hotel that has been run by the same family since 1921, Durrants has a lot going for it, not least of all its proximity to the Wallace Collection and Regent's Park. But mainly, it's a hotel that gives very good value for the money. The rooms are more spacious than comparably priced places and they certainly are more lovely than most, furnished with genuine antique pieces, as well as bright soft furnishings. The atmosphere in the hotel is that of a leather-chaired gentleman's club with oil paintings and gas fires. There's a tiny bar called The Pump Room, where women used to not be allowed, which gave license for the hotel to feature paintings of nudes on the walls. Breakfast (an expensive breakfast) is served by waiters in a very charming breakfast room, and the restaurant on the other side of the lobby is of a good quality. The hotel is a great location for shopping on Oxford and Bond Streets, going to Regent's or Hyde Park, and running in and out of the free Wallace Collection any time of the day.

SETTINGS & FACILITIES

Location Marylebone. **Nearest Tube Station** Bond Street. **Quietness Rating** A. **Dining** The restaurant has the best booths in the world and decent food besides. **Amenities** Pump Room, lounges with fireplaces, bar downstairs. **Services** Concierge, 24-hour room service, bellhop, laundry, airport transfer, baby-sitting.

ACCOMMODATIONS

Rooms 92. **All Rooms** Telephone, TV, hair dryer, iron, writing desks. **Some Rooms** Minibars, sitting chairs. **Bed & Bath** New mattresses in all rooms, newly remodeled bathrooms that are nice and relatively spacious. **Favorites** Suite number 305 is a two-room pleasure: The sitting room has lots of conversation areas and is beautifully decorated with old portraits. **Comfort & Decor** Top-notch; the antiques warm up the cleanliness of the hotel decor. There's an effortlessness that is very appealing, and the comfort is part of this.

PAYMENT, RESERVATIONS, & RESTRICTIONS

Deposit Credit card; must cancel by noon on the day before arrival hour. **Credit Cards** All major, except DC. **Check-In/Out** 2 p.m./noon. **Pets** Not allowed. **Elevator**

Two. **Children** Yes; baby-sitting and cribs can be arranged. **Disabled Access** One room with wheelchair access and porters to help; call ahead.

EDWARD LEAR HOTEL £60–£89

OVERALL ★ | QUALITY ★★★½ | VALUE ★★★★★ | ZONE 14

28–30 Seymour Street, W1; (0207) 402-5401; fax (0207) 706-3766; www.edlear.com

The Edward Lear Hotel is a simple place, at a low price. The rooms can be dark and not extremely appealing, but the hotel does offer more amenities than comparative hotels, such as telephone and satellite TV. It's clean, well run, and provides a good breakfast in its price. Only 100 yards from Oxford Street and within a short walk of Hyde Park, the Edward Lear Hotel is popular among budget travelers, but not so attractive to those who like more luxury. The decoration includes charming drawings and limericks by the famous Victorian artist and poet Edward Lear, who once lived here. The exterior has greenery spilling from every window, which lends a nice homey touch.

SETTINGS & FACILITIES

Location Marble Arch. **Nearest Tube Station** Marble Arch. **Quietness Rating** B in back, C in front. **Dining** Breakfast room. **Amenities** Full English breakfast, two lounges. **Services** Breakfast.

ACCOMMODATIONS

Rooms 30. **All Rooms** Telephone, satellite TV, radio, tea and coffee. **Some Rooms** Shower/toilet. **Bed & Bath** Rooms without toilets and showers en suite do have them nearby and they are clean; beds are satisfactory. **Favorites** Rooms in back, triples with shower/toilet. **Comfort & Decor** Plain, cheerful, clean, and decorated with Edward Lear's marvelous drawings and nonsense poems and limericks. Smallish rooms.

PAYMENT, RESERVATIONS, & RESTRICTIONS

Deposit Credit card; 24-hour cancellation policy. **Credit Cards** VISA, MC. **Check-In/Out** 1 p.m./11 a.m. **Pets** Not allowed. **Elevator** No. **Children** Yes. **Disabled Access** No.

11 CADOGAN GARDENS £145–£215

OVERALL ★★★★★ | QUALITY ★★★★ | VALUE ★★★ | ZONE 11

11 Cadogan Gardens; (0207) 730-7000; fax (0207) 730-5217; www.number-eleven.co.uk

This is a perfectly delightful hotel tucked away behind Sloane Street in the expanses of red-bricked Victorian town houses. It was built in the 1860s, has been a hotel for 40 years, and has a certain quiet, non-hotelish charm. The building has held on to all of its oak-paneled walls, which are perfectly set off by the William Morris–style wallpaper. The antiques are of high quality, and the walls are filled with fascinating portraits of people from the past few centuries—worthies on every wall. The drawing room has a genuine clubby atmosphere, and one could get extremely comfortable sitting before the fireplace with a book. Number 11 is popular for its brand of discreet, efficient service. The hotel has a rare feature for this type of hotel: a decent gym room in the lower ground floor, with a couple of StairMasters, a treadmill, two bikes, and a whole lot of weight equipment. All the rooms are different—in size, in decor, in views. The hotel is so impressive overall that any room will no doubt suit you just fine. Breakfast is not included in the price of the room and is quite expensive, but you are very near many cafés in Chelsea.

SETTINGS & FACILITIES

Location Knightsbridge/Chelsea. **Nearest Tube Station** Sloane Square. **Quietness Rating** A. **Dining** A dining room serves breakfast, lunch, and dinner. **Amenities** Drawing room, exercise room, aromatherapy, massage. **Services** Concierge, 24-hour room service, bellhop, laundry.

ACCOMMODATIONS

Rooms 62. **All Rooms** Telephone, satellite TV, safe, hair dryer, excellent antiques. **Some Rooms** Writing desk, views, air-conditioning. **Bed & Bath** Bathrooms are marble and provide Moulton Brown toiletries; beds are comfortable; many single rooms have double beds. **Favorites** The ones in front with the view of the garden are nice, but the best is definitely the biggest suite in the hotel, which is more like a stately flat, with high ceilings, four-poster bed, limited kitchenette, big windows, and plenty of room for a family of four. **Comfort & Decor** Exquisite decor suggesting a graceful bygone age; extremely comfortable.

PAYMENT, RESERVATIONS, & RESTRICTIONS

Deposit Credit card. **Credit Cards** All major. **Check-In/Out** 1 p.m/noon. **Pets** Not allowed. **Elevator** Yes. **Children** Yes. **Disabled Access** Will accommodate.

FIELDING HOTEL £76–£100

OVERALL ★ | QUALITY ★★★ | VALUE ★★★ | ZONE 7

4 Broad Court at Bow Street, WC2; (0207) 836-8305; fax (0207) 497-0064; www.thefielding-hotel.co.uk

The Fielding is like a college dormitory: completely utilitarian and inoffensive. It even manages a small amount of charm; certainly the exterior is pretty with the ivy-covered leaded windows. The fact that the hotel sits on a pedestrian court with nineteenth-century lamps in the shadow of the Royal Opera House renders it extremely attractive. It's all cheap pine and hard beds inside, but you don't share bathrooms, and everything is as clean and simple as you could ask for at the price. The superior double rooms in front are a bit nicer than the double suite, which actually costs more. The Fielding is around the corner from Covent Garden and is within walking distance of the City, the British Museum, the Thames, and Piccadilly. It's a good location at a very low price.

SETTINGS & FACILITIES

Location Covent Garden. **Nearest Tube Station** Covent Garden. **Quietness Rating** A. **Dining** Breakfast room. **Amenities** Breakfast at a very low price, honor bar. **Services** Helpful reception desk.

ACCOMMODATIONS

Rooms 24. **All Rooms** Telephone, five-channel TV with remote control, toilet. **Some Rooms** Sitting area, writing desk. **Bed & Bath** Hard beds, clean bathrooms with showers only. **Favorites** Superior doubles in the front of the building have the most space and light. **Comfort & Decor** Somewhere between utilitarian and spartan.

PAYMENT, RESERVATIONS, & RESTRICTIONS

Deposit One night's rate; 72-hour cancellation policy. **Credit Cards** All major. **Check-In/Out** Noon/11:30 a.m. **Pets** Not allowed. **Elevator** No. **Children** No children under age 13. **Disabled Access** No.

FIVE SUMNER PLACE HOTEL   £130–£152

OVERALL ★★ | QUALITY ★★★ | VALUE ★★★★★ | ZONE 11

5 Sumner Place, South Kensington, SW7; (0207) 584-7586; fax (0207) 823-9962; www.sumnerplace.com

Five Sumner Place has those most formidable of qualities: good value and good location. It is on the small side, as one would expect from a Victorian town house, but it makes much of its size, and the prices are good for the neighborhood. It was twice awarded the British Tourist Association Best Small Hotel prize and would probably have won it more often, except they stopped giving out these awards. The place is modest but comfortable and extremely clean and well kept. A couple of good rooms at the front have a scenic Mary Poppins–type view of a white row of town houses. Breakfast (included in the price) is served in the conservatory, which doubles as a sitting area at other times. The owners made a conscious decision to forgo cable TV (you do get five channels), the thinking being that, as the place is so intimate, it wouldn't do to have some jet-lagged wide-eyed traveler staying up till 3 a.m. watching CNN or MTV at high volumes. There are a lot of repeat customers, so book well ahead. You can get a 10% discount during January and February.

SETTINGS & FACILITIES

Location South Kensington. **Nearest Tube Station** South Kensington. **Quietness Rating** A. **Dining** Breakfast; tons of restaurants and a 24-hour grocery nearby. **Amenities** Daily newspapers, magazines, conservatory. **Services** Concierge services, laundry, bellhop, tea and coffee.

ACCOMMODATIONS

Rooms 13. **All Rooms** Telephone, TV, radio. **Some Rooms** Refrigerator. **Bed & Bath** Very good beds and showers, some baths. **Favorites** Numbers 4 and 6 have balconies. Number 5 is a surprisingly spacious-feeling single. **Comfort & Decor** It's not luxury, but it's not spartan either; in some rooms the decor is very comely, and in all rooms, clean and fresh. Some of the original moldings from 1848 have been beautifully preserved.

PAYMENT, RESERVATIONS, & RESTRICTIONS

Deposit Credit card; 14-day cancellation policy. **Credit Cards** All major, except DC. **Check-In/Out** 11 a.m. **Pets** Not allowed. **Elevator** Yes. **Children** No children under age 6. **Disabled Access** Two ground-floor rooms; no wheelchair access.

FLEMINGS   £199–£233

OVERALL ★★★ | QUALITY ★★★½ | VALUE ★★★★ | ZONE 8

10 Half Moon Street, W1; (0207) 493-2088; fax (0207) 499-1817;
www.flemings-mayfair.co.uk

Flemings is seven old houses strung together, with the result that the rooms are of all different shapes and sizes, mostly of the smaller variety. It's a friendly place, with a very homey atmosphere. The junior suites are nice, as are the common sitting areas. The decoration is an interesting pastiche of periods, a kind of art deco meets Victorian, which is more attractive than it sounds. The hotel has a restaurant and a bar downstairs, and the rooms are equipped with all the amenities you could want (except for a minibar). However, the rooms and the beds are small, which prevents Flemings from being really good value for the money.

SETTINGS & FACILITIES

Location Mayfair. **Nearest Tube Station** Green Park. **Quietness Rating** A in back, B in front (double-glazed windows). **Dining** Flemings Restaurant serves European food with a good wine selection; the Claridge Bar is downstairs, and tea is served in the lounges. **Amenities** Restaurant, bar, modem connections for British and American plugs, bathrobes. **Services** Concierge, 24-hour room service, bellhop, laundry.

ACCOMMODATIONS

Rooms 121; apartments available as well as rooms. **All Rooms** Telephone, satellite TV, air-conditioning, hair dryer, iron, tea and coffee, in-house movies, writing desk. **Some Rooms** Four-poster bed. **Bed & Bath** Bathrooms are made of marble and are nicely appointed; beds are on the small side—ask for a twin put together for a king. Doubles are good only for one or two very thin and short people. **Favorites** The junior suites. **Comfort & Decor** Victorian paneled wood, art deco cast-iron sculptures, nice art on the walls, great smell in the hotel. Small rooms, but very comfortable, and the owners aim to please.

PAYMENT, RESERVATIONS, & RESTRICTIONS

Deposit Credit card; must cancel on day of arrival by 4 p.m. **Credit Cards** All major. **Check-In/Out** 2 p.m./noon. **Pets** Not allowed. **Elevator** Yes. **Children** Yes. **Disabled Access** Limited, but possible.

FRANKLIN HOTEL   £188–£225

OVERALL ★★★★ | QUALITY ★★★½ | VALUE ★★★★ | ZONE 10

*28 Egerton Gardens, Knightsbridge, SW3; (0207) 584-5533, in U.S. (800) 473-9487;
fax (0207) 584-5449, in U.S. (800) 473-9489; www.franklinhotel.co.uk*

The Franklin Hotel is a small, elegant hotel situated on (and with access to)
Egerton Gardens, which is a beautiful expanse of greenery wild with bright
blooms in the spring. The hotel's almost sylvan peace is uncompromised by
the fact that the bustling Brompton Road lies mere steps away. The magnificent Brompton Oratory, a Catholic Church, is a neighbor, and you can
visit the nearby Victoria and Albert Museum a few times a day. The atmosphere is serene, with antique furniture and art decorating the sitting rooms.
The two sitting rooms look onto the garden, and a fire is kept blazing
while you read the complimentary newspapers. There is an honor bar, and
people like to congregate in the leather-chaired drinks room before dinner, or read the paper in one of the beautiful sitting rooms. This hotel,
owned by the same people who gave us Dukes and the Egerton Garden
Hotel (right down the street), is a real favorite with Americans, who
return again and again; even the queen of Sweden stays here for its comfort, decor, and excellent service. The hotel has a clean, elegant Georgian
feel to it, and though the rooms may be on the small side, they are perfectly appointed. Check the website for special offers; or talk to the manager for upgrades or deals. They are very accommodating and friendly.

SETTINGS & FACILITIES

Location Border of Knightsbridge and South Kensington. **Nearest Tube Station**
South Kensington. **Quietness Rating** A in garden-facing rooms, B in front rooms. **Dining** Breakfast only. **Amenities** Honor bar, access to gardens, breakfast in breakfast
room or bedroom, nonsmoking rooms, small computer room for use of guests. **Services** Concierge, 24-hour room service, butler, valet.

ACCOMMODATIONS

Rooms 50. **All Rooms** Direct-dial phones, modem lines, optional fax, cable TV, minibar, hair dryer, iron, heated towel racks. **Some Rooms** Garden view and entrance,
four-poster bed, sitting area, two TVs, bay window. **Bed & Bath** Great beds with cotton sheets; all baths are marble and include power showers. **Favorites** There are two
rooms that are split level and spacious, number 24 and number 26. Number 1 has an
entrance to the gardens and a four-poster. Number 3 is on the lower ground floor, but
is very spacious and pleasing. Number 5 has a long view of the gardens; number 19 is
just about two rooms, with a wall dividing the bedroom and the sitting room. **Comfort
& Decor** Excellent decor, homey feeling, extremely comfortable.

PAYMENT, RESERVATIONS, & RESTRICTIONS

Deposit Credit card; 48-hour cancellation policy. **Credit Cards** All major. **Check-
In/Out** Whenever possible/noon. **Pets** Not allowed. **Elevator** Yes. **Children** Yes. **Disabled Access** Steps in front, but help can be arranged.

THE GAINSBOROUGH   £88–£141

OVERALL ★★★ | QUALITY ★★★ | VALUE ★★★★ | ZONE 11

7–11 Queensberry Place, SW7; (0207) 838-1700, in U.S. (800) 270-9206;
fax (0207) 970-1805; www.eeh.co.uk

This is very similar to its sister hotel across the street, The Gallery, except
that it's slightly less expensive, which makes for good value. There are no
large sitting rooms, but the hotel is extremely serviceable and well decorated. The smallish rooms are comfortable and tasteful. You can feel quite
at home here without spending all your money on lodging—not an easy
feat in London. The staff is helpful and friendly. There is a hearty breakfast included in the price, set out each day in the bright room off the
lobby that becomes a tearoom/bar in the afternoon. Walk out of the
hotel and you'll see the magnificent Natural History Museum—one of
three museums on your doorstep. This is a very good location.

SETTINGS & FACILITIES

Location South Kensington. **Nearest Tube Station** South Kensington. **Quietness
Rating** A in back, C in front and on lower floors. **Dining** Breakfast room and snack/
sandwich room service. **Amenities** Breakfast room and bar, fax in lobby, discount at two
fitness clubs nearby. **Services** Concierge, room service, laundry, breakfast, bellhop.

ACCOMMODATIONS

Rooms 49. **All Rooms** Telephone, cable TV, tea and coffee, safe, hair dryer, iron. **Some
Rooms** French windows, balcony, bigger TVs, air-conditioning. **Bed & Bath** Beds are a
bit hard. Singles all have shower stalls in the bathrooms, and doubles have shower/tub
combinations. Very nicely decorated bathrooms. **Favorites** Number 112 has a balcony
and French windows and seems a little bigger than the others. **Comfort & Decor**
Rooms are small, but everything is clean and nicely presented. The decor is subdued,
individual in each room, but homey.

PAYMENT, RESERVATIONS, & RESTRICTIONS

Deposit Credit card; 24-hour cancellation policy. **Credit Cards** All major. **Check-
In/Out** 1 p.m./noon. **Pets** Not allowed. **Elevator** Yes. **Children** Yes. **Disabled Access**
Wheelchair access planned, call ahead.

THE GALLERY HOTEL   £141–£153

OVERALL ★★★ | QUALITY ★★★½ | VALUE ★★★★ | ZONE 11

8–10 Queensberry Place, SW7; (0207) 838-1700, in U.S. (800) 270-9206;
fax (0207) 970-1805; www.eeh.co.uk

This is a good hotel in the heart of South Kensington, with the imposing
Natural History Museum at the end of the street, the tube a two-minute
walk away, and Kensington Gardens/Hyde Park a five-minute walk away.
The rooms are not big, except for the fabulous suite, number 502
(£235), which has a private garden terrace! There is a very good breakfast

room (breakfast is included) with a well-stocked buffet. Upstairs you'll find a pleasant sitting room with a bar and a chess board. Newly refurbished, the decor is attractive; everything shines and sparkles, especially the mahogany-and-marble bathrooms. Check website for deals.

SETTINGS & FACILITIES

Location South Kensington. **Nearest Tube Station** South Kensington. **Quietness Rating** A in back, C in front. **Dining** Breakfast room; room service of sandwiches and snacks. **Amenities** Minibars, cable TV, iron, tea and coffee, safe, writing desk, fitness club nearby, music in bar on occasion, fax in lobby. **Services** Concierge, 24-hour room service.

ACCOMMODATIONS

Rooms 36. **All Rooms** Cable TV, hair dryer, safe. **Some Rooms** Air-conditioning, fax, couches, Jacuzzi. **Bed & Bath** Excellent on both counts. Baths in doubles and suites, shower stalls in singles. **Favorites** Number 502 is a penthouse suite with a huge bed, a private garden terrace, a dining table, two couches, and three phone lines. **Comfort & Decor** Care has been taken to ensure all comforts, and the decor is individual and restful, a bit on the plain side, but clean and pleasing to the eye.

PAYMENT, RESERVATIONS, & RESTRICTIONS

Deposit Credit card; 24-hour cancellation policy. **Credit Cards** All major. **Check-In/Out** 1 p.m./noon. **Pets** Not allowed. **Elevator** Yes. **Children** Yes. **Disabled Access** No wheelchair access.

THE GORE   £141–£223

OVERALL ★★★★ | QUALITY ★★★★½ | VALUE ★★★★ | ZONE 11

189 Queen's Gate, SW7; (0207) 584-6601; fax (0207) 589-8127; www.gorehotel.com

We raved so much about this hotel in our first edition that visitors to the Gore were disappointed and unimpressed. There were complaints by three readers that The Gore did not live up to our description, so we shall tone it down a bit. The Gore was the brainstorm of two antiques dealers who had started their hotel career with the wonderful Hazlitt's in Soho. They bought this fine old mansion on Queen's Gate, steps from Kensington Garden, in which to hang 4,500 prints and paintings and house their serious collection of antiques. The Tudor Room could be part of a National Trust property, and its sixteenth-century bed could easily find a home in a museum. Even the single rooms are extraordinary, with beds and furnishings from the nineteenth century. The bathrooms are good, with attention paid to details. There is a restaurant, Bistrot 190, that serves excellent food and good breakfasts and is bright and cheerful. On the lower ground floor is the more formal and pricey restaurant known simply as 190. The Gore has two sister hotels—Hazlitt's in Soho and The Rookery in the City. The Gore's location is good for lovers of Hyde Park and is also walking distance from South Kensington, the Albert Hall, and

Kensington High Street. A word of caution: The beds are genuine Victorian antiques, and some of the larger guests have a problem with the size. If you are extremely tall or particularly overweight, the beds may pose a problem to you. Talk to the concierge about your needs.

SETTINGS & FACILITIES

Location South Kensington/Kensington border. **Nearest Tube Station** Gloucester Road. **Quietness Rating** A in back and top floors, B in lower front floors. **Dining** Two restaurants: Bistrot 190 and Restaurant 190. The first is informal but with an excellent menu, and the second is more formal and expensive. Both are excellent restaurants. **Amenities** Use of two nearby fitness centers. **Services** Concierge, 24-hour room service, bellhop, laundry.

ACCOMMODATIONS

Rooms 48. **All Rooms** Minibars, limited cable TV, antiques and art, genuine Victorian beds, fans, writing desks. **Some Rooms** Stained-glass windows, French doors and balconies, sitting area, fireplace. **Bed & Bath** The beds may be too small for some people used to king-size modern hotel beds. Try the twin-bedded rooms if you can't fit into a double with your partner. The bathrooms are amazing: Many of them have the old-fashioned loo chair around the toilet—a genuine "throne." In one of the suites, there is a shower head as big as a dinner plate. **Favorites** The Tudor is astonishing: a Victorian re-creation of an Elizabethan gallery, complete with huge stone fireplace (using gas) and stained glass of the queen herself. Carved lintels of heads and gargoyles are not for the faint of heart. Miss Ada's room (number 207) has a lovely Victorian theme and the aforementioned enormous shower head. It's masculine and mahogany, with a very good double bed and a bust of Queen Victoria at the foot of it. In the Venus Room, a very feminine and well named room, you can sleep in an antique rococo bed once owned by Judy Garland. The Dame Nelly suite is wonderful, and as for singles, number 108 has an ornate bed and airy atmosphere. **Comfort & Decor** There is a sense of easy comfort throughout the hotel, and the decor is endlessly fascinating, although a minimalist would run screaming from its portals.

PAYMENT, RESERVATIONS, & RESTRICTIONS

Deposit Credit card; 48-hour cancellation policy. **Credit Cards** All major. **Check-In/Out** 1 p.m./11:30 a.m. **Pets** Not allowed, exceptions made for guide dogs and perhaps well-behaved lap dogs. **Elevator** Yes. **Children** Yes. **Disabled Access** No.

GORING HOTEL   £229–£288

OVERALL ★★★★★ | QUALITY ★★★★½ | VALUE ★★★★ | ZONE 9

Beeston Place, SW1; (0207) 396-9000; fax (0207) 834-4393; www.goringhotel.co.uk

The Goring is a lovely hotel, pure elegance and comfort a few steps from Victoria Station and within easy reach of the wonders of Westminster Abbey and Buckingham Palace. It has the great benefit of being on a tiny street where most of the traffic belongs to the hotel; in the back there's a lawn that is a real oasis of peace, even though you can only look at it. Sometimes that's enough, especially when St. James's Park is so nearby.

The hotel is justifiably proud of having remained in the same family since 1911, and it does indeed call to mind a fine country club of the early 1900s. It doesn't have any Victorian frippery, just a cool Edwardian elegance and comfort, from the bright yellow and marble of the beautiful lobby to the lounge tables that look like they've seen quite a few bridge games in their day. There's a finely carved fireplace and a wall of windows through which you can view the garden, and drinks and light food are served there all day. The dining room is of a high quality, as are the rooms themselves. Strangely but appealingly, there are adorable stuffed sheep in the rooms, which also have lovely furniture and excellent bathrooms outfitted with Penhaligon's toiletries. The Goring plays to a lot of repeat customers—generations of them—and it's easy to see why. Special weekend rates are available.

SETTINGS & FACILITIES

Location Victoria. **Nearest Tube Station** Victoria. **Quietness Rating** A/B (double-glazed windows). **Dining** Beautiful dining room, plus garden bar and drawing room for teas and light meals. **Amenities** Dining room, a very attractive and capacious drawing room and bar, a splendid expanse of lawn out back to admire, complimentary membership in nearby health club. **Services** Concierge, 24-hour room service, bellhop, laundry.

ACCOMMODATIONS

Rooms 75. **All Rooms** Individual temperature control (including air-conditioning), telephone, cable TV, hair dryer, writing desk. **Some Rooms** Balcony overlooking garden, fax. **Bed & Bath** Beautiful wood-and-marble bathrooms and good-size beds in all the rooms. **Favorites** There are a few rooms with balconies that overlook the garden. These are fantastic and quite a rarity in London (or in any big city for that matter). **Comfort & Decor** The decor is extremely well done, suggesting a quite pleasing Georgian elegance and cheerfulness. All the common areas and the individual rooms are bright and warmly welcoming.

PAYMENT, RESERVATIONS, & RESTRICTIONS

Deposit Credit card. **Credit Cards** All major. **Check-In/Out** Noon. **Pets** Dogs and birds not allowed (since 1911, when, judging from the posted restriction, apparently many people traveled with birds in hand). **Elevator** Yes. **Children** Yes. **Disabled Access** Yes.

GRANGE WHITE HALL HOTEL   £183–£194

OVERALL ★★★ | QUALITY ★★★½ | VALUE ★★★★ | ZONE 2

2–5 Montague Street, WC1; (0207) 233-7888; fax (0207) 630-9897;
www.grangehotels.co.uk

This is a pleasant and well appointed hotel literally in the shadow of the British Museum (which just doesn't look quite as magnificent from the back—the red bricks are less impressive than the front's stone sheath), with an exquisite and large garden. There's a glassed-in (air-conditioned) conservatory in the garden that can be used for afternoon teas or private functions. The rooms are as small as most London hotel rooms, but if you require space, ask for the lower ground (basement) rooms—some have more space for the same price as an upstairs room. The ambience is pleasing, and although all the furniture is reproduction, the decor still has a certain cleanliness and order that is attractive. There are some really lovely touches, such as the elaborate molding in every room that has been painstakingly painted, the stencils on the walls, the glass and brass elevator, and the sumptuous curtains. There are a number of money-saving schemes—one of which is to book through the hotel's website, though you can also call and negotiate a deal.

SETTINGS & FACILITIES

Location Bloomsbury. **Nearest Tube Station** Russell Square. **Quietness Rating** A on garden in back, B+ in front (double glazing helps). **Dining** Breakfast, lunch, and dinner in the gorgeous English Garden Restaurant; The Museum Wine Bar is attached to the hotel, but with a separate entrance. **Amenities** Garden, minibar, TV with BBC and Sky News, in-house movies, buffet breakfast, smoking and nonsmoking rooms, daily newspaper. **Services** Concierge, 24-hour room service, bellhop, laundry, fitness center two-minute walk away.

ACCOMMODATIONS

Rooms 50. **All Rooms** Telephone, TV, minibar, iron, tea and coffee, hair dryer, writing desk, computer modem. **Some Rooms** Four-poster beds, balcony, garden view, French doors, sofa bed. **Bed & Bath** Bathrooms are in perfect condition; beds are OK and some are wonderful, such as the four-posters. **Favorites** Number 109 has a four-poster bed and a balcony on the garden; number 106 has a sofa bed and also a balcony on the garden. All the rooms on the first floor have high ceilings and French doors. **Comfort & Decor** Decor is quite rich and handsome, and there is a surprising amount of light for a period conversion building. Care has clearly been taken to make this hotel visually gratifying, although it lacks a certain authenticity (not a lot of real antiques). It is comfortable enough, even though rooms are of the usual smallish variety.

PAYMENT, RESERVATIONS, & RESTRICTIONS

Deposit Credit card; 24-hour cancellation policy. **Credit Cards** All major. **Check-In/Out** 2 p.m./11 a.m. **Pets** Not allowed. **Elevator** Yes. **Children** Yes. **Disabled Access** Limited.

GREAT EASTERN HOTEL   *£265–£311*

OVERALL ★★★★ | QUALITY ★★★★ | VALUE ★★★★ | ZONE 3

Liverpool Street, EC2M 7QN; (0207) 618-5000; fax (0207) 618-5000; www.great-eastern-hotel.co.uk

The Great Eastern Hotel is one of the best—not that it has much competition—full-service hotels in the Square Mile, as the financial center of the city is known. This is a great boon to business travelers, and for those who want to stay further east than the usual pleasure visitor does. Liverpool

Street Underground and Trail Station, a major hub of London travel (with a direct train to Stansted Airport), is adjacent to the hotel, and while the neighborhood is not as charming as many others in London, there is the growing trendiness of nearby Hoxton Square and Spitalfields. The Great Eastern was one of the grand old Victorian train-station hotels, built in 1884 and expanded in 1901. Recently, it was closed for three years for a massive renovation, and all the millions spent really show. Luckily, many of the fine Victorian period elements were left in place, the best being the stained-glass dome in the restaurant Aurora. The hotel has everything a traveler could want, including 24-hour massages and a special jet-lag treatment. (It's not cheap, we hardly need add.) There is also a guide to the hotel that gives you two maps and plenty of up-to-date local information. Beware of the suggestions to go to any of Sir Terence Conran's (the hotel's co-owner) many restaurants or to buy his book on London—it's clearly a bit of in-house publicity. The health club is top of the line.

SETTINGS & FACILITIES

Location Liverpool Street, by the City and the East End. **Nearest Tube Station** Liverpool Street or Bishopgate. **Quietness Rating** C. **Dining** Huge selection: Myabi for Japanese, the Fishmarket for guess what, the George for ye olde England pub-style food, Aurora for fancy European dining under an amazing stained-glass dome, and Terminus is a good brasserie type restaurant with wonderful desserts and a large menu. You'll never go hungry, day or night. Prices are high. **Amenities** Aromatherapy in-room amenities, business center, health club with treatment facilities; see below for what's included in each room. **Services** Concierge, room service, same-day laundry, mobile-phone rental, shoe-shine, shops, valet parking.

ACCOMMODATIONS

Rooms 267, including 21 suites. **All Rooms** Ergonomically designed workstation with two-line telephones, fax, modem, ISDN, voice mail, and all the usual amenities such as cable TV, hair dryer, minibar, safe, CD player, DVD player, and DVD library. **Some Rooms** Fireplaces, high ceilings, big windows; others are more of a modern loft effect. **Bed & Bath** Splendid, with Frette sheets and the latest bathroom fittings. **Favorites** The rooms on the lower floors of the east block are best because they have more Victorian features; the higher floors are more modern. **Comfort & Decor** As you'd expect from furniture magnate Terence Conran, the decor is modern, solid, and comfy, with clean lines and relaxing colors.

PAYMENT, RESERVATIONS, & RESTRICTIONS

Deposit Credit card. **Credit Cards** All major. **Check-In/Out** 2 p.m./noon. **Pets** Not allowed. **Elevator** Yes. **Children** Yes. **Disabled Access** Yes.

HAZLITT'S HOTEL   £205–£240

OVERALL ★★★½ | QUALITY ★★★★ | VALUE ★★★ | ZONE 7

---

6 Frith Street, Soho Square, W1; (0207) 434-1771; fax (0207) 439-1524;
www.hazlittshotel.com

Hazlitt's Hotel was the first establishment of the creators of The Gore and The Rookery. Hazlitt's, which happens to be author Bill Bryson's favorite home away from home, is a perfect evocation of another time, with handsome antiques and decor in the Georgian style. For those allergic to Victoriana, Hazlitt's is the perfect alternative to The Gore, and it is in the heart of Soho, where sleepy London tends to stay awake. It is a simple hotel, without an elevator and with only a tiny sitting room for communal amenities. Staying here is more like staying at a particularly well-appointed rooming house from days gone by. The house was built in 1718, and the floors sag and droop as you would, too, if you'd been trod on for close to 300 years. The rooms are luxuriously comfortable, with beautiful antique bedsteads and cotton sheets. Busts sculpted by one of the owner's relatives grace many of the bathrooms and rooms, and antique prints adorn the walls. The period verisimilitude is strict, and the house of a writer like William Hazlitt would not have been overdone. And Hazlitt's attracts writers like honey draws flies. In the sitting room is a bookcase with signed copies of books written by guests, and it's an impressive collection: Seamus Heaney, Ted Hughes, Vikram Seth, Jostein Gardner, Susan Sontag, Dava Sobel, and scores of others. Of course, the brilliant Bill Bryson's books are there; he sent the phones ringing off the hook when he mentioned his favorite hotel in his hilarious book on England, *Notes from a Small Island.* Hazlitt's attracts a loyalty—or eccentricity—hardly ever met with: One of the regulars paid for double glazing to be put on the windows of his favorite room. This is not to say that you will like Hazlitt's; it's for a particular type of person, one who likes the noise and action of the present-day West End as much as the atmosphere of long-ago Soho. Book way, way in advance.

SETTINGS & FACILITIES

Location Soho. **Nearest Tube Station** Tottenham Court. **Quietness Rating** C/D in front during weekend nights, A/B in back at all times. **Dining** No. **Amenities** Writing desks and modems, cotton sheets, continental breakfast at extra charge. **Services** Receptionist, bellhop, laundry, 24-hour room service.

ACCOMMODATIONS

Rooms 23. **All Rooms** Telephone, satellite TV, bathtub, antiques, writing desk. **Some Rooms** Ornamental fireplace, four-posters, high ceilings. **Bed & Bath** Superb on both counts. Victorian tubs; one bathroom has a dinner plate–size Victorian shower head. Beds are comfortable, big, and cotton sheeted. **Favorites** The suite on the ground floor, the double-glazed Jonathan Swift room, and a small room in the back are best. Really, there are no rooms here that aren't charming and inviting; the high ceilings are on the first and second floors. **Comfort & Decor** Top-notch comfort (unless you require an elevator), and the decor is pleasing to the eye and soul.

PAYMENT, RESERVATIONS, & RESTRICTIONS

Deposit Credit card; 48-hour cancellation policy. **Credit Cards** All major. **Check-In/Out** 2 p.m./noon. **Pets** Not allowed. **Elevator** No. **Children** Yes. **Disabled Access** No.

HILTON LONDON MEWS   £151–£187

OVERALL ★★★★ | QUALITY ★★★★ | VALUE ★★★★ | ZONE 8

2 Stanhope Row, Park Lane, W1; (0207) 493-7222, in U.S. (800) 774-1500;
fax (0207) 629-9423; www.hilton.com

This is not an inexpensive hotel exactly, but it is less than the big Hilton
and it's right around the back from it. The neighborhood is extremely
posh, and the hotel itself is very attractive and beautifully appointed.
There are 72 rooms with all the amenities you could possibly want, and
you are welcome to use all the facilities at the big Hilton: beauty salon,
fitness center, treatment rooms, business support. And of course, Hyde
Park and Piccadilly, with all their various delights, are nearby.

SETTINGS & FACILITIES

Location Mayfair. **Nearest Tube Station** Green Park. **Quietness Rating** A. **Dining**
Small 32-seat restaurant and lounge for tea and drinks. **Amenities** All the facilities at
the big Hilton (fitness, beauty, hair stylist, restaurants) are at your disposal. **Services**
Concierge, 24-hour room service, bellhop, laundry, rental computers and printers, business support.

ACCOMMODATIONS

Rooms 72. **All Rooms** Two-line telephone, modem, voice mail, cable TV, in-house
movies, air-conditioning, iron, hair dryer, tea and coffee. **Some Rooms** Mayfair Suite
has lounge and private entrance. **Bed & Bath** Top-notch. **Favorites** The more expensive doubles are quite nice. **Comfort & Decor** Upscale hotel style, with more than a
touch of jolly olde England and all the comforts of a Hilton.

PAYMENT, RESERVATIONS, & RESTRICTIONS

Deposit Credit card; must cancel by 4 p.m. on day of arrival. **Credit Cards** All major.
Check-In/Out 2 p.m./noon. **Pets** Not allowed. **Elevator** Yes. **Children** Yes. **Disabled
Access** No, stairs in lobby.

HOLIDAY INN MAYFAIR   DISCOUNT RATES–£255

OVERALL ★★ | QUALITY ★★★½ | VALUE ★★★ | ZONE 8

3 Berkeley Street, W1; (0207) 493-8282; fax (0207) 629-2827;
www.mayfair.holiday-inn.com

In the United States, the name Holiday Inn has the connotation of a
budget-to-moderate kind of a place, which is why we had to gasp when we
saw a Holiday Inn rack rate of £255! But hang on, that's not what you'll
end up paying if you are smart and join the Priority Club or take advantage
of any of the many packages and deals available here and on the website.
They don't even have a tariff card to give out (nor will you get very far with
them on the phone unless you have definite dates in mind), because there
are so many possible combinations of discounts and promos. The neighborhood is excellent, and the rooms have pretty much everything you

want. OK, the place is not dripping with charm, but it's attractive and well decorated with pictures and furniture. If you want to stay in the beautiful Mayfair, give the hotel a call or go to their website to see if you can get a good rate.

SETTINGS & FACILITIES

Location Mayfair. **Nearest Tube Station** Green Park. **Quietness Rating** A in back, B in front (double-glazed windows). **Dining** Nightingale's Restaurant serves international cuisine. **Amenities** Bar, very small fitness room. **Services** Concierge, 24-hour room service, bellhop, laundry.

ACCOMMODATIONS

Rooms 184. **All Rooms** Telephone, modem lines and Internet access, cable TV, minibar, air-conditioning, hair dryer, iron, tea and coffee, in-house movies, writing desk. **Some Rooms** Suites have two rooms, two bathrooms, two TVs. **Bed & Bath** Bathrooms are fine; beds are comfortable. **Favorites** The suites and executive rooms, which have the most space. **Comfort & Decor** Hotel style, but not at all drab; major refurbishment has been ongoing and plans are that it will continue.

PAYMENT, RESERVATIONS, & RESTRICTIONS

Deposit Credit card; must cancel by 6 p.m. on the day of arrival. **Credit Cards** All major. **Check-In/Out** 2 p.m./1 p.m. **Pets** Not allowed. **Elevator** Yes. **Children** Yes. **Disabled Access** Two disabled rooms available.

L'HOTEL   £165–£176

OVERALL ★★★★★ | QUALITY ★★★★ | VALUE ★★★★★ | ZONE 10

28 Basil Street, SW3; (0207) 589-6286, in U.S. (800) 926-3199; fax (0207) 823-7826; www.capital-london.net/lhotel

This is essentially a bed-and-breakfast owned by the neighboring Capital Hotel, and it only has 12 rooms. Speak up early if you want to book here—it's very popular among the cognoscente. The hotel is located 50 meters from Harrods and 250 from Hyde Park, with Sloane Street right down the way. The rooms are all quiet and simple, in a French country style that may come as a relief to those who find the English traditional too floral. Pine furniture and neutral colors accented by elegant artwork and bibelots make it a restful and aesthetic experience. The staff is friendly and helpful—reception will act as concierge and help out wherever needed. Best of all, there are three rooms and one suite that come with gas fireplaces, and these are the rooms that need booking well ahead. The price, for the area and the quality, is good. All the rooms are double, with no extra charge for the second person.

SETTINGS & FACILITIES

Location Knightsbridge. **Nearest Tube Station** Knightsbridge. **Quietness Rating** A (double glazing throughout). **Dining** Le Metro is a wine bar that serves breakfast, lunch, and dinner with cool modern style. **Amenities** Continental breakfast is included in price and can be served in room; fax and iron on request. **Services** Concierge, breakfast room service only, laundry.

ACCOMMODATIONS

Rooms 12. **All Rooms** Minibar, telephone, cable TV, in-house movies, hair dryer, tea and coffee, writing desk, ceiling fan. **Some Rooms** Fireplace. **Bed & Bath** 100% Egyptian cotton Frette sheets and perfect bathrooms. **Favorites** Number 302, a room with a fireplace, and the suite. **Comfort & Decor** Dedicated to comfort and simplicity of decor. A good feeling pervades.

PAYMENT, RESERVATIONS, & RESTRICTIONS

Deposit Credit card; 72-hour cancellation policy. **Credit Cards** All major. **Check-In/Out** 2 p.m./noon. **Pets** Not allowed. **Elevator** Yes. **Children** Yes. **Disabled Access** One ground-floor room.

JURY'S   £210–£235

OVERALL ★★★ | QUALITY ★★★½ | VALUE ★★★ | ZONE 11

109–113 Queen's Gate, South Kensington, SW7; (0207) 589-6300;
fax (0207) 581-1492; www.jurysdoyle.com

The best things about Jury's are the location and the lobby. The rooms run a fairly wide gamut from much too small and dull to rather grand, with French windows looking out on the white stucco town houses of Queen's Gate. This hotel provides an airport shuttle bus for a fee, a nonsmoking floor, and a great reading room with a fireplace. All the restaurants, shops, and public transportation of South Kensington are at its doorstep, as are Hyde Park and the museums. This is a large enough corporation that it offers deals; call to ask about them, and definitely get an upgrade, because we saw a couple of so-called doubles that were very small. The staff is friendly and helpful.

SETTINGS & FACILITIES

Location South Kensington. **Nearest Tube Station** South Kensington. **Quietness Rating** B. **Dining** Copplestone's Restaurant; Kavanaugh's Irish Pub. **Amenities** Elegant lobby and reading room for tea and drinks. **Services** 24-hour room service, business services, same-day laundry.

ACCOMMODATIONS

Rooms 156. **All Rooms** Satellite TV, tea/coffee-making facilities, iron. **Some Rooms** Minibars and modems in suites only. **Bed & Bath** Clean, if boring. **Favorites** Executive suite looking out on Queensgate and Manson Place. **Comfort & Decor** Comfortable, if small; decor is standard, dull hotel-chain style.

PAYMENT, RESERVATIONS, & RESTRICTIONS

Deposit Credit card; cancellations by 4 p.m. day of arrival. **Credit Cards** All major. **Check-In/Out** 2 p.m./11 a.m. **Pets** Not allowed. **Elevator** Yes. **Children** Yes. **Disabled Access** Yes.

LONDON MARRIOTT HOTEL COUNTY HALL   £170–£269

OVERALL ★★★★½ | QUALITY ★★★★½ | VALUE ★★★ | ZONE 5

County Hall, SE1; (0207) 928-5200; toll free in U.S. (888) 236-2427; toll free internationally +44-80-221-221; fax (0207) 928-5300; www.marriotthotels.com

This hotel has the largest rooms of any Marriott in London, and it has all the amenities you'd expect from the chain, but with one major difference: It's located in the old County Hall building right on the Thames and has spectacular, postcard-perfect views of Parliament, Big Ben, the London Eye, and the tower of Westminster Abbey. You may feel a bit cut off from a sense of a neighborhood; Waterloo Station is at the rear, and across the bridge is Westminster, which tends to roll up the sidewalks at night and on weekends, but it doesn't matter, as the South Bank has plenty to look at and the stroll along the river path is wonderful. The hotel has a 25-meter pool and an excellent gym; beauty and health treatments are available. There are some delightful eating and lounging areas, which you should visit even if you don't stay here—the view is magnificent, especially at night. The library has been preserved from when it was part of the County Hall, and the books are all the original volumes. There are wood-paneled walls everywhere and all kinds of interesting architectural features in this historical, listed building. And the beds are huge. Ask for deals and promotions, as the price is steep.

SETTINGS & FACILITIES

Location South Bank. **Nearest Tube Station** Westminster or Waterloo. **Quietness Rating** A. **Dining** County Hall Restaurant has English cuisine and an oyster-and-seafood bar, plus great views of the Thames—be sure to make reservations. Library Lounge has tea and snacks. There is also Leaders Cocktail Bar. **Amenities** Restaurant, lounge, bar, views of Parliament and Big Ben, health club with pool, disabled rooms, valet parking at good payment for London. **Services** Concierge, 24-hour room service, valet parking, bellhop, laundry.

ACCOMMODATIONS

Rooms 186. **All Rooms** Telephones, voice mail, cable TV, air-conditioning, minibar, hair dryer, tea and coffee, iron, personal safes. **Some Rooms** Separate sitting rooms, views of river. **Bed & Bath** Excellent bathrooms; beds are queen- or king-size. **Favorites** Rooms with a river view are superior. **Comfort & Decor** Comfort is high, decor is high-standard hotel type, with some unfortunate choices in fabrics.

PAYMENT, RESERVATIONS, & RESTRICTIONS

Deposit Credit card; must cancel by 4 p.m. on day of arrival. **Credit Cards** All major. **Check-In/Out** 2 p.m./noon. **Pets** Not allowed. **Elevator** Yes. **Children** Yes. **Disabled Access** Six disabled rooms of a very high standard.

MERIDIEN RUSSELL   £190–£205

OVERALL ★★★ | QUALITY ★★★ | VALUE ★★★★ | ZONE 2

Russell Square, WC1; (0207) 837-6470; fax (0207) 837-2857; www.lemeridien.com

Recently bought and aggressively upgraded to the tune of untold millions by the Meridien group, this is a grand old edifice looking out on Russell Square in Bloomsbury. It's got a lot of space, unlike so many hotels in London, plus all the services one expects from a Meridien hotel. The multimillion-pound renovation has made a big difference in the ambience and decor of this long-lived hotel, and the high standards of Meridien service have been reached. The hotel attracts a business crowd due to its conference facilities, and so is accustomed to demanding customers. The restaurants are good and quite convenient, and it's close to the West End, the City, and the British Museum. It's a magnificent building—one of the great Victorian hotel palaces.

SETTINGS & FACILITIES

Location Bloomsbury. **Nearest Tube Station** Russell Square. **Quietness Rating** C in front (double glazing), A in back. **Dining** Fitzroy's Doll Bar-Restaurant serves European and British food; Virginia Woolf's Brasserie serves burgers, pastas, and so on. The King's Bar and Lounge has a club atmosphere (fireplace, red leather) and drinks. **Amenities** Full business support, executive floor with lounge and continental breakfast. **Services** Concierge, 24-hour room service, bellhop, laundry, conference ready.

ACCOMMODATIONS

Rooms 357. **All Rooms** Telephone, cable TV, hair dryer, iron, tea and coffee. **Some Rooms** Minibar, writing desk, bathrobes, balcony. **Bed & Bath** Excellent; some bathrooms are quite big. **Favorites** Number 347 is a suite with a sitting room and French doors in both rooms looking out onto Russell Square. Ask about the French-window rooms. **Comfort & Decor** Deluxe, with old-fashioned huge hallways, high ceilings, and big rooms. The common areas are appealing, with a beautiful Victorian lobby and a grand staircase.

PAYMENT, RESERVATIONS, & RESTRICTIONS

Deposit Credit card; must cancel before 2 p.m. on day of arrival. **Credit Cards** All major. **Check-In/Out** 2 p.m./noon. **Pets** Not allowed. **Elevator** Three. **Children** Yes. **Disabled Access** As a Grade II building, they can't alter structure for built-in ramps, but management can help a lot.

THE MILESTONE HOTEL   £295–£340

OVERALL ★★★★½ | QUALITY ★★★★ | VALUE ★★★ | ZONE 11

1 Kensington Court, W8; (0207) 917-1000; fax (0207) 917-1010;
www.themilestone.com

The Milestone is a fine hotel that works hard to offer the best in services to international travelers and businesspeople. Don't be put off by the rack

rate; they have many affordable deals available. It is beautifully decorated, especially the common areas, and although all the rooms may not
suit all tastes, they are all carefully and imaginatively put together, with
lovely antiques and fine furnishings. Comfort and convenience are of an
unusually high standard here, and the location is wonderful for park
lovers: It is directly across the street from Kensington Gardens. Some of
the rooms have excellent views of Kensington Palace. There is a room
specially designed for disabled guests. The hotel offers the very latest in
business-support systems, not to mention a snooker table that turns into
a conference table. The lounge is a fine place to hang out, and there's a
bar that has a leathery pub atmosphere.

SETTINGS & FACILITIES

Location Kensington. **Nearest Tube Station** High Street Kensington. **Quietness
Rating** A in back, B in front (double glazing on all but corner room, 102, which has
leaded windows protected by landmark status). **Dining** Chenistons Restaurant.
Amenities Sleeping sound machines on request, sitting room, bar, breakfast room,
health club. **Services** Concierge, 24-hour room service, business support.

ACCOMMODATIONS

Rooms 57. **All Rooms** Telephone, voice mail, cable TV, air-conditioning, minibar,
modem station, in-house movies, CD player, U.K./U.S. video player. **Some Rooms**
Video-conferencing cables, pop-up TVs, electronic blinds, Jacuzzi, fireplace, four-posters,
fax machine. **Bed & Bath** Excellent, the highest quality. **Favorites** Number 509 has
bay windows and a park view; number 106 has the most panoramic view of Kensington
Gardens. Number 102 suite has two fireplaces, red velvet sofas, crystal chandeliers,
leaded-glass windows, the works. **Comfort & Decor** Very beautifully decorated by
owner and extremely comfortable in all ways.

PAYMENT, RESERVATIONS, & RESTRICTIONS

Deposit Credit card; 24-hour cancellation policy. **Credit Cards** All major. **Check-
In/Out** 2 p.m./noon. **Pets** Not allowed. **Elevator** Yes. **Children** Yes. **Disabled Access**
Specially designed disabled room and entrance.

MILLENNIUM HOTEL MAYFAIR   £225–£323

OVERALL ★★★★ | QUALITY ★★★★ | VALUE ★★★ | ZONE 8

Grosvenor Square, W1; (0207) 629-9400; fax (0207) 629-7736; www.mill-cop.com

The 319-room Millennium Britannia Mayfair faces Grosvenor Square, a
most peaceful and dignified old part of London, with the glaring exception of the modern American embassy at one end. It's a perfect hotel for
people who have a problem with noise. Piccadilly, Park Lane, and Oxford
Street are all within a few blocks. The neighborhood is full of magnificent buildings from all different periods, and walking around is a delight.
The hotel has most of the amenities of a four-star, deluxe hotel and is
associated with a Japanese restaurant next door. The fitness room is no

more than a couple of bikes, a treadmill, a stepper, and some weight machines, but for London that's not bad. The rooms are all a good size, and the decor is pleasing if unadventuresome. There are various promotions that you should certainly investigate, as the rack rate is high, though perfectly in keeping with the posh neighborhood. There's an executive lounge that businesspeople will find attractive.

SETTINGS & FACILITIES

Location Mayfair. **Nearest Tube Station** Green Park or Bond Street. **Quietness Rating** A. **Dining** Restaurant, Shogun Japanese Restaurant, two bars. **Amenities** 24-hour fitness room, business center, 24-hour valet, free modem access in rooms, reduced rate at National Car Park. **Services** Concierge, 24-hour room service and valet, bellhop, laundry.

ACCOMMODATIONS

Rooms 319. **All Rooms** Telephones with free modem access, cable TV, in-house movies, air-conditioning and individual climate control, minibar, writing desk. **Some Rooms** Tea and coffee, iron, fax, safe. **Bed & Bath** Marble baths with phone in them, good-size beds. **Favorites** The Millennium Rooms are the best size before you get into suites; those rooms overlooking the Square are nice. **Comfort & Decor** Decor is uninspired, but of a good hotel standard.

PAYMENT, RESERVATIONS, & RESTRICTIONS

Deposit Credit card; must cancel by 2 p.m. on day of arrival. **Credit Cards** All major. **Check-In/Out** 2 p.m./noon. **Pets** Not allowed. **Elevator** Three. **Children** Yes. **Disabled Access** Yes, but limited.

MILLER'S RESIDENCE   £176

OVERALL ★★★ | QUALITY ★★★★ | VALUE ★★★★ | ZONE 13

111A Westbourne Grove, W2 (entrance on southeast side of Hereford Road);
(0207) 243-1024; fax (0207) 243-1064; www.millersuk.com

Miller's Residence has become one of London's worst-kept secrets; it opened in 1997 and has been quietly drawing strength from the numbers of people who love it and keep going back and the newspaper and magazine writers who keep writing about it. Martin Miller, of *Miller's Antique Guide,* and Kay Raveden have created an eccentric and beautiful "rooming house" in Notting Hill Gate, filled to bursting in the common areas with sublime antiques (there's a covered sedan chair in the front hall and an old sled on the wall, to name only two of the first things to hit your eyes). The drawing room is wonderful, with a fireplace that is stunningly well carved, and still more antiques. The couple has clearly spent years successfully scavenging in markets like Portobello and Bermondsey and at many a country auction. The seven rooms are all named after English Romantic poets and have lines from the poems of these masters on the back of each door. The Coleridge Room has an old model of the HMS

Bounty, and the "Rime of the Ancient Mariner" is quoted on the door. Guests who book long stays will get a discount. Book well in advance. The house is on a busy stretch of Westbourne Grove, not a tremendously charming street, but full of restaurants and interesting shops, and the health-food store Planet Organic down the street has a great juice bar.

SETTINGS & FACILITIES

Location Notting Hill Gate. **Nearest Tube Station** Bayswater. **Quietness Rating** B/C. **Dining** Breakfast only. **Amenities** Amazing drawing room with coffee and tea and a fireplace, all lit up with candles at night, and another lounge, equally pleasant. **Services** Reception acts as concierge, limited room service (from local restaurants), laundry.

ACCOMMODATIONS

Rooms six; two apartments. **All Rooms** Telephone, voice mail, satellite TV, wonderful antiques. **Some Rooms** Four-poster, even more wonderful antiques. **Bed & Bath** Beds are of good quality, and the bathrooms are of a high standard. **Favorites** All rooms are different and very cool. Try the red Coleridge Room or the lighter Tennyson Room. **Comfort & Decor** Comfort is fine, except for the lack of a lift and the possibility of a hot day or two without air-conditioning. The decor has to be seen to be believed. The owners have spent their time amassing the most amazing antiques and they have spread them wildly and well all over this wonderful rooming house.

PAYMENT, RESERVATIONS, & RESTRICTIONS

Deposit Credit card; must cancel within seven days of arrival. **Credit Cards** All major. **Check-In/Out** 2 p.m./12 a.m. **Pets** Not allowed. **Elevator** No. **Children** Yes. **Disabled Access** No.

THE MONTAGUE ON THE GARDENS   £229–£288

OVERALL ★★★★ | QUALITY ★★★½ | VALUE ★★★ | ZONE 2

15 Montague Street, Bloomsbury, WC1; (0207) 637-1001, in U.S. (800) 424-2862; fax (0207) 637-2516; www.montaguehotel.com

A deluxe hotel, The Montague on the Gardens features the type of sumptuous interior design that uses fabric as wallpaper and cleverly combines fine antiques with bold patterns and pleasing colors. It provides all the services one would expect of a deluxe hotel and then some. There's a garden in the back that you can enjoy while sitting on the patio off the Terrace Bar, and the restaurant is of very good quality at reasonable (for London) prices. It's also across the street from the British Museum, and within walking distance of the West End. The delightful decor of the rooms can't conceal the small size of most, but each one does tend to divert one's attention from it. The Montague is made from eight Grade II town houses strung together, so the rooms are all of different sizes and shapes. Some of the suites are comprised of three different levels, which might be good if you have a need for privacy from your roommate, but each one has less floor space than you might have if it were all on one floor. There are a couple of deluxe kings that are spacious (numbers 317 and 319). Ask about promotional deals. It's a bit pricey for the neighborhood—unless you simply *have* to be near the West End or the British Museum and want a full-service hotel.

SETTINGS & FACILITIES

Location Bloomsbury. **Nearest Tube Station** Russell Square. **Quietness Rating** A in garden rooms, B on street. **Dining** Blue Door Bistro is a three-star restaurant serving breakfast, lunch, and dinner, with a very pleasing and elegant interior. **Amenities** Smoking and nonsmoking rooms, bar, restaurant with piano music, bathrobes, in-room express checkout via TV system, executive room with business-related amenities, mobile phones for rental, fax machines on request, healthy guest rooms featuring a Nordic exercise bike. **Services** Concierge, 24-hour room service, bellhop, laundry, business support.

ACCOMMODATIONS

Rooms 104. **All Rooms** Telephone, voice mail, cable TV, in-house movies, hair dryer, air-conditioning, writing desk, iron, tea and coffee. **Some Rooms** Minibars, fax lines, CD players and CD selection. **Bed & Bath** Beautiful beds, most with elaborate canopies and handsome duvets and curtains. The bathrooms are first rate. **Favorites** Number 219, The Duchesse, is a fine suite that has a sky painted on the ceiling. **Comfort & Decor** They aim to please here, so the comfort factor—even adjusting for the size of the rooms—is particularly high. The decor is quite impressive, if a bit over the top in places.

PAYMENT, RESERVATIONS, & RESTRICTIONS

Deposit Credit card; 24-hour cancellation policy. **Credit Cards** All major. **Check-In/Out** 2 p.m./noon. **Pets** Large pets not allowed (small pets conditional). **Elevator** Yes. **Children** Yes. **Disabled Access** Ramps for main stairs, and the people here are very helpful, but since it's a Grade II listed building, they can't create total wheelchair access.

MORGAN HOTEL £80–£95

OVERALL ★★ | QUALITY ★★★½ | VALUE ★★★★★ | ZONE 2

24 Bloomsbury Street, WC1; (0207) 636-3735; fax (0207) 636-3045

Make your reservation well in advance to get a room at this extremely popular family-run bed-and-breakfast/budget hotel. Practically on the doorstep of the British Museum and within walking distance of the West End, this is the place discerning cheapskates love to go. It's an easy, informal sort of a place, run by a family who seem to do absolutely everything themselves, and nicely, too. The breakfast room is the jewel here: It's done up in booths and decorated with an extraordinary collection of English ceramics, some very interesting pieces. Clearly, someone here has the taste to make a budget place look inviting and interesting, or maybe it's because they got started on decorating the place when they opened it over 20 years ago, back when you could still get a deal on Portobello Road. All the rooms have a private shower and toilet.

SETTINGS & FACILITIES

Location Bloomsbury. **Nearest Tube Station** Tottenham Court. **Quietness Rating** A in back, B+ in front (double-glazed windows). **Dining** Breakfast, which is included in price. **Amenities** Breakfast in delightful dining room. **Services** Bellhop.

ACCOMMODATIONS

Rooms 21 hotel rooms and 4 flats. **All Rooms** Telephone, TV (BBC and CNN), hair dryer. **Some Rooms** Tea and coffee, air-conditioning, writing desk, bath, TV and VCR in apartments. **Bed & Bath** Highest cleanliness and comfort. **Favorites** Number 1 is a good size, with lots of drawers. Room B is a favorite; and Flat 1 is a nice apartment, with eat-in kitchen, pleasant decoration, and good space. **Comfort & Decor** The decor is superior to most of the local B&Bs in this price range, with really interesting pictures on the walls and a fine collection of English porcelain. The family is well versed in making visitors comfortable.

PAYMENT, RESERVATIONS, & RESTRICTIONS

Deposit Credit card; 72-hour cancellation policy. **Credit Cards** Most major. **Check-In/Out** Noon/10:30 a.m. **Pets** Not allowed. **Elevator** No. **Children** Yes. **Disabled Access** No elevator.

NUMBER SIXTEEN   £152–£240

OVERALL ★★★★ | QUALITY ★★★★ | VALUE ★★★★ | ZONE 11

16 Sumner Place, South Kensington, SW7; (0207) 589-5232,
in U.S. (800) 592-5387; fax (0207) 584-8615; www.numbersixteenhotel.co.uk

This town-house hotel, an old favorite among visitors who love South Kensington, has been taken over by the Firmdale group (which owns the Pelham, Charlotte Street, Covent Garden, and other hotels) and has undergone a renovation that may have some of the former customers feeling a bit uncomfortable: Gone is the chintz of yesteryear, as well as the old descriptive names of the rooms. It's now a modern, but not minimalist, boutique hotel, whose prices have also caught up to the present. There are quirky ethnic decorations around, huge birdcages, driftwood lamps, and the like, which work marvelously well in the formerly staid conservatory. The garden is as gorgeous as ever, and is often used for fashion shoots. The bathrooms have been seriously upgraded, with gray granite and power showers, and the bedrooms are all individually decorated. What they couldn't upgrade is the size of the rooms, which are pretty small, except for the superior deluxes. The lower ground floor has a few rooms with their own entrance to the garden, which is a big plus. There's no breakfast room, but food will be brought to your room, the conservatory, or one of the public sitting areas, 24 hours a day. Beds are big and draped in cotton sheets, which appeals to the 80% American clientele. Good service. Ask about promotional deals.

SETTINGS & FACILITIES

Location South Kensington. **Nearest Tube Station** South Kensington. **Quietness Rating** A/B. **Dining** 24-hour room service. **Amenities** Air-conditioning, voice mail, modem points, cable TV, DVD player (card to nearby video store), mobile phone rental, minibar, safe, access to health club nearby (for fee). **Services** Concierge, laundry.

ACCOMMODATIONS

Rooms 42. **All Rooms** Air-conditioning, telephone with voice mail, modem point, minibar, DVD player, cable TV, safe, hair dryer. **Some Rooms** Balcony, French doors. **Bed & Bath** Of a very high standard; big beds, great bathrooms. **Favorites** Number 3 is on lower ground, but has space and huge bed; 306 is red and elegant, if small; ask for rooms that look over garden, as they're quieter. **Comfort & Decor** Decor is eccentrically elegant, with faux stone painted walls and interesting artwork and knickknacks; comfort is top-notch.

PAYMENT, RESERVATIONS, & RESTRICTIONS

Deposit Credit card; 48-hour cancellation policy. **Credit Cards** All major. **Check-In/Out** 3 p.m./noon. **Pets** Not allowed. **Elevator** Yes. **Children** Yes. **Disabled Access** Four ground-floor rooms, three stairs outside.

PARKES HOTEL   £229–£282

OVERALL ★★★½ | QUALITY ★★★★ | VALUE ★★★★ | ZONE 10

41 Beaufort Gardens; (0207) 581-9944; toll free in U.S. (800) 306-5054;
fax (0207) 581-1999; www.parkeshotel.com

You'll find pristine English elegance at this hotel, a mere stone's throw from Harrods on a tree-lined, dead-end street off the busy Brompton Road. It's not at all stuffy, but it does seem to have high standards for decor and service. There are plenty of maids and bellhops, and very friendly they are, too. There is no restaurant, but there is a breakfast room with a full English breakfast for £5, and you can get room service. But the best thing is that all the rooms have kitchens, so you can feast from Harrods Food Halls without any difficulty. Parkes had long prided itself on not offering any deals, yet always being solidly booked, but these days, even Parkes Hotel needs to fill rooms and will offer upgrades, or other money-saving deals.

SETTINGS & FACILITIES

Location Knightsbridge. **Nearest Tube Station** Knightsbridge. **Quietness Rating** A. **Dining** Breakfast room. **Amenities** Sitting room, complimentary newspaper, kitchens. **Services** Concierge, room service, bellhop, laundry, chauffeur service and airport transfer.

ACCOMMODATIONS

Rooms 33. **All Rooms** Kitchen, cable TV and in-house movies, tea and coffee, hair dryer, iron, minibar, double bed, iron, safe, bath. **Some Rooms** Fax, writing desk, sitting area, chandeliers, fireplaces (electric). **Bed & Bath** Excellent. **Favorites** Number 32 is a front-facing junior suite, and number 37 is a fine one-bedroom suite with huge crystal chandeliers, high ceilings, and French windows in the bedroom and the sitting room. They are switching some things around, making smaller suites out of the three-bedroom ones, so the room numbers may change. The doubles are a bit small, but the junior suites are a good size. **Comfort & Decor** Pains have been taken to make the rooms comfortable, and the decor is well composed and pleasant.

PAYMENT, RESERVATIONS, & RESTRICTIONS

Deposit Credit card; 48-hour cancellation policy. **Credit Cards** All major. **Check-In/Out** 2 p.m./noon. **Pets** Allowed by arrangement. **Elevator** Yes. **Children** Yes. **Disabled Access** No wheelchair access, lots of stairs and small hallways.

THE PELHAM   £177–£211

OVERALL ★★★★ | QUALITY ★★★★½ | VALUE ★★★★ | ZONE 11

15 Cromwell Place, SW7; (0207) 589-8288, in U.S. (800) 553-6674;
fax (0207) 584-8444; www.firmdale.com

The Pelham Hotel is a beautiful hotel. Each room is unique and exquisitely decorated by the deft hand of the owner, and the hotel's size (46 bedrooms and suites) guarantees the guest the most punctilious and personal service. The atmosphere is that of a luxurious town house, with all the amenities you could desire. There are two sitting rooms with fireplaces, mahogany paneling, artfully arranged flowers, stunning furniture, and deep, comfy chairs and sofas. The views in the front are of the town of South Kensington, and there's not much to look at out of the rear windows except for the French Lycee playground. The location is excellent, with the museums of South Kensington just steps away, three tube lines across the street, buses that stop in front of the hotel, and the shops of Knightsbridge within a five-minute walk. The staff is friendly, helpful, and knowledgeable. They can get you anything you need at any time— baby-sitter, massage therapist, tickets, tours, airport transfer. Call about the special deals they offer. Breakfast is included with some rooms.

SETTINGS & FACILITIES

Location South Kensington. **Nearest Tube Station** South Kensington. **Quietness Rating** A in rear, C in front (the front has double glazing twice). **Dining** Kemp's Restaurant has an excellent menu that changes every few weeks. The room is quite comfortable and as beautiful as you'd expect from this exquisite hotel. **Amenities** Sitting rooms with fireplaces, champagne and hors d'oeuvres on Wednesdays, honor bar and coffee and tea in back sitting room. **Services** 24-hour room service, concierge, laundry, anything you can think of.

ACCOMMODATIONS

Rooms 46. **All Rooms** Satellite TV, two telephones, mobile phone, voice mail, minibar, sitting area. **Some Rooms** Video, sofa, balcony, four-poster. **Bed & Bath** Twin, double, king (which can be turned into twin) are all very comfortable; all private bathrooms, big tubs, good showers, granite and mahogany decor. **Favorites** Number 101: front-facing luxury double, with French doors leading to balcony; number 204 is a deluxe double, pleasingly decorated; number 409 is a luxury double; number 406, a new deluxe, has walk-in wardrobes, two sinks in bathroom, and shower cubicle as well as tub; rooms 405 and 305 are also new and distinguished. **Comfort & Decor** The comfort factor is what we'd all like to achieve in our own homes, and the decor is like stepping into the pages of *Architectural Digest.*

PAYMENT, RESERVATIONS, & RESTRICTIONS

Deposit Credit card; 48-hour cancellation policy. **Credit Cards** All major, except DC. **Check-In/Out** 1 p.m./noon. **Pets** Not allowed. **Elevator** Yes. **Children** Yes. **Disabled Access** Yes, except stairs into hotel must be negotiated with assistance.

PEMBRIDGE COURT HOTEL   £125–£160

OVERALL ★★★ | QUALITY ★★★★ | VALUE ★★★★★ | ZONE 13

34 Pembridge Gardens; (0207) 229-9977, in U.S. (800) 709-9882;
fax (0207) 727-4982; www.pemct.co.uk

This is an excellent town-house hotel within easy reach of Portobello Road: You only need slip out the back of the house and through an alley and you're there. The atmosphere of this Victorian house is bright and friendly, with the resident cats adding a lovely homey touch. They roam freely and, if they take a liking to you, may hang out in your room with you. The rooms are of a decent size—some bigger than others—and decorated in ingenious ways: Antique gloves, dresses, belts, fans, and other accessories are beautifully framed and hung all around. There's a very pleasant sitting room with a library and fireplace, and downstairs you'll find a bar/restaurant called Caps that used to be open to the public until the success of the hotel made the owners decide to keep it as a private place for guests only. The bar will stay open as long as you need, though they try to close it at 11 p.m. or midnight. A full English breakfast is included in the price. There's nothing precious or pretentious about this place; it's just good value and good vibrations in a beautiful setting.

SETTINGS & FACILITIES

Location Notting Hill Gate. **Nearest Tube Station** Notting Hill Gate. **Quietness Rating** A. **Dining** The Caps Restaurant has a limited but fine menu. **Amenities** Full English breakfast included, sitting room, arrangements with nearby health club, fax on request. **Services** 24-hour room service, limited menu, bellhop, laundry.

ACCOMMODATIONS

Rooms 20. **All Rooms** Telephone, satellite TV, writing desk, iron. **Some Rooms** Air-conditioning. **Bed & Bath** Bathtubs in all but four rooms (which have showers), some four-poster beds. **Favorites** They're all different, but they're all good. If you want a lot of space, look for the ground-floor room, or any of the suites. The rooms at front have marvelous large windows. **Comfort & Decor** Very comfortable, and the decor is charming.

PAYMENT, RESERVATIONS, & RESTRICTIONS

Deposit Credit card; 48-hour cancellation policy. **Credit Cards** All major. **Check-In/Out** 2 p.m./noon. **Pets** Dogs allowed as long as you don't leave them cooped up in the room. **Elevator** Yes. **Children** Yes. **Disabled Access** Steps in front.

THE PORTOBELLO HOTEL   £120–£160

OVERALL ★★★★ | QUALITY ★★★½ | VALUE ★★★ | ZONE 13

22 Stanley Gardens, W11; (0207) 727-2777; fax (0207) 792-9641;
www.portobello-hotel.co.uk

This is a trendy place with corporate accounts held by a number of modeling, music, and film agencies. It's in an old Victorian terrace house, and the rooms are each completely different from one another, and admirably so. The rooms in the rear look out over a communal garden into which you may not go, but which provides a sublime view. The Portobello has a lot of charm, with whimsical and traditional decor blending nicely. There's a sitting room that looks out over the garden and a small breakfast room on the ground floor. Continental breakfast is included in the price and is sent to your room. The ambience is pleasant, especially if you get one of the larger rooms, but the singles are cell-like, despite the gracious decor, and there is no space to do anything other than sleep. The most imposing room, number 16, features a big round bed and a balcony on the garden, with an antique copper bathtub right in the room; it's great for romance. Number 13 has a huge, high four-poster bed that requires a footstool to mount. The hotel is within walking distance of Portobello Road, which makes it good for committed Portobello and Kensington Church Street shoppers, but it's not terribly well situated for general sight-seeing due to its distance from public transportation.

SETTINGS & FACILITIES

Location Notting Hill Gate. **Nearest Tube Station** Notting Hill Gate. **Quietness Rating** A. **Dining** Very small breakfast room. **Amenities** Tiny basement restaurant with a few tables for breakfast and lunch; drawing room with fireplace and view of garden; health-club facilities are a four-minute walk away; computer in most rooms. **Services** Concierge, 8 a.m.–4 p.m. room service, continental breakfast sent to room, laundry.

ACCOMMODATIONS

Rooms 24. **All Rooms** Telephone, satellite TV. **Some Rooms** Balcony, couches, minibar, air-conditioning, four-poster. **Bed & Bath** Beds are divinely comfy; baths range from a huge clawfoot tub to tiny shower stalls, but all are clean and user friendly. **Favorites** Number 16, with the balcony overlooking the garden and the big round bed, is everyone's favorite. We also like the Asian-style number 46, also with a garden view. The single number 38 is very small, but has a good feeling to it. The first-floor rooms with the large French windows are spacious and fine. **Comfort & Decor** The decoration here is extraordinary and includes a range of furnishings, from traditional English antiques to exotic Asian and Middle Eastern treasures. Comfort is as high a priority as style.

PAYMENT, RESERVATIONS, & RESTRICTIONS

Deposit Credit card; 48-hour cancellation policy. **Credit Cards** All major. **Check-In/Out** After noon/noon. **Pets** Not allowed for a long stay. **Elevator** Yes, but only to third floor. **Children** Yes. **Disabled Access** No.

QUALITY HOTEL   £125–£150

OVERALL ★★ | QUALITY ★★★½ | VALUE ★★★★ | ZONE 9

82–83 Eccleston Square, SW1; (0207) 834-8042; fax (0207) 630-8942;
www.hotels-westminster.com

The hotel is standard, without any charisma or glamour, but the rooms are tidy and reasonably sized. There is a small restaurant and a self-service coffee area. It's the kind of place that has an automatic shoe shiner near the public telephones, a video slot machine in the bar, and a condom dispenser in the ladies' room. But it's also the kind of place that has a marble-floored lobby, with plants in the windows. There's a fax/Internet laptop in the lobby for your use, a sitting area, and a bar that opens at 5 p.m. Apparently, guests can get a key to Eccleston Square, a charming garden with benches and flora across the street. You can also walk to many of the great sights of London, such as Westminster Abbey and Buckingham Palace. There are many promotional deals offered in conjunction with the Choice Hotels Europe Group, which has over 3,000 hotels worldwide.

SETTINGS & FACILITIES

Location Victoria. **Nearest Tube Station** Victoria. **Quietness Rating** A/B. **Dining** Connaught's Brasserie serves delicious breakfast, lunch, and dinner. **Amenities** Dining room, bar, airport transfer, key to private gardens across the street. **Services** Reception functions as concierge, limited room service, bellhop, laundry.

ACCOMMODATIONS

Rooms 107. **All Rooms** Telephone, satellite TV, ceiling fans, iron, tea and coffee, writing desk. **Some Rooms** Minibar, teletext TV; some triples have two rooms. **Bed & Bath** Standard hotel style. **Favorites** Go for a premier double or triple. **Comfort & Decor** Standard hotel style, inoffensive and restful.

PAYMENT, RESERVATIONS, & RESTRICTIONS

Deposit Credit card. **Credit Cards** All major. **Check-In/Out** 2 p.m./noon. **Pets** Small pets allowed conditionally. **Elevator** Yes. **Children** Yes. **Disabled Access** Steps outside, but people to help.

THE RADISSON EDWARDIAN HAMPSHIRE   £169–£244

OVERALL ★★★★ | QUALITY ★★★★ | VALUE ★★ | ZONE 7

Leicester Square, WC2; (0207) 839-9399, in U.S. (800) 333-3333;
fax (0207) 930-8122; www.radissonedwardian.com

Housed in a magnificent building right on Leicester Square behind the half-price theater-ticket booth, The Hampshire is a five-star hotel run by the Radisson group. It has all the amenities you'd expect from a five-star inn, though, as with so many of London's hotels, not quite as much space in some of the standard rooms as you would want. The rooms are well appointed and there's a kind of Asian theme to the decor—check out the grandfather clock in the lobby. The lobby is gorgeous, with walnut paneling everywhere, offering a quiet sitting place far from the madding crowds of Leicester Square, yet with them still in view. There's a bar attached, a restaurant, and Oscar's Wine Bar with seating right on the square from which you can watch the milling crowds. There's a small fitness room with a few machines. The four-poster bedrooms are beautiful, and all the junior suites are of reasonable size. Some of the rooms have views over Trafalgar Square and Leicester Square. Leicester Square isn't for everyone; it's noisy and people packed, and the sleaze factor can be high on the weekends after the pubs close. Ask about the theater packages and other Radisson-related deals. There are so many variables in price at the Radisson hotels, we hesitated to even list the costs. Call or visit the website to see what a wide array of prices they have.

SETTINGS & FACILITIES

Location Leicester Square. **Nearest Tube Station** Leicester Square. **Quietness Rating** Triple glazing in all the windows on the Leicester Square side makes those desirable rooms quiet, but beware of the Carnival Fair that comes to the square occasionally—you may want to be in the back. **Dining** Apex Bar and Restaurant and Oscar's Wine Bar, both for good food and ambience. **Amenities** Room safes, small fitness room, bathrobes, telephones in bathrooms, fully air-conditioned. **Services** Concierge, 24-hour room service, bellhop, laundry, business support.

ACCOMMODATIONS

Rooms 124. **All Rooms** Minibar, telephones with modem lines, satellite TV, in-house movies, hair dryer, bathrobe, tea and coffee, iron, writing desk. **Some Rooms** Four-posters, views, floor-to-ceiling windows. **Bed & Bath** High quality. **Favorites** Number 705 is a four-poster suite with a view over Trafalgar. Any junior suite is fine. **Comfort & Decor** Five-star-hotel-style comforts and interesting decor, mixing eighteenth-century reproductions with Asian artwork.

PAYMENT, RESERVATIONS, & RESTRICTIONS

Deposit Credit card; 24-hour cancellation policy. **Credit Cards** All major. **Check-In/Out** 2 p.m./11 a.m. **Pets** Not allowed. **Elevator** Yes. **Children** Yes. **Disabled Access** Yes.

RADISSON EDWARDIAN PASTORIA HOTEL   £239–£272

OVERALL ★★ | QUALITY ★★★ | VALUE ★★ | ZONE 7

3 St. Martin's Street, Leicester Square, WC2; (0207) 930-8641; toll free in U.S. (800) 333-3333; fax (0207) 451-0191; www.radisson.com/londonuk-pastoria

The Radisson hotels offer many deals, frequent-flier tie ins, and all the services and amenities that Radisson Hotels offer all over the world. Internet deals here are currently well below the rack rate: You can get a single room for around £125. This hotel serves a large American clientele and, in response to the overwhelming demand, has installed air-conditioning in every room. The visitors at this hotel can use the fitness room at the Radisson Hampshire across the street. The rooms are very small, and the singles in back are awful; but every basic need is attended to in the rooms. The location is great for action seekers; it's right on Leicester Square, which is host to hordes of people all weekend—buskers, tourists, criminals, drunks, you name it. You'll either love or hate staying on the Square; noise-phobics need not apply. Of the six floors, you'll find the high front rooms are the most quiet and bright. There's a small restaurant attached called Flicks Brasserie.

SETTINGS & FACILITIES

Location Leicester Square. **Nearest Tube Station** Leicester Square. **Quietness Rating** C in front, low-floor rooms, A in back (double glazing throughout). **Dining** Flicks Brasserie serves burgers, salads, and pasta. **Amenities** Small sitting area, in-house movies. **Services** Concierge, 24-hour room service, bellhop, laundry.

ACCOMMODATIONS

Rooms 58. **All Rooms** Telephone, modem plug, satellite TV, in-house movies, writing desk, tea and coffee. **Some Rooms** iron, chairs. **Bed & Bath** Standard and clean. **Favorites** The singles are not great, very small and cramped, so for the extra money get a double. **Comfort & Decor** As you'd expect: inoffensive decor, good beds, and reasonable comfort in small rooms.

PAYMENT, RESERVATIONS, & RESTRICTIONS

Deposit Credit card; 72-hour cancellation policy. **Credit Cards** All major. **Check-In/Out** 2 p.m./11 a.m. **Pets** Not allowed. **Elevator** Yes. **Children** Yes. **Disabled Access** Very limited, with small elevator and narrow hallways.

THE REMBRANDT HOTEL   £190–£215

OVERALL ★★★ | QUALITY ★★★½ | VALUE ★★★★ | ZONE 11

11 Thurloe Place; (0207) 589-8100; fax (0207) 225-3476; www.sarova.co.uk

The three main reasons to stay at the Rembrandt are location, location, location. It's across the street from the Victoria and Albert and a hop, skip, and jump from the Science Museum, the Natural History Museum, and Harrods. It is also a four-minute walk from the South Kensington tube station, where one can access the Piccadilly (which goes to Heathrow), Circle, and District lines. There are three useful buses within shouting distance, and taxis are a breeze to hail. The hotel has a pleasant feeling to it, with a big lobby that has a fireplace, bar service, and plenty of couches to go around. The staff is plentiful and courteous. The rooms are nice enough and very clean, but without much character. Reservationists usually advise Americans to go for the double executive room since they're accustomed to lots of space. The Rembrandt attracts a lot of business conferences, and is at the top of many package tours' hotel lists. Ask about upgrading rooms.

SETTINGS & FACILITIES

Location South Kensington, on the border of Knightsbridge. **Nearest Tube Station** South Kensington. **Quietness Rating** A at the rear and top floors; C/D front lower floors (double glazing is not 100% effective, but the traffic roar quiets down at night). **Dining** The Masters Restaurant serves traditional breakfast, lunch, and dinner. **Amenities** Lobby with bar and fireplace, big dining room and small conservatory, tour bus pick-up, health club with pool (£5 charge), conference rooms, professional business services. **Services** Concierge, 24-hour room service, bellhop, laundry, fax and Internet in lobby, baby-sitting.

ACCOMMODATIONS

Rooms 195; two floors nonsmoking. **All Rooms** Telephone, cable TV, in-house movies, minibar on request, tea and coffee, hair dryer, writing desk. **Some Rooms** Air-conditioning, iron, bidet, sitting area. **Bed & Bath** Beds are so-so; bathrooms are clean and spacious by London standards. Jacuzzi on request for executive doubles. **Favorites** Executive-double front rooms on first floor facing Victoria and Albert Museum—you can admire the statues that you can't see from street level. The only drawbacks are street noise and fumes. **Comfort & Decor** The lobby is appealing, with a fireplace and plenty of seating, as well as a bar, but the rooms are somewhat dull, if clean. The decor could be described as unimaginative but safe.

PAYMENT, RESERVATIONS, & RESTRICTIONS

Deposit Credit card; 48-hour cancellation policy. **Credit Cards** All major. **Check-In/Out** 2 p.m./noon; express checkout available. **Pets** Not allowed. **Elevator** Two. **Children** Yes. **Disabled Access** Yes, but with three front stairs to be negotiated; doormen will gladly help.

RIVERSIDE HOTEL   £50–£70

OVERALL ★★ | QUALITY ★★★ | VALUE ★★★★★ | ZONE 12

23 Petersham Road, TW10; (0208) 940-1339; fax (0208) 948-0967; www.smoothhound.co.uk

Richmond is a very beautiful town, and it would behoove anyone who wanted to see a bit of the lovelier nearby parts of the Thames to take a trip out there on the tube or by rail. If you wanted to be sure of comparatively clean air, you might even want to stay there. A five- to ten-minute walk from the tube along Richmond High Street is the Riverside Hotel, a Victorian building right smack dab on the Thames, with pretty views and easy access to all the shops and amenities of Richmond. Richmond has a lot to enjoy: a historic theater, an arts center, nearby golf course, swimming pools, tennis and squash courts, plenty of pubs and restaurants and shops, not to mention the huge park. The hotel is well priced and well located, and the owners are willing to help you find your way to and from central London. It's a homey place, and it's recently been refurbished and upgraded. Some of the rooms are smaller than others, as is the case with the old Victorian conversions, so discuss with the owners exactly what you need when booking. June and July are very busy times, what with Wimbledon nearby, so be sure to book well in advance. Full English breakfast is included. Ten percent discount applies for stays of over a week.

SETTINGS & FACILITIES

Location Richmond. **Nearest Tube Station** Richmond (or BritRail). **Quietness Rating** C in front (double-glazed windows), A in back. **Dining** Breakfast and dinner. **Amenities** Breakfast and dinner room, bar. **Services** Helpful reception, one-day laundry service.

ACCOMMODATIONS

Rooms 22. **All Rooms** Shower and toilet, telephone, satellite TV, hair dryer, tea and coffee. **Some Rooms** View over river, balcony, garden access, four-poster bed. **Bed & Bath** Clean and satisfactory; about half have shower stalls only. **Favorites** Big rooms and balcony rooms with river view; the Riverside Room is the best. **Comfort & Decor** Eclectic decor; all rooms different, some very small.

PAYMENT, RESERVATIONS, & RESTRICTIONS

Deposit Credit card; 48-hour cancellation policy. **Credit Cards** All major, except DC. **Check-In/Out** 2 p.m./11 a.m. **Pets** Allowed by arrangement. **Elevator** No. **Children** Yes; younger than age 5 stay free. **Disabled Access** No.

THE ROOKERY   £223–£265

OVERALL ★★★★ | QUALITY ★★★★½ | VALUE ★★★ | ZONE 3

Peter's Lane, Cowcross Street, EC1; (0207) 336-0931; fax (0207) 336-0931; www.rookeryhotel.com

The Rookery is a charming hotel owned by the talented team of Peter McKay and Douglas Blain, who brought you The Gore and Hazlitt's. The hotel is in Clerkenwell, a short distance from the City, which makes it perfect for the businessperson. This is not the usual area where tourists stay, but it is definitely a viable choice, especially if you have an interest in the "real" historic London. Dr. Johnson would find himself completely lost in the postwar city of London, but you should be able to navigate from St. Paul's to the Old Bailey (both of which are visible from some of the hotel's windows). However, it is not only the neighborhood that lends appeal; the building itself is a conglomeration of restored eighteenth-century town houses that make for an intimate, delightful accommodation. All the modern conveniences are here, but they pale next to the glories of the past carefully culled from auction houses, flea markets, and antiques markets that litter the place. Like Hazlitt's, the exterior gives no hint of what wonders lie within: The old brick buildings are nondescript, located down a little lane and through an alley that cows used to cross making their fatal way to the Smithfield Meat Market. Look for lanterns and a discreet sign—no waving banners here. There are two common areas: a library and a conservatory that looks out onto a little garden. The rooms are of a decent size, and the bathrooms are unique. A great choice for the businessperson, the antiques freak, or one in search of a very good representation of old London. Sticking to the period theme, there is no elevator for the four floors.

SETTINGS & FACILITIES

Location Clerkenwell. **Nearest Tube Station** Farringdon. **Quietness Rating** A. **Dining** No. **Amenities** Conservatory, meeting rooms, personal safes in each room; you can take your breakfast in the lounge or in your room. **Services** Concierge, 18-hour room service, bellhop, laundry.

ACCOMMODATIONS

Rooms 33. **All Rooms** Telephones, satellite TV, fans on request, hair dryer, writing desk, personal safe. **Some Rooms** Views, four-poster. **Bed & Bath** Amazing. **Favorites** The Rook's Nest has a view of St. Paul's and the Old Bailey, and if you squint your eyes to remove the modern eyesores, you can really get the measure of Old London town. **Comfort & Decor** Of the highest quality on both scores, except for the lack of an elevator.

PAYMENT, RESERVATIONS, & RESTRICTIONS

Deposit Credit card. **Credit Cards** All major. **Check-In/Out** 1:30 p.m./11:30 a.m. **Pets** Not allowed. **Elevator** No. **Children** Yes. **Disabled Access** No.

RUSKIN HOTEL £43–£62

OVERALL★ | QUALITY ★★½ | VALUE ★★★★★ | ZONE 2

23–24 Montague Street, WC1; (0207) 636-7388; fax (0207) 323-1662; www.accomodata.co.uk

The Ruskin Hotel has been run by the same Spanish family for the past 22 years, and it has very much the feel of an inexpensive hotel in Barcelona. It also has the loyalty of many return customers. Unlike many of the budget bed-and-breakfasts in London, the Ruskin has an elevator to all floors, accepts all major credit cards, and is clean and friendly. The owner is not interested in customers who want to argue about services and room size, but is happy to house the kind of sensible souls who welcome a square deal that's across the street from the British Museum (the rooms in front have a view of the museum's side). The sitting room has a beautiful painting from 1801 by John Ward, a painter for the Duke of Bedford, whose estate still owns all the land around here. The house is quite old, having started out as a private residence before it served as a warren of offices where Sir Arthur Conan Doyle was reputed to have worked on his Sherlock Holmes stories. For a no-frills B&B/budget hotel, the Ruskin is a good bet. The single rooms have no en suite toilets; you will need to get a double for that.

SETTINGS & FACILITIES

Location Bloomsbury. **Nearest Tube Station** Russell Square. **Quietness Rating** A in back, B in front (double-glazed windows help). **Dining** Breakfast room. **Amenities** Breakfast included; generous portions served by waiters in a nice breakfast room. **Services** *Se habla español;* they can manage a few other languages as well.

ACCOMMODATIONS

Rooms 33; 6 with shower and toilet. **All Rooms** Telephones, hair dryer, tea and coffee. **Some Rooms** Garden view, bathroom. **Bed & Bath** Both communal and private bathrooms are in good shape; the beds are comfortable, though the doubles might be a squeeze for large Americans. **Favorites** Number 102 is a pleasant family room. **Comfort & Decor** The exuberance of the many plants and flowers on the outside may betray the utilitarian decor within: strip lights over beds, Naugahyde, fake wood, and plastic furniture, plus pink walls that mimic but don't quite match the Mediterranean concept of pink walls. Sensitive souls might shrivel at the decor, frankly, but if you can close your eyes to it, you might find time to admire certain features like friezes and the sitting-room mural.

PAYMENT, RESERVATIONS, & RESTRICTIONS

Deposit One night nonrefundable, unless they can re-let room. **Credit Cards** All major. **Check-In/Out** 1 p.m./11:30 a.m. **Pets** Not allowed. **Elevator** Yes. **Children** Yes. **Disabled Access** Yes.

ST. MARGARET'S HOTEL   £52–£95

OVERALL ★ | QUALITY ★★½ | VALUE ★★★★★ | ZONE 2

26 Bedford Place, Russell Square, WC1; (0207) 636-4277; fax (0207) 323-3066; www.stmargaretshotel.co.uk

This is a place that you can't help but like, even if it has no frills. What it lacks in amenities and style, it more than makes up for in good intentions, friendliness, amazingly low prices, and a very fine dining room overlooking some lovely gardens, which you are welcome to enjoy at any time. It has the feeling of a penzione, appropriately, as the owners are Italian. The senior Marazzis started it when they arrived in London after the war, and their son and his bride took it over. Mrs. Marazzi's daughter is now entering the family business, which makes it a real family affair and a labor of love. The place is informal but very clean, and although most of the single rooms don't have en suite bathrooms, the shared conveniences are spotless. It's a big place and the management renovates rooms one after another, so there are always improvements being made.

This is the kind of inexpensive hotel that people continue to come to time and time again for the friendliness, the British Museum around the corner, the relative spaciousness of the rooms, and the sensible cost. Be warned, though, that this is a low-cost, bed-and-breakfast-type hotel—if you're looking for elegance and three- or four-star service, you need to pay a lot more than they're charging. Also be warned that there are lots of stairs and no elevator.

SETTINGS & FACILITIES

Location Bloomsbury, off Russell Square. **Nearest Tube Station** Russell Square. **Quietness Rating** A. **Dining** A bright and very pleasant dining room overlooking gardens (for breakfast only, which is included in the price). **Amenities** Breakfast in dining room, tea and coffee served anytime, safe in office, fax available for use. **Services** 24-hour receptionist.

ACCOMMODATIONS

Rooms 64; 12 with en suite bathrooms, more planned for future. No singles have toilets at present. **All Rooms** TV, phone. **Some Rooms** En suite bathrooms, hair dryers, French doors and high ceilings, view of gardens. **Bed & Bath** Beds are reasonably comfortable; baths are spotless in both communal and en suite bathrooms. **Favorites** Number 53 is a room that looks over the garden and features a glassed-in conservatory. Book this one well in advance, as it is the favorite of regulars. Number 40 is a fine family room with enough space for four to sleep comfortably, as is number 45. Rooms on the first floor all have high ceilings and long French windows. **Comfort & Decor** The decor is utilitarian, but would offend the very sensitive souls or those used to the Ritz. It feels like a place your sensible, thrifty grandma would put together for you.

PAYMENT, RESERVATIONS, & RESTRICTIONS

Deposit One night's charge, £6 administration fee for cancellation at any time. **Credit Cards** All major. **Check-In/Out** Check in whenever room is available; out at noon. **Pets** Not allowed. **Elevator** No. **Children** Yes. **Disabled Access** There are two rooms on ground floor, but there are steps to reception. Not good for wheelchairs, as there are no porters.

THISTLE HOTEL HYDE PARK   £246–£281

OVERALL ★★★★ | QUALITY ★★★½ | VALUE ★★★★★ | ZONE 14

Lancaster Gate, W2; (0207) 262-2711; toll free from U.S. (800) 847-4358; fax (0207) 262-2147; www.thistlehotels.com/hydepark

If you really want to be on Hyde Park but don't want to shell out the kind of dough the luxury hotels on Park Lane charge, this is one of the many hotels along Bayswater that can solve your problem (not that it's cheap, it's just less than the Dorchester). As a Thistle Hotel, it has all the amenities you can expect from a good hotel group: room service, a restaurant, newspaper at your door, packages and promotions, business facilities, minibars. What it doesn't have is loads of charm, but that may be made up for by its location and the possibility that you'll get a good deal. There's a sitting room with leather chairs and a piano, and a conservatory that looks out across Bayswater to Kensington Gardens and Hyde Park. The traffic of Bayswater's four lanes can be stiff in the daytime, but it becomes relatively quiet at night—the higher the floor, the quieter the room and the better the view. Nearby Queensway has lots of restaurants and shops.

SETTINGS & FACILITIES

Location Lancaster Gate (Bayswater Road). **Nearest Tube Station** Queensway. **Quietness Rating** A on high floors and in back; C on low floors and front. **Dining** The restaurant offers white-linen service (and prices). **Amenities** Restaurant, fax in reception, fitness center next door, piano in sitting room. **Services** Concierge, 24-hour room service, bellhop, laundry.

ACCOMMODATIONS

Rooms 54. **All Rooms** Telephone, minibar, cable TV, air-conditioning, hair dryer, iron, safe. **Some Rooms** Balcony, park views, sitting area. **Bed & Bath** Good beds, perfect baths. **Favorites** Number 405 is a big room that gets lots of light, is very quiet, and has the most spectacular views over Kensington Gardens and Hyde Park. Any on the park are nice. **Comfort & Decor** Very comfortable; decor is of the up-market hotel style.

PAYMENT, RESERVATIONS, & RESTRICTIONS

Deposit Credit card; must cancel by noon on day of arrival, except for group bookings. **Credit Cards** All major. **Check-In/Out** 2 p.m./noon. **Pets** Not allowed. **Elevator** Yes. **Children** Yes; near one of the playgrounds in Kensington Gardens. **Disabled Access** Planning a wheelchair ramp.

THISTLE HOTEL KENSINGTON PALACE   £176–£268

OVERALL ★★★ | QUALITY ★★★½ | VALUE ★★★★ | ZONE 13

DeVere Gardens, Kensington, W8 5AF; (0207) 937-8121; fax (0207) 937-2816; www.thistlehotels.com

Now that DeVere, the budget hotel across the street, is being gutted for a future fancy hotel, the Thistle Hotel Kensington Palace is the next best place. The prices are a good deal for the area and for what you get. The common areas are nicely put together, and the rooms are pleasant enough. Runners and park lovers will appreciate having Kensington Gardens and Hyde Park across the street, and shopaholics will love having the stores of Kensington High Street and the antiques of Kensington Church Street only steps away. Plenty of buses go by the hotel, too. The restaurant isn't much to speak of, but Kensington has tons of good restaurants. Ask about or check the website for details and promotions.

SETTINGS & FACILITIES

Location Kensington, across from Kensington Gardens. **Nearest Tube Station** Kensington High Street. **Quietness Rating** C on park side, B in rear rooms. **Dining**

Café/restaurant on the premises called Fox &Hendersons. **Amenities** The usual for a chain hotel, cable TV, telephone, tea and coffee facilities. **Services** Concierge, room service.

ACCOMMODATIONS

Rooms 285. **All Rooms** Cable, telephone, hair dryer, iron, coffee and tea in room. **Some Rooms** View of Kensington Palace and Gardens. **Bed & Bath** Rooms are a reasonable size, with American-size beds; bathtubs in some, showers in others; clean and pleasant. **Favorites** Any of the rooms on the Kensington Gardens side over the first floor are best. **Comfort & Decor** Comfort is of good standard, decor is nothing to write home about, but possesses a cheerful and tasteful uniformity.

PAYMENT, RESERVATIONS, & RESTRICTIONS

Deposit Major credit card. **Credit Cards** All major. **Check-In/Out** 2 p.m./noon **Pets** No. **Elevator** No. **Children** Under age 16 free. **Disabled Access** Steps out front, doormen available to help.

THISTLE HOTEL VICTORIA £245

OVERALL ★★★★★ | QUALITY ★★★★ | VALUE ★★★★ | ZONE 9

Buckingham Palace Road; (0207) 834-9494; fax (0207) 630-1978; www.thistlehotels.com

This is one of those massive, grand Victorian hotels that makes your eyes pop when you enter it, and by the time you reach the middle of the vast dome with the huge chandelier swinging from it, you've unconsciously straightened your posture. The hotel was built to accommodate the visitors coming to see the Great Exhibition of 1851, and it was built to impress. There are stained-glass windows, wrought-iron staircases, columns, marble floors and walls, carved busts on the interior and exterior walls, potted plants, and huge windows. The rooms are in excellent shape, the common areas are impressive, and the Galleria, which rings the huge lobby one level up, is one of the finest hotel sitting areas in London. It's a Thistle Hotel, so it provides all the services one can expect from a hotel group with global standards: modems, fax on requests, cable TV, nonsmoking floors, complimentary newspapers, business support, and so on. It's near Victoria, Westminster Abbey, and Buckingham Palace—a central location that is also rather noisy during the day. The rear rooms have unfortunate views over Victoria Station, but they are very quiet. There are two sections: the "new" wing, built in the 1870s, has more standard-size rooms, whereas the old wing was built at a time when the guest would require a couple of rooms plus one for the maid or valet, so those conversions have left the sizes of rooms rather disparate. If you're visiting with a group or taking more than one room, ask for the new wing so there are no disappointing comparisons. Ask about the Leisure Breaks and Pound for Dollar promotions.

SETTINGS & FACILITIES

Location Victoria. **Nearest Tube Station** Victoria. **Quietness Rating** A in back, C in front, D in lower floors with huge windows, but that doesn't stop people from requesting these rooms again and again. **Dining** Very stately dining room, big enough to seat the occupants of the whole hotel; Harvard Bar; Galleria and lounge for tea and meals. **Amenities** The above, plus modems in some rooms, many different pillows available, newspaper. **Services** Concierge, 24-hour room service, bellhop, laundry.

ACCOMMODATIONS

Rooms 364. **All Rooms** Telephone, cable TV, hair dryer, iron, tea and coffee, in-house movies, writing desk. **Some Rooms** Minibar, modem, four-poster and half-tester (half a four-poster, with canopy) beds, huge windows, and high ceilings. **Bed & Bath** 100% cotton sheets on the bed, and you can request pillows of all kinds. The bathrooms are perfect. **Favorites** The big rooms at the front in the old wing with the big windows— noisy, but gorgeous. **Comfort & Decor** High quality; all rooms individually decorated in nice colors and furniture.

PAYMENT, RESERVATIONS, & RESTRICTIONS

Deposit Credit card. **Credit Cards** All major. **Check-In/Out** 2 p.m./noon. **Pets** Dogs allowed conditionally. **Elevator** Yes. **Children** Yes. **Disabled Access** No; many steps.

Part Four

Arriving and Getting Oriented

Entering the Country

You should have been issued an arrival card on the plane; make sure it has been filled out, and stick it in your passport along with your customs form. Arrival cards must be completed by each passport holder in your family. Fill it out on the plane and stash it in your passport. If for some reason they don't give you the landing cards on board, you can get them at immigration. The walk from plane to immigration may be very long, so try to keep your carry-on luggage light and easy to handle.

Immigration

Keep your eyes on the signs and make sure you are heading for the right immigration line. If you have been traveling in first or business class, you can usually head straight for the Fast Track line and show your Fast Track Pass or boarding ticket. Fast Tracks often close at night—check with the flight attendant so a closed Fast Track doesn't slow you down. There are two other lines: one for EU passport holders and one for all other nationalities. Have your passport ready, as the line can move pretty swiftly. You may be asked pointed questions about what you're doing here and where you're staying. Answer honestly and solemnly; immigration is a serious business in this country with national health service and other quality-of-life attractions. Nationals from the United States, Canada, Australia, New Zealand, South Africa, Japan, or Switzerland can get in without a visa as long as they are on vacation. Anyone carrying another passport should check with the British consulate in their country before making plane reservations.

Customs

Next, you will be sent into the luggage hall to collect your bags. Grab a free trolley, and after you have retrieved your luggage, follow signs for customs. The Goods to Declare exit is red, the Nothing to Declare exit is green, and the European Union exit (for anyone arriving from the continent) is blue. For our readers who may be traveling abroad for the first time, you'll decide which exit to use based upon what you have brought along with you that was purchased outside England.

The guidelines for what you can bring into England are divided into two categories: one for goods bought within the European Union, and the other for items purchased outside the EU. The likelihood that you will bring large jewels or luxury goods to London is remote, but you may want to save some money by bringing in your own instruments of vice. So, you may bring in, duty free:

- 200 cigarettes, 100 cigarillos, 50 cigars, or 250 grams of tobacco
- 2 liters of table wine and 1 liter of alcohol over 22% by volume (most spirits) and either 2 liters of alcohol under 22% by volume (fortified or sparkling wine or liqueurs) or 2 more liters of table wine
- 50 milliliters of perfume
- Other goods up to a value of £145 (about $250)

You may not bring in controlled drugs (any medication you have should be in its original bottle with your name on it), firearms and/or ammunition, obscene material, threats to public health and the environment, plants and vegetables, fresh meats, or any kind of animals.

If you have any questions about import and export issues, contact the Excise and Inland Customs Advice Centre (Her Majesty's Customs and Excise; (0845) 010-9000; www.hmce.gov.uk).

If you have to pay duty, you can pay in pounds sterling or by Master-Card or Visa. You have rights, which Her Majesty's customs officers are supposed to make perfectly clear to you, such as receiving help in repacking bags if they make you unpack them, appealing on the spot to a senior officer against a proposed search, and claiming compensation if they have damaged any of your property. If you want to appeal a written tax or duty decision, let the officer know at the time. If you don't do so at the time, you must write to them within 45 days; they will give you a leaflet that explains how to appeal. If you have any complaints about how you were treated, you can get assistance from the Adjudicator's Office (Haymarket House, 28 Haymarket, London, SW1 4SP; phone (0207) 930-2292; fax (0207) 930-2298).

The customs hall is often unstaffed, or there will be only one or two people there. Assuming you have nothing to declare, march quickly through the appropriate exit. There are large two-way mirrors in some of the airports here, and someone will definitely be watching. If you are stopped—occasionally random checks are carried out—*never* make jokes about the contents of your bags. You could be arrested, detained, and possibly deported. This is a nation that has had its share of terrorist bombings, and the officials are extremely and understandably jumpy. *Never* leave your bags unattended.

Make sure you have some English pounds to pay for your transportation from the airport. Cash machines are found in all airports and train stations, and they will give you the best exchange rate. They are known as "cashpoints" here, and they abound in London. Most of them are on the Cirrus or MacPlus system and will take money straight from your checking account at home. If you only have a credit card, make sure before you leave that you have a four-digit PIN for use in the cashpoints. There are seldom letters on the machines, so memorize your PIN numerically.

Getting into London

Car Rentals

There are car rental counters at all the airports, with most of the major companies represented: Hertz, Avis, or Europcar. You can rent a car when you arrive if necessary, but it's best to reserve ahead. You must be over age 23 and have a valid license from your country. You will need to use a parking lot in London, as there are only metered spots and restricted parking on the streets. For reservations, visit www.hertz.com, www.avis. com, or www.europcar.com.

From Gatwick Airport (phone (0870) 000-2468)

It's a long drive into London from Gatwick, with a good chance of bad traffic. Taking a taxi to central London is not smart, as it costs as much as £90, and can take over an hour. By far the best way is the **Gatwick Express** (phone (0845) 850-1530), which leaves every 15 minutes and takes you right to Victoria Station in half an hour, where you can catch a taxi, tube, or bus to your final destination. Follow signs and take the escalator down to the platform. The Gatwick Express is clearly marked. You pay on board the train, where they take cash and most credit cards. The fare is £11.50 one way, £21.50 round trip, half price for children between the ages of 5 and 15, and free for children under age 5.

Connex South Central (phone (0845) 000-2211, www.connex.co.uk) has trains running every 15 minutes between Gatwick and Victoria, and although the trip takes slightly longer than the Gatwick Express, it costs less, at £8.50 for a single trip, £17 return.

Thameslink (phone (0845) 748-4950, www.thameslink.co.uk) is another train line that has stops throughout the city: Blackfriars, City Thameslink, London Bridge, Farringdon, and King's Cross. So if you're staying in the east or north, it's a good choice. Tickets are £10 single journey, £20 return. Tickets must be purchased at the ticket office, and the trains don't run as frequently as the Gatwick Express.

Hotelink (phone (0129) 353-2244, www.hotelink.co.uk), at £22, is much cheaper than a taxi and you'll be met at the plane and taken to your hotel, which is comforting after a long flight.

From Heathrow Airport (phone (0870) 000-0123, www.baa.co.uk/heathrow)

By Taxi Heathrow has a number of excellent options for getting into London. The most expensive is the black-cab taxi, which can run from £40 for a no-traffic, west London drop off, to upward of £60 for a bad-traffic, central or north London destination. The best thing about the black cabs is that they are allowed to drive in the bus lanes, which saves time in rush hour.

There are also car services known as "minicabs." They are normal-size cars, but the name differentiates them from the black cabs. They don't run on a meter; they are slightly cheaper than the black cabs, but they can be unreliable. Unless it's a reputable outfit like Addison Lee (phone (0207) 387-8888, www.addisonlee.com) that you must call in advance or book through the Internet, they will likely not know London as well as the black cabs, and they cannot drive in bus lanes. Take advantage of the safe and spacious black cabs, whose drivers have the "Knowledge" (a long and stringent study of London's roads) to get you anywhere you want to go. Driving time varies with traffic, but it will generally take between 45 minutes and an hour to reach most central London locations.

By Bus National Express (phone (0870) 580-8080, www.gobycoach.com) has buses that run from Heathrow to Victoria Station from 6 a.m. to 9:30 p.m., and leaves from Heathrow's Central bus station every half hour. It's £8 one way and £12 round trip, half price for children, and takes about 50 minutes to central London. Depending on traffic, it can take approximately 50 to 90 minutes to get from Heathrow to central London.

By Underground (Tube) The Piccadilly line originates at Heathrow and is a fast and inexpensive way to get into the city, with convenient stops—Hammersmith, Earl's Court, South Kensington, Chelsea, Knightsbridge, Hyde Park Corner, Piccadilly, Leicester Square, Blooms-bury, King's Cross, Finsbury Park, and even beyond to the northern sub-urbs. This is a great option if you aren't carrying a lot of baggage and it's not rush hour. Be careful about the train—there are some trains from which you have to get out and change trains at Acton Town—a pain that can add a sizable chunk of time to your trip (normally it takes about 45 minutes). Buy the correct ticket—you'll be going to Tube Zone One (not to be confused with this book's zones; it's a London Underground defini-tion)—and hold onto it. You need it when you leave the tube station. Tickets cost £3.70 one way, and can be purchased right outside the tube entrance. Look for signs to Underground. If you have the wrong ticket, you can be fined £10 on the other end. You can take the tube into town and then hail a taxi on the street to get to your hotel for a fraction of what a taxi would cost straight from the airport. Barring delays or train changes, it takes about an hour to get from Heathrow to Piccadilly Circus. The tube is the least expensive option and the best bet for large groups of travelers.

By Heathrow Express Train   (phone (0845) 600-1515; www.heathrow express.co.uk) Run and owned by British Airways, this train is the fastest way into London—at 100 miles an hour, it takes only 15 minutes, and it leaves every 15 minutes. The standard round-trip fare is £22, £12 one way from the ticket counter; round-trip fare is £24, £14 one way on the train. If you book on their website you will save a couple of quid. The first-class price of £40 round trip apparently makes it the most expensive public transport in the world per mile and minute traveled, even more than the Concord. There are plenty of taxis at Paddington, where you arrive; and returning to Heathrow via the express is wonderful if your airline has a counter there. You can check in right there and ride luggage free with boarding pass in hand to the airport. Unfortunately, due to security concerns, American-based airlines no longer allow such ease of passage and have closed their check-in desks there, but you can check in if you're on British Airlines, Lufthansa, Singapore, Quantas, Varig, Air Canada, FinnAir, British Midlands, or Austrian Airlines. Paddington is in zone 14, and its Underground station connects with four tube trains, as well as overland trains that go west.

From Stansted Airport (phone (0845) 850-0150, www.baa.co.uk/stansted)

This is a relatively new airport and functions quite smoothly. As it's 35 miles outside of London, a taxi is prohibitively expensive; luckily, the Stansted Express train is very fast: You'll arrive at Liverpool Street Station in 45 minutes. Just follow signs down one floor to the train platform and catch the train to Liverpool Street, which is a major rail hub and tube station. Journey time is 45 minutes, and the fare is £13 one way, and £23 for round trip. Trains run every 30 minutes. A taxi takes over an hour and costs close to a hundred pounds; the Airbus A6, (0870) 580-8080, takes over an hour and a half and costs only £3 less than the train. We don't recommend these options—just take the train.

From Luton Airport (phone (0158) 240-5100, www.londonluton.co.uk)

Luton deals mostly with British charter flights or cut-rate budget airlines. Getting into London from Luton (which is about 30 miles north) by taxi can take up to 90 minutes in traffic and costs around £65. It is, however, the best option for those in a hurry or with lots of baggage. There is a Luton Airport Parkway Station that is nearby, but not in the station, so you have to deal with a shuttle bus after dealing with the Thameslink (see info above) train, which takes about 40 minutes from King's Cross, leaves every 20 minutes, and costs £10 one way and £20 round trip. Train time is about 40 minutes. The National Express (see info above) coach company runs a 24-hour bus service from Victoria to Luton, every half-hour for £7 one way, and £12 return; children are half price. Greenline Buses travel between Victoria Station in London and Luton for £8 one way, £11.50 round trip. There are discounts if you are flying EasyJet. Call (0870) 608-7261 for times. Bus travel time is approximately an hour and a half.

From London City Airport (phone (0207) 646-0000, www.londoncityairport.com)

This is the closest airport to central London (nine miles east of Docklands), but it deals mostly with European short hops. It is a good, well-run airport, and the transportation is quite convenient: A black-taxi ride to London runs about £25; and shuttle buses leave every 20 minutes or so for Canary Wharf (£3 one way) and Liverpool Street (£6).

By Eurostar (phone (0123) 361-7575, www.eurostar.com)

This high-speed train is a fast, though not necessarily cheap, way to get from the heart of Paris or Brussels to London's Waterloo Station. All leisure tickets are now subject to availability, with lowest price £59 (first-class £139) round trip, for a nonrefundable, non-changeable ticket, staying over one Saturday. To get these great fares, you must book about two weeks in advance, and you should do so on the website in order to avoid a £3 per ticket handling fee. The website also gives you a chance to check out the various rates available. If you want to pop over for a one-night stand on the spur of the moment, it costs £298 for a fully refundable, fully negotiable ticket (first-class £415). Waterloo Station is on the south side of the Thames across from Westminster and is served by the tube's Northern line, buses, and taxis (taxis are reasonably priced for a trip to central London). The great advantage of the Eurostar over the plane or ferry is that it is absolutely the most convenient way to get to and from the continent—three and a half hours from London to the Gare du Nord in Paris. (Don't forget to take your passport and fill out an arrival card for immigration at Waterloo Station.) The train travels at 185 miles per hour on French soil, but must slow down in England because the British don't have the high-speed tracks yet. They are in the process of laying down the track, which will give the Eurostar access to and from St. Pancras Station.

By Car from the Continent

Renting a car on the European continent to drive into Britain is expensive and a bit risky. There is compulsory insurance, and the European car will have the steering wheel on the "wrong" side of the car, which will make driving in England much more difficult. You will have to park in a lot in central London because most of London's parking is by meter or residential parking permit. There are car-rental companies at all the major ports, most of which will allow you to drop off at other locations, though there may be a drop-off fee. It's important to buy a good road atlas of Great Britain if you plan to drive from any of the ports (Dover, Folkestone, Newhaven, Southampton, Harwich, or Ramsgate) into London. The signs are confusing at times, with more information on them than you may be able to take in at once, directing you off roundabouts. But this is the beauty of a roundabout: Keep going around about it until you're sure what direction to go.

By Ship from America

If you're phobic about air travel, have plenty of time and money, or want to see what a transatlantic crossing is like, you can call Cunard at (800) CUNARD, or look for fares and schedules on www.cunard.com. A round trip from New York to London starts at $1,000. The crossing on the *Queen Elizabeth 2* takes six days. They also offer a one-way trip with a free economy air ticket for the return, starting at $1,600.

Getting Oriented in London

Post Codes

As we explained in the introduction, London is divided into post codes, which instantly identify an area to those in the know. You'll see the post codes on maps, street signs, and addresses. This system is very helpful for the visitor, who may want to stay in the same post code as a particular museum, or for the business traveler who wants to be near the office. These are not arbitrary; they represent compass directions: W1 is west and WC is west central, just as E1 is east and EC is east central. The closer an area is to central London, the lower the code number—all "1s" abut central London. These post codes can encompass more than one "town" and vice versa; SW1 includes Victoria, Pimlico, and Westminster, and Chelsea extends into districts SW3, SW7, and SW10. You'll quickly figure it out, and you'll have your own favorite post code before you know it.

Grasping London's Geography   The most important feature of London's geography is the rolling Thames River. It snakes through the city, bending around boroughs and post codes, and though it may not be the great and busy highway through London that it once was, it is still the major water artery. Starting in the east, the Thames slows down at the hairpin turn around the Isle of Dogs, with Greenwich on the south side of the river. Canary Wharf is on the Isle of Dogs, and at the next bend of the river is the East End. The river straightens out for the section that includes the Tower of London, Tower Bridge, and the City of London. To the south of this portion of the river is Southwark, turning into the South Bank to the west, with the Globe's thatched roof and the mighty London Eye Ferris wheel visible. Continuing westward, the river slows down again for another curve; on this curve, along Victoria Embankment, you'll see the Temple, Cleopatra's Needle, Big Ben, the Houses of Parliament, and at Lambeth Bridge, on the opposite bank, is the medieval Lambeth Palace. Radiating north from this important stretch of the river is Soho, then Bloomsbury, and slightly northwest is Regent's Park. Come back down to the river and follow it past Westminster and Pimlico to Chelsea, where it will continue to flow west through Fulham, Hammersmith, and Chiswick, toward Richmond and Hampton Palace. North of Chelsea you'll find South Kensington, Hyde Park, Bayswater, and Marylebone, and run into Regent's Park again. North of that is Hampstead Heath.

Hyde Park is another landmark that helps visitors to get a handle on London's geography. The park is surrounded by central London; to the north is Bayswater, to the east lie Marble Arch and Mayfair, to the southeast are Belgravia and Knightsbridge, to the southwest is South Kensington, and to the west are Kensington and Holland Park.

London is a huge city, but it is divided into enough discrete areas that you can start to differentiate between parts of it rather easily, using the river and Hyde Park as baselines. Study the map of the whole city, see how the zones intersect; look at the tube map, bearing in mind that it's highly stylized, but it can help you get a grip on this vast metropolis. Look especially at the yellow Circle line, which circles around central London. The tube map was streamlined from a mess of meandering lines into what you see now. It works and it's readable, but it's not geographically exact. For instance, if you look at the tube map, the distance between Lancaster Gate to Paddington Station looks significant; in fact, it is only a four-minute walk. However, a walk from Marble Arch to Lancaster Gate looks pretty easy on the tube map, but it would take about 12 minutes. Use the street map to determine distance, not the tube map.

The *London A to Z Book,* pronounced "a to zed" by the British, is essential to you, as it is to any Londoner. There are other street atlases, by Collins and by Nicholson, which are also fine, but the *A to Z* is the most commonly used. It's not for tourists only. In fact, Londoners probably rely even more on these maps than tourists do, because they know how devilishly devious the streets here are. Not only are there streets of the exact name in different post codes but there are major arteries that change names as they charge ahead through various areas. Thus the A4 from Heathrow becomes the Great West Road, then Talgarth Road, then Cromwell, Thurloe Place, Brompton Road, Knightsbridge, and Piccadilly, all without making a single turn.

Some of the major thoroughfares in London are of rather ancient vintage—old Roman commercial routes of strict design—and all the streets, mews, alleys, dead ends, cul-de-sacs, terraces, and crescents that later made a mess of Rome's plans were often cowpaths, driveways, back passageways to a high street, or footpaths between neighborhoods and pubs. This city was never brought to heel by planners in the way New York and parts of Paris were, which is what makes it so much fun to explore. For seeing the best of London by foot, there is nothing better than to just get lost. Indeed, it is highly unlikely that you won't do so unintentionally at least once when you're here. But as long as you carry an *A to Z* book and persist in one direction or another, you are bound to eventually hit some recognizable landmark . . . or a taxi.

In Covent Garden there's a fantastic shop called Stanford's (zone 7; 12–14 Long Acre; (0207) 836-1321; www.stanfords.co.uk; tube: Covent Garden) that has every map known to London. Here you can find walking maps, cycling maps, backstreet maps for avoiding the large thoroughfares, and maps of the old city. For your purposes, it is best to get the big picture with a fold-out map that is relatively simple, listing the major attractions and streets, and keep the pocket street atlas for narrowing down your route.

Things the Locals Already Know

Getting the Lowdown on What's Up

For the latest information on current plays, movies, art exhibits, clubs, fairs, museum tours, lectures, walking tours, or whatever, pick up a *Time Out* magazine. It's more thorough than its competitor, *What's On,* although *What's On* is a little simpler to read. On Thursday, the *Evening Standard* newspaper includes a magazine, *Metro Life,* which is the least expensive of the three and is quite comprehensive.

If you want to get a copy of *Time Out* before you arrive, e-mail them at net@timeout.co.uk, or call their distribution department at (0207) 813-6060. Check out their website at www.timeout.com. If you're in a big city, try a newsstand that carries foreign newspapers and magazines; they might carry the weekly *London Time Out.*

Tipping

In many restaurants, there is a service charge of between 12% and 15% added on; make sure you examine your menu and your bill to see if it has already been added. If it has, and you still get a credit card receipt with an empty gratuity line, just run a slash through it. If you pay with cash, you can leave some change from the bill if you feel like it. If service is not included, it will be mentioned in some obvious manner on the bill. Twelve to fifteen percent is appropriate for tipping in restaurants, twenty percent if the service was fantastic.

Taxi drivers do appreciate a tip and in many cases really earn it by helping with bags, taking a smart route, and giving information. Anything from 50p to £1 is usual in short-haul trips, and after £10, a tip of 10% to 15% is fine. You won't be abused for giving a lousy tip, and you may be warmly thanked for a good one. In the good hotels, you can tip the staff as you feel they deserve. £1 or £2 a bag for bellhops, a fiver for the maid, whatever you think the concierge deserves for whatever service he or she provides. Check to see if service is added to your bill, in which case you may feel free to tip only those who have been especially helpful.

London's Media

Newspapers

London has a huge selection of newspapers, from the solemn to the sleazy. Make a point of reading at least a couple of them while you're here.

The Times   Now owned by media king Rupert Murdoch, it aspires to be a great newspaper, but falls short of the mark. It does have a big Sunday edition that has something for everyone.

The Independent   A decent broadsheet with some good writing and a very good Sunday edition.

The Observer   A Sunday-only paper with all the sections you'd expect; a fine read.

The Guardian   A well-written liberal newspaper.

The Daily Telegraph   Right-wing broadsheet with big Saturday and Sunday editions.

Financial Times   Printed on pink paper; a must for the businessperson.

International Herald Tribune   This is the fluff-free paper of choice for American expats—it features the best of the *New York Times* and has no advertising. Great editorial section with weekly contributions from America's favorite columnists, and Doonesbury, too. It recently dissolved its longstanding partnership with *The Washington Post* and may be changing its name in the near future.

Evening Standard   Tabloid-size afternoon newspaper; a little light on news, but features good local stories and entertainment listings, plus the Metro Life entertainment supplement on Thursdays and the *Evening Standard Magazine* on Friday.

Daily Mail   Usually manages to have a star, a royal, or a socialite on the cover. Fairly good money section. Relatively free of hard news.

Daily Express   Conservative middle-brow newspaper, not unlike the *Mail.*

The Sun   Sleazy tabloid. This is the home of the famous Page Three Girl, the gratuitous photo of a topless woman placed on the third page. Its content is similarly absurd. Read it and laugh.

There are the other tabloids that you may not want to be caught dead reading, like *The Daily Star* or *The Sun*, full of the important news of women's breasts, murder, and sex scandals; and the *Sport*, which doesn't even bother to pretend it's anything but a titillation rag.

Magazines

The Big Issue   You must buy this magazine. It provides the homeless with some income (feel free to give the vendor a tip when buying it), and it has some of the most interesting articles on London you can find. It's often guest-edited by some literary or media worthy.

The Economist   Very serious and informative conservative mag on money and politics.

Harpers and Queen   Glossy magazine devoted to the rich, famous, and beautiful; a bit like the *Tatler* in its social diary, but with more beauty articles.

Hello!   Weekly rag that makes *People* look like *The New Yorker.* Lots of Hollywood celebs, minor royalty, gossip, puzzling media creations, and a weekly television and radio guide. Seems to be the family photo album for people like Sarah Ferguson and Posh Spice. *O.K.* is its closest competitor, and it's easy to get them mixed up; the same photos appear in both these weeklies.

The Literary Supplement   Like the *New York Times Review of Books,* this is a ripping good intellectual read, with articles and book reviews written by some of the brightest people in the world of letters. After you've read a few pieces you'll wonder how you've lived without it.

Private Eye   Funny political satire—it's the scourge of the establishment, any establishment. Might be obscure for nonresidents, but worth a try.

Punch   Now owned by Mohammed Al Fayed, it's sold throughout Harrods and has certainly lost its punch. Don't bother, unless you happen across editions from the nineteenth century.

The Spectator   Entertaining, with intelligent wit; politically to the right.

Tatler   House (or castle) organ of aristocrats, social climbers, and wannabes. Features such edifying articles as guides to eligible rich bachelors and bachelorettes. Endless pages of photos of dull social gatherings of marquises, dukes, and barons. Good info on how to spend all your money in one day.

Time Out   The most comprehensive weekly magazine on what's going on in London.

W. H. Smith, the bookstore chain, has an enormous range of magazines and newspapers from all over the world.

Television

TV in England is paid for by subscription to the tune of £119 a year. This means that there are no commercials on BBC 1 and BBC 2, except for advertising for BBC's own shows and products. It's a lovely change of pace from American television. BBC 1 is the weakest of the British TV stations, with lots of cheaply produced cooking shows, talk shows, and animal programs. BBC 2 used to be very stuffy, but now regards itself as quite hip. It produces some good drama, imports the occasional good movie, and has some good current-affairs shows. The independent station ITV is on channel 3 and currently produces the most expensive dramas seen on British TV. It's funded by commercials, which only appear (mercifully) every 15 minutes. Channel 4 is also a commercial station, but it's definitely the hippest. Conscientiously irreverent and envelope pushing, it has an hour of nightly news at 7 p.m. There's a movie channel on 5.

Cable, found in all the good hotels, provides Sky One, which has CNN, MTV, and plenty of movies and television programs from the United States. Do yourself a favor and watch some of the BBC—there are some truly wonderful shows on it, such as adaptations of Dickens or less recognized English authors.

Radio

The radio is mostly BBC, which has five national networks. The radio is in many ways quintessentially British: Until the 1950s, BBC radio presenters were required to wear dinner jackets when reading the news. This Britishness is best heard on BBC Radio 3 and 4. Try to catch the shipping forecast at 6 p.m. daily on Radio 4. It is eccentric and incomprehensible to the layperson, and it articulates perfectly the voice of an old island culture.

The local listings in newspapers and magazines will tell you what is on when.

- **Radio 1** Pop music at 98.8 FM
- **Radio 2** Light entertainment at 89.2 FM
- **Radio 3** Classical music and related topics at 91.3 FM
- **Radio 4** To our mind, the best thing in British media. Like National Public Radio, but much more, with short stories, serials, dramatizations, interviews, quizzes, comedies, and plays. The hackles of every Radio 4 lover were raised recently when there were rumors of the Beeb's intention to "dumb down" the unusually intelligent programs to appeal to more people. No word on if this plot has been launched as of yet. Listen to it, and you decide.
- **Capital FM** Top-ten pop music on 95.8 FM and oldies on Capital Gold on 1548

kHz

- **Classic FM** More classical music on 100.9 FM (an English friend told me that no Brit will ever complain about classical music played at ear-deafening decibels)
- **Jazz FM** Great jazz and blues, at 102.2 FM
- **Newstalk** All news all the time, with phone-in commentary that can be quite interesting, at 97.3 FM

Telephones

Criminally, some pinheads at British Telecom (BT) decided to remove and sell off the majority of the red phone boxes that were such a pleasing and distinctive hallmark of London. They have been kept in many of the tourist areas, but mostly you'll see soulless and ugly glass boxes with tons of sex-trade advertising (it's the specific job of one person to remove these cards each week, but they go back up immediately). The public phone booths here take either coins or BT phone cards. Just to make things more confusing, there's a competitor, Mercury, which has its own phone booths and phone cards. Coins are your best bet, and you can make a very quick call for 10p. Some of the public phones in restaurants have a system in which you wait for the call to be answered before putting the money in—otherwise you lose it. Read the directions before using a pay phone.

The telephone jacks in England will not fit an American modem cord, so if you have your laptop and want to get online, ask the hotel for an adapter or buy one at a department store (Harrods, John Lewis, Peter Jones, Dixons, and small electronic shops carry them). Important: If you are calling England from overseas, you must drop the 0 at the beginning of the number. When in the country, you use the 0.

International calls are made by dialing 00, then the country code, area code, and local number. To call through a long-distance service, dial their access lines and follow directions, using your credit-card number:

AT&T Direct (0800) 890-011   Australia (0800) 890-061

MCI World Com (0800) 890-222   New Zealand (0800) 890-064

Canada Direct (0800) 890-016

SOME IMPORTANT NUMBERS

- **00** International dialing code; that is, if calling outside England, dial 00 + 1 for U.S. and Canada, 61 for Australia, 64 for New Zealand
- **100** General operator
- **112** Emergency for police, fire, or ambulance
- **153** International-directory inquiries
- **155** International operator
- **118118** U.K. directory inquiries

■ **999** Emergency for police, fire, or ambulance

Public Toilets

London has earned the admiration of its tourists and the appreciation of its dwellers by its plentiful and clean public conveniences, also called WCs or loos. The secret may be that there's usually a small charge for their use, and people tend to be more respectful when they've invested some money. Twenty pence gets you 15 minutes in a free-standing cubicle, which is washed and sterilized automatically after each use. There always seems to be toilet paper in these loos as well as in the free lavatories found in the parks and in some tube stations and squares. Although we can't tell you it's OK to walk into a pub, hotel, or a restaurant and use the toilet if you aren't a customer, it is true that many people here aren't too uptight about that.

Mail

Get your stamps for postcards and letters from a newsagent or a Mail Boxes shop. The post offices can be extremely crowded, as lots of people pay their bills there. If you want to get special-edition stamps, you will have to queue up at the post office. An overseas postcard stamp costs between 42p and 47p, and an overseas letter is 68p to 84p, depending on weight. Remember to put the air-mail sticker on your mail and don't forget to write "USA" or the name of the destination country at the bottom of the address. I once had a letter addressed to New York, New York, returned because I didn't write the country on it. Post offices are open Monday through Friday, 9 a.m.–5 p.m., and Saturday, 9 a.m.–12:30 p.m. (www.royalmail.com).

Store Hours

This is where you get to really appreciate the American way: Many retail shops here are on a rather old-fashioned schedule of 10 a.m.–6 p.m. and closed on Sundays. However, much to the dismay of the more traditional who deplore the Yankee incursions on their way of life (and to the delight of anyone with a 9-to-5 office job), stores, especially the clothing chains, are now open on Sundays. Some supermarkets and convenience stores are opening 24 hours a day, and even the great hold-outs—Harrods, John Lewis, and Peter Jones—are open later on Wednesdays and Thursdays. (Later only means until 7 or 8 p.m.) Call and check before you take off for any shop, especially on a Saturday, when strange hours such as noon–5 p.m. may be in effect.

Crime

There's a perception of London as one of the safest cities in the world, fostered by the fact that the bobbies (policemen) don't carry guns. Also, because of the strict gun laws in England, there just aren't the number of gunshot fatalities that plague the United States. Compared with other European cities, London is among the least violent, with one of the lowest homicide rates. But women take note: The statistics for rape are high. Try not to travel alone at night, and avoid minicabs.

There is definitely a disturbing trend on the streets of London toward the commission of crimes more violent than the usual purse snatchings. There have been a number of muggings involving knives and bodily harm. Shouting matches on the street are not an uncommon sight, and they frequently degenerate into fisticuffs. I lived in New York for many years, but I had to come to London to see grown men brawling in the street over a road rage incident. As in all cities, there's a lot of stress, and bad behavior often follows on its heels. Do keep a sharp eye out, and try to avoid areas with a high concentration of pubs (Leicester Square, Soho) late at night. If you take a night bus, sit downstairs; the rowdies congregate on the upper deck. I don't wish to frighten anyone, but we need to be realistic about life in the big city.

Here are some tips:

- Keep your pocketbook close at all times; sling it across your chest if possible, and don't leave it sitting unattended in public places.

- Don't put your wallet in a backpack unless it's in an inside, zipped pocket.

- Put your wallet in a front pocket.

- Use a money belt when carrying large sums.

- Don't hang around counting your money after using an ATM.

- Watch your belongings on the tube and on buses.

- Don't wear flashy jewelry or an expensive wristwatch.

- Avoid night buses after midnight; use a taxi or minicab instead. Women may be happier using the women's minicab company formed after a spate of minicab-related rapes. Call Lady Cabs, (0207) 254-3501; or a black taxi Dial a Cab, (0208) 253-5000; or Radio Taxis (0207) 272- 0272. The car service Addison Lee is highly recommended, (0207) 387-8888.

- Never allow yourself to be picked up by a minicab on the street.

- Leave your passport in a safe at the hotel and carry a photocopy of the information page.

- Ignore any implausible story you might hear on the street; this town is full of talented con artists.

- Stay out of the parks after dark.

- Late at night, travel in groups if possible.

- If you buy something at a very expensive store, don't parade around with the bag too long—get it back to your hotel or put the bag in a less ritzy one (there are jewelers on Bond Street who now offer a plain bag to their customers).

- The emergency phone number is 999; *don't* use it unless it is truly an emergency.

To report a crime, call directory assistance at 118118 for the number of the nearest police station.

The Homeless and Beggars

The best way to help the homeless is to buy *The Big Issue* magazine, which is sold on the street by licensed vendors. Part of the money goes to the vendor, and you would be kind to also give the vendor a tip. They work hard in all weather for very little money. It's also an excellent magazine. There are an estimated 100,000 homeless persons on the streets of London, an enormous increase from only a couple of years ago. I'm happy to give money to the people sitting on sleeping bags asking for spare change, especially when I consider the sums I spend just to get the basics in London, but many people are opposed to giving cash on various grounds. Giving a sandwich or some food is a good alternative.

Religion

Here are some phone numbers of various churches, synagogues, mosques, or meetinghouses of the listed denominations to help you find a place to worship in your own way. If you're not picky, feel free to drop into any of the wonderful churches all over London for a bit of beauty and peace.

Anglican
  St. Paul's Cathedral, (0207) 236-4128, or Westminster Abbey, (0207) 222-5897

B'hai (0207) 584-2566

Baptist (0207) 221-7039

Buddhist (0207) 834-5858

Catholic
  Brompton Oratory, (0207) 808-0900, or Westminster Cathedral, (0207) 798-9055

Christian Science (0207) 499-1271

Evangelical (0207) 207-2100

Greek Orthodox (0207) 723-4787

Hindu (0208) 961-5031

Islamic (0207) 724-3363

Jewish
  Liberal Jewish Synagogue, (0207) 286-5181, or United Synagogue, (0208) 343-8989

Methodist (0207) 222-8010

Pentecostal (0207) 701-1658

Quaker (0207) 387-3601

Gay London

When Oscar Wilde was arrested at the Cadogan Hotel in the last days of the nineteenth century on charges of homosexuality, that afternoon's boat to Calais was so crowded with single gentlemen that it almost sank. The law banning homosexuality was often enforced more for political reasons than anything else, but it made being a homosexual in England fraught with real danger. And it was all the more peculiar because of the tacit acceptance of homosexual dalliances in the male segregated school system of the upper classes. Homosexuality was seen by many as an adolescent phase that one outgrew. In 1967, the outdated law was finally changed, and London can now boast the most happening gay scene in Europe. There are gay hotels, bookshops, health clubs, religious groups, bars, nightclubs, cafés, travel agencies, publications, and even a taxi company. The best neighborhoods are in Soho (Old Compton Street in particular) and Earl's Court. Clapham Common, Hampstead Heath, and the Brompton Cemetery are popular green spaces for hanging out and meeting people—and maybe doing a little cruising.

There is an excellent book by Graham Parker called *Gay & Lesbian London* (published by Metro Publications, P.O. Box 6336, London N1 6PY), which can be found in most bookstores and tourist centers. It lists and reviews every possible venue or service for the gay community in London. Unless you have an updated edition (latest edition is May 2002), it might be wise to check club, pub, and other information against the more current weekly magazines.

Here are a few gay-friendly organizations and businesses you may want to seek out:

Gay.Com (www.gay.com) is a good place to start on the Internet. In the United States, call the International Gay Travel Association, in Florida at (305) 292-0217, or leave a message at (800) 448-8550, for information about gay-friendly tours and services. Pick up or call for a copy of *Out and About,* a magazine that offers reviews of the best hotels, clubs, gyms, and so on in the world; call (800) 929-2215.

London Lesbian and Gay Switchboard can be reached 24 hours a day, 365 days a year at (0207) 837-7324 or www.llgs.org.uk. They can offer help, information, or counsel on any issues related to being gay in London.

Philbeach Hotel is a reasonably priced and fun gay hotel where a crossdressing party erupts once a week. It is located in zone 11, at 30–31 Philbeach Gardens, Earl's Court, SW5 (phone (0207) 373-1244; www.philbeachhotel.freeserve.co.uk; tube: Earl's Court).

Number Seven is a Victorian townhouse in Brixton with eight suites ranging from £60 to £129 and located in zone 5, at 7 Josephine Avenue, SW2 (phone (0208) 741-6740; tube: Brixton).

Gay's the Word is the first—and to date the only—specifically gay and lesbian bookshop in the United Kingdom and can be visited at 66 Marchmont Street, Bloomsbury, (phone (0207) 278-7654, zone 2; tube Russell Square).

The **Clone Zone** has two conveniently located shops, one at 64 Old Compton Street (phone (0207) 287-3530, zone 7; tube: Leicester Square) and one at 266 Old Brompton Road (phone (0207) 373-0598) zone, 11; tube: Earl's Court). You'll find books, cards, magazines, sex toys, clothes, and—most importantly—people to answer questions you may have about what's up in London.

The **Sauna Bar** is a luxury spa for men in the heart of Soho, in zone 7, at 29 Endell Street (phone (0207) 836-2236; tube: Covent Garden).

You can check out the scene in *Time Out,* or in the following free mags distributed in London's clubs and pubs:

Boyz—phone (0207) 296-0026

QX *(Queer Extra)*—phone (0207) 379-7887 or www.qxmag.co.uk

Lost/Stolen Credit Cards

Report missing credit cards to both the police and the 24-hour lost-or-stolen-card bureaus below:

American Express (0127) 369-6933

Diners Club (0800) 460-800

Mastercard/Eurocard (0800) 964-767

Switch (0113) 277-8899

Visa (0800) 895-082

Part Five

Getting around London

Public Transportation

The most important thing to take out with you in London is a good map and/or the pocket-size *London A to Z Book*—the map for the overall big picture and the *A to Z* for the small streets. You won't regret the extra weight in your bag. A camera is a must because you never know when you'll run into a horse-drawn carriage or a battery of the queen's guards outfitted as if waiting for the Battle of Waterloo. Strange details on buildings or gates will call out to be recorded, and you may never pass that way again. Bring extra film. Also, be sure to carry a few 20p coins for the public toilets.

Like all big modern cities, London's biggest problem is transportation and traffic. The congestion charge initiated in February 2003 was an attempt to limit cars in a certain central area by charging drivers £5 a day to drive inside its perimeters. The idea was to get more people to leave their cars at home and use public transportation. The money generated by the congestion charge is to be used to improve underground and bus service. Unfortunately, public transportation is still a mess, so the extra people using it as a result of the congestion charge has made commuting in London just that much more hellish. There are constant delays and interruptions of service on the tube, and on the weekends repairs are made, which causes whole lines to be shut down. Buses, when not stuck in traffic, have an infuriating habit of arriving at long last in packs. But having said that, as visitors, you will be more tolerant than regular commuters, and will be able to travel during off-peak times. Eight times out of ten, the tube will get you wherever you're going quickly and efficiently, and the double-decker buses are a fun way to see London. Just avoid public transport during rush hours, and resign yourself to taking a cab late at night.

For any questions you might have regarding London travel information, call London Transport at (0207) 222-1234. You can get information on any facet of travel, including how everything (or *if* everything) is running.

Travel Zones

London Transport has divided London into six travel zones (which have nothing to do with the zones outlined in this book). Zone 1 is in the middle of central London, and the rest radiate outward in circles that end at zone 6 in the suburbs and at Heathrow in the west. Most of what you'll be doing in London will fall within zones 1 and 2. Bus and tube fares rise with zone numbers. For years, the transportation experts have discussed the possibility of simplifying fares by making one flat fee, but the size of London and the cost of gas unfortunately make such a master stroke impractical.

Travel Cards

The best deal for traveling on public transportation is the Travel Card, which gives you unlimited travel on the tube, buses, and most overland rail services in Greater London, including the Docklands Light Railway. The Travel Card will save you time and money. A one-day off-peak Travel Card for zones 1 and 2 (bought after 9:30 a.m.) costs only £4.10, whereas a round-trip tube ticket in the same zones costs £4. A weekend card is £6.10 for zones 1 and 2, and a weekly card costs £19.60 for zones 1 and 2—a very good deal if you're planning on being in London for a week. You'll need a passport-size photo to get the weekly card. Most stations have photo machines for precisely this purpose.

The Family Travel Card is also a great deal: £2.70 per adult for zones 1 and 2 on a one-day off-peak card and 80p per child. The family must consist of at least one adult and one child between the ages of 5 and 15; they need not be related. Family cards are valid only after 9:30 a.m. Monday–Friday and all day on weekends. For visitors, alas, there are no senior or student discounts; you have to be a London resident. Travel Cards can be bought at tube stations and also at certain newsagents. Travel Cards can be used on buses within the same travel zones.

Buses

There is no better view in the world than that of London from the top first-row seat of a double-decker bus. Many of the old buildings seem to have been designed expressly for the view from the top of the bus; the statues and gargoyles that decorate some of the fine architecture of the city are at eye level when you're riding up top. There are 17,000 bus stops all over London, so you should be able to get pretty close to whatever your destination may be. See pages 155–158 for some of the best London-viewing, double-decker public buses. The European Union forbids double-decker buses, and there is a threat that they may be removed from the London streets to comply with idiotic continental regulations. Let's hope the government keeps its head in this case and tells Brussels exactly what bus they can get on. The mayor has been plotting to get rid of the handy change-making facility of the present-day bus and, in fact, you will see some bus ticket machines at bus stops in central London. You can also buy bus tickets at some newsagents. These stops will require you to buy a ticket from the machine, so keep a one-pound coin handy.

Types of Buses

- **Routemaster** This is the old-style double decker. You get on at the rear, take your seat, and wait for the conductor to come collect your fare. These are becoming rarer each year, so enjoy them while you can.

- **Double-decker front-entry buses** These are the newer buses, used solely by some routes and for all-night buses. You get on in front, pay the driver, and take your seat. Try to have change for the sake of convenience. A Travel Card makes paying much less of a hassle.

- **Single-decker buses** These tend to be for shorter journeys through London. Same price as the others, less room inside. Pay upon entering or use Travel Card.

- **Night buses** Night buses tend to cost more than buses in the day; they follow the same routes, but run less often. They have an N before the route number, and run from around 11 p.m. to 6 a.m. They are the only all-night public transport, as the tube stops running around midnight. Most night buses have a stop at Trafalgar Square. It is advised that you not sit alone on the top of a night bus late at night; there are many drunks and more sinister types out then.

Here's how the buses go 'round and 'round:

Get on the Bus   Most bus-stop shelters have a big map of London displaying the bus routes. There is also a list of the stops of each number bus on the route. Be careful that you're standing at the correct bus stop—on Oxford Street or Hyde Park Corner, for example, there are many buses and many stops. If your bus number is not written on the red-and-white sign, it won't stop there. The bus stop with a red symbol on a white background indicates a compulsory stop, and the signs with a white symbol on a red background are known as request stops. Supposedly, a bus will always stop at a compulsory stop, but don't believe it. When you see your bus, wave your hand to flag it down, or it may just sail sedately by (if it's full, it will definitely sail by, so don't take it personally). When preparing to get out, ring to stop the bus in advance of your stop. Ask for help if you're not sure where your stop is.

Paying Your Way   The fares of the buses are determined by how far you travel, so you should know the name of your destination. The fares go up every year, but at time of publication, the fare for zone 1 was £1, for zones 2–4, £1.20, etc. You can buy a SaverTicket book of six zone 1–2 bus tickets for £3.90, or a bus day pass for only £2. They can be purchased at a Travel Information Center, Underground station, or newsagent. You can also use the tube Travel Card. Children under age 5 ride free; children ages 5–16 pay a child's fare of 40p in zones 1 and 2 until 10 p.m., after which they pay full fare. Fourteen- and fifteen-year-olds must carry child-rate photo cards, and if your child looks borderline you may be hassled by some persnickety conductors. Photo cards are available in any post office; take a passport-size photo and proof of age.

The Tube

The first tube line ran in 1863 and carried 40,000 people the first day. It now carries millions of passengers a day; at rush hour it feels as if there are millions in your train car alone. Avoid it at peak times if possible.

It is the best possible way to get around London, even with the breakdowns and delays. The streets are just so choked that buses are too iffy when you need to get somewhere quickly. The tube's most outstanding failing is that it doesn't run 24 hours a day. The last trains leave central London around midnight and begin again around 5:30 a.m. You pay according to transport zones, as outlined above (and remember, these zones have nothing to do with this book's tourist zones), with zone 1 costing £1.60, zones 1–2 £2, zones 1–3 £2.30, zones 1–4 £3.70. Your best bet is the Travel Card as described above, or buying something called a Carnet, for which you receive ten zone-1 tickets for £11.50 (£5 for kids). The ten tickets come in a handy holder with a tube map on it. *Beware:* If you are traveling with an invalid ticket (such as trying to leave a zone-3 station with a zone-1 ticket) you are liable to be fined £10 on the spot. You will certainly be asked to pay the difference. Look on one of the big maps posted near the vending machines and ticket windows—it will show you what stations fall in which zones.

Tickets Please   Buy a ticket for your trip at the ticket window or use one of two machines. There is a big machine, which has in alphabetical order all the possible stations you might wish to go. You pick your station and the type of ticket you want (adult single journey, child single, adult return, and so on), and the machine will tell you how much money to insert. The other machine is simpler, but assumes you know how much your ticket will cost and what travel zones you'll be in. You will most likely be buying the £1.60 ticket for zone 1. You can choose one way (single) or round trip (return).

Put the ticket in the front of the turnstile, magnetic stripe down. It will come out at the top of the turnstile. Don't lose it; put it in a convenient pocket because you will need to put it into another turnstile as you exit your destination. A lost ticket will cost you £10, so hold onto it.

Reading the Map   The tube map is an amazing feat of workmanship. Before it was standardized in 1931 by transport hero Harry Beck, it looked like an explosion in a string factory, with lines snaking all over central London. The map is not an accurate geographical representation of London, and much time and grief will be saved if you look at the *A to*

Z first. Locate your destination and identify the color or pattern for each Underground line. Look for the key to the lines at the right bottom of the map. There are 12 tube London lines; to change lines, you must find the station connecting the lines, which are indicated by white circles outlined in black. The conductor may tell you while you're on board which lines you can catch at the next station, but you're better off using your map and your head. If you get on a train and are totally confused, look at the map above the windows—it's a straight line of the stops on that particular train and is much easier to read than the big map.

Which Way?   Be aware of what direction you're traveling. Each platform has a sign indicating direction. See where you are on your map and figure out which direction you want to go in and go to the correct platform.

Check the front of the train for its destination! There are a few lines, as you will see on the map, that split off into different directions. Look at the map to see where your line terminates, and make sure you get on the train with that name; the final stop is posted on the front of the train.

Tube Etiquette

A cardinal rule is to always stand to the right of the escalators to allow free passage to people who want to walk. Failure to observe this rule will always be met with an impatient reprimand. As in any big city, rush hour is a nightmare, and it is best to try to avoid the tube at this time.

You must never leave a bag unattended at a tube station. This is not so much an invitation to thieves (although it is certainly that) as it is an alarm to the commuters who will treat it as a possible explosive device. London has a history of terrorist bombings, and people tend to be cautious. You may notice that there are no trash cans on any London tube platform—trash cans are a good place to hide a bomb.

There is no smoking allowed on the tube platforms or trains.

Taxis

The famous black taxi cab of London is not always black now—many are besmirched by advertising painted all over the body, a disturbing sight indeed. This is also becoming common on buses. The taxis in London cruise the streets or line up in queues. If they are available, the yellow light atop the car will be on, and you may wave them down. You can usually get a taxi on the opposite side of the road to stop for you, so don't despair if none are going your way. They are famous for being able to make U-turns on a dime—or on a 5p piece. If there are zigzagging lines running along the curb, the taxi cannot legally stop. Move to where those lines end to get picked up.

Seekers of the Knowledge   As much a part of the London scene as their automobiles, the taxi drivers are a respected part of the work force. They have remarkable powers of navigation, of which they are justifiably proud. They train for three to five years, memorizing every street and landmark in London. You'll sometimes see people on mopeds, with maps clipped to the handlebars, looking around and making notes. These are student cab drivers. They have to learn, by heart, 60,000 routes across and around London. During their exams they have to recite these "runs" to their examiner, citing traffic lights, one-way systems, roundabouts, and landmarks. During this recital, the examiner will do everything he can to distract the student, often playing a difficult customer, hurling insults, singing, or arguing. Those who pass this stringent test are said to have "the Knowledge."

How to Take a Taxi It may be because of the respect to which drivers feel entitled that the preferred etiquette is that you do not enter the cab until you have told the driver, from the curb through the window, where you want to go. Do not ask if he knows the way; he's trained to know and what's more, he will not admit it if he doesn't (we say "he" because there are not so many women cab drivers at this time)—although to be fair, plenty of cabbies will gracefully turn to their oversize *A to Z*. When getting out of the cab, you are likewise expected to pay through the window, standing on the curb. This works to both your and the cabbie's advantage; you can get out and reach easily into your pocket or purse, and the driver doesn't have to turn around and reach through the partition. Smoking is prohibited in taxis, although if you see the driver light up, you can ask him if you might as well. Don't eat or drink in a taxi. Many cabbies own their cars—which cost upward of £27,000—and are fiercely protective of their well-being.

It is our sad duty to report that in recent years, some cab drivers, when hearing a foreign accent, will sometimes take a less than direct route to bump up the fare. These people are definitely the exception rather than the rule, and with the serpentine routes usually taken quite legitimately by a taxi, it's often hard to tell if they are playing games. Personally, American accent and all, I have never been run around like this—at least I don't think so. In his hilarious, best-selling book about England, *Notes from a Small Island,* Bill Bryson observes that, although London taxi drivers are absolutely the most excellent in the world, they do have a couple of idiosyncrasies. One is that they are incapable of driving for any distance in a straight line: "no matter where you are or what the driving conditions, every 200 feet a little bell goes off in their heads and they abruptly lunge down a side street." My own experience with London cabbies is that they are absolute geniuses at getting from point A to point B with the least amount of traffic and in the shortest amount of time. They know London better than anyone.

Worth (Almost) Every Pound I learn more about London and its roads when I take a cab, so much that I can justify the expense, which can be considerable. A short trip will cost about £5; a trip from central

London to, say, Hampstead, will be about £20 plus. Although, barring a breakdown, the tube is usually a quicker bet, it's always a pleasure to jump in a taxi and watch London go by from the dark comfort of the cab's very civilized interior. Sometimes you can also get a great conversation out of the deal.

Some drivers, on hearing an American voice, will want to tell you about their experiences in the United States or give you a heads up as to what to expect in England. Cabbies are a talkative and opinionated lot, so much so that *Private Eye,* the satirical magazine, often runs op-ed pieces by "Lord Justice Cabdriver."

You can call a black taxi if you're staying in a place where they don't cruise regularly or if it's late at night. Some companies charge extra for booking over the phone or using a credit card—ask when you call.

Computer Cabs (0207) 286-0286   **Data Cab** (0208) 964-2123

Dial a Cab (0207) 253-5000   **Radio Taxis** (0207) 272-0272

Minicabs

Minicabs are a much less reliable option than the black cabs, but they are cheaper and come in very handy in many instances, such as when you find yourself far from a tube stop in an outlying area or when you need to get back to your hotel very late at night and there's not a black cab in sight. There are plenty of reputable minicab companies, including some that have only women drivers. You can't hail a minicab on the street; in fact, do *not* get into one that stops and offers you a ride. It's not at all kosher; there are a lot of scams and dicey drivers out there. You must call to book a car; in that way you have some recourse should anything go wrong. Minicab drivers are not required to have "the Knowledge," which may be made abundantly clear by how lost they can get, but because there's a flat fee, there's at least no economical downside to this. Make sure you agree on a price when booking the cab, and confirm it with the driver when you get in. Tipping is normally between 10% and 15%. The cars are often two-door compacts—nowhere near as roomy as the black cabs—so if you have four large or five regular people, get a black cab, or ask if the minicab company has a people carrier (minivan). Addison Lee regularly uses them, which is one reason the company is so popular. Here are some good minicab companies:

A & A Chauffeurs Ltd.   **Greater London Hire Ltd.**
   (0208) 958-3344   (0208) 444-2468

Addison Lee (0207) 387-8888   **Pegasus** (0207) 622-2222

College Cars (0208) 955-6666   **Lady Cabs** (0207) 254-3501

Motorcycle Taxis

Motorcycle taxis are a new travel twist, currently also enjoying success in Paris, another clogged European city. The bike will get you through the worst possible traffic in a very short time, and the helmets are equipped with microphones so you can tell the driver to slow down. Not for the faint of heart. Call Addison Lee Taxybike (their motto: "Safe, Sedate, and You Won't Be Late") at (0207) 387-8888, or visit www.addisonlee.com.

Rail Services and Docklands Light Rail

Travel Cards can be used on some of the local commuter lines in London. The North London line is a good way to cross greater London as it cuts a swath from west (Richmond) to east (Woolwich); it stops at various tube stations along the way. It's above ground, which is a nice change of pace from the mole tunneling of the tube. Call (0845) 748-4950 for all train inquiries.

If you are using British Rail to get out of London, ask about the discounts it offers. There are a number of discount cards, which you may not think apply to you, as they are good for a year, but the savings can be enormous. Ask at any major rail station or travel agency. You can apply for the discount at the same time you buy your tickets.

The Docklands Light Rail (phone (0207) 363-9700) is clean, quiet, and rides above the ground. It services the East End, Canary Wharf, Greenwich, the *Cutty Sark,* and ends in Lewisham. It is also becoming a tourist option, and special tickets that combine rail travel with riverboat trips, plus deals on certain attractions, such as the National Maritime Museum at Greenwich, are offered. These special trains leave from Tower Gateway and Bank every hour on the hour starting at 10 a.m., and you will hear interesting commentary from a guide as you ride.

Getting around on Your Own

Renting a Car and Driving in London

It's not a good idea to rent a car to drive around London. London is a confusing, frustrating, and dangerous place to drive, even for those who are already used to driving on the left. Although you need only present a valid driving license from any country or state to rent a car, traffic laws and driving customs are quite different from those of other countries. If you are driving out to the country and must rent a car, it might be best to take the tube out to Heathrow or Gatwick and rent a car from there to avoid the problems of central London's notorious traffic.

If you do find yourself driving in England, here's a tip: The best way to remember which side of the road you're supposed be on is to just keep yourself and your steering wheel (which is on the right side of the car) in the middle of the road, and not hugging the side of the road, and you'll always be in the right place. This is the same principle in countries that drive on the left—the driver is always in the middle of the road. As for traffic roundabouts, the saying is "right has might, left is bereft"; that is to say, yield to the person on the right. And don't let the way the cars are parked throw you—you can park facing any old direction in England.

In London, the parking regulations are strict—look at lampposts to find signs outlining them. You can't park on a double yellow line ever; your car will be clamped with a Denver boot or towed. If you're clamped, there will be a sticker telling you where to pay for its removal and the additional fine; if you're towed, call (0207) 747-7474 to find out where your car was taken.

There are resident permits for parking in most neighborhoods, and you cannot park in these areas except at night and Sunday. Read the signs carefully. There are meters and Pay and Display spaces for visitors to use. Pay and Display works like this: Park your car; find the ticket machine; pay the correct amount for the desired time; and display the ticket on your windshield or dashboard. There are a number of National Car Parks (signs say NCP) around central London: call (0870) 606-7050, or go to their website at www.ncp.co.uk for locations.

The central numbers for the big rental companies (cars will cost about £60 a day) are as follows:

Alamo (0870) 400-4508;
www.alamo.com

Avis (0207) 917-6700;
www.avis.co.uk

Budget (0800) 181-181;
www.gobudget.com

Enterprise (0125) 235-3620;
www.enterprise.com

Europcar (0870) 607-5000;
www.europcar.co.uk

Hertz (0870) 844-8844;
www.hertz.co.uk

Expect to pay about £40 to fill up the tank with gas.

Bicycling

As a way of getting around London, biking is beyond nerveracking, and possibly just slightly suicidal. Between the fright and fury at the cavalier behavior of the motorists, and the filth of diesel fumes and other pollutants, it can't be good for you. But if you want to take advantage of the great parks and vehicle-free paths in London for fun and exercise, by all means do. Just look mighty sharp as you're riding through the streets. Although there are no bike-riding helmet laws in London, it won't hurt to wear one. Call the London Cycling Campaign at (0207) 928-7220 for information about renting bikes, cycling routes, safety, and security.

Motorbike Hire

On the off chance that you might want to up the two-wheeling ante, about £25 per day you can rent a motorbike or moped at Scooter, 48–50 Shepherd's Bush Road, W6; phone (0207) 610-4131; www.eel. store.co.uk. All you need is a driving license . . . and nerve.

Motorcycles don't have to pay the congestion charge, and their numbers on the streets of London have predictably gone up.

Walking

Please do. You'll be surprised at how far you can go by foot—a lot faster at times than on the bus, and certainly more pleasantly than on the tube. You'll get to see small architectural curios, drop into inviting shops and restaurants, and find alleys and mews that you wouldn't see by cab. Keep your *A to Z* handy and go ahead and get lost. You'll thank yourself for it.

Remember the maniac drivers, and be aware that your instincts when crossing the streets are all wrong. Take it slowly and *don't* try to outrun a walking light—the drivers will scare the devil out of you.

The zebra crossings, however, are where you get your own back—they belong to the pedestrian. When you see a flashing yellow light and a cross path marked with white stripes, you are in the right of way—cars *must* stop for you. There may be one or two foreigners who haven't quite got the hang of this system, so don't stride out without sensible caution.

Around big intersections such as Piccadilly Circus, Marble Arch, and Hyde Park Corner there are "subways," which are walkways beneath the street. They are well indicated with signposts, so you'll be able to know which way to go. Some are actually quite interesting—Hyde Park Corner has painted tiles giving you the goods on the duke of Wellington (whose house is right there) and the parks of London. Some of them use exit numbers and seem to go on forever. Avoid them late at night; some of the subways become little villages of sleeping homeless people.

Walking is the most interesting, healthy, revealing, ecologically sound, and inexpensive way to get around London; so bring the most comfortable shoes you have.

LOST AND FOUND

If you have left something in one of the above public conveyances, which is easily done when you're tired and jet-lagged, take heart: You just might get it back. For insurance claims you must inform the police of your loss. Do not call the emergency number; find the nearest police station by dialing 118118 information. Here are the numbers for lost property:

Buses (0207) 486-2496

Black taxis (0207) 918-2000

Train stations (railroad) (0870) 000-5151

Tube trains (0207) 486-2496

Part Six

Sight-Seeing and Tours

An Embarrassment of Riches

A trip to London surely must be on every dedicated traveler's wish list. For the indefatigable sightseer, there is an endless itinerary to follow. For one in need of a little R and R, there are theaters to enjoy and parks to kick back in. For the scholar, there is so much to learn, so much to swoon over. For more trendy types, there are clubs and shops that rival those in New York and Paris. There's so much to see and do in London that you must try to restrict yourself to only that which you find fascinating, or you'll find yourself very, very tired. There are the obvious tourist attractions—the Tower of London, the British Museum, Covent Garden, Westminster Abbey—and then there are the other bits that make London so wonderful: the parks, the themed walking tours, the obscure collections, and the marketplaces. Only you can determine what is most interesting to you and your companions, but we can help you to make your decisions.

Dissension in the Ranks

In a place like London, with so many varied attractions, you can easily disagree with your traveling companions as to what are the most important sights. You may think that visiting the Globe Theatre without seeing a play is a yawn, and your spouse may be bored silly by the very idea of a design museum. There are two ways to go about solving these fundamental problems of taste, time, and touring. One is to compromise: You see one of mine, and I'll see one of yours. This at least addresses honestly the issue of not being keen on the attraction, instead of going along grudgingly and being clearly uninterested. The other is to split up and go your own way. This has the great advantage of making it less likely that you will grow tired of each other's company, and ensures ready store of dinner conversation as you each recount your experienc

Know Thy Limits

Everyone has a threshold at which sight-seeing moves from being a joy to a torture. Your feet hurt, the lines are too long, the weather is appalling, you're hungry. These thresholds vary from person to person, but for the disabled, the elderly, and the very young, the passage over it can be uncomfortable as well as risky. There are a number of attractions in London in which you'll find no wheelchair access, or in which there are incredibly steep stairs, or where all the exhibits are too high for the young or a wheelchair user to see. You do not want to put yourself (or your companions if they are any of the above) in the position of finding out too late that the attraction just won't work. Although in our listings we try to tell you whether a place is disabled or child friendly, it is always a good idea to call first and find out for sure. There are improvements being made all the time in the interests of easier access at most attractions, museums, churches, and stately homes, so check ahead. Also, there are some places that call themselves disabled friendly, but in reality have a limit on the number of wheelchairs allowed in at a time. For children, you might want to find out if the museum you're visiting has any activities for kids. The Victoria and Albert and the British Museum are just two of the "grown-up" museums that are trying to keep the children entertained, but they do so only on weekends or school holidays (see Part Seven, "Children's London," for more specifics about touring the city with children).

Tourist Information Centers

The **London Tourist Board** has as many extremely well-stocked tourist centers as befits a city so supported by visitors. You can pick up an armful of pamphlets, brochures, maps, and fliers, and reserve tickets, tours, and hotel rooms. Before you arrive, visit their website at www.visit london.com. It's a magnificently useful and complete source. Center locations include:

Heathrow Airport Terminals 1, 2, 3. All open daily, 8:30 a.m.–6 p.m.

Liverpool Street Underground Station is in zone 3 and is open Tuesday–Saturday, 8:15 a.m.–6 p.m.; Sunday, 8:30 a.m.–5 p.m.; and Monday, 8:15 a.m.–7 p.m.

Victoria Station, in zone 9, houses a center in its forecourt that is open from 8 a.m. to 7 p.m. Winter hours may be shorter.

LondonLine will provide recorded details of events; phone (0906) 866-
but beware: It's charged at 60p per minute, plus whatever the hotel

Touring

Jump on the Bus

The best thing to do on the first day in a city is to take advantage of a hop-on, hop-off bus tour. This gives you the lay of the land, and if the day is bright, the open top of a double-decker bus is the best place to get the sunlight that helps you get over jet lag. They make stops at most of the major attractions/intersections, such as the Tower of London, Madame Tussaud's, Green Park, Hyde Park Corner, Harrods, in front of the Victoria and Albert Museum, and so on. You can pick up the buses at almost any of the significant attractions; check with your hotel to determine the closest stop. Tickets can be bought on the bus or from the bus employees at some of the bus stops. It is crucial that you get on the bus as early as possible to avoid the crushing traffic jams (congestion charging has only slightly eased them) that can make the tour a carbon monoxide-scented bummer. If you see traffic building up while you're touring, you can always hop off and continue your tour the next day or later in the afternoon, as the tour tickets are often good for 24 hours, which is great—you can break up the tour nicely. You can get your tickets online, although that seems rather extreme pre-planning to me, even with the £1 discount for online booking. Your move. Both companies offer fast-track attractions tickets to the more overcrowded spots, such as Madam Tussaud's and the Tower of London, which are well worth getting. Both of the following companies have basically the same routes and services, with tickets good for 24 hours.

Big Bus Company (phone (0207) 233-7244; www.bigbustours.com) has a Red Tour that starts at Green Park and lasts approximately two hours, and a Blue Tour that commences at Marble Arch and goes for three hours. In the summer the buses run every 15 minutes or so; in winter they go about every half hour, stopping at all the major (and minor) attractions. Tickets are £17 for adults and £8 for children ages 5–15. The Big Bus Company offers three walking tours, a river cruise, out-of-town excursions, theater tickets, and accommodation reservations.

The Original London Sightseeing Tour (phone (0208) 877-1722; www.theoriginaltour.com) offers tours in eight languages, fast-entry tickets, and four different touring options, including a river tour as part of the ticket price. Tickets are £15 for adults and £7.50 for children ages 5–15. Tickets are good for 24 hours. This company features a kids' activity pack and Kid's Club commentary.

On Your Own

You don't have to spend all that much to get a decent double-decker bus ride. There is the famous **number 11** bus that takes you past many of the same sights the tourist buses pass, for a mere fraction of the cost. Pick it up at the King's Road at World's End or the Chelsea Town Hall stops, and you'll have a good look at that famous mod street, go through Victoria, past Westminster Abbey, Whitehall, Trafalgar Square, up the Strand to St. Paul's Cathedral, and finish in the East End at Liverpool Street. All this costs less than £2.

The **number 15** is also wonderful. I met a couple of elderly Londoner ladies on it once, and they told me they often get on it to take in the sights and visit with one another without having to spend money (British seniors, or old-age pensioners, as they're called, ride free). Pick up the 15 at Paddington and ride to Marble Arch, up Oxford Street, down Regent to Piccadilly Circus, down Haymarket to Trafalgar Square, up the Strand (which turns into Fleet Street), St. Paul's Cathedral, the Tower of London, and end up at Petticoat Lane (Middlesex Street), which has a market on Sunday mornings, as well as some stalls during the week.

The **number 14** goes from Tottenham Court Road (by the British Museum) over the Thames and west to Putney Heath, passing Piccadilly, Knightsbridge, the museums of South Kensington, and the antiques shops of Fulham.

Bus **number 24** will take you north, from Victoria Station all the way to Hampstead Heath and Highgate, from which you can get an amazing view of London.

To get a look at some of South London, take the **number 2** bus from either Marylebone Station, Marble Arch, or Hyde Park Corner and ride across the Thames through Brixton, up Tulse Hill to Crystal Palace Park, where you can get out and look at the prehistoric creatures imagined and modeled by the Victorians.

Get a bus map at any tourist center or hotel lobby and check out these routes and any others that look interesting to you. If, as you're traveling, you feel you are going too far afield, just get off and jump on a bus going in the opposite direction to get back to London.

Private Tours

The **Classic Coach Company** offers a small bus in a classic design with room for 11 passengers, who are given a three-hour guided tour for £17 per seat, or you can hire the entire vehicle for £110 and up. The advantage to this coach tour is that, because it's smaller than the double-deckers, it can take you into small streets and squares that you couldn't see on the other tours. And it's very cool looking, with plenty of windows to gape from. Tours go daily at 8:30 a.m., 10 a.m., and 1 p.m. Call (0208) 390-0888, 24 hours a day, or ask your hotel to book you a spot.

You can also hire a black cab to take you around London, creating your own tour, seeing only those sights that interest you most. Call **Black Taxi**

Tours of London at (0207) 935-9363, or visit their website at www.blacktaxitours.co.uk. A two-hour tour, day or night, will cost about £75, and you can have a maximum of five people. The great thing is that you can avoid traffic jams and get into the squares, mews, and backstreets to which no tour bus can take you.

Seeing the Highlights

The double-decker bus tours are designed for seeing the sights of London in a general way. You can see where everything is in relation to everything else, perhaps find out how long the lines are for certain attractions, figure out what can be done in a day or a week, and determine which areas seem most intriguing. Taking a general tour first thing will help you make plans more efficiently for the days ahead. You'll learn that you won't be able to do the Tower of London on the same day you take a walk in Hampstead Heath, which is so far away that it's off any standard London tour itinerary. Or you will note that a trip to the National Gallery can be combined with a visit to any or all of the following: the adjacent National Portrait Galley, St. Martin-in-the-Fields, Trafalgar Square, Leicester Square, and Covent Garden, topped off by a trip to the theater.

Sight-Seeing Companies

There are a lot of tour companies in London doing very similar out-of-town and London tours for roughly the same amount of money. You can find their brochures in any hotel lobby. A word of caution: They have many courtesy hotel pick-up points in London, which sounds very convenient—who doesn't want to fall out of their hotel room into a waiting coach at 8 a.m.? But yours may just be the first stop of 15, and if you get stuck in the normal London traffic, you can be on the bus for an hour before you actually get started on the tour. You'll probably find it less annoying to meet your bus at the final departure point. When you reserve your seat, find out where the bus will actually leave for the tour, then take the tube or a taxi to get there. The downside to this evasive action is that you may not get the seat you want on the bus. The best seats are clearly the top-floor front row.

The tour companies offer half-day, morning, night, full-day, or two-day tours of London, plus tours to such places as Windsor and Leeds Castles, Eton, Hampton Court, Stonehenge, Bath, Stratford-upon-Avon, Oxford, Cambridge, Salisbury, Brighton, Dover, Canterbury, York, Chester, Warwick Castle, the Lake District, Scotland, and even Paris and Amsterdam. The price of the tour almost always includes entrance fees for the attractions and the cost of meals, and in the case of the overnight trips, the cost of accommodations.

Here are some of the tour companies; do take a look at their websites:

Astral Travels (phone (0700) 078-1016 or (0870) 902-0908; fax (0707) 071-2035; www.astraltravels.co.uk) courts small groups on mini coach day tours and won the London Tourist Board Award for Best Sight-seeing Tours from London in 2000.

Evan Evans can be reached by phone (0207) 950-1777, fax (0207) 950-1771, or www.evanevans.co.uk.

Frames Rickards can be reached by phone at (0207) 828-9720, or at www.framesrickards.co.uk.

Golden Tours Deluxe can be reached by phone (800) 456-6303 in U.S., (0207) 233-7030 in the U.K. or www.goldentours.co.uk.

Visitors Sightseeing can be contacted by phone at (0207) 636-7175, by fax at (0207) 636-3310, or at www.visitorsightseeing.co.uk.

For tours along the river: call **Catamaran Cruisers** at (0207) 987-1185, or visit www.catamarancruisers.co.uk; or **City Cruises** at (0207) 740-0400 or see www.citycruises.com. For boat rides along the canals of Little Venice and Camden Lock, call **London Waterbus Company** at (0207) 482-2550 or (0207) 482 2660, or visit their website at www.little venice.co.uk/waterbus.

Outside London

Although just getting a taste of London's richness can take all of even a long vacation, it may be a great change of pace to get out into the famous English countryside. The foot-and-mouth epidemic in 2001 resulted in many public footpaths being closed and some may still remain closed to hikers. But a trip to the country can still be wonderful, even without rambling around the countryside. There are so many delightful medieval towns and inspiring cathedrals to see. The above tour companies conduct such trips conveniently and trouble free.

You may want to rent a car to do your sight-seeing, but sometimes it's just easier to let others do the driving. Astral Tours, especially, is a good option if you're not fond of big buses with lots of people. Taking a train will work for going to Bath, Oxford, Salisbury, Cambridge, or Stratford-upon-Avon, where you can get a hotel room and walk around town, but for trips to Stonehenge or to places such as the town of Laycock or Warwick Castle, you are better off going with a tour. Go on any of the of the above companies' websites to decide where you want to go. Ask how many people have already booked—perhaps you can find a day when it will only be a handful of people. Arrange to meet the tour bus at its last stop so you don't have to tack on too much sitting time while the bus picks people up.

Some Good Side Trips

Note: All the travel times given below are for British Rail train service.

Bath is about one-and-a-half hours from Paddington Station (170 miles) and is a gorgeous Georgian town with Roman relics, famous for its Sally Lunn cakes. Jane Austen once lived there.

Brighton is one hour from Victoria station (53 miles). Brighton makes for jolly seaside and amusement-park fun, with its little shopping streets and alleys, the Brighton Pavilion, and the Oriental fantasy of George IV.

Cambridge is one hour from King's Cross Station (85 miles). Cambridge is a quiet university town, with beautiful river views and significant buildings.

Canterbury is 80 minutes from Victoria Station (50 miles). The old pilgrimages used to come to the cathedral, in which Saint Augustine converted King Ethelbert in 597, and Thomas à Becket was murdered.

Hatfield House is 20 minutes from King's Cross Station (20 miles). This is where Queen Elizabeth I spent her childhood.

Oxford is one hour from Paddington station (56 miles). Oxford is the university city of "dreaming spires" and a good jumping-off place for the Cotswolds.

St. Albans is 30 minutes from King's Cross Station (25 miles). St. Albans is an old Roman stronghold, with ruins and rose gardens.

Salisbury is one-and-a-half hours from Waterloo Station (84 miles), with a magnificent cathedral, military museum, and beautiful flower-filled neighborhoods around the Cathedral. Stonehenge is a short drive away.

Stratford-upon-Avon Paddington Station to Stratford takes about three hours (91 miles). This is Shakespeare's town—he was born, married, and buried there—and the town is devoted to him, but has other attractions as well.

Windsor is 30 minutes from Waterloo Station (20 miles), and you can see the storybook castle by the Thames, plus a fine old town with good pubs. The playing fields of Eton are nearby.

NOT TO BE MISSED IN LONDON: A Highly Subjective List

- The British Airways London Eye (see page 176)
- The British Museum (see page 178)
- The Globe Theatre (see page 190)
- Hampton Court Palace (see page 193)
- Museum of London (see page 209)
- The National Portrait Gallery (see page 213)
- St. Paul's Cathedral (see page 223)
- The Science Museum (see page 224)
- The Tate Modern (see page 231)
- The Tower of London (see page 233)
- Victoria and Albert Museum (see page 235)
- Westminster Abbey (see page 239)

NOT TO BE MISSED IN LONDON: A Highly Subjective List *(continued)*

- Hyde Park on Sunday (see page 246)
- St. James's Park (see page 250)
- A street market on the weekend (see page 352)

Romantic London

One really doesn't associate romance with London in the way one might with Paris or Venice, but that's not to say there aren't some romantic places to seek out with your beloved. Judging by the snogging (kissing) that goes on in Hyde Park, we'd have to say that taking a blanket, a jug of wine, and your special someone to the park for a lie around in the sun is one of London's favorite pastimes for couples, and it's free. If you need exercise, get in a paddleboat built for two and tool around the Sepentine. Take a night cruise along the Thames, or sit on a bench at sunset on the Thames at the end of Oakley Street, watch the birds circling overhead, and wait for the lights to illuminate the spectacular Albert Bridge.

A romantic restaurant would be **Momo** (zone 8; 25 Heddon Street, off Regent Street, W1; (0207) 434-4040; tube: Oxford Circus); it's a Middle-Eastern restaurant done exquisitely in *Arabian Nights* fantasy style. The quite expensive **Pont de la Tour** (zone 5; Butler's Wharf, 36D Shad Thames, SE1; (0207) 403-8403; tube: London Bridge or Tower Hill) has good food and wonderful views of Tower Bridge, which can be pretty romantic, unless you truly only have eyes for each other.

The most romantic hotels are **The Portobello** (ask for the room with the round bed) and **The Gore** (request The Venus, the Tudor, or the Miss Ada suite). And, of course, you can't go wrong at the **Ritz** for romance—check out the weekend break prices and tell them you want a honeymoon-type room or, better still, a suite (see Part Three, "Hotels," for more information).

Agent Provocateur (zone 10; 16 Pont Street, SW1; (0207) 235-0229; tube: Sloane Square) sells *very* sexy underwear that's erotic and sophisticated at the same time. And for chocolate massage-oil bars and bath salts for two, go to **Lush** in Covent Garden (zone 7; Unit 11, Central Piazza; (0207) 240-4570; tube: Covent Garden) or in Chelsea (zone 11; 123 King's Road, SW3; (0207) 376-8348; tube: Sloane Square).

Oh, Such a Perfect Day

What constitutes a perfect day in London will naturally depend on who's in your party and what your keenest interests are. One person's poison is another one's mead, as they say. But if I were to try to conjure up a day that would hit as many of my personal favorite high notes as possible, it would go something like this:

I would want to start my day with the best cappuccino in London, which would be near my hotel in the Knightsbridge or South Kensington area: Orsini's Café (zone 11, 8a Thurloe Place; phone (0207) 581-5553 tube: South Kensington) is across the street from the Victoria and Albert Museum and just east of the Rembrandt Hotel. It's a friendly family-run café that feels like a little slice of Italy in London. I love having a cappuccino and toasted bread at a pavement table. If you require a more hearty breakfast, go up the street to Patisserie Valerie—the croissants are unlike those anywhere else, and they serve a large selection of hot breakfasts (zone 10, 215 Brompton Road (phone (0207) 823-9971; tube: Knightsbridge).

After breakfast, go look at the Brompton Oratory Church (zone 11; 1 Thurloe Place; tube: South Kensington). It's an amazing edifice, with small chapels lining the enormous hall, and a rotunda to rival St. Paul's. Go through the churchyard and out to Ennismore Gardens, which you'll take up to Hyde Park, a couple of blocks away. Amble around the park, and go to the riding ring and see if any of the queen's guards are exercising their horses or rehearsing any ceremonies. Go feed a duck or two at the Serpentine.

Exit the park at Exhibition Road and head for the Victoria and Albert Museum down the street (opens at 10 a.m.). Wander around the stained-glass windows upstairs, sit in the Fakes and Forgeries Statue Court, and go admire the William Morris tearoom. If the weather's good, sit in the Pirelli Courtyard for a spell, then walk or take a taxi up Sydney Street to the Chelsea Town Hall. Across from the hall is the Bourbon-Handy Antiques Centre for browsing or buying; next to it is Daisy and Tom's, a wonderful place to buy British books for your little friends. And then, if the weather's warm, have lunch outside at one of the restaurants at the Chelsea Marketplace, or try the Vietnamese noodles at Phat Phuc for an inexpensive and healthy lunch. Within the marketplace is a good health-food store, Neal's Yard Remedies shop, and a marvelous garden center.

Stroll down the King's Road toward Sloane Square, maybe do a little window-shopping, and catch the 11 bus wherever possible. Take the 11 past all the great sights: Westminster Abbey, Big Ben, Whitehall, Trafalgar Square, up Fleet Street, to St. Paul's. If you have the energy, climb up to the top of St. Paul's and enjoy the view. If not, just have a seat in the church and admire the craftsmanship that went into this magnificent building, or perhaps rest in the courtyard of the church and watch the tourists. Catch a bus toward Trafalgar Square and go to Leicester Square to buy half-price theater tickets at the kiosk there for that evening. There's no saying what plays will be available, but it's always great to see

an Oscar Wilde or Noël Coward play if possible: so very, very English.
Check to see what stars are performing: You may get the pleasure of seeing Judi Dench, one of the Redgraves, or Maggie Smith tread the boards.

Then, depending on the time, your next move would be a toss-up
between having tea at the Ritz (no blue jeans allowed) or Fortnam and
Masons, or doing some brass-rubbing in the crypt at St. Martin-in-the-
Fields'. It's a real treat: You pick out one of the many medieval brass plates
with engraved images, get a piece of paper and some waxy chalk, and rub
the chalk over the plate, making a print of the design. Take your time with
the rubbing, enjoying the atmosphere and the pastime. Buy some gifts in
the wonderful shops (one at the brass-rubbing area and one in the other
part of the crypt). Then walk over to Covent Garden and watch the
buskers (street entertainers) at work. Dinner at last. For the atmosphere
and the Yorkshire pudding, try Rules, the oldest surviving restaurant in
London (zone 7; 35 Maiden Lane, WC2; (0207) 836-5314; tube: Charing
Cross). Yes, it's a tourist trap, but it is also redolent of a long-gone era, with
the photos and cartoons on the wall charting its history since it opened in
1798. And where else can you get grouse, woodcock, and partridge?

You will love the play, especially because you will have paid half price
for some perfectly decent seats. You will love how they sell delicious ice
cream right in the theater at the intermission, and you will be proud of
yourself for already ordering your refreshments before the play started
and finding them waiting for you at the bar at intermission. When the
play gets out at 10:30 or 11 p.m., walk over to Ronnie Scott's (zone 7; 47
Frith Street, W1; (0207) 439-0747; tube: Tottenham Court Road) and
listen to jazz until it's time to call a minicab and go back to your hotel.

Walking in and around London

Walking is by far the best way to experience London. Grab a map and
your camera, select a starting point, and just begin to explore. You never
know what you may find once you move off of London's bustling main
thoroughfares: a cobbled alleyway with a quaint café, a medieval church,
or even a dreamy view across the river. Below are a number of suggested
walks covering a diverse range of areas. Many cross the paths of some
great London attractions and can create an entire day's worth of wandering if you decide to stop off and visit some of the sights along the way.

You might also want to try out **The Original London Walks** (phone
(0207) 624-3978; www.walks.com), which offers 120 weekly themed
walks dedicated to Jack the Ripper, ghosts of London, lost palaces, The
Beatles, rock and roll, literary London, the swinging 1960s, Princess
Diana, Charles Dickens, and so many more. You can pick up a leaflet at
most hotels or check for daily events in *Time Out*. Another company is
Stepping Out (phone (0208) 881-2933; fax (0207) 405-6036).

Walking on Your Own

If you prefer to walk at your own pace, try the walks we've outlined here.

ZONE 3 City of London: Through the Centuries

Time to Allow 3–4 hours depending on indoor visits

Distance Approximately 1½ miles

Sights Museum of London; St. Botolph, Aldersgate; Postman's Park; St. Bartholomew-the-Great Church; National Postal Museum; Christ Church, Greyfriars; St. Paul's Cathedral; Guildhall (including Guildhall Clock Museum and Guildhall Art Gallery); St. Lawrence Jewry

Tube St. Paul's or Barbican

This walk gives just a glimpse of the vast array of architecture that has evolved in London over the centuries, from the ancient Roman wall that once enclosed the fourth-century city of Londinium, to the skyscrapers of the modern financial district. Begin your wanderings at the Museum of London, looking out from the museum's terrace, where you are sur-rounded by concrete and glass. This is twentieth-century London, with heavy traffic and office buildings. This is a London that would make a Londoner from the last century (or even from just before the Blitz) weep with confusion and sorrow. However, if you know where to look, you will glimpse bits of Old—the London of medieval peasants, Renaissance grandeur, and Victorian sentimentality. A stop at the museum is great for getting your bearings on London's diverse historical eras.

After enjoying an engaging few hours of history, head across the traffic circle to Aldersgate. Locate Little Britain Street on the right; St. Botolph Church is on the corner. The church's classical Georgian interior is a glo-rious contrast to its bland and unassuming exterior. Turn right as you exit the church and enter Postman's Park. This hidden churchyard was dedi-cated by the Victorians in 1900 as a memorial to "heroes of everyday life" who died in acts of bravery. In the center of the intimate park, you will find the protected wall of memorials. One epitaph reads, "Saved a lunatic woman from suicide at Woolwich Arsenal, but was himself run over by the train." Exiting the park on the opposite side, turn right onto King Edward Street, then follow Little Britain around to the left to where it deposits you in Smithfield Square.

In medieval times, the marketplace of Smithfield Green was thriving with merchants, peddlers, peasants, and livestock. Jousts, tournaments, horse fairs, and hangings have all been held here. To your left is St. Bartholomew's Hospital. Begun in 1123 as a priory and hospice, it is London's oldest hospital. Out front is a memorial to Sir William Wallace, known as Braveheart, the Scot who defied a king and was torn in quar-ters by four horses for the crime of treason. If you venture inside the hos-pital's main entrance, you will find the small hospital church of St.

Bartholomew-the-Less and an eighteenth-century courtyard. Back out on the square and to your right you will see a half-timbered, Tudor gatehouse. Through here is a gem of medieval London, the Priory Church of St. Bartholomew-the-Great, also dating back to 1123. Don't miss the opportunity to take a look at this breathtaking example of original twelfth-century Norman architecture.

Making your way back to Little Britain, turn right onto King Edward Street, using the dome of St. Paul's Cathedral before you as a guide. Past Postman's Park and the National Postal Museum, at the end of Little Britain, are the remains of Christopher Wren's Christ Church, Greyfriars. Originally built in 1691, it was destroyed during air raids in World War II. Today, the tower and walls enclose a lovely trellised garden marking the original location of the church columns and center aisle. Cross Newgate Street and turn left. Beyond the tube station entrance is the churchyard of St. Paul's Cathedral. Vastly different from medieval St. Bart's, Christopher Wren's Renaissance masterpiece is the second largest cathedral in the world. Stop here to see the glorious interior or perhaps climb the dome for unparalleled city views.

Wandering back through the churchyard, turn right and head east on Cheapside. Cross over and make a left on Wood Street and then follow Milk Street as it bears to the right. This area was another of London's medieval marketplaces, although the only remnants are the street names—Bread Street, Milk Street, Honey Lane—to remind you of its past. Just ahead is the entrance to Guildhall, the headquarters for the Corporation of London. Behind the bleak twentieth-century facade lies the impressive Great Hall, open 10 a.m.–4:30 p.m. Monday through Friday. Next door, the Guildhall Library houses a clock museum (open 9:30 a.m.–4:30 p.m., Monday through Friday) and a remarkable art collection. Also, if you can catch it open, be sure to stop in and see the spectacular interior of the Church of St. Lawrence Jewry located on the main road. The name is derived from its location on the site of London's early Jewish ghetto. Finally, follow King Street south to Victoria Street. Turn right and end your walk at Mansion House tube station.

ZONE 1 Old Hampstead Village

Time to Allow 2 hours

Distance Approximately 1½–2 miles

Sights Church Row, St. John's-at-Hampstead, Fenton House, Admiral's House, Burgh House, Flask Walk and Well Walk, Downshire Hill, Keats House, Hampstead Heath, Hampstead High Street

Also Nearby Freud Museum, Kenwood House

Tube Hampstead

The history of Hampstead has always been tied closely to its hill, its heath, and its healthy environment, and in the early 1700s, Hampstead became a booming spa town. The area's iron-rich water was said to cure all manner of ailments and you could purchase flasks of the vile-tasting stuff for 3p a bottle or bathe in it at one of the local bathhouses. Today, narrow streets lined with lovingly restored eighteenth-century homes help the village retain much of its charming Georgian atmosphere.

Arriving in Hampstead via the underground, you come up London's deepest (and creakiest) elevator shaft near the top of Hampstead Hill in the village center. Heath Street and Hampstead High Street stretch before you, lined with shops, cafés, and restaurants—definitely a great area in which to stop for tea at the end of your walk. Exiting the tube station, cross over and turn left on Heath Street, then right on Church Row, one of the best-preserved streets in London. Notice the grand wrought-iron work, the remains of early eighteenth-century oil lampstands, and the intricately detailed windows over many of the homes' main entrances. These fanlights, illuminated from behind by candles, helped identify one's home after dark in the days before street lighting. Famous residents here included George du Maurier and H. G. Wells. At the end of the line of trees sits St. John's-at-Hampstead, consecrated in 1747. Take some time to wander the graveyard and church then head up Holly Walk.

At the top of the hill on the right, St. Mary's Church is nestled among a row of homes. One of London's oldest Roman Catholic churches, its discreet location is due to its existence before religious tolerance was granted in 1829. Make a right and follow Mount Vernon down to where it meets up with Hampstead Grove. Turn left. Another worthwhile stop is Fenton House on the right. This wonderfully preserved seventeenth-century home today houses an exquisite collection of Asian, European, and English china, needlework, and furniture, but its finest attraction is its unique collection of early musical instruments, including Handel's harpsichord. Beyond Fenton House, turn left onto Admiral's Walk. Look carefully at the house and you will see the nautical alterations made by Lt. Fountain North in 1775. North adapted the roof to resemble the deck of a ship, complete with flagstaff and cannon, which were fired to celebrate naval victories. P. L. Travers and Walt Disney fans should find this all vaguely familiar; the character and home of Admiral Boom in *Mary Poppins* was based on this eccentric individual.

At the end of Hampstead Grove, where it runs into the main thorough-fare of Heath Street, you will find a small reservoir on your left. Whitstone Pond, built in 1856, allowed Londoners who had successfully navigated the steep muddy roads to the hilltop to clean their carriages by walking their horses down the ramps and through the pond. Crossing Heath Street, begin your journey down the hill and alongside Hampstead Heath, turning right at Squire's Mount and passing some lovely cottages, which date to 1704. Continue on Cannon Lane, turning left on Well Road, so named for the spring that gave the town its reputation for health. Famous residents here included D. H. Lawrence, J. B. Priestly, and John Constable. Turning left on New End Square brings you past Burgh House, the 1703 home of Hampstead Spa's physician, William Gibbons. Today the building is a lovely local museum, meeting place, and exhibition space. There is a small tearoom downstairs if you are needing a snack or rest. To your left is Well Walk and to your right, Flask Walk. Just up Flask Walk on your right is a bathhouse that was actually in use by some locals until the late 1960s. Cross Well Walk and enjoy a downhill stroll on Willow Road. At the bottom, turn right on Downshire Hill.

Another picturesque street lined with nineteenth-century homes and gardens, its centerpiece is St. John's-at-Hampstead Church, opened in 1823. If open, it is worth taking a quick peek inside. Turning left on Keats Grove brings you to our last stop. John Keats lived in Hampstead from 1818 to 1820, and it is here that he produced many of his most famous works. The home is carefully restored and decorated as Keats would have known it, and the intimate museum is a wonderful tribute to his short, tragic life. Upon leaving Keats House, turn left and head back up Keats Grove, then left again on Downshire Hill. Make a right on Rosslyn Hill and enjoy some window-shopping or stop in one of the many cafés on your way back toward the Hampstead tube station, just a five-minute walk up the road.

ZONES 7 AND 9 Royal London: From Palace to Parliament

Time to Allow 3–4 hours

Distance Approximately 2½ miles

Sights Royal Mews, Queen's Gallery, Buckingham Palace, St. James's Park, Cabinet War Rooms, Admiralty Arch, Trafalgar Square, National Gallery, National Portrait Gallery, St. Martin-in-the-Fields Church, Royal Horse Guards, Banqueting House, 10 Downing Street, Cenotaph, Houses of Parliament, St. Margaret's Church, Westminster Abbey

Tube Victoria

This walk takes you past many of London's most popular sights. London's history, royalty, and fabulous architecture are thoroughly represented as we travel throughout Westminster, the home to London's monarchy and Parliament. The walk affords plenty of opportunities to stop along the way, so the length of the walk depends entirely on your stamina.

Begin your walk at Victoria tube station. Turn right on Buckingham Palace Road, following signs for the palace. Just beyond Lower Grosvenor Place you will find the entrance for the Royal Mews on the left. Housed here in the palace stables is an impressive display of royal carriages; the oldest, made in 1762 for George III, is still used for coronations. Just past the Royal Mews is the Queen's Gallery, recently renovated and upgraded to display even more of the royal monarch's incredible collection of privately owned works of art. Continuing, you will soon arrive in the palace forecourt.

Buckingham Palace has been the official London residence of the sovereign since George III bought the place from Lord Buckingham in 1762. The palace is home and office for Her Majesty, and its elaborately decorated rooms are in continuous use for state affairs, official receptions, ceremonial occasions, and Parliamentary meetings. See the attractions listing for opening times; it is currently open to the public only from August through October. North of the palace is Green Park, but you need to locate St. James's Park, to the right of The Mall, as that is our next area to explore.

Enter the park by Birdcage Walk, and wander east along the pond's edge. St. James's is the oldest of London's parks. It started life as part of the private grounds of St. James's Palace, but was opened to the public during the reign of the Stuart monarchs. Cross over the bridge, stopping to take in the stunning views of the palace to the west and the Horse Guards Parade to the east. As you continue to walk along the path beside the lake, the London Eye Ferris wheel, Westminster Abbey, and St. Stephen's Clock Tower can be seen through the trees, wildlife skitter past or glide by on the water, and if you're lucky, the sun will shine a few rays through the clouds above. Charles II, Samuel Pepys, and John Milton have all enjoyed such views (except for that of the London Eye, of course, that has an elegance we are sure they would have loved). The most famous residents of the park are the pelicans, who have delighted visitors there since the seventeenth century. Every afternoon they parade across the lawn on Duck Island to receive their daily fish dinner, and they thoroughly enjoy the sanctuary provided here, along with the 20 or more other species of duck and goose that call St. James's home.

As you reach the other side of the park, cross Horse Guards Road. Just in front of you, King Charles Street ends in a pedestrianized stairway, and to the right of this is the entrance to the Cabinet War Rooms. Winston Churchill and his cabinet carried out operations here during World War II. From the War Rooms, turn right on Horse Guards Road, passing the Horse Guards Parade, where the Changing of the Guard occurs daily at 11:30 a.m. (Sunday at 10 a.m.). Never take the daily changing of the guard as a given: It is frequently cancelled (call (0906) 866-3344 for recorded information). Turn right on The Mall and walk under Admiralty Arch and into Trafalgar Square. In the center stands Nelson's Column, the memorial to Britain's best-loved national hero, Admiral Lord

Horatio Nelson, who defeated Napoléon at the Battle of Trafalgar in 1806. The square is the location for frequent political demonstrations, London's annual Christmas tree lighting, and New Year's countdowns. The famous feeding of pigeons was outlawed a few years ago to the relief of the cleaning crew and the disappointment of the ornithologically courageous. Behind is the National Gallery, where you could spend hours enjoying one of the world's greatest art collections. To the right is the eighteenth-century church of St. Martin-in-the-Fields, definitely worth a stop. Its simple but elegant interior offers free lunchtime concerts. Downstairs, the church's Café-in-the-Crypt provides soups and sandwiches.

Leaving Trafalgar Square, walk down Whitehall (the street directly opposite the National Gallery). You will pass the front of the Horse Guards Building, with its guards at attention, and almost directly opposite is the Banqueting House, all that remains of the great palace at Whitehall, which burned to the ground in 1698. Prior to this loss, the palace was the site of numerous historical events, such as the marriage of Henry VIII to Anne Boleyn and the execution of Charles I during the English Civil War. Others who have lived here include Cardinal Wolsey, Oliver Cromwell, Charles II, and William III and Mary II. Further along on the right is 10 Downing Street, home of Britain's prime minister, although you are not likely to see much, because the street is guarded and gated. The Cenotaph, in the middle of Whitehall, is Britain's memorial to those who died in World War I. It is the focal point of the country's Remembrance Day ceremonies, which include two minutes of silence throughout the entire country on the 11th minute of the 11th hour of the 11th day of the 11th month each year.

Not far ahead, you will begin to see the towers of the Palace of Westminster coming into view. Once you have arrived in Parliament Square, you have a number of choices before you. You can wander out onto Westminster Bridge for the best views of Westminster Palace and St. Stephen's Tower. You can sit in on debates in the Houses of Parliament or explore the sixteenth-century St. Margaret's Church (where Sir Walter Raleigh is laid to rest). And take the opportunity at walk's end to enjoy inspiring hymns sung by the Westminster Boys Choir during the daily choral evensong at Westminster Abbey, possibly the most visited tourist sight and certainly one of the most beautiful churches in London.

For Museum Lovers

If you love going to museums, you already have a lot in common with typical Londoners. London is crammed with wonderful museums, many of which are free of charge.

There's a remarkable website that details current and upcoming exhibitions at 2,000 museums in London and across the country; it also offers virtual tours of the permanent collections of the museums featured. It's a great way to see some of the smaller, harder-to-visit museums without leaving your desk. The website's goal is to represent Britain's entire cultural history—no small undertaking. Visit it at www.24hourmuseum.org.uk.

Saving Money on Museum Admissions

There are ways to save on the admission fees of museums. The London-pass, a program launched by the London Tourist Board in 1999 affords fast-track, reduced, or free entry into more than 50 fee-charging attractions, free travel on tubes, trains, and buses; discounts at a number of restaurants; free phone rental; discounts on film developing; free walking tours; and a plethora of other incentives to buy. They had to pull out all the stops on making the Londonpass attractive since so many museums dropped their entrance fees in late 2001. It's not exactly inexpensive, at a starting price for a one-day pass of £23 (without transport or the 17.5 percent VAT) for adults and £15 for children, but if you are planning to go to, say, the Tower of London, at £13.50 for adults and £9 for children, and then want to take a river cruise to Hampton Court or see the Tower Bridge Experience, it may be worth it, especially with all the extras, such as free skating or bowling at Firstbowl Queensway, or £4.50 worth of free brass rubbing at St. Martins. Passes can be purchased at www.london pass.com or at the British Visitor Centre (1 Regent Street, south of Piccadilly Circus).

Name	Type	Author's Rating
LONDON ATTRACTIONS		
Zone 1: North London		
Burgh House	Museum with exhibition and concert space	★★
Freud Museum	Historic home and museum	★★★
Kenwood House (The Iveagh Bequest)	Georgian villa and art gallery	★★★★
Zone 2: Bloomsbury and Holborn		
British Museum	Among the most famous museums in the world	★★★★★
Dickens House	Historic home and museum	★
Dr. Johnson's House	Historic home and museum	★★
Sir John Soane's Museum	Historic home and museum	★★★★
Somerset House	Historic home and art galleries	★★★★★

LONDON ATTRACTIONS (continued)

Name	Type	Author's Rating
Zone 3: The City and Barbican		
Bank of England Museum	Museum of money and banking	★★
Millennium Bridge	Footbridge across the Thames	★★★
The Monument	Commemorating the Great Fire of 1666	★★★
Museum of London	Museum of the city's history	★★★★★
Old Bailey	London's central criminal courts	★★★
St. Paul's Cathedral	London's most prominent cathedral	★★★
Tower Bridge	Offers terrific views	★★
Tower of London	Ancient fortress	★★★★★
Zone 4: East End		
Bethnal Museum of Childhood	Large museum of toys	★★★
Windsor Castle	Queen's country house in Hertfordshire	★★★★
Zone 5: South London		
The British Airways London Eye	Observation wheel	★★★★★
Clink Exhibition	Recreation of a medieval prison	★★★
Dali Universe	Surrealist master's works	★★★★
Design Museum	Changing exhibits of exemplars of design	★★
The Globe Theatre	Reconstructed Shakespearean theater	★★★★
HMS *Belfast*	Royal Navy battle ship from WWII	★★
Imperial War Museum	British military experience	★★
London Aquarium	Wonderland of fish	★★★★
London Dungeon	Horror attraction	★★★
Millennium Bridge	Footbridge across the Thames	★★★
Old Operating Theatre, Museum, and Herb Garret	Museum of old medical equipment	★★★★
Saatchi Gallery	Best of young British modern art	★★★
Southwark Cathedral	Small medieval church	★★★
Tate Modern	Museum of international modern art	★★★★
Tower Bridge	Offers terrific views	★★
Zone 6: Greenwich and Docklands		
Cutty Sark	Restored sailing clipper ship	★★★
National Maritime Museum and Queen's House	Largest maritime museum in the world	★★★★
Royal Greenwich Observatory	Location of world's prime meridian	★★★

LONDON ATTRACTIONS (continued)

Name	Type	Author's Rating
Zone 7: Soho and the West End		
Guildhall	Corporate headquarters for the City of London	★★
London Transport Museum	Interactive museum of trams, buses, and trains	★★★★
National Gallery	Art gallery	★★★★★
National Portrait Gallery	Famous faces of England	★★★★★
Zone 8: Mayfair and Piccadilly		
Apsley House (The Wellington Museum)	Historic home and museum	★★★
Royal Academy of Arts	Museum and exhibition venue	★★★★
Zone 9: Victoria and Westminster		
Big Ben Clock Tower	Monument	Not rated
Buckingham Palace	Stately home of the queen	★★★
The Cabinet War Rooms	Secret WWII headquarters	★★★
Changing of the Guard	Grand old tradition	★★
Houses of Parliament	Britain's working chambers of government	★★
Queen's Gallery, Buckingham Palace	Art gallery	★★★
Royal Mews, Buckingham Palace	Where royal carriages and queen's horses are kept	★★★
Tate Britain	Museum of English painters	★★★★
Westminster Abbey	Historically important church	★★★★
Zone 10: Knightsbridge and Belgravia		
The Wellington Arch	Small, specialty museum of architecture	★★
Zone 11: Chelsea and South Kensington		
Carlyle's House	Historic home and museum	★★★
Natural History Museum	Old and modern exhibits	★★★
Science Museum	Huge, excellent museum	★★★★
Victoria and Albert Museum	Museum of decorative arts	★★★★★
Zone 12: West London		
Chiswick House	Stately home and gardens	★★★
Hampton Court Palace	Royal palace and gardens	★★★★★
Hogarth's House	Historic home	★★

Name	Type	Author's Rating
LONDON ATTRACTIONS *(continued)*		
Zone 13: Kensington, Holland Park, Notting Hill		
Albert Memorial	Outdoor memorial	★★
Kensington Palace State Rooms	Stately home of Kensington Gardens	★★★★
Leighton House Museum and Art Gallery	Historic home	★★★
Linley Sambourne House	Historic home	★★★
Zone 14: Bayswater, Marylebone, Little Venice, St. John's Wood		
Madame Tussaud's Waxworks	World-famous wax museum	★★
Pollock's Toy Museum	Adventure into toys past	★★★★
Sherlock Holmes Museum	Museum	★★★★
Wallace Collection	Private collection of 19th-century Anglo-French art	★★★
Zone 15: Regent's Park and Camden Town		
British Library at St. Pancras	Multidisciplinary cultural collection	★★★★
London Zoo	Modernized old zoo	★★★

Museums and Attractions

Important note: Please be sure to call the following places before you go; opening times can be subject to change without notice.

For a look into London's parks and green spaces, see "Green and Pleasant Lands: Parks of London" on page 242. Also, at the end of this chapter is a profile of Greenwich.

Albert Memorial

Type of Attraction Outdoor memorial to a beloved prince consort

Location Zone 13; Kensington Gardens, west of Exhibition Road, SW7; tube: High Street Kensington

Admission Free

Hours Daily, dawn to dusk

When to Go A sunny day, or at night when the floodlights are on

Special Comments Bring binoculars so you can see the amazing detail of the high parts of the memorial.

Overall Appeal by Age Group

Pre-school ★★		Teens ★★		Over 30 ★★
Grade school ★★		Young Adults ★★		Seniors ★★

Author's Rating ★★

How Much Time to Allow 20 minutes, plus time to hang around on the steps. It's a good people-watching place, where talented inline skaters congregate on weekends.

Description and Comments This memorial, built by a grieving Queen Victoria after her husband's death from typhoid at the age of 42, is no small thrill to see, as it had been covered in plastic and scaffolding for over a decade while being restored. It had been stripped of its gold in 1915, so we are in the privileged position of being the first generation in almost a century to see it in all its exuberant neo-Gothic gilded glory (it cost three times as much to build as one of the finest churches in Kensington built at the same time and caused an uproar in Parliament). There are some Londoners who find the entire thing hideous and are appalled at the millions of pounds spent for its conservation. But whatever one might think of its artistry, it is a visual knockout. Check it out at night with the floodlights on it to appreciate a view the Victorians were denied.

The memorial can be seen from many angles in Hyde Park and Kensington Gardens, but don't imagine you have experienced its full flavor until you have looked the buffalo square in the eye.

Touring Tips Make this part of your Kensington Palace/Gardens and Hyde Park day.

Apsley House (The Wellington Museum)

Type of Attraction Former home of the duke of Wellington

Location Zone 8; 149 Piccadilly, W1; tube: Hyde Park Corner

Admission £4.50 for adults; free for children under age 16

Hours Tuesday–Sunday, 11 a.m.–5 p.m.; last entry at 4:30 p.m.

Phone (0207) 499-5676

Website www.vam.ac.uk

When to Go Anytime

Special Comments There is no wheelchair access, but there are steps into the house and between floors. If you walk along the pedestrian subway below Hyde Park Corner, you can see the story of Apsley House and the duke of Wellington rendered on the tiles on the wall, a good way to prepare for the visit to the house.

Overall Appeal by Age Group

Pre-school ★		Teens ★★		Over 30 ★★★
Grade school ★★		Young Adults ★★★		Seniors ★★★

Author's Rating ★★★

How Much Time to Allow 45 minutes to an hour; more if you really love old masters

Description and Comments This grand house was given to the duke of Wellington as a splendid reward for his military successes in the Napoléonic Wars. While the Hyde Park Corner traffic circle whirls in front of the house, the windows in the back of Apsley House look out onto a serene vista of Hyde Park, the rose gardens, and the occasional horseback riders. Apsley is of interest to art lovers for the works it houses of such old masters as Velázquez, Goya, and Rubens, along with some lesser luminaries. The basement houses a collection of political cartoons that will teach you about the duke and his times.

Touring Tips This is a very small, quick-hit kind of place, and it fits in well with a walk through Hyde Park and a visit to the Wellington Arch, before moving on through Green and St. James's Parks.

Bank of England Museum

Type of Attraction Historical displays tracing the rise of banking

Location Zone 3; Threadneedle Street, EC2 (museum entrance on Bartholomew Lane); tube: Bank

Admission Free

Hours Monday–Friday, 10 a.m.–5 p.m.; closed weekends and bank holidays

Phone (0207) 601-5545

Website www.bankofengland.co.uk

When to Go Anytime

Special Comments Disabled friendly, with portable ramps available on request

Overall Appeal by Age Group

Pre-school —		Teens ★★		Over 30 ★★
Grade school ★★		Young Adults ★★		Seniors ★★

Author's Rating ★★

How Much Time to Allow 1 hour

Description and Comments This is the only part of the massive fortress that is the Bank of England, known as The Old Lady of Threadneedle Street, that mere mortals can enter. One display shows the evolution of the banknote from 1694—when the bank was formed to lend money to the government to pay for King James II's war against France—to the present; much of the currency used over time can be viewed here. Another display is modeled after the first bank and includes mannequins of wigged clerks and a huge fireplace behind mahogany counters. A video shows real footage from the building of the present bank in the 1930s, and there are interactive computer screens that provide a lot of information. Be warned: The displays require quite a bit of reading, as well as a particular interest in money and banking.

Bethnal Museum of Childhood

Type of Attraction Largest museum of toys in the world

Location Zone 4; Cambridge Heath Road, E2; tube: Bethnal Green

Admission Free

Hours Daily, 10 a.m.–5:50 p.m.; closed Friday

Phone (0208) 980-2415

Website www.museumofchildhood.co.uk

When to Go Anytime

Special Comments Call ahead to arrange wheelchair access (phone (0208) 983-5205). Art workshops for children over age 3 and a soft play area for children ages 5 and under are available only on weekends.

Overall Appeal by Age Group

Pre-school ★★★	Teens ★★★	Over 30 ★★★
Grade school ★★★	Young Adults ★★★	Seniors ★★★

Author's Rating ★★★

How Much Time to Allow 90 minutes

Description and Comments Housed in a building directly across the street from the Bethnal Green tube station, the Museum of Childhood is part of the Victoria and Albert Museum. It has an unparalleled collection of children's toys and accessories: dollhouses from as far back as the seventeenth century, model trains, hobby horses, old mechanical games and toys (you must pay 20p to use them), dolls of every possible kind, teddy bears, and even old-fashioned prams and nursery furniture. Not surprisingly, the children seem to prefer pumping the mechanical toys full of coins to admiring the antiques behind glass.

Big Ben Clock Tower

Type of Attraction Look-only clock tower; enduring symbol of London

Location Zone 9; Parliament Square, SW1; tube: Westminster

Admission One cannot enter the tower

Hours 24 hours a day

Website www.londontouristboard.com

When to go When you're in the area

Description and Comments Big Ben is not an attraction, but just a beautiful piece of architecture that you can set your watch to. It is the most recognizable symbol of the city, and replicas of Big Ben are at the top of most visitors' must-have souvenir list.

In 1834, the old Palace of Westminster burned to the ground and Parliament decided to build itself a Gothic-style replacement. The clock tower was part of the grand plan, but due to its exacting specifications, construction took some time and was beset by difficulties. Big Ben refers in fact to the actual bell that chimes, and it was Big Trouble from the start. The first bell cast cracked almost immediately—possibly due to the weight of the clapper—and had to be recast in a smaller format. The clock's hands were too heavy to move, and also had to be replaced. The bell cracked again, and was silent for three years, until a solution was found in 1862. Big Ben has been ringing out the famous Westminster chimes ever since.

The British Airways London Eye

Type of Attraction The world's biggest observation wheel

Location Zone 5; in Jubilee Gardens, next to County Hall by Westminster Bridge, on the south bank of the Thames; tube: Westminster or Waterloo

Admission £11 for adults; £10 for seniors and the disabled; £5 for children ages 5–16; free for kids under age 5; 10% discount for parties of ten or more

Hours May–June, daily, 9:30 a.m.–8 p.m., weekends till 9 p.m.; July–September, daily, 9:30 a.m.–10 p.m.; October–December, 9:30 a.m.–8 p.m.; closed for three weeks in January.

Phone (0870) 500-0600

Website www.ba-londoneye.com

When to Go Best on a sunny day or clear night; avoid on very hot days

Special Comments This is not for those suffering from vertigo; it is very high and can make one feel quite exposed. It is disabled friendly. No baby stroller unless it folds up small; they can loan you a baby carrier.

Overall Appeal by Age Group

Pre-school ★★★	Teens ★★★★★	Over 30 ★★★★★
Grade school ★★★★★	Young Adults ★★★★★	Seniors ★★★★★

Author's Rating ★★★★★

How Much Time to Allow If you haven't ordered tickets ahead of time, you may have to wait in line, depending on the season and the weather. If you have reserved tickets (by phone or website), you can pick them up easily, and then you must wait about a half hour for boarding. The rotation takes 30 minutes.

Description and Comments Definitely London's most successful attraction designed to celebrate the new millennium, the London Eye is a colossal (450 feet high) silver wheel sprouting clear pods that hang off the frame. Originally planned to last for a five-year period, its wild popularity has ensured it a place among the most traditional of London's attractions. There have been constant improvements in the running of it, and now it boasts a gift shop, a free guidebook, and a much more efficient system of ticket-buying and boarding. You can pay extra to have a private pod, which comes with a guide, and they have special champagne "flights" (British Air uses aeronautical terms rather endearingly). Each of the 32 pods carries about 25 people, with benches for those who wish to sit. The design and the effect are surprisingly elegant and graceful; the wheel soars above the old buildings of Westminster and the South Bank. It moves slowly and majestically up, until its zenith of 450 feet, at which point passengers can see a good 25 miles away on a clear day. It's an amazing view of London.

Touring Tips If you order tickets ahead of time on the website or by telephone, you choose the day and the time you wish to "board"; then you show up with your credit card and retrieve your tickets from the center in the City Hall Building—follow the signs to it. A word of caution: The glass pods can be hot on sunny summer days. Combine your visit with a trip to the aquarium, Dali's Universe, or lunch at the Marriott Hotel's dining room with the river view.

British Library at St. Pancras

Type of Attraction New location of reading rooms (manuscript-archive collections) formerly housed in the British Museum (see profile below)

Location Zone 15; 96 Euston Road, NW1; tube: King's Cross

Admission Free

Hours Daily: general admission, 10 a.m.–5 p.m.; special exhibition times are varous

Phone (0207) 412-7000

Website www.bl.uk

When to Go Anytime

Special Comments Full wheelchair/disabled access

Overall Appeal by Age Group

Pre-school —	Teens ★★	Over 30 ★★★
Grade school ★★	Young Adults ★★★	Seniors ★★★★

Author's Rating ★★★★

How Much Time to Allow 1 hour

Description and Comments The embattled (and expensive: £500 million!) project to move the reading rooms from their beautiful, longtime niche at the British Museum was one of those necessary concessions to age that no one really wanted to make. However, since the opening, visitors and readers have been grudgingly admitting that it is a vast improvement over the cramped old quarters. Even Prince Charles, who scorned the exterior as "a collection of brick sheds groping for significance," was impressed with the interior. The fact is that, however lacking in aesthetics the place may be, it's still a veritable Aladdin's cave of treasures, and an improved one at that. Manuscripts such as the Lindisfarne Gospels from the tenth century, James Joyce's first draft of *Finnegan's Wake,* a copy of the Magna Carta from 1215, the Gutenberg Bible, and plenty of documents related to the greatest English writer of all, Shakespeare, are only some of the magnificent materials on view here.

The library offers to the public a fine bookstore, a café, and three exhibition galleries. There's the John Riblat Gallery, in which are displayed some of the library's most ancient and valuable manuscripts and maps. There's a wondrous room called "Turning the Page" in which a computer allows you to virtually flip through four texts: the Lindisfarne Gospels, the Diamond Sutra, da Vinci's notebooks, and the Sforza Hours. You can listen to James Joyce and other authors reading from their work, and to music of all types, too. In the Pearson Gallery of Living Words are educational exhibits, one of which explores the history of writing; another is a reading area, with a good display of children's literature. There are a few interactive, fun things to do, such as design a book or check out the evolution of recorded music.

Touring Tips This is not really a tourist attraction; it is for people who love and respect books, so take care who you take along with you. Sign up for a guided tour to see the parts of the library not open to the public.

The British Museum

Type of Attraction Colossal museum housing treasures of the British empire

Location Zone 2; Great Russell Street, WC1; tube: Tottenham Court Road

Admission Free

Hours Saturday–Wednesday, 10 a.m.–5:30 p.m.; Thursday–Friday, 10 a.m.–8:30 p.m. (selected galleries only open after 5:30 p.m.)

Phone (0207) 636-1555

Website www.british-museum.ac.uk

When to Go Early mornings

Special Comments Obtain a leaflet from the information desk for details about wheelchair accessibility; wheelchairs are also available to borrow. Queen Elizabeth II Great Court opened in December 2000 and has improved the museum immensely.

Overall Appeal by Age Group

Pre-school ★★★★	Teens ★★★★★	Over 30 ★★★★★
Grade school ★★★★	Young Adults ★★★★★	Seniors ★★★★★

Author's Rating ★★★★★

How Much Time to Allow 2–4 hours

Description and Comments This venerable old institution houses more than 50,000 items in 100 galleries, and receives upward of 7 million visitors a year. It all began when Sir Hans Sloane bequeathed his remarkable collection of art and artifacts to the state in 1753, and the earl of Oxford's rare manuscripts were added to the mix. The collection grew rapidly, as it became the scholarly and patriotic thing to do to leave one's finest possessions to the museum, and the museum repeatedly benefited from England's greatest empire-booty-looting years. Even the stolen goods of Napoléon's empire-building campaigns were placed here after the British defeated the French at Alexandria during the Napoléonic Wars.

At the British Museum, you can travel to the ends of the globe, throughout centuries of humankind's time on earth, and see just about every little thing that we've thought up along the way: mummies, pottery, clocks, painting, tools for war and peace, sculpture, personal decoration, household goods, treasures of gold and precious stones, and far more. Not only are there artifacts from practically every civilization throughout time, but they are of the greatest import. The Rosetta Stone, the Lindow Man, the Egyptian mummies, and prehistoric pieces are just a few of the finds that have literally changed history and now reside here.

The building itself contributes to the museum's appeal. Recently remodeled, it features at its center the Queen Elizabeth II Great Court, which is the largest covered square in Europe, with over 3,000 panes of glass sheltering an area the size of a soccer field. This courtyard has not always been accessible, because it was slowly filled with the materials of the round, domed Reading Room of the British Library. When the library was removed to St. Pancras in 1997 (see preceding profile), the courtyard space was reclaimed.

The museum also offers numerous gift shops, many benches and tables on which to rest your tired bones, and a restaurant at the top of the courtyard that lends wonderful views. It's lovely on a sunny day, and quite atmospheric during more typical English weather. To make the most of your visit, do study the website, which will have all the hours of all the shops, cafés, restaurants, exhibitions, and special lectures.

Touring Tips It's far too big to try to cover in one visit, so consult the map and the interests of your group before heading to the galleries, and use the compass multimedia system in the Reading Room to help plan your tour. There's a good guidebook sold in the excellent bookstore. And as with most museums, getting there before the school buses arrive is key. It is hard to gaze with the proper wonder at the Rosetta Stone when you're being jostled by an army of uniformed schoolchildren.

Buckingham Palace

(see profiles for Queen's Gallery and Royal Mews, both on premises)

Type of Attraction Stately home of the queen

Location Zone 9; Buckingham Palace Road, SW1; tube: Green Park

Admission £12 for adults; £5.50 for children ages 5–16; free for children under age 5; £30 for a family ticket (£1 service charge for booking over the phone or website)

Hours August–September, daily, 9:30 a.m.–4:30 p.m.

Phone (0207) 766-7300

Website www.royal.gov.uk

When to Go If you purchase tickets from the ticket office in Green Park, go at 9 a.m. The queues can be murder.

Special Comments Wheelchair users are required to arrange a visit in advance. I personally wouldn't inflict this tour on a preschooler, although they assure me that the young ones seem to love it.

Overall Appeal by Age Group

Pre-school ★		Teens ★★		Over 30 ★★★
Grade school ★★		Young Adults ★★★		Seniors ★★★

Author's Rating ★★★

Description and Comments Buckingham House was purchased by King George III in 1761 from the duke of Buckingham. Like most real estate, the three most attractive features were location, location, location. Situated between St. James's and Hyde Parks, with a tree-lined avenue affording views of Westminster and even St. Paul's Dome, it was like a country estate in the city (or near the city, as west of the house was still country). It was a private residence, the official court remaining—as it does to this day, if only in name—that of St. James's. When George IV ascended the throne, he had his favorite architect, John Nash, remodel it in the grandiose style you see today.

There are only two months in which you can view the state rooms at Buckingham Palace, so plan accordingly. In 1996, Queen Elizabeth II decided to open some of the palace to the public to pay for the restoration of Windsor Castle, which was severely damaged by a fire in 1992. I suspect that they may have paid for the work several times over by now.

It's an amazing spectacle, even more so when you ponder that for all the years of the palace's existence, loyal subjects of the Crown never had a prayer of setting foot in these august precincts, and now they're letting the likes of you and me in to eyeball the queen's goods. And what goods they are: treasures of painting, sculpture, furniture, and decoration beyond description, so I won't even try. (Neither do they. You have to buy the official guidebook to know what you are looking at; there are no signs anywhere.) I will say that after a while, I felt rather unsettled, if not revolutionary, by the endless, priceless display. And there are hundreds of other rooms you're not allowed to see. The views through the numerous French doors are magnificent; you can look out along the back garden rolling regally along, a piece of ye olde English countryside within earshot of the roar of Hyde Park Corner.

Warning: This is not an attraction for everyone, not least because of the ridiculous lines you have to wait in. It's a lot of money and a lot of effort for what is essentially an inert stately home. You could feel equally, if not more, satisfied with a good book on the palace.

Touring Tips Don't bring in any bags, so you can avoid the baggage security check. Before your tour time, do go buy the official guide from the gift shop next to the palace at the Queen's Gallery—you'll save yourself a wait on the way into the palace. I repeat: It's important to get this book if you want to know what is what, because just as in your own home, there are no labels on the goods. The guides are there to answer questions, and they're very knowledgeable. There's no guided tour per se; you just go in and follow the group. The time designated for your entry will be printed on your ticket; don't bother lining up until about 15 minutes beforehand. You might wander around the gift shop or St. James's Park in the meantime.

Burgh House

Type of Attraction Lovely period home/arts center providing exhibitions, concerts, and lectures

Location Zone 1; New End Square, Hampstead, NW3; tube: Hampstead

Admission Free

Hours Wednesday–Sunday, noon–5 p.m.; bank holidays, 2–5 p.m.

Phone (0207) 431-0144

When to Go Anytime

Overall Appeal by Age Group

Pre-school ★		Teens ★		Over 30 ★★
Grade school ★		Young Adults ★★		Seniors ★★

Author's Rating ★★

How Much Time to Allow One hour to see Hampstead Museum exhibit; other times depend on lecture or concert lengths

Description and Comments The meandering streets of Flask Walk and Well Walk are picturesque reminders of when Hampstead was a thriving spa village. To step out of the sometimes brisk Hampstead breeze, you might stop at this well-maintained Queen Anne home, where a modest museum of local history along with other, changing exhibitions are housed. The house is much more well known among the locals for its ongoing series of concerts, including opera, chamber music, and jazz. (Call for a current schedule.) There is also a charming tearoom downstairs.

Touring Tips See our walking tour of Old Hampstead Village (pages 164–166) for other sights worth visiting in the area.

The Cabinet War Rooms

Type of Attraction World War II shelter for Churchill and his cabinet

Location Zone 9; Clive Steps, King Charles Street, SW1; tube: Westminster or St James's Park

Admission £7 for adults; free for children under age 16; £5.50 for seniors and students; admission includes audioguide

Hours April–September, daily; 9:30 a.m.–5:15 p.m.; October–March, daily; 10 a.m.–5:15 p.m.

Phone (0207) 930-6961

Website www.iwm.org.uk, click on Cabinet War Rooms

When to Go Anytime

Special Comments Good disabled access, including wheelchairs on loan and accessible toilets

Overall Appeal by Age Group

Pre-school ★		Teens ★★★		Over 30 ★★★
Grade school ★★		Young Adults ★★★		Seniors ★★★★

Author's Rating ★★★

How Much Time to Allow 1 hour

Description and Comments This is the shelter in which Winston Churchill met with his staff, heads of state, and military personnel during the six years of World War II, when Hitler's bombs rained with grim regularity on London. Churchill's historic broadcasts to buck up the public were made from this site, and desperate decisions that could have turned the war against the Allies were strategized in these rooms. From the sandbags that line the front of the shelter to the old telephones and notepaper on Churchill's desk, this is an unusually close encounter with the reality of the war in London. When the war ended, the lights were turned off and the door shut, and the rooms remained exactly as they were left until the 1980s, when they were opened to the public. In 2003, the Churchill suite was opened to the public; this was where Winston and his wife, Clementine, slept, dined, and entertained during the long nights of the Blitz. The attraction offers a good audio tour, or you can get a booklet with which to go through the rooms. This is a must for the WWII veteran or buff.

Touring Tips Combine with a visit to St. James's Park.

Carlyle's House

Type of Attraction Queen Anne home of the sage of Chelsea

Location Zone 11; 24 Cheyne Row, SW3; tube: Sloane Square

Admission £3.70 for adults; £1.80 for children under age 16

Hours March 29 through November 2: Wednesday–Sunday and bank holidays, 11 a.m.–5 p.m.

Phone (0207) 352-7087

When to Go Anytime it's open

Special Comments It's an old house with steep stairs; no wheelchair access

Overall Appeal by Age Group

Pre-school ★	Teens ★★	Over 30 ★★★
Grade school ★★	Young Adults ★★★	Seniors ★★★

Author's Rating ★★★

How Much Time to Allow 1 hour

Description and Comments It's likely that the name Thomas Carlyle may not mean anything to most people these days; he was a great essayist and historian in his own time (1795–1881), known and admired by all the Victorian literati. His house was a salon of luminaries such as Charles Dickens, George Eliot, Alfred Lord Tennyson, and Frederic Chopin, drawn as much by the sage of Chelsea's wisdom as by the famous wit of his wife, Jane. What is marvelous about the house, in the absence of any great feeling for its former owner, is that it was made a museum not too long after Carlyle's death, and so has an abundance of authentic minutiae—a hat hung on a hook, clothing in a drawer—that is lacking in most literary shrines of this sort. There's a wonderful garden reflecting the Victorian reverence for controlled nature. All the furnishings are authentic, and the atmosphere is beyond the wildest dreams of a Victoriana-phile.

Touring Tips Be sure to look at all the blue plaques around here to see the kind of neighbors Carlyle enjoyed.

Changing of the Guard

Type of Attraction A grand old London tradition

Location Zone 9; in the forecourt of Buckingham Palace, at the end of Pall Mall, SW1; tube: Green Park, then walk directly through the park to the palace

Admission Free

Hours April–July, daily at 11:30 a.m.; August–March, every other day at 11:30 a.m.; be sure to call for information

Phone (0906) 866-3344

Website www.royal.gov.uk

When to Go Arrive by 10:30 a.m. to get a good place by the railings or on the statue of Victoria, especially in the summer on a nice day.

Special Comments The pageant is cancelled in very wet weather.

Overall Appeal by Age Group

Pre-school ★		Teens ★★		Over 30 ★★
Grade school ★★		Young Adults ★★		Seniors ★★

Author's Rating ★★

How Much Time to Allow The actual ceremony lasts 40 minutes, but if you want to get a good vantage point, you may want to show up an hour earlier.

Description and Comments: The Queen's Guard, often accompanied by a band, leaves Wellington Barracks at 11:27 a.m. and marches along Birdcage Walk to the Palace, where they . . . well, change. I'm not crazy about this attraction even though I love horses and history. There's something so annoying about the hordes of people standing around, very few of whom can get a good look at the ceremony, and the ones pressed up against the railings looking relatively miserable for all the waiting they've had to do. That said, I can recommend the statue of Victoria for a vantage point that isn't quite as desperate and uncomfortable as the scene around the palace railings. (I'm talking about the summer months; in the winter, it's not quite so bad.) If it's too crowded for you around the palace, go to the Horse Guards Parade on Horse Guards Parade Road, which is on the far eastern perimeter of St James's Park (tube: Embankment or Charing Cross). There is a less-elaborate ceremony at 11 a.m. Monday–Saturday and at 10 a.m. on Sunday. The Queen's Life Guards leave the Hyde Park Barracks at 10:30 a.m. Monday–Saturday and at 9:30 a.m. on Sunday, and march most impressively through Hyde Park Corner, Constitution Hill, and The Mall.

Touring Tips If it's too crowded one day and you can't get a good view, save it for the next. There's a small Guard's Museum at the Wellington Barracks on Birdcage Walk that is open daily from 10 a.m. to 4 p.m.; entrance fee £2; (0207) 414-3271. It may be of interest to military enthusiasts, and it has a decent gift shop of Guards' memorabilia.

Chiswick House

Type of Attraction Stately home with major gardens in west London

Location Zone 12; Burlington Lane, W4; tube: Turnham Green, or Chiswick by rail

Admission £3.50 for adults; £2 for children under age 16

Hours April–September, daily, 10 a.m.–6 p.m.; October–March, Wednesday–Sunday, 10 a.m.–4 p.m.

Phone (0208) 995-0508

When to Go In good weather; the garden is splendid

Special Comments Limited disabled access; call for details

Overall Appeal by Age Group

Pre-school ★	Teens ★	Over 30 ★★
Grade school ★	Young Adults ★★	Seniors ★★

Author's Rating ★★★

How Much Time to Allow 1 hour

Description and Comments It's a bit of a hike from either the train station in Chiswick or the tube at Turnham Green, but for anyone interested in Palladian design and eighteenth-century, over-the-top splendor, this is the place. Built in 1725 by Lord Burlington and William Kent, it has at its heart an octagonal room with a dome that is classically symmetrical. Its original purpose was more to show off Burlington's extensive art collection than to live in, but alas, most of those treasures have long since been retired to museums. However, the decoration, carvings, and statuary that remain are magnificent, and the William Kent ceilings are as sumptuous as those he did at Kensington Palace. In summer, the gardens are spectacular, filled with wonderful follies—mock ruins that were all the rage in the eighteenth and nineteenth centuries, ponds, statues, benches, and formal gardens.

Touring Tips This can be combined with a trip to Hogarth's House.

Clink Exhibition

Type of Attraction Re-creation and exhibition of a medieval prison

Location Zone 5; 1 Clink Street, SE1; tube: London Bridge

Admission £4 for adults; £3 for seniors, students, and children under 16

Hours Daily, 10 a.m.–6 p.m.

Phone (0207) 403-6515

Website www.clink.co.uk

When to Go Anytime

Special Comments This attraction is not accessible to those in wheelchairs or baby strollers, as the entrance to the basement site is down a rather dark flight of stairs, and the exhibit itself includes a number of narrow doorways that must be stepped over.

Overall Appeal by Age Group

Pre-school †		Teens ★		Over 30 ★
Grade school ★		Young Adults ★		Seniors ★

† *Too creepy for preschoolers*

Author's Rating ★★★

How Much Time to Allow 30 minutes

Description and Comments Be warned: This place is a rip-off. The Clink began as a dungeon for disobedient clerics, debtors, and prostitutes. The exhibition presents itself as a re-created medieval dungeon and includes some dismal cell re-creations, diagrams of medieval torture devices, and fact boards on some of the prison's prior inhabitants. Though one might think that the ghoulish subject matter would be of high interest to grade-school kids and teens, most of the information must be read from the mounted displays, something kids seem to grow weary of too quickly.

Touring Tips If you do decide to explore this area, be sure to include a stop at Southwark Cathedral and Shakespeare's Globe Theatre, both within only a few minutes' walk of the Clink Exhibition.

Cutty Sark

Type of Attraction Last of the great sailing clipper ships, restored

Location Zone 6; Greenwich Pier; Docklands Light Railway: Greenwich

Admission £3.95 for adults; £2.95 for children, students, and seniors; £10 for family

Hours Daily, 10 a.m.–5 p.m.; last admission at 4:30 p.m.

Phone (0208) 858-3445

Website www.cuttysark.org.uk

When to Go Early

Special Comments Access for the disabled is limited to the entrance level of the ship, as the ship contains stairways that may prove difficult for some to maneuver.

Overall Appeal by Age Group

Pre-school ★★		Teens ★★★		Over 30 ★★★
Grade school ★★★★		Young Adults ★★★		Seniors ★★★

Author's Rating ★★★

How Much Time to Allow 45–90 minutes

Description and Comments First launched in 1869, the *Cutty Sark* spent seven years in the China tea trade, but actually became famous as a wool-merchant ship in the years that followed, able to sail from England to Australia in only 72 days. The ship's main hold contains a history of this well-known tea clipper (there's a small gift shop there, too), but it is the lower hold that most impresses with the largest collection of merchant-ship figureheads in Britain. Captain John Cumbers of Gravesend, better known as Long John Silver, amassed the colorful display. Tours of the ship can be arranged at no additional charge simply by asking. Children love to explore the restored ship's cabins, which give an alarming indication of the difference in class between captain and crew.

Touring Tips From the *Cutty Sark's* bow you can also see the much smaller *Cutty Sark Gipsy Moth IV*, in which Francis Chichester first sailed solo around the world.

Dali Universe

Type of Attraction Restrospective of surrealist master

Location Zone 5, County Hall Gallery, Riverside Building, South Bank; tube: Westminster or Waterloo

Admission £8.50 for adults, children ages 10–16, £4.95 for children ages £1 for children 3–9, concessions £7.50

Hours Daily, 10 a.m.–5:30 p.m.; open one hour later in July and August

Phone (0207) 620-2720

Website www.daliuniverse.com

When to Go Anytime

Special Comments Wheelchair access available at entrance along Queens Walk

Overall Appeal by Age Group

Pre-school ★★★		Teens ★★★★		Over 30 ★★★★
Grade school ★★★★		Young Adults ★★★★		Seniors ★★★★

Author's Rating ★★★★

How Much Time to Allow 1 hour

Description and Comments This is a wonderful gallery honoring the surrealist master Salvador Dali. While certainly not as impressive as the Dali

Museum in Fuergeras, Spain, it is certainly as, if not more, comprehensive as the one in Paris. Over 500 of his works include the famous red-lips sofa, the lobster telephone, and many of his best-known and -loved canvases, along with some personal artifacts. Dali Universe contains the largest collection of his sculptures from the years between 1935 and 1984, and the gift shop sells copies of many of them, almost impossible to resist. It is an intelligently and creatively curated exhibit, making the most of lighting and backgrounds to create a temple that Dali would most likely have approved.

Touring Tips Combine with visits to any of the South Bank attractions, such as the London Aquarium, the London Eye, or the Saatchi Gallery

Design Museum

Type of Attraction Four floors featuring the design of everyday items

Location Zone 5; 28 Shad Thames, Butler's Wharf, SE1; tube: Tower Hill or London Bridge

Admission £6 for adults; £4 for children; £16 for a family ticket (2 adults and 2 children)

Hours Daily, 10 a.m.–5:45 p.m.; Friday, open till 9 p.m.

Phone (0207) 378-6055

Website www.designmuseum.org

When to Go Anytime

Special Comments Wheelchair/disabled accessible

Overall Appeal by Age Group

Pre-school ★	Teens ★	Over 30 ★★
Grade school ★	Young Adults ★★	Seniors ★★

Author's Rating ★★

How Much Time to Allow 60–90 minutes

Description and Comments The Design Museum strongly features changing exhibits of design from all possible areas of life. One of the most popular was a recent show of Manolo Blahnik's shoe designs, which highlighted his cunning skill and artistry.

The museum is well attended and appreciated by Londoners and tourists, who flock here to look at the mass-produced designs of the twentieth century that we've lived with, perhaps without even noticing what they really looked like. One need only look at the collection of evolving TV sets to see that our household items have their own histories, which are inextricably linked to our domestic memories. Cars, office furniture, radios, and household utensils are all part of a permanent collection, which is added to regularly. New ideas and design breakthroughs are highlighted here. The Design Museum was created by restaurant and furniture king Terence Conran, on the south bank of the Thames by Tower Bridge, and the café and restaurant have splendid views.

Touring Tips Walk around the Thames waterfront; it's an interesting, old London kind of place.

Dickens House

Type of Attraction Literary shrine to the great Charles Dickens

Location Zone 3; 48 Doughty Street, WC1; tube: Russell Square

Admission £4 for adults; £3 for children

Hours Monday–Saturday, 10 a.m.–5 p.m.; Sunday, 11 a.m.–5 p.m.

Phone (0207) 405-2127

Website www.dickensmuseum.com

When to Go Anytime

Special Comments The house contains numerous steps and no wheel-chair access.

Overall Appeal by Age Group

Pre-school ★	Teens ★	Over 30 ★★
Grade school ★	Young Adults ★	Seniors ★★

Author's Rating ★

How Much Time to Allow 40 minutes

Description and Comments I am a big Dickens fan, and I was hoping for more from this museum; it is sad that London, the city that Dickens made real for so many readers, doesn't have a better temple to him. Dickens actually only lived in this house for two years, so his spirit certainly does not walk these floors the way you sense Carlyle's does in his house. There are manuscript pages that are exciting to see, lots of wonderful illustrations from his books and portraits of the writer, and these can make it worth the trip. The gift shop sells some fine old and new editions of Dickens and some of his contemporaries. Watch the video in the base-ment first; it's very good.

Touring Tips If you happen to be visiting between May and September, go on Wednesday evening for the one-man show, "Sparkler of Albion," which starts at 7:30 p.m. and costs £14 per ticket; come at 6 p.m. for a free glass of wine.

Freud Museum

Type of Attraction English home of famous psychoanalyst Sigmund Freud

Location Zone 1; 20 Maresfield Gardens, South Hampstead, NW1; tube: Finchley Road

Admission £5 for adults; £2 concessions

Hours Wednesday–Sunday, noon–5 p.m.

Phone (0207) 435-2002

Website www.freud.org.uk

When to Go Anytime

Special Comments Limited access for disabled; no lift to upper floor

Overall Appeal by Age Group

Pre-school ★	Teens ★	Over 30 ★★
Grade school ★★	Young Adults ★★	Seniors ★★

Author's Rating ★★★

How Much Time to Allow 2 hours

Description and Comments The house at 20 Maresfield Gardens, Hampstead, was the home of Dr. Sigmund Freud, the father of psycho-analysis, for the last year of his life, after he fled the Nazis in Vienna in 1938. It continued to be home to his daughter, Anna, until her death in 1982, and on her request, it now celebrates the life and work of her father. Inside, each room is carefully decorated as it had been in 1938, and the museum contains all of the possessions from Freud's former home in Vienna in which he had lived for over 47 years. The exhibition's centerpiece is Freud's library and study, including his famous analytic couch and numerous antiquities.

Touring Tips A wonderfully informative video is available for viewing upstairs. The 45-minute film, partially narrated by Anna Freud, contains silent black-and-white footage of Freud at home in Vienna as well as a description of the family's harrowing escape in 1938.

(Shakespeare's) Globe Theatre

Type of Attraction Magnificently reconstructed Shakespearean theater

Location Zone 5; 21 New Globe Walk, Bankside, SE1; tube: Mansion House or Blackfriars

Admission The Globe Exhibition and guided tour cost £8 for adults, £6 for seniors and students, £5.50 for children ages 6–16, and are free for children under age 5; a family ticket is £24; tours run every half hour. Prices for performances run from £5 (standing room) to £29 (tiered seating).

Hours Daily, 10 a.m.–5 p.m.; check with the box office for performance times and dates

Phone (0207) 401-9919

Website www.shakespeares-globe.org

When to Go Anytime

Special Comments The exhibition is easily accessible for individuals in wheelchairs.

Overall Appeal by Age Group

Pre-school ★		Teens ★★		Over 30 ★★★★
Grade school ★★		Young Adults ★★★		Seniors ★★★★

Author's Rating ★★★★

How Much Time to Allow 1–2 hours for museum and tour

Description and Comments Brilliantly reconstructed as an almost exact replica of its former self (and founded by the late American actor and director Sam Wanamaker), The Globe officially opened in 1998 and is a delightful place to learn about the world's greatest playwright, William Shakespeare. In his day, Shakespeare's plays were also performed at The Rose and occasionally The Swan, but it was at The Globe that Shakespeare made his literary name. The tour of the theater, often led by actors and very well done, describes marvelous details about Elizabethan theater and the notorious Bankside area. Performances run in the summer months, and are held outdoors under natural light, as they used to be. The Globe Exhibition was opened in 2000 and is located beneath the theater. The exhibit contains a fact-filled museum on the life and times of the Bard, and includes some of the impressive reproductions of medieval tools used to make the building. It focuses as well on the actors and the audiences who have made Shakespeare's plays so enduring. The complex also contains a café, as well as a more upscale restaurant with a view of the river and the city.

Touring Tips The box office says that the best seats for performances are not seats at all but the standing area in front of the stage, where the "groundlings" stand, the actors may mingle, and the rain may pour (don't worry; they sell rain ponchos). Personally, we prefer the seats.

Guildhall (including Clock Museum, Art Gallery, and Library Bookshop)

Type of Attraction Corporate headquarters for the City of London

Location Zone 7; Gresham Street; tube: St. Paul's, Mansion House, or Bank

Admission Free

Hours Guildhall: Monday–Friday, 10 a.m.–5 p.m.; Guildhall Clock Museum and Library Bookshop: Monday–Saturday, 10 a.m.–5 p.m., Sunday, noon–4 p.m.

Phone (0207) 332-1456

Website www.cityoflondon.gov.uk

When to Go Anytime

Special Comments Partial access for disabled

Overall Appeal by Age Group

Pre-school ★	Teens ★★	Over 30 ★★
Grade school ★★	Young Adults ★★	Seniors ★★

Author's Rating ★★

How Much Time to Allow 1–1½ hours

Description and Comments Guildhall has witnessed traitors' trials and heroes' welcomes, freedom ceremonies and glittering state occasions. The seat of London's municipal government for over 800 years, it is still used for official ceremonies, state banquets, and the annual installation of the lord mayor of London. Although surrounded by twentieth-century government offices and largely reconstructed after a World War II bombing, the Great Hall still impresses. Its walls are original and date to the fifteenth century. An array of monuments lines the hall in honor of national figures from the past three centuries, and banners of the 12 Great Livery Companies hang from above. The complex itself also houses over 700 examples of timekeeping in its rather small Clock Museum; its Art Gallery houses the Corporation of London's impressive collection of works depicting London life from the fifteenth century to the present.

Touring Tips The fifteenth-century crypt and nineteenth-century Old Library are generally off-limits to the public, but it is well worth asking if it might be possible to see them. Guided tours include these spots.

HMS Belfast

Type of Attraction Perfectly preserved Royal Navy battleship from World War II that is permanently moored in the Thames

Location Zone 5; Morgans Lane, Tooley Street, SE1; tube: London Bridge

Admission £5.80 for adults; free for children under age 16

Hours March–October, daily, 10 a.m.–6 p.m.; November–February, daily, 10 a.m.–5 p.m.

Phone (0207) 940-6328

Website www.iwm.org.uk

When to Go Weekdays; call to see if any class trips are scheduled

Special Comments Ship accessible to disabled, but there are many areas that are impassable for wheelchairs.

Overall Appeal by Age Group

Pre-school ★★	Teens ★★★	Over 30 ★★
Grade school ★★★	Young Adults ★★	Seniors ★★

Author's Rating ★★

How Much Time to Allow 90 minutes

Description and Comments A bit of floating history, the HMS *Belfast* was built in 1938 and pressed into service at the D day landings. Decommissioned in the 1960s, the HMS *Belfast* is run by the Imperial War Museum. It's a popular tourist attraction, although its appeal is not universal. You can explore all seven levels of this huge battleship and check out the boiler room, the cabins, and the gun turrets, as well as exhibitions and videos about life on board in 1943 and the history of the Royal Navy. Children of all ages tend to love this ship, and those very interested in World War II may find it an enlightening experience.

Hampton Court Palace

Type of Attraction London's most impressive royal palace

Location Zone 12; East Molesey, Surrey, approximately 12 miles outside of central London; tube: Richmond, then R68 bus; British Rail (accessible from Waterloo Station): Hampton Court)

Admission £11.30 for adults; £7.40 for children ages 5–15; £34 for families; prices include admission to the gardens and maze

Hours March 25–October 27, Monday, 10:15 a.m.–6 p.m. and Tuesday–Sunday, 9:30 a.m.–6 p.m.; October 28–March 24, the palace closes on Monday at 4:15 p.m. and at 4:30 p.m. all other days

Phone (0208) 781-9500

Website www.hrp.org.uk

When to Go Anytime

Special Comments Disabled access, including ramps to the Tudor kitchens, access to some areas of the gardens, lifts to the first floor, and equipped toilets

Overall Appeal by Age Group

Pre-school ★★	Teens ★★★★★	Over 30 ★★★★★
Grade school ★★★	Young Adults ★★★★★	Seniors ★★★★★

Author's Rating ★★★★★

How Much Time to Allow Head out early to give yourself the full day to enjoy Hampton Court and time to arrive back in London for dinner or perhaps a trip to the theater.

Description and Comments One of the nicest things about Hampton Court Palace is its location. If you have been running all over the city of London, deciphering bus schedules and tube maps, a trip outside this fast-paced metropolis is a relaxing treat.

The powerful and influential lord chancellor to Henry VIII, Cardinal Wolsey, built Hampton Court Palace in 1516 and proceeded to live there quite lavishly. In 1528, after Henry commented on the extravagance of such a home for a member of the clergy, Cardinal Wolsey offered it to the king. After Wolsey failed to secure from the pope Henry's much-desired annulment from Catherine of Aragon in 1529, Henry accepted his offer, no doubt with malicious glee. Henry created the enormous Tudor kitchens and redesigned the chapel. Alterations were also made by the great architect Christopher Wren, under the direction of William and Mary, and further changes were instigated by Queen Anne. The result allows palace visitors to clearly distinguish some of the most important design styles in England's history.

The palace is organized into six walking tours, and then there are still the gardens and maze in which to wander. With all this to see, your best bet is to decide whether you want to start inside or out. I usually find that after an hour or two inside the vast halls I need to get outside for a bit and can then return to more fully enjoy the rest of the palace. Costumed guides offer tours of Henry VIII's apartments, the King's and, in summer, Queen's apartments at no additional charge; this is always a good way to start your visit, as the fascinating story of Hampton Court is immediately brought to life by these experienced historians. If you prefer to head out on your own, audio guides of Henry's apartments and the Tudor kitchens are also available at no additional cost.

Of significant interest in Henry's Great Hall are the hammer-beam ceiling and stunning medieval tapestries. The rather plain hallway leading to the king's chapel is the Haunted Gallery and claims to be the wandering ground for the ghost of Henry's fifth wife, Catherine Howard.

Outside, you have a wide choice of garden styles to match the rooms they surround. The grandest of these is William III's Fountain Garden; on the south side is the Privy Garden. Beyond this are the sunken Pond Gardens and Tudor-style Knot and Herb Gardens, while on the opposite side of the palace you can venture into the less manicured Wilderness with its evergreens and the ever-popular maze, originally laid out in 1714.

Touring Tips A sunny day makes Hampton Court's ornate gardens a fantastic picnic spot for families. Alternately, you might head to the Tiltyard Tearoom for an enjoyable light meal, or wander beyond the Lion Gates for a number of cozy pubs, all serving some wonderfully traditional lunchtime fare. Hampton Court is easily reached by train from Waterloo or Wimbledon Stations, but if you have time, the best way to approach the palace is by water. Boat tours up the Thames run in the summer months from Richmond (for a half-hour ride) or Westminster (for an hour-long excursion). Approaching the palace in this manner affords an unequaled view of the majestic King's Apartments, the magnificently cultivated Privy Gardens, and the vast park areas that once served as Henry's private hunting grounds. For river-tour schedules and pricing information call (0207) 930-4721.

Hogarth's House

Type of Attraction The satirist and painter's summer home and engravings

Location Zone 12; Hogarth Lane, Great West Road, W4; tube: Turnham Green or British Rail to Chiswick

Admission Free

Hours April–October, Tuesday–Friday, 1–5 p.m., Saturday and Sunday, 1–6 p.m.; November–March, Tuesday–Friday, 1–5 p.m. Closed Monday and the month of January

Phone (0208) 994-6757

When to Go As part of a day in Chiswick (Chiswick House is a short walk away)

Special Comments Disabled accessible

Overall Appeal by Age Group

Pre-school ★	Teens ★★	Over 30 ★★
Grade school ★	Young Adults ★★	Seniors ★★

Author's Rating ★★

How Much Time to Allow 1 hour

Description and Comments If you go to Chiswick House in the morning, you might want to visit Hogarth in the afternoon. It used to be a quiet country retreat for the brilliant painter and satirist William Hogarth, but is now located on a particularly busy section of the A4 motorway, known as the Hogarth roundabout. More than 200 of Hogarth's most famous prints are here, including *Marriage à la Mode, A Rake's Progress,* and *A Harlot's Progress.* It's quite delightful to take your time over them in this setting that the master called home for 15 years, until his death in 1764.

Touring Tips Make this visit part of your trip to Chiswick House.

Houses of Parliament: House of Lords and House of Commons

Type of Attraction Britain's working chambers of government

Location Zone 9; Parliament Square, SW1; tube: Westminster

Admission Free, except for prebooked tours

Hours House of Lords: the public is admitted to the Strangers' Gallery Monday–Wednesday, beginning at 2:30 p.m., Thursday beginning at 3 p.m., and occasionally on Friday, beginning at 11 a.m. To the House of Commons, Monday–Wednesday, 2:30–10:30 p.m., Thursday, 11:30 a.m.–7:30 p.m., and Friday, 9:30 a.m.–3 p.m. Check whether the House is sitting by calling (0207) 219-4272. Question Time (accessible by special prebooked tickets) takes place Monday–Wednesday, 2:30–3:30 p.m., and Thursday, 11:30 a.m.–12:30 p.m. The prime minister answers questions 3–3:30 p.m.

Phone Commons info at (0207) 219-4272; Lords info at (0207) 219 3107

Website www.parliament.uk (go to Index and click on the letter "V" for visits)

When to Go When the Houses are not in recess (they recess at Christmas, at Easter, and from August to the middle of September)

Special Comments Security is very tight. Allow plenty of time to clear security checks. Do not bring food, drinks, mobile phones, or pagers. They will allow you in with a camera as long as it stays in your bag; absolutely no photography is permitted.

Overall Appeal by Age Group

Pre-school †		Teens ★★		Over 30 ★★★
Grade school †		Young Adults ★★		Seniors ★★★

† *Not appropriate for young children.*

Author's Rating ★★

How Much Time to Allow 1–2 hours, depending on how long you'd like to observe the debates (allowing at least 30 minutes to clear security)

Description and Comments The first Parliament was convened in 1254 and consisted of lords, bishops, abbots, knights, and local citizens. Today's Parliament, closely based on its predecessors, includes the sovereign, the House of Lords (which used to be made up of hereditary peerage members, but now must be elected or appointed to their positions) and the House of Commons (members elected from their respective English, Welsh, Scottish, and Northern Irish communities). The current buildings in which they meet, built between 1840 and 1860, have become the most recognized trademarks of London. Parliament burned down in the mid-nineteenth century, and was built in its present neo-Gothic splendor by an architect named Pugin, who went mad after years of working on what must have been an exhausting project—just look at all the details of the exterior. You can see Parliament in session on CSPAN and certain BBC channels, and it is a most refreshing sight: The Prime Minister will be questioned, chastised, or challenged directly by the ministers in often rowdy sessions that seem much more of an exercise of democracy than the carefully controlled press conferences of the American president.

Touring Tips Do use the website to plan your visit, because admission policies are currently being updated and the place may be temporarily closed to visitors. Call to get the latest information. If you want to do more than witness debates, consider arranging in advance to receive permits that allow you unchaperoned access as you follow a printed guide through splendidly decorated lobbies, corridors, the grand Westminster

Hall, and the two Houses. If the Houses are in recess, tours will be granted Monday–Saturday, 9:15 a.m.–4:30 p.m. When the Houses are in session, tours will be scheduled only for Friday (you can also pay £25 for a personal guide). For tours while the Houses are in session, you must write a few months in advance to: Parliamentary Education Unit, Norman Shaw Boulevard (North), London SWIA 2TT. Be sure to include the exact dates of your visit, the total number in your party (not to exceed 16 people), your home address, and your London address and telephone. Permits will be mailed, so be sure to allow enough time.

If you can't get into the Houses of Parliament for any reason, visit Jewel Tower (zone 9; Abingdon Street, by Westminster Abbey; phone (0207) 222-2219), where you can see, for a small fee, an interactive virtual reality tour of both Houses. It's open 10 a.m.–4 p.m. in winter and 10 a.m.–6 p.m. in summer.

Imperial War Museum

Type of Attraction Highlights twentieth-century British military actions

Location Zone 5; Lambeth Road, SE1; tube: Elephant and Castle or Lambeth North

Admission Free

Hours Daily, 10 a.m.–6 p.m.

Phone (0207) 416-5320

Website www.iwm.org.uk

When to Go Anytime

Special Comments Limited access for disabled; wheelchairs can be booked by calling (0207) 416-5397

Overall Appeal by Age Group

Pre-school ★		Teens ★★		Over 30 ★★
Grade school ★		Young Adults ★★		Seniors ★★

Author's Rating ★★

How Much Time to Allow 1 hour

Description and Comments Housed in the famous former lunatic asylum known as Bedlam, the Imperial War Museum is an oddly appropriate present tenant, dedicated to the madness that is twentieth-century war. It is a sobering museum, especially the section on the liberation of Belsen, part of the permanent exhibit on the Holocaust completed in 2000. Overall, it was hard not to be upset by the blithe displays of the awful hardware of destruction: guns, tanks, zeppelins, V2 rockets, bombers. You are given insight into the horror of war by the re-creation of the sights and sounds and smells of the Blitz, a clock counting down the numbers of war deaths in this century, and the nightmare of life in a

World War I trench, but then it seems you are invited to appreciate the machinery of it.

Touring Tips After experiencing war, go bask in the Peace Garden which shares the grounds with the Imperial War Museum, and which was dedicated by the Dalai Lama in May 1999.

Dr. Johnson's House

Type of Attraction Literary attraction in historic house

Location Zone 2; 17 Gough Square, EC4; tube: Blackfriars

Admission £4 for adults; £3 for children ages 10–16; free for children under age 10; £9 for families

Hours May–September, Monday–Saturday, 11 a.m.–5:30 p.m.; October–April, Monday–Saturday, 11 a.m.–5 p.m.

Phone (0207) 353-3745

Website www.drjohnsonshouse.org

When to Go Anytime

Special Comments No wheelchair access; steep stairs

Overall Appeal by Age Group

Pre-school ★★	Teens ★★	Over 30 ★★
Grade school ★★	Young Adults ★★	Seniors ★★

Author's Rating ★★

How Much Time to Allow 27 minutes for video, 10–15 minutes for the house

Description and Comments I like Samuel Johnson more than the average bloke on the block, but even I wasn't overly impressed by this house, the only surviving domicile of the 17 he lived in. I might have felt differently had the admission been free; however, I do respect and support the fact that this house on prime property has managed to avoid the wrecking ball for 250 years. This alone makes it worth the visit and the price. Dr. Johnson spent 11 years in this house working on his famous dictionary, as well as bopping around London with his biographer Boswell at his heels, dropping bons mots and shillings in the coffeehouses and taverns of his beloved London. The collection of mezzotints and books on Johnson are impressive. You must watch the video, very well done and interesting, which does make the remarkable Johnson, and Boswell, come to life.

Kensington Palace State Rooms

Type of Attraction Stately home in the middle of Kensington Gardens

Location Zone 13; Kensington Gardens, Broad Walk; tube: High Street Kensington

Admission £10.20 for adults; £6.60 for children ages 5–16; free for children under age 5; £31 for families

Hours April–September, daily, 10 a.m.–5 p.m.; October–March, daily, 10 a.m.–4 p.m.

Phone (0207) 937-9561

Website www.hrp.org.uk

When to Go Mornings in summer; anytime in winter

Special Comments There are wheelchair-accessible toilets and a ramp to Orangery, but many steps inside the palace. Upstairs is inaccessible.

Overall Appeal by Age Group

Pre-school ★★	Teens ★★★★	Over 30 ★★★★
Grade school ★★★	Young Adults ★★★★	Seniors ★★★★

Author's Rating ★★★★

How Much Time to Allow 1½ hours

Description and Comments Kensington Palace is the former home of Princess Diana, and the place where Princess Victoria was told that she had become queen. It's not a grandiose palace like Buckingham, which makes it in many ways more interesting. It was built in 1605 and sold to King William and Queen Mary in 1689 as a country escape from the noxious fumes of Whitehall, which were aggravating the king's asthma. The monarchs immediately hired Christopher Wren and Nicholas Hawksmoor to improve the house. Queen Anne later added more improvements, such as the Orangery, which was her "summer supper house," and acres of gardens. George I turned what was essentially a country estate into a palace, and it's fascinating to note the difference between the homey oak-paneled dining room of William and Mary and the over-the-top decor of William Kent's innovations. King George II and Queen Caroline made extensive additions to the gardens that can be enjoyed today, such as Broad Walk, the Round Pond, and the Serpentine. In 1841, the gardens were opened to the public, when the palace became a source of "grace and favour," apartments for offshoots of the royal family, such as the late Princess Margaret.

You can see the bedroom in which Princess Victoria lived with her mother, the duchess of Kent, until she was made queen at 18. There are fine examples of furniture and brilliant trompe l'oeil ceiling paintings and murals by William Kent. Two oddities that must be seen are the wind dial by which King William III could tell how fast his ships might be approaching, and the massive clock in the Cupola Room that used to play tunes by Handel, Corelli, and Geminiani, and which, even minus this feature, represents a marvelous marriage of sixteenth-century technology and art.

Touring Tips Make this part of a day in the park. Early birds get the worm here, but it's also nice to come later in the day and follow up your visit with tea at the Orangery next door. Be sure to take advantage of the audio tour, as it's very thorough and interesting.

Kenwood House (The Iveagh Bequest)

Type of Attraction World-class art gallery in an elegant Georgian villa

Location Zone 1; Hampstead Lane, Hampstead Heath, NW3; tube: Archway or Golders Green

Admission Free

Hours April–September, daily, 10 a.m.–5:30 p.m.; October–March, daily, 10 a.m.–4 p.m.

Phone (0208) 348-1286

Website www.english-heritage.org.uk

When to Go Anytime, but preferably on weekdays and in good weather so you can enjoy the heath

Special Comments Limited wheelchair access for ground floor only

Overall Appeal by Age Group

Pre-school ★	Teens ★★★	Over 30 ★★★
Grade school ★★★	Young Adults ★★★	Seniors ★★★

Author's Rating ★★★★

How Much Time to Allow 2 hours in the house, plus time for tea or a walk around the grounds and on the heath. It's a good day out.

Description and Comments Kenwood is the most elegant exponent of architects Robert and James Adams's early Georgian design. It is gorgeous, with Adams and Chippendale furniture and decoration, the stunning masterpieces on the walls, and exceptional views all year long.

Built in 1700, the house changed hands several times, until brewery magnate Edward Guinness, earl of Iveagh, purchased it to display his extensive collection of seventeenth-century Dutch and Flemish and late eighteenth-century British paintings, including works by Sir Joshua Reynolds, George Romney, J. M. W. Turner, Gainsborough, and Raeburn. There are a number of absolutely unmissable old masterpieces here, such as Rembrandt's *Self-Portrait* and Vermeer's *The Guitar Player*. As an art gallery, it is right up there in the top ten of London. A number of somewhat quirky displays of miniature portraits, jewelry, ceramics, and 1,300 Georgian shoe buckles have also been donated by a variety of collectors.

Touring Tips Combine this visit with a trip to Hampstead Village and the heath. If you're visiting in the summer, combine it with the weekend concerts.

Leighton House Museum and Art Gallery

Type of Attraction House of pre-Raphaelite painter Lord Frederick Leighton

Location Zone 13; 12 Holland Park Road; tube: High Street Kensington, then bus 9, 10, 27, 33, or 49 to Odeon Cinema, then walk through Holland Park

Admission £3 adults, £1 children

Hours Monday–Saturday, 11 a.m.–5:30 p.m.; closed Tuesday

Phone (0207) 602-3316

Website www.rbkc.gov.uk/leightonhousemuseum

When to Go Anytime

Special Comments Not wheelchair accessible; many steps to top floor

Overall Appeal by Age Group

Pre-school ★		Teens ★★		Over 30 ★★
Grade school ★		Young Adults ★★		Seniors ★★

Author's Rating ★★★

How Much Time to Allow 30 minutes

Description and Comments If you are a true lover of the pre-Raphaelites (Edward Burne-Jones, John Millais, Frederick Leighton, and others) this is a must-see. Lord Leighton, whose magnificent painted hallway can be seen in the Victoria and Albert Museum, dedicated his home as "a private palace devoted to art." The main attraction is the Arab Hall, which is a Victorian fantasy of the Middle East, with Isniuk tiles, elaborately carved and gilded woodwork, and the mosaic frieze. There is a wonderful sunken fountain in the middle of the room, which furthers the impression of a courtyard straight out of the pages of *The Arabian Nights.* The top floor is Leighton's old studio, and the huge windows, skylights, and dome are clearly the heart's desire of any nineteenth-century painter. There's a good collection of Victorian paintings on the lower floor, including Leighton's *Roman Mother;* upstairs you can see temporary exhibits of a widely varied nature. The house is sadly lacking in furniture and knickknacks, and despite the stuffed peacock in the hall, one wishes for more of the decorative exuberance that must have resided when Lord Leighton lived here.

Touring Tips Combine this with a trip to Holland Park and the Linley Sambourne House.

Linley Sambourne House

Type of Attraction Perfectly preserved home of Victorian punch cartoonist

Location Zone 14; 18 Stafford Terrace, Kensington, W8; tube: High Street Kensington

Admission £3 for adults; £1 for children

Hours Daily, 11 a.m.–5:30 p.m.; closed Tuesday

Phone (0207) 602-3316

Website www.rbkc.gov.uk/linleysambournehouse

When to Go Weekends

Special Comments Lots of stairs and no wheelchair access

Overall Appeal by Age Group

Pre-school ★	Teens ★★	Over 30 ★★★
Grade school ★★	Young Adults ★★★	Seniors ★★★

Author's Rating ★★★

How Much Time to Allow 1 hour

Description and Comments This place is a veritable time machine, plunking one smack down in the middle of the late Victorian–early Edwardian era, with the sumptuous clutter that incited the backlash of modernism. William Morris designs adorn both walls and floors, and there are a few stained-glass windows to love. A predominant thought on seeing the vast collection of clocks, vases, gimcracks, and knickknacks was of pity for the poor servant in charge of dusting. The immense aesthetic weight of all the pretty possessions can be a bit tiring, but it is an amazing piece of preservation, and the tours conducted by guides in period costume are fun.

Touring Tips Combine with a trip to Holland Park and/or to the Leighton House Museum.

London Aquarium

Type of Attraction Wonderland of fish on the bank of the Thames

Location Zone 5; County Hall, Riverside Building, Westminster Bridge Road, SE1; tube: Westminster or Waterloo

Admission £8.75 for adults; £5.25 for children; free for children under age 3; £25 for families

Hours Daily, 10 a.m.–6 p.m. (last entry at 5 p.m.)

Phone (0207) 967-8000

Website www.londonaquarium.co.uk

When to Go Avoid weekends and school holidays if possible; go early.

Special Comments Fully accessible for disabled persons. To avoid steps, go around building to Belvedere Road to reach entrance. Picnic area available.

Overall Appeal by Age Group

Pre-school ★★★★	Teens ★★★	Over 30 ★★★
Grade school ★★★★	Young Adults ★★★	Seniors ★★★

Author's Rating ★★★★

How Much Time to Allow 2 hours

Description and Comments In a most unlikely conversion, a portion of London's County Hall (also the former home of the Greater London Council) became three dimly lit and atmospheric floors of enormous tanks filled with sea life and freshwater fish of every kind. The Atlantic tank holds 800,000 liters of water and tons of sharks, eels, and stingrays. It's most impressive, although I felt badly for the magnificent sharks whose snouts have been damaged by hitting the glass walls. There's a petting pool for kids to stroke manta rays, who actually seem to invite these caresses. In the Pacific tank, even bigger than the Atlantic, reside more sharks, rays, groupers, and smaller fish. The piranha tank is interesting, especially at dinnertime, when you get to see what a real-life feeding frenzy looks like (call ahead to find out feeding times for various fish).

This is not the most amazing aquarium in the world by a long shot, and if you have access to a good one where you live, you might as well leave this off your list, but it has been proven to me time and again that, when it comes to taming small children, fish take the cake.

Touring Tips There's a McDonald's next door, with its own entrance to the aquarium. There's also a wonderful gift shop for every budget.

London Dungeon

Type of Attraction Yuck-fest with historical pretensions

Location Zone 5; 28–34 Tooley Street, SE1; tube: London Bridge

Admission £12.95 for adults; £11.25 for students; £8.25 for children ages 5–14

Hours July–August, daily, 10 a.m.–7:30 p.m.; September–June, daily, 10:30 a.m.–5:30 p.m.

Phone (0207) 403-7221

Website www.thedungeons.com

When to Go Weekdays as soon as it opens; it gets pretty crowded midday

Special Comments Wheelchair access; don't bring small children

Overall Appeal by Age Group

Pre-school †		Teens ★★★★		Over 30 ★★
Grade school ★		Young Adults ★★		Seniors ★

† *Too scary for preschoolers.*

Author's Rating ★★★

How Much Time to Allow 90 minutes

Description and Comments I am the first one to line up for the weird and horrible—the only thing I didn't yawn over at Madame Tussaud's was the Chamber of Horrors—but this place hit me the wrong way. The relentless gore without context was disturbing, and the "Jack the Ripper Experience"

was just plain offensive. The hordes of French teenage boys who were there during my visit seemed to find it hilarious. They cheered wildly when we saw a dummy guillotined. There's a little boat ride that takes you on a trip to Traitor's Gate, which at least gets you off your feet for a bit. The best part was the gift shop, where I picked up a life-size skull candle and some fun Halloween stuff.

Touring Tips Drop off the teens here and go wait for them in one of the restaurants in the area, or take a look at nearby Southwark Cathedral while the youngsters do their thing.

London Transport Museum

Type of Attraction A fun, interactive museum of trams, buses, and trains of old and new London

Location Zone 7; 39 Wellington Street, off Covent Garden Piazza, WC2; tube: Covent Garden, Leicester Square

Admission £5.95 for adults; free for children

Hours Daily, 10 a.m.–6 p.m.; opens at 11 a.m. on Friday

Phone (0207) 379-6344

Website www.ltmuseum.co.uk

When to Go Anytime

Special Comments Wheelchair and stroller access; café and gift shop

Overall Appeal by Age Group

Pre-school ★★★★	Teens ★★★	Over 30 ★★★
Grade school ★★★★	Young Adults ★★★	Seniors ★★★

Author's Rating ★★★★

How Much Time to Allow 1 hour

Description and Comments This is one of the best venues for kids in London, and adults love it, too. Although many might yawn at the idea of a museum dedicated to that most prosaic feature of urban life, public transportation, this museum is so cleverly and earnestly organized that it's impossible not to get swept up in the fun of it. From horse-drawn stage-coaches and omnibuses that you can climb on, to buses that you can pretend to drive and underground switches you can pretend to throw, this is an interactive museum that most kids will love. You're given a ticket to be stamped at numbered sites until you've filled up your card and seen all there is to see. There are videos of old-time trams and buses and a wonderful short film on the touching last trip of the last tram in London, with everyone singing "Auld Lang Syne." There's so much for adults to learn here, too, such as why the fares on buses and trains in London have to be so complicated; and that 40,000 people took the first underground line on its first day. (Alas, we don't find out why you can wait forever for your bus and then three will come all at once.)

The gift shop has a huge selection of great postcards and underground posters and a wealth of books about London's transport. You can get just about anything with the London Underground map on it, even slippers.

Touring Tips Buy the museum guide if you have children under age 12—there's a fun pull-out section with games and educational pursuits in it. Combine this trip with a visit to Covent Garden, also fun for the kids, especially on weekends. Call or visit their website to check for lectures, tours, films, and family activities.

London Zoo

Type of Attraction Modernized old zoo set at the edge of Regent's Park

Location Zone 15; Regent's Park; tube: Camden Town

Admission £12 for adults; £9 for children ages 3–15

Hours Daily, 10 a.m.–5:30 p.m.

Phone (0207) 722-3333

Website www.zsl.org

When to Go When it's warm and not raining

Special Comments Wheelchair access

Overall Appeal by Age Group

Pre-school ★★★★	Teens ★★★	Over 30 ★★★
Grade school ★★★★	Young Adults ★★★	Seniors ★★★

Author's Rating ★★★

How Much Time to Allow 2 hours

Description and Comments The London Zoo has had some financial headaches for some time now, as there are no significant subsidies from the government to help it operate. It is trying its best, and the education that it provides on endangered species is invaluable, as is the experience of seeing Asian lions, lemurs, and rhinos in the flesh; it makes the possible loss of these animals to extinction all the more horrific. The zoo has tried hard to be the best it can be and has created a small but full environment of hooved, winged, and four-legged friends, but it may have already seen its day. Of course this might just be true for all zoos that have been unable to completely conform to the new ideas of keeping wild animals in captivity in a humane way—a concept that could be considered a contradiction in terms.

Opened in 1828, the zoo has clearly evolved from the old animals-in-cages standard, but it can't be all things to all animals, as is clear from the Bactrian camel, used to the torrid aridity of the Gobi Desert, standing listlessly in the chilly, damp air of London or from the gorilla rocking back and forth, giving his viewers reproachful looks. On a brighter note, the reptile house—which appeared in the first Harry Potter book, when he discovered he could talk to a snake—is magnificent, with cobras, pythons, and even alligators in nicely designed environments, plus a teaching center with snakeskins and things made from the hides of unfortunate animals. The aquarium is also quite comprehensive and well housed. There are a lot of monkeys and a petting zoo for children. The shop is fantastic and will fulfill all your animal-paraphernalia needs, with books, stuffed animals, knickknacks, gimcracks, and geegaws.

Madame Tussaud's Waxworks and the London Planetarium

Type of Attraction World-famous display of wax dummies, chosen most arbitrarily

Location Zone 14; Marylebone Road, NW1; tube: Baker Street

Admission £19.95 for adults; £14.50 for children under age 16; £15.80 for seniors; free for children age 4 and under. This breathtaking entry fee includes tickets to the London Planetarium.

Hours Daily, 9 a.m.–5:30 p.m. Opens at 9:30 a.m. on weekends, bank holidays, and summer weekdays

Phone (0870) 400-3000 to book tickets in advance and avoid the queue (for £1 extra on each ticket) or (0207) 935-6861

Website www.madame-tussauds.com

When to Go They advise that you go in the afternoon, but there always seems to be a line there, no matter what the time, even a half hour before it opens. Go a day before or book over the phone and get a ticket so you can get in the prepaid, timed line. Forget the weekends.

Special Comments Limited wheelchair access: call in advance (0207) 935-6861

Overall Appeal by Age Group

Pre-school ★★		Teens ★★		Over 30 ★★
Grade school ★★		Young Adults ★★		Seniors ★★

Author's Rating ★★

How Much Time to Allow 2 hours

Description and Comments I am not the one to talk to about Madame Tussaud's, because I found it ridiculous—I might have been more pleased with it if it were not for the lines, the price, and the milling hordes inside. I also think that it may have been more interesting in the days before film, when one really didn't know what the personages of the day looked like. However, I have many friends who loved it, so I decided to try to give it the benefit of the doubt. It's certainly one of London's most visited attractions. I liked the section on the history of the waxworks, where you got to see the unfortunates who'd been decommissioned and decapitated and ended up with their heads on the shelf: Liza Minelli, Nikita Krushchev, Sammy Davis Jr., and W. C. Fields were but a few. Some of the newer dummies are frighteningly real, down to the gleam in the eye. One can't say for sure about the verisimilitude of the old ones, like Voltaire, but I must say that Princess Diana's is a pretty good imitation. I loved the surreal display of the duke of Wellington staring down at the wax effigy of his old nemesis, Napoléon, an event that actually transpired.

There is a pretty silly ride in a miniature black taxi that rushes you through the history of London (from Elizabeth I till now) at a breakneck pace. All you can do is giggle as you fly along. Things improved (for me anyway) in the Chamber of Horrors, over which is the Dante inscription "All Hope Abandon, Ye Who Enter Here!"—a sentiment perhaps more fitting for the end of the queue outside. It is a sobering and disturbing exhibit, which manages to even approximate the smell of unwashed bodies and despair (also reminiscent of the queue outside) in the prison section. But of all the horrors, murderers, and bloodiness, there is surely nothing more chilling than the display of Madame Tussaud herself, lantern held aloft, searching a mountain of decapitated bodies for the head of her former employer, Marie Antoinette. I think they should dump the celebrities and make the museum all about the madame: The young Marie Grosholtz Tussaud started out in the late 1700s assisting a doctor who specialized in making wax anatomy forms. Her talent for portraiture was so extraordinary that she was hired to teach art to the children of the doomed king and queen of France. When the French Revolution came, she was imprisoned (rooming with the future Josephine Bonaparte) and marked for the guillotine. Marie was saved by those who thought to have her make death masks of the aristocrats, many of whom she had known. She spent many a night poking through the bloody corpses for the heads she was commissioned to work on. What a way to make a living.

Touring Tips Book a ticket in advance by phone or in person, so that you can avoid the lines, or at least minimize waiting time.

Millennium Bridge

Type of Attraction A footbridge across the Thames linking the Tate Modern with St. Paul's Cathedral

Location Zones 3 & 5; Upper Thames Street on north bank of river; Bankside on south side of river; tube: Mansion on north, London Bridge on south

Admission Free

Hours 24/7

Phone London Tourist Board for info: (0207) 932-2000

Website www.londontouristboard.com

When to Go Anytime, but sunny days are best

Special Comments Wheelchair accessible

Overall Appeal by Age Group

Pre-school ★★★	Teens ★★★	Over 30 ★★★
Grade school ★★★★	Young Adults ★★★	Seniors ★★★

Author's Rating ★★★

How Much Time to Allow 15 minutes to cross it very slowly

Description and Comments The Millennium Bridge opened to great fanfare in 2000, but when the people spilled over its shimmering expanse, it started swaying dangerously, throwing some people to the ground, and it had to be closed for re-engineering. It's the first new bridge to be built over the Thames since 1894, and it's closed to motor vehicles. The original cost of £16 million kept going up as the engineers and architects tried to address its instability. It was amusing to watch the architect blame the engineers and the engineers blame the architect when the bridge started swinging to and fro. Now that it's stable, it certainly is pleasing, forming what architect Lord Norman Foster envisioned as a "blade of light," and providing great views as well as an efficient way to cross the Thames.

Millennium Dome

The Millenium Dome exhibition has come and gone, and the fate of the bulbous growth has yet to be determined—maybe sports arena, visitors center, or technology park; we shall see.

The Monument

Type of Attraction Tower commemorating the Great Fire of 1666

Location Zone 3; Monument Street, EC3; tube: Monument

Admission £2 for adults; £1 for children under age 16

Hours Daily, 9:30 a.m.–5 p.m. (last admission at 4:30 p.m.)

Phone (0207) 626-2717

When to Go Any time you feel perky enough to climb the stairs

Special Comments Not for claustrophobes, acrophobes, or the infirm.

Overall Appeal by Age Group

Pre-school —	Teens ★★★	Over 30 ★★★
Grade school ★★	Young Adults ★★★	Seniors *Depends*

Author's Rating ★★★

How Much Time to Allow 20 minutes

Description and Comments The Monument at 202 feet high was once as visible as St. Paul's Dome, which was certainly no coincidence, as Christopher Wren designed both. It was built to commemorate the Great Fire of 1666 that was actually responsible for making Wren, King Charles II's chief surveyor, one of London's most prolific architects. If laid down on its side, the Monument would reach directly to the spot on Pudding Lane where the fire started. It also has a precise linear relationship to St. Paul's, no doubt a touch that Wren relished.

The 311 steps to the top take about five minutes to walk, though it seems much longer. The stairs are pie shaped, which makes passing on them a little delicate. There is no stated etiquette for who takes which part of the steps as the climbers and descendants squeeze by each other, but the guard assured me that good manners and awareness are all that's necessary to negotiate the pass. I went on a rainy day when only a few hardy souls were to be seen, and I had no problem with passing the few that I did. There are three or four window seats on which to take a little breather while ascending. The view is quite fine—spectacular in fact—and the best possible place from which to see Tower Bridge. Sadly, the views of the Tower of London and the whole of St. Paul's have been severely compromised by newer buildings. I was assured by a taxi driver that the view used to be much more amazing. He also told me that his 4-year-old son was completely freaked out by the height. Look down the stairwell when you get to the top—it's like an Escher drawing or something out of Alfred Hitchcock's *Vertigo*.

Touring Tips Bring a camera, and don't forget to pick up your certificate as you leave, commending you on your climb.

Museum of London

Type of Attraction Museum covering thousands of years of London history

Location Zone 3; London Wall and Aldersgate; tube: St. Paul's or Barbican

Admission Free; fee for special exhibits

Hours Monday–Saturday, 10 a.m.–6 p.m., Sunday, noon–5:50 p.m.

Phone (0207) 600-3699 or 600-0870

Website www.museumoflondon.org.uk

When to Go Anytime, although you may be navigating around large groups of schoolchildren if you go too early on weekdays while school is in session; after 2:30 p.m., they're gone

Special Comments Good handicapped accessibility with a number of ramps and lifts for all floors

Overall Appeal by Age Group

Pre-school ★★	Teens ★★★	Over 30 ★★★
Grade school ★★★★	Young Adults ★★★	Seniors ★★★

Author's Rating ★★★★★

How Much Time to Allow 2–3 hours

Description and Comments The Museum of London tells the story of London from its first settlers back in 4,000 B.C. to the present, using a variety of eye-catching displays and fascinating reconstructions. Its chronologically themed tour route allows visitors to explore more closely the time periods each finds most intriguing. This museum is kid friendly, with some interactive or tactile displays. A few not-to-be-missed exhibits include a large section of London's fourth-century town wall, located outside but incorporated into the museum's Roman London exhibition through a window overlook, the 1757 gilded Lord Mayor's Coach, and re-created nineteenth-century street scenes and shops.

There are exhibits here that can be quite fascinating—a recent one had to do with Londoners' bodies over the centuries and displayed skeletons, corsets, and bones ravaged by such diseases as rickets and syphilis. It is a very well-presented museum, and it manages to make London's history feel quite intimate. There's a real cell from Newgate Prison that is perfectly chilling, and the Victorian shops give one the strangest sense of déjà vu. The displays about the years of the Blitz are riveting. If you are even slightly interested in London's history, this museum is a must-see; if you're not, you will be after a visit. The gift shop has a huge assortment of books on London and English history for all ages. There's a good café, too.

Touring Tips For an introduction to many of the exhibitions and information on current exhibits check out the museum's website. Also, call ahead to find out how many schools are booked on the day of your visit—if there are a lot, come after 2:30 p.m.

National Gallery

Type of Attraction Splendid art gallery of 700 years of European painting

Location Zone 7; Trafalgar Square, WC2; tube: Leicester Square or Charing Cross

Admission Free, though there is a charge for special exhibits

Hours Daily, 10 a.m.–6 p.m.; late view, Wednesday till 9 p.m.

Phone (0207) 839-3321

Website www.nationalgallery.org.uk

When to Go Anytime, but avoid major exhibits on weekends

Special Comments Wheelchair accessible

Overall Appeal by Age Group

Pre-school ★	Teens ★★★	Over 30 ★★★★★
Grade school ★★★	Young Adults ★★★★★	Seniors ★★★★★

Author's Rating ★★★★★

How Much Time to Allow As much as you can physically handle

Description and Comments This is one of those amazing art museums, like The Louvre, in which you get to see the original of some utterly familiar image—Holbein's *The Ambassadors,* Van Gogh's *Sunflowers, or* Monet's *Water Lily Pond*—practically every time you turn around. It is the repository of about 2,300 works from 700 years of European art; you can spend hours gazing at paintings by Titian, Rembrandt, Caravaggio, Vermeer, Velazquez, Michelangelo, da Vinci, Van Eyck, and other old masters too numerous to mention. As if that weren't enough, the East Wing is filled with Impressionists, featuring some 50 paintings on a sort of permanent loan from the Tate Gallery. You'll see Seurat, Pissarro, Gauguin, Degas, Corot, and others. The collection is laid out quite methodically, and excellent inscriptions accompany each painting. The special exhibits are always worth the fee, and do get yourself a headset to listen to the tour.

The National Gallery was founded in 1824 under King George IV, when the government purchased 38 important paintings—from artists such as Raphael, Van Dyck, and Rembrandt—from the estate of John Julius Angerstein. The building was commissioned with a few strange requirements, such as the cupola crowning the front portico, initially ridiculed as a mustard pot, with the two bell towers on either side looking like pepper shakers. The architect, William Wilkens, was also asked to use a portion of a former royal palace in his design, so the slightly ungainly appearance may be due to these requests.

The modern Sainsbury's Wing houses the oldest paintings, dating from 1260 to 1510. Don't miss Jan Van Eyck's Arnolfini Marriage, and look for the artist reflected in the mirror. The West Wing has paintings dating from 1510 to 1600, including Tintoretto's St. George and the Dragon. The North Wing (paintings from 1600 to 1700) has dedicated Room 27 to Rembrandt and includes other seventeenth-century geniuses whose paintings have an almost supernatural power that no reproduction can capture. The East Wing takes us from 1700 up to 1920, with Canaletto and Turner's land- and seascapes giving way to the English portraits and social scenes of Gainsborough, Reynolds, and the prodigious Hogarth, whose series *Marriage à la Mode* can be seen here. Rooms 43–45 are always crowded with Impressionism fans looking at Rousseau's *Tropical Storm with Tiger,* Renoir's *Umbrellas,* Van Gogh's *Chair,* and so many more. Picasso is represented in Room 46, though there are no really major items here, except for *Minotauromachia*.

There's a food shop in the basement with excellent sandwiches and salads, and in the Sainsbury Wing is a more upscale restaurant serving decent food. The gift shops are filled with the most wonderful collection of books, postcards, and calendars, and must be visited. Try to get your hands on the National Gallery Advent calendar.

Touring Tips Take advantage of the lectures and recorded tours available here; they are great aids. There is also a computer in the Micro Gallery, where you can look up and print out information about the art and artists.

National Maritime Museum and Queen's House

(see also profile for Royal Greenwich Observatory)

Type of Attraction Largest maritime museum in the world

Location Zone 6; Romney Road, Greenwich (Docklands Light Railway: Greenwich)

Admission Free; fee for special events and exhibits

Hours Daily, 10 a.m.–5 p.m.

Phone (0208) 312-6565

Website www.nmm.ac.uk

When to Go Anytime on weekdays; early in the day on weekends

Special Comments Fully accessible with lifts for disabled, touch-talks for visually impaired and sign-interpreted talks. Call for details.

Overall Appeal by Age Group

Pre-school ★★★	Teens ★★★	Over 30 ★★★★
Grade school ★★★★	Young Adults ★★★★	Seniors ★★★★

Author's Rating ★★★★

How Much Time to Allow 2–3 hours for the museum and 1–2 hours for Queen's House Millennium Exhibition

Description and Comments The National Maritime Museum was restructured and revitalized just in time for the new millennium, and it now fashions itself as part of the larger "Maritime Greenwich World Heritage Site," which includes the Queen's House and the Royal Observatory. Its new galleries include lots of interactive displays exploring the impact of the oceans on our daily lives, as well as our destructive impact on the seas. Exhibitions include the re-creations of steerage and first-class cabins and deck sections from an ocean liner, thousands of ship models, hundreds of navigational instruments, and galleries devoted to the history of British naval conquests and accomplishment. Of particular interest to adults is the elaborate Horatio Nelson exhibition, which pays homage to the famous admiral who defeated Napoléon at the Battle of Trafalgar. Kids, however, will have to be dragged out of the All-Hands Gallery, a fascinating interactive collection of exhibits, tools, and experiments of nautical principles. The fun includes raising and lowering signal flags, working a crane to load a ship's cargo, or attempting some deep-sea engineering.

The Queen's House, adjacent to the museum, has undergone major refurbishment and presents an architectural triumph of seventeenth-century architect Inigo Jones. The Queen's House is now a venue for the appreciation of maritime-related artwork, with exhibits regularly mounted, such as the comprehensive exhibition on Queen Elizabeth I, friend to sailors and pirates alike. The interior of the house has been restored to the days of Charles II, and the Royal Apartments on the upper floor are especially dazzling.

Touring Tips The museum offers a wide range of children's educational workshops and activities, many free of charge. There are Pirate Workshops, the Crowsnest Club for those under age 6, and Shipmates for those age 7 and older. For details and a full schedule of planned events, call (0208) 312-6608, or check the excellent website.

The National Portrait Gallery

Type of Attraction Collection of the most famous faces in British history
Location Zone 7; 2 St. Martin's Place, W2; adjacent to the National Gallery; tube: Leicester Square or Charing Cross
Admission Free; £4–£8 for special exhibits
Hours Monday–Wednesday and Saturday–Sunday, 10 a.m.–6 p.m.; Thursday and Friday, 10 a.m.–9 p.m.
Phone (0207) 306-0055
Website www.npg.org.uk
When to Go Anytime
Special Comments Very accessible to disabled individuals
Overall Appeal by Age Group

Pre-school ★	Teens ★★★★	Over 30 ★★★★
Grade school ★★	Young Adults ★★★★	Seniors ★★★★

Author's Rating ★★★★★
How Much Time to Allow 2–3 hours
Description and Comments Of all the museums that London has to offer, the National Portrait Gallery holds particular appeal, as it's in the middle of a very interesting area. It's across the street from St. Martin-in-the-Fields Church, and sits next to the National Gallery, just off Trafalgar

Square. It's quite manageable in a couple of hours, unlike the eight miles of the Victoria and Albert or the grand halls of the National Gallery. Its size allows for relaxed browsing without the feeling that you must rush or you won't see everything. The NPG gives the casual student of England a direct line to its history through the faces of its most interesting and important people. It's a veritable Who's Who of England that includes the lean faces of the early medieval kings; the Tudors, with Holbein's images of Henry VIII and his many wives; the Stuarts in the seventeenth century; the nineteenth-century Victorians; and, finally, portraits and photos of the current royal family.

As you take this visual voyage through the ages, notice the changing styles of portraiture and what kinds of people each age deemed worthy of portraiture. You will see people from various disciplines—science, literature, politics, art, and entertainment—whose contributions to English life reached far beyond this small island. With the help of the NPG sound guides, the amount of history you absorb will change how you perceive London's most famous sights. There's a good restaurant on the top floor offering glorious views over Trafalgar Square and beyond.

Touring Tips In addition to the more pricey roof restaurant, there is also the Portrait Café in the basement. Combine your visit with a trip to the National Gallery next door.

Natural History Museum

Type of Attraction Exhibits on the history of the natural world

Location Zone 11; Cromwell Road, South Kensington, SW7; tube: South Kensington

Admission Free

Hours Monday–Saturday, 10 a.m.–5:50 p.m.; Sunday, 11 a.m.–5:50 p.m.

Phone (0207) 942-5000

Website www.nhm.ac.uk

When to Go Weekends can be quite crowded, so go early.

Special Comments Complete disabled access

Overall Appeal by Age Group

Pre-school ★★★	Teens ★★★	Over 30 ★★★
Grade school ★★★★	Young Adults ★★★	Seniors ★★★

Author's Rating ★★★

How Much Time to Allow 2 hours or more

Description and Comments As part of the South Kensington cultural revolution of the nineteenth century, the Natural History Museum was formed by the British Library's collections of Sir Hans Sloane, which were divvied up and sent to South Ken in the 1860s. It's a grand old institution, housed in a majestic building that, in itself, makes the visit worthwhile. Notice the animal statues on the outside, and the terra-cotta monkeys and other beasts climbing on stone vines in the lobby. It has all the hallmarks of a Gothic cathedral, an impression that architect Alfred Waterhouse intended, to inspire the proper reverence for nature. It is a huge place, full of many surprises and some really fine examples of educational curation, such as the Ecology Gallery in which you walk through a rain forest, and the new Darwin Centre with 22 million specimens of everything from amoebas to monkeys. It has plenty of interactive, permanent displays and temporary exhibits, some of which have been very good, such as the one on human biology. The newly remodeled Earth Galleries (entrance on Exhibition Road) are entered via a long escalator that goes through a model of the earth and features a re-creation of a convenience store in the Kobe earthquake. The Earth Galleries are full of see-and-touch educational exhibits, which is fine with kids, but perhaps not so wondrous for adults. I am much more impressed with some of the older artifacts: dioramas of exotic animals, including the extinct dodo bird, and cabinets full of butterflies, all the bounty brought back from the far-flung reaches of the empire, much of which is utterly irreplaceable and of great scientific importance. The dinosaur exhibit is quite good, and of interest to old and young alike. It is set out in such a way that one follows along paths and climbs up stairs, which keeps the kids active and happy, while the parents can take the time to read the information posted there. The gift shops are excellent for children's educational toys and books, as well as geological booty.

Touring Tips Be sure to look at the entire front of the building on Cromwell Road: In a witty reflection of the statues of artists that adorn the front of the neighboring Victoria and Albert Museum, the Natural History Museum has statues of animals on its facade. If the line at the Cromwell Road entrance is long, enter at the Earth Galleries on Exhibition Road.

Old Bailey (Central Criminal Courts)

Type of Attraction London's bastion of justice

Location Zone 3; Old Bailey Street, EC4; tube: St. Paul's

Admission Free; children under age 14 not admitted

Hours Monday–Friday, 10:30 a.m.–4:30 p.m.; closed for lunch from 1–2 p.m.

Phone (0207) 248-3277; ask for List Office

Website www.courtservice.gov.uk

When to Go Arrive for the times given. The public gallery in each courtroom has a limited number of seats, and bailiffs may not allow access once court is in session.

Special Comments Security searches are routine. Do not bring backpacks, cameras, food, cell phones, or pagers. These items are prohibited and there is no cloak room for storing them.

Overall Appeal by Age Group

Pre-school †		Teens ★★		Over 30 ★★★
Grade school †		Young Adults ★★		Seniors ★★★

† *Not appropriate for children*

Author's Rating ★★★

How Much Time to Allow As much time as your interest in the proceedings dictates

Description and Comments Although most interesting to those with a background in law, the cases held in London's Old Bailey are criminal cases, and just about anyone will find both the content of the cases and the etiquette of the British courtroom intriguing for some length of time. Wigged and traditionally robed barristers address each other as "friend" and the judge as "milord," and politely assert their cases while the defendant sits at the rear of the courtroom, visibly separated from the "gentlemen's proceedings" going on in front of him.

The Old Bailey was built on the site of Newgate Prison, the noxious and notorious prison that held criminals and public executions from the twelfth century until it was destroyed in 1902. Not the best feng shui for a court, one might say, with God only knows how many desperate ghosts hanging around. This court saw the spectacle of Oscar Wilde's trial— "the butterfly broken on a wheel"—as well as those of the Yorkshire Ripper and the wife-killer, Dr. Crippen.

Touring Tips The entrance to the public galleries is off of Newgate Street and down Old Bailey, past the original courts building and its contemporary addition, to Warwick Passage on the left. Call ahead to find out what cases are currently on the docket and at what point in the proceedings they are. Dial the number above and ask for the List Office.

Old Operating Theatre, Museum, and Herb Garret

Type of Attraction Haunting museum of old medical equipment and an early Victorian operating theater

Location Zone 5; 9A St. Thomas's Street, SE1; tube: London Bridge

Admission £4 for adults; £2.50 for children; £10 for a family

Hours Daily, 10:30 a.m.–5 p.m.

Phone (0207) 955-4791

Website www.thegarret.org.uk

When to Go Anytime

Special Comments The stairs in this old house are very, very steep. There is no wheelchair access.

Overall Appeal by Age Group

Pre-school †		Teens ★★		Over 30 ★★★
Grade school ★		Young Adults ★★★		Seniors ★★★

† *Not appropriate for preschoolers.*

Author's Rating ★★★★

How Much Time to Allow 1 hour

Description and Comments In a tiny old house in a street by London Bridge is one of the most fascinating medical museums in London. You must climb up some rather treacherous steps to reach the musty old attic in which you'll find displayed many of the gruesome medical instruments used before the days of anesthesia. Around the room are sheaths of herbs—comfrey for healing bones, pennyroyal for nausea, willow bark from which aspirin was derived, and elderflowers for what ails you.

The centerpiece of the museum is the operating theater from the early nineteenth century, a case study for postoperative infection from the days before Dr. Lister figured out the germ theory. The table is made of wood, and under it is a box of sawdust, which the surgeon would kick where necessary to catch the blood; there's a small washbasin in which hands were washed after the operation. The room is ringed by semicircular levels of observation areas into which medical students would be crammed like sardines to stand and watch. This is not a place for the faint of heart. The gift shop is packed with interesting books on herbal remedies.

Pollock's Toy Museum

Type of Attraction Adventure into toys of the past

Location Zone 14; 1 Scala Street, W1P; tube: Goodge Street

Admission £3 for adults; £1.50 for children

Hours Monday–Saturday, 10 a.m.–5 p.m.

Phone (0207) 636-3452

Website www.pollocksweb.co.uk

When to Go Anytime, but call and check to see if a school group is planned

Special Comments This museum consists of six rooms on three floors connected by very steep stairs; it is not disabled or wheelchair accessible.

Overall Appeal by Age Group

Pre-school ★★		Teens ★★★		Over 30 ★★★★
Grade school ★★★★		Young Adults ★★★		Seniors ★★★★

Author's Rating ★★★★

How Much Time to Allow 1 hour

Description and Comments I can't say it better than Robert Louis Stevenson: "If you love art, folly, or the bright eyes of children, speed to Pollock's."

OK, so he was actually referring to Benjamin Pollock's famous toy theaters of the nineteenth century, but he probably would have been just as hearty in his approval of the Toy Museum. It contains not only Mr. Pollock's cunning toy theaters but five further rooms of toys of every description, as well as displays along the steep staircases. There is probably not one square foot in the place that doesn't display some charming toy, poster, or board game. You'll see rocking horses, American automatic money boxes, magic lanterns, ancient jack-in-the-boxes, toy soldiers, folk dolls from around the world, dollhouse rooms, puppets, teddy bears, even space toys. There are no interactive displays, but it's small and delightful enough to keep children well entertained for the time it takes to look through, though adults may want to linger longer. There's a shop on the ground floor with books, toy reproductions, and other fun stuff. Buy generously and support this priceless collection.

Touring Tips Combine this with a trip to the nearby British Museum

Queen's Gallery, Buckingham Palace

Type of Attraction Rotating exhibition of a fraction of the queen's treasures

Location Zone 9; Buckingham Palace, SW1; tube: Victoria, Green Park, or St. James's Park

Admission £6.50 for adults; £3 for children; £5 concessions

Hours Daily, 10 a.m.–4:30 p.m.; occasionally closed between exhibitions, so call ahead

Phone (0207) 766-7301

Website www.royal.gov.uk

When to Go Anytime, but it can be very crowded in summer

Special Comments A new wing opened in spring 2002 to celebrate the Queen's Golden Jubilee, and is disabled friendly.

Overall Appeal by Age Group

Pre-school ★	Teens ★★	Over 30 ★★★
Grade school ★	Young Adults ★★★	Seniors ★★

Author's Rating ★★★

How Much Time to Allow 1 hour

Description and Comments The new Queen's Gallery is an impressive piece of renovation and curating. Entirely new wings have been built in the grand style of the Buckingham Palace state rooms, and are completely modern and practical. Total wheelchair access has been added, which is impossible to do in many renovations of old buildings. It is certainly a triumph. There are sketches by da Vinci and paintings by old masters. There is extraordinary furniture—don't miss the silver table and mirror if they are still there; understandably, not much silver furniture has made it intact through the ages. There are gold table services, sculpture, porcelain, and treasures from every corner of the empire. Unlike Buckingham Palace, this gallery has comprehensive explanatory signs describing the marvels, and it would appear that the bulk of the current exhibits were accumulated under Charles II and mad George III, whom you would think certainly had other things on their minds besides bibelots and art. You will always be impressed by whatever the Queen's Gallery is showing because there is such bounty to choose from: 20,000 drawings by old masters, such as Holbein, Canaletto, da Vinci, Michelangelo, Carracci, and more; 10,000 old masters' paintings, including such artists as Rembrandt, Vermeer, Holbein, Brueghel, Van Dyck, and Rubens; royal portraits by Gainsborough, Reynolds, and Wilkie, as well as George Stubbs's magnificent equine portraits; 30,000 English watercolors, a possible half-a-million prints, and countless sculptures, glass and porcelain works, books, and Fabergé trinkets. Excellent gift shop on the site with lots of royal memorabilia.

Touring Tips Leave your backpacks and pocketbooks at the hotel: There is a very slow security drill in place in which your bags are examined and you must check them into the coatroom. The gallery is great but nothing is worth that length of time and that kind of hassle to enter.

Royal Academy of Arts

Type of Attraction Venue for the world-famous Summer Exhibition of contemporary artists, record-breaking exhibitions of major artists and art themes, and a small but fine permanent collection of past academicians

Location Zone 8; Burlington House, Piccadilly, W1; tube: Piccadilly Circus, Green Park

Admission £6–10 for adults, depending on exhibition; £2.50 for children ages 12–18; £1 for children ages 8–11

Hours Daily, 10 a.m.–6 p.m.; open until 10 p.m. on Friday

Phone (0207) 300-5760 or (0207) 300-5761

Website www.royalacademy.org.uk

When to Go The largest crowds will be when there's a very popular exhibition; weekends are normally crowded. Go in the morning if possible.

Special Comments Wheelchair access

Overall Appeal by Age Group

Pre-school ★		Teens ★★★		Over 30 ★★★★
Grade school ★		Young Adults ★★★★		Seniors ★★★★

Author's Rating ★★★★

How Much Time to Allow It depends on the exhibit, but 2 hours is a good estimate

Description and Comments The academy is housed in the beautiful old Burlington House, off Piccadilly. The courtyard usually features some exhibit of sculptures, often marvelously at odds with the Palladian grandeur of these last few surviving eighteenth-century palazzos. This was England's first art school, founded by Gainsborough and Reynolds, among others, in 1768. To be counted among the academicians was the highest mark of success. Today, it continues its tradition as a venue for new artists by hosting the 200-year-old Summer Exhibition, in which painters and sculptors compete for the honor of displaying their work to an appreciative audience, many of whom come to buy. It's a bit of a hodgepodge and scorned by many of the chattering classes (critics and journalists) and most of the artists who don't get in the exhibit. But everyone keeps trying to win a place on the wall.

The exhibits are usually excellent. One record-breaking exhibit was the Monet show in which people had to be let in on a timed basis, and for the last couple of days, they had to keep the academy open for 24 hours. A less popular but no less interesting show was of the whimsical Victorian paintings of fairies. A permanent collection includes work from past academicians, as well as its most significant treasure, Michelangelo's marble frieze of Madonna and child.

Touring Tips For £48, you can become a Friend of the Royal Academy, which allows you use of the very pleasant Friends' Room, free admission plus a guest, and, most importantly, you can jump the queue for the blockbuster exhibitions. You also get to feel quite virtuous as a much-needed patron of the arts. Call the academy ahead of time, or just come to the Friends' Desk and sign up.

Royal Greenwich Observatory

Type of Attraction Location of the world's prime meridian (0 degrees longitude)

Location Zone 6; Blackheath Avenue, hilltop of Greenwich Park; Docklands Light Railway: Greenwich

Admission Free; fee for special events, exhibits, and planetarium shows

Hours Daily, 10 a.m.–5 p.m.

Phone (0208) 312-6565

Website www.nmm.ac.uk

When to Go Anytime

Special Comments Not all observatory buildings are fully accessible.

Overall Appeal by Age Group

Pre-school ★	Teens ★★★	Over 30 ★★★
Grade school ★	Young Adults ★★★	Seniors ★★★

Author's Rating ★★★

How Much Time to Allow 1–2 hours

Description and Comments In 1675, Charles II appointed John Flamsteed his Astronomer Royal, with the specific mandate to create better navigational maps for the British empire. Christopher Wren then designed and built an observatory for him on the highest point of the king's royal hunting grounds in Greenwich. Today, this small complex of buildings is a popular museum. You can place yourself in two hemispheres at the same time as you straddle the prime meridian, a favorite photo op for visitors. The museum's oldest part, Flamsteed House, is the restored home of the first Astronomer Royal. Its main galleries tell a variety of the bizarre methods once used to help ships' captains determine their location at sea and the increasingly important race to discover longitude. The remaining buildings contain a number of astronomical tools and telescopes, including Britain's largest, in the impressive Telescope Dome.

Touring Tips Planetarium showsoccur at 2:30 p.m. on weekdays.

Royal Mews, Buckingham Palace

Type of Attraction Where the royal carriages and queen's horses are kept

Location Zone 9; Buckingham Palace Road, SW1; tube: St. James's Park or Victoria

Admission £5 for adults; £2.50 for children

Hours Monday–Thursday, noon–4 p.m. During Palace State Rooms opening in August and September, Monday–Thursday, 10:30 a.m.–5 p.m. Closed Friday–Sunday. Subject to sudden closures, so be sure to call first.

Phone (0207) 766-7302

Website www.royal.gov.uk

When to Go See hours above

Special Comments Disabled are free, and there is good wheelchair access. Call (0207) 839-1377 for disabled info.

Overall Appeal by Age Group

Pre-school ★★		Teens ★★		Over 30 ★★
Grade school ★★		Young Adults ★★		Seniors ★★

Author's Rating ★★★

How Much Time to Allow 40 minutes

Description and Comments It's a small attraction and only open a few hours a week, but I urge any horse-and-carriage fancier to go take a look, if only to see the most elegant, cleanest stables in the entire world. Designed by John Nash, the stables retain a Georgian perfection, with freshly painted stalls of a pale yellow and lovely wrought-iron lamps. The horses are just as magnificent as you would expect: strong, well-bred, and glossy. How they handle the oddly narrow riding ring is anyone's guess, but what the ring lacks in practicality, it makes up for in beauty. The royal coaches and automobiles are just mind-boggling, especially the gold state coach built for George II in 1761, which is still in use. There's a room with some of the most admirable tack and saddles ever made, with sketches and photos of royal public occasions also on display.

Touring Tips Try to make this part of your trip to Buckingham Palace and/or the Queen's Gallery.

Saatchi Gallery

Type of Attraction Collection of young British artists

Location Zone 5; County Hall, South Bank, SE1; tube: Waterloo or Westminster

Admission £8.50; family ticket £25; concessions £6.50

Hours Daily, 10 a.m.–6 p.m.; Friday and Saturday, open until 10 p.m.

Phone (0207) 823-2363

Website www.saatchi-gallery.co.uk

When to Go Anytime, although weekend days can be crowded

Special Comments Complete disabled access; entrance at Belvedere Road

Overall Appeal by Age Group

Pre-school ★	Teens ★★★★	Over 30 ★★★
Grade school ★★	Young Adults ★★★	Seniors ★★★

Author's Rating ★★★

How Much Time to Allow 2 hours

Description and Comments It's not just the well-done renovation of 40,000 square feet of the old County Hall that makes one favorably disposed toward this gallery; nor is it only the newsworthy opening blast attended by the city's leading citizens and the performance-art piece of 200 naked people happily mingling with the celebs that make one feel like cheering modern art. It's more a combination of the above and the long-term speculation about the wisdom of the Young British Artists' patron Charles Saatchi plunking down thousands of pounds for artworks such as Damien Hirst's shark in formaldehyde and Tracey Emin's unmade bed being somewhat resolved by the robust attendance at this new gallery, opened in June 2003. One goes along to this gallery with a sense of humor, and one is not disappointed. There is plenty to be amused by here, and the cheekiness of the young (or rather, now aging) British artists, known as the Britpack, exhibited in some of these pieces can only be admired. The first exhibit featured Damien Hirst, whose animal cadavers caused such a hue and cry in the 1990s, and although Charles Saatchi's collection is heavy with such contemporary British artists, his intention for his new gallery is to make it a center for modern art that will rival the Tate Modern. It is a good opportunity to make up your own mind about the art that the media has been tut-tutting about for the past ten years, and to realize how powerful some of these pieces are.

Touring Tips Combine a visit with any of the other Southbank attractions, such as the London Eye, Dali Universe, or the London Aquarium. Friday and Saturday late nights are appealing because you can enjoy the night lights of Westminster's sights from a good vantage point outside County Hall.

St. Paul's Cathedral

Type of Attraction London's most prominent cathedral

Location Zone 3; Ludgate Hill, EC4; tube: St. Paul's or Mansion House

Admission Cathedral, galleries, and crypt entry: £6 for adults; £5 for seniors and students; £3 for children. Self-guided tours (with cassette) and guided tours are available for an extra fee.

Hours Visitors to cathedral: Monday–Saturday, 8:30 a.m.–4:30 p.m.; galleries open at 9:30 a.m.; choral evensong occurs weekdays at 5 p.m. and Sunday at 3:15 p.m. Call the cathedral for other mass times, and for information on closures due to weddings or baptisms.

Phone (0207) 236-4128

When to Go Early in the day on weekdays to avoid the crowds and catch the best chances for clear-sky views from the dome

Special Comments Good disabled access to cathedral's nave and crypt, but there is no lift access to the galleries

Overall Appeal by Age Group

Pre-school ★	Teens ★★	Over 30 ★★★
Grade school ★★	Young Adults ★★★	Seniors ★★★

Author's Rating ★★★

How Much Time to Allow 30 minutes to 1 hour, depending on whether you plan to climb to the top of the dome

Description and Comments There was once a Roman temple to the goddess Diana on the site of the present St. Paul's, but even such ancient sanctity did not put the succeeding buildings out of harm's way; the first church was destroyed by fire around 660. The second was demolished by Vikings. The huge wooden cross was struck by lightning in 1382, and in 1561 a spire was also toppled by lightning. During Henry VIII's reformation, the church turned into a kind of public marketplace. A bishop described the nave in 1560: "The south side for Popery and Usury; the north for Simony (buying and selling pardons); and the horse-fair in the middle for all kinds of bargains, meetings, brawlings, murders, conspiracies; and the font for ordinary payments of money." The Great Fire of 1666 destroyed the third incarnation of St. Paul's Cathedral, along with four-fifths of the city. King Charles II's surveyor-general, Christopher Wren, became responsible for designing its replacement, and this became his masterpiece. The cathedral was finished in a mere 35 years (the first cathedral to be completed by a single architect), and its stone English baroque style, despite being dwarfed by the encroachments of skyscrapers, still dominates the neighborhood. At 360 feet, the dome is one of the highest in the world and second in size only to St. Peter's Basilica in Rome. Its lantern weighs a massive 850 tons.

Inside the cathedral, there are mosaics and frescoes, the *Light of the World* by Holman Hunt, Jean Tijou's grand sanctuary gates, and the intricate choir-stall carvings designed by the most skilled woodcraftsman of the day, Grinling Gibbons. The crypt is the resting place of—among other notables—Lord Admiral Horatio Nelson, the duke of Wellington, and Wren himself, whose son composed the Latin inscription on his tomb: "Reader, if you seek his monument, look around." Also in the crypt are the cathedral shop and a small café.

The 530 steps that take you to the top of St. Paul's are worth the effort, especially if you are lucky enough to have a clear, or even sunny, day. It is an easy walk to the Whispering Gallery, the first of the three levels, where words whispered on one side of the gallery can be clearly heard on the other. On the second level, the external Stone Gallery provides telescopes and benches, but it is the uppermost Golden Gallery that offers the most spectacular views of London. To see them, however, you must submit to considerably more nerve-racking climbing.

Touring Tips If your interest in Christopher Wren is inspired by St. Paul's, there are a number of other charming examples of his seventeenth-century work, many of which are just around the corner. Some of those closest to the cathedral include: St. Mary-le-Bow (Cheapside), St. Bride's (Fleet Street), and Christ Church (Newgate Street), that has only its tower remaining. A lovely garden now fills what was once the nave. Also visit St. Bartholomew the Great, in Little Britain Street; it's London's oldest monastic church (telephone (0207) 606-5171).

The Science Museum

Type of Attraction Abundant collection of scientific/technological odds and ends that add up to a fascinating experience

Location Zone 11; Exhibition Road, SW7; tube: South Kensington

Admission Free; charge for Imax and special exhibits

Hours Daily, 10 a.m.–6 p.m.

Phone (0207) 942-4000

Website www.sciencemuseum.org.uk

When to Go Avoid school holidays and weekends, unless you're there at 10 a.m. It's one of London's most popular museums, so go early or on weekdays.

Special Comments Wheelchair access and facilities

Overall Appeal by Age Group

Pre-school ★★★★	Teens ★★★★	Over 30 ★★★★
Grade school ★★★★	Young Adults ★★★★	Seniors ★★★★

Author's Rating ★★★★

How Much Time to Allow As much as you can spare—you could easily spend all day here, there's so much to see. If you're with children who want to play in the interactive areas, plan to spend at least 2 hours.

Description and Comments You don't need any particular interest in things scientific to love this most comprehensive collection displaying the progress of technology and science from the dawn of time to today. It is dauntingly large and there is a lot to read, but it allows you to travel, from an early hourglass in the time gallery to the Apollo 10 Command Module in the exploration-of-space exhibit. Moving exhibits include a miniaturized field with examples of plowing carried out by a number of small tractors, and a stupendously huge mill engine in the middle of the East Hall. You can watch Foucault's pendulum swinging away in the staircase by the East Hall, or check out a replica of a turn-of-the-century pharmacy in the area that focuses on the art of medicine. The supermarket Sainsbury's has contributed a "Food for Thought" exhibit that examines every aspect of nutrition, the strangest being the mannequins of a young man and a young woman, showing what food they consumed in a month, how much sweat, feces, and urine they excreted, and how much their hair and nails grew.

Downstairs in the basement is a wonderful place to bring the young children: There's a hands-on gallery where children between ages 3 and 6 can splash around (hands only) in a water sluice and build things with giant Legos, to name only two of its many attractions. You'll never get them out of there, which may be why the museum suggests starting at the top and moving downward.

Touring Tips If you arrive and find a line, go across the street to the Natural History Museum, and come back late in the afternoon when the families have taken their tired kids home.

Sherlock Holmes Museum

Type of Attraction Re-creation of fictional Victorian bachelor's house

Location Zone 14; 221B Baker Street, NW1; tube: Baker Street

Admission £6 for adults; £4 for children under age 16; free for children under age 7

Hours Daily, 9:30 a.m.–6 p.m.

Phone (0207) 935-8866

Website www.sherlock-holmes.co.uk

When to Go Anytime, especially if you're waiting for Madame Tussaud's to open or are on your way to the London Zoo

Special Comments No wheelchair access; numerous, steep stairs

Overall Appeal by Age Group

Pre-school ★		Teens ★★★		Over 30 ★★★
Grade school ★		Young Adults ★★★		Seniors ★★★

Author's Rating ★★★★

How Much Time to Allow 30–40 minutes

Description and Comments I am a Sherlock Holmes fan, and I am also a sucker for anything from the nineteenth century. But even if you are neither of the above, I think you'll find this a charming, if expensive, little stop. The self-guided (and short) tour through the little house is like stepping back in time: There are fires laid in all the rooms, which are bursting with curios and furniture, much in the way described in the stories by Sir Arthur Conan Doyle. It is a funny experience, seeing this fictional place brought to life; by the time you leave you may think there really was a Sherlock Holmes. The decor is wonderful. There's the violin he so famously played close at hand in the study, leg irons on the bed by a valise half packed, a medical corner for Dr. Watson, a remarkable early typewriter, and a turn-of-the-century telephone. Even the attic is perfect, stuffed with leather goods, hatboxes, and other household items we're all too young to remember. Props from the stories are displayed with appropriate quotes from the books, and there's an extraordinary chess set in gold and silver with characters from the books as the pieces.

Touring Tips Time your visit so you can have a traditional tea in the charming Hudson's Victorian Dining Room on the ground floor of the museum.

Sir John Soane's Museum

Type of Attraction Fascinating, eccentric collection of sculpture, art, and antiquities belonging to neoclassical architect Sir John Soane

Location Zone 2; 13 Lincoln's Inn Fields, WC2; tube: Holborn, Central and Piccadilly lines

Admission Free

Hours Tuesday–Saturday, 10 a.m.–5 p.m.; open the first Tuesday of each month 6–9 p.m.

Phone (0207) 405-2107

Website www.soane.org

When to Go Anytime, although there is an excellent tour of the museum on Saturday at 2:30 p.m., which is limited to 20 people and costs £3

Special Comments The museum is not handicapped accessible, because it was formerly the private home of Sir John Soane and was directed to be left as he had it. You will even be asked to leave backpacks at the front desk so there is less chance of knocking over any of the hundreds of items that can be seen in each room. This attraction is not recommended for very young children with the tendency to touch everything.

Overall Appeal by Age Group

Pre-school †		Teens ★★★		Over 30 ★★★★
Grade school ★		Young Adults ★★★★		Seniors ★★★★

† *Not appropriate for young children.*

Author's Rating ★★★★

How Much Time to Allow 1½–2½ hours

Description and Comments Many in London consider this their favorite museum. As small as it is, you can visit this nondescript residence numerous times, with treasures in every conceivable cranny, and discover new things to love about this collection each time. Situated just a stone's throw from one of the early Inns of Court, Sir John Soane bought and reconstructed the Georgian homes at 12, 13, and 14 Lincoln's Inn Fields and began filling them with a rather eccentric collection of art and antiquities. His architectural talent is seen in much of the unique floor plan of number 13, which includes a glass-domed roof and central atrium that lights three floors as well as in the Soanes' dining room and breakfast parlor, both of which incorporate an unusual display of mirrors that reflect light and add illusions of space.

Other remarkable aspects of the collection include the series of paintings by William Hogarth, entitled the *Rake's Progress* and *Election,* in an impressive picture gallery of false and hidden walls; a mock medieval monk's parlor containing gloomy casts and gargoyles; and the sarcophagus of Seti I surrounded by rows of antique statuary. Saturday's hour-long tour takes you through all of this and into number 12 as well, where you can see Soane's enormous research library, complete with architectural plans for the Bank of England, Whitehall, and parts of the treasury, along with numerous models of Pompeiian temples.

Touring Tips If you can't manage the Saturday tour, definitely strike up a conversation with any of the museum curators. They are very friendly and love to talk about the plethora of items acquired by Sir John Soane. It is the only way to really appreciate the amount and variety of items you see housed in this small town house. Call about the candlelit late opening.

Somerset House (including Courtauld Institute Gallery, Gilbert Collection, and Hermitage Rooms)

Type of Attraction Magnificent edifice with river views, a classical courtyard, a river terrace, and three separate art galleries

Location Zone 2; Strand, WC; tube: Covent Garden, Holborn, Temple (except on Sunday)

Admission Free for Somerset House and grounds. Courtauld Institute Gallery: £5 for adults, £4 for seniors; admission is free on Monday between 10 a.m. and 2 p.m. Gilbert Collection: £5 for adults, free for children under age 18 (an audio guide and magnifying glass are included in the price). Combined-admission adult tickets for the Courtauld Gallery and Gilbert Collection are £8. Hermitage Rooms: Prices depend on the current exhibit and will range from free to £8 for adults. Children under age 18 are admitted free of charge to all galleries.

Hours Somerset House and all galleries are open daily, 10 a.m. to 6 p.m. and on Sunday from noon to 6 p.m. During the summer, the house itself and its terrace and courtyard stay open on Friday till 10 p.m.

Phone Somerset: (0207) 845-4600; Courtauld: (0207) 848-2526; Gilbert: (0207) 420-9400; Hermitage: (0207) 845-4630

Websites www.somerset-house.org.uk; www.courtauld.ac.uk; www.gilbert-collection.org.uk; www.hermitagerooms.com

When to Go The courtyard and terrace of the house are splendid on a sunny day; inside galleries are great anytime, but see special comments about the Hermitage Rooms.

Special Comments The house and the galleries are all wheelchair accessible. Special sign-language talks are also offered occasionally; call (0207) 848-2549 for details. Because the Hermitage Rooms are small, the tickets are sold for timed slots, on the hour and on the half hour; about 60 at a time can go in. Also, check the Hermitage website to be sure they are not in the middle of staging a new exhibit; the exhibits are shown in ten-month cycles.

Overall Appeal by Age Group

Pre-school ★★★	Teens ★★★	Over 30 ★★★★★
Grade school ★★★	Young Adults ★★★★★	Seniors ★★★★★

Author's Rating ★★★★★

How Much Time to Allow This depends on whether you go to any or all of the art galleries and on how long you stroll around or linger in the cafés or on the terrace. You could spend the day here.

Description and Comments Somerset House is one of the great jewels in London's architectural and historical crown. It was opened to the public in 2000, after a lengthy and expensive renovation that included adding the Gilbert Collection and the Hermitage Rooms to its long-standing Courtauld Gallery Institute. The site of Somerset House has a long history, going back to 1547. In addition to the galleries, it now houses a fair number of cafés, gift shops, and places to sit and watch the Thames flow by. In winter, the courtyard fountain is turned into a skating rink.

The Courtauld Gallery is an integral part of the Courtauld Institute of Art. The gallery originated out of textile magnate Samuel Courtauld's private collection from the 1930s, but has grown considerably since that time. It is most famous for its priceless Impressionist works, which include Van Gogh's *Self-Portrait with Bandaged Ear,* Degas's *Two Dancers,* Renoir's *La Loge,* and Manet's *Déjeuner sur l'herbe.* It is worth noting, however, that the medieval and early Renaissance works in galleries 1 and 2 are also quite impressive, with paintings by Brueghel, Bellini, and Rubens.

The Gilbert Collection is a museum of decorative arts, housing Sir Arthur Gilbert's mammoth collection of gold, silver, and mosaics. There are silver items here to rival the Victoria and Albert's collection, and I don't know where in the world there could be more "micro-mosaic" tables, artwork, and snuff boxes. A staggering amount of work went into these pieces, and I would advise that you take the offered magnifying glass to fully appreciate what's here.

In the Hermitage Rooms are exhibited selections from the great Hermitage Museum of St. Petersburg, Russia. If you are a museum lover, this is a must go; it's a long way to St. Petersburg.

Touring Tips The Courtauld offers a fantastic educational booklet called "Courtauld Gallery Trail," available at the admissions desk, that instructs children (ages 5–12) in the study of the gallery's fine-art collection by asking practical questions about how to look at and learn from the paintings.

Southwark Cathedral

Type of Attraction Small medieval cathedral with famous literary ties

Location Zone 5; Montague Close, Southwark, SE1; tube: London Bridge

Admission Combined exhibition and audio tour: £6 for adults; £2 for children under age 12

Hours Monday–Saturday, 10 a.m.–6 p.m.; Sunday, 11 a.m.–5 p.m.

Phone (0207) 367-6700

Website www.dswark.org

When to Go Anytime

Special Comments Disabled access; permits must be obtained from welcome desk for photography or videotaping

Overall Appeal by Age Group

Pre-school ★★	Teens ★★	Over 30 ★★★
Grade school ★★★	Young Adults ★★★	Seniors ★★★

Author's Rating ★★★

How Much Time to Allow 1–2 hours

Description and Comments Although it has only been a cathedral since 1905, parts of this building date back to the twelfth century, when it was the Augustinian priory church of St. Mary Overie. In the time span between, the cathedral has been frequented by many notables of the day. William Shakespeare attended mass here regularly, and his brother, Edward, is interred in the choir aisle. A chapel is dedicated to the founder of Harvard University, John Harvard, who was born in Southwark and baptized in the church in 1607. In addition, there is the tomb of poet John Gower, a contemporary of Chaucer, and a memorial to Shakespeare that includes a glorious twentieth-century stained-glass window depicting almost two dozen of Shakespeare's most famous characters.

As part of the £10.9 million Southwark Cathedral Millennium Project, there is a new exhibition using technology such as computers to look at artifacts and films, interactive cameras contrasting today's view from the top of the cathedral tower with views since the sixteenth century, and an amazing 24-hour time-lapse 360-degree view from London Bridge. There's also a shop and a restaurant.

Touring Tips Southwark Cathedral makes a nice stop if you are wandering around the Southwark area, especially if you have already been to Shakespeare's Globe Theatre.

Tate Britain

Type of Attraction Museum of English painters

Location Zone 9; Millbank, on Thames, SW1; tube: Pimlico

Admission Free, though donations are eagerly accepted; there's a charge for special exhibits

Hours Daily, 10 a.m.–5:50 p.m.

Phone (0207) 887-8008

Website www.tate.org.uk

When to Go Anytime, but avoid midday if there's a big exhibition

Special Comments Access-for-disabled leaflet is available at information desks. Parking spaces and wheelchairs are available, but must be booked in advance.

Overall Appeal by Age Group

Pre-school ★	Teens ★★★	Over 30 ★★★★
Grade school ★★	Young Adults ★★★★	Seniors ★★★★

Author's Rating ★★★★

How Much Time to Allow 2 hours or more

Description and Comments The old Tate Gallery was changed in the spring of 2000, when the international modern art was moved across the river to the new Tate Modern (see separate profile) at the Bankside Power Station. This left a completely marvelous collection of English painters and sculptors from the sixteenth to the early twentieth century here at Tate Britain. The building itself is quite impressive, with Poseidon situated between a lion and a unicorn on the roof, stately columns adorning the entrance, and halls of beautiful marble and design. In October 2001, a new extension opened five new galleries, another entrance and shop, and better visitor facilities. There are plenty of benches from which to enjoy the paintings and the ambience. All the great British artists are here: Hogarth, Stubbs, Reynolds, Blake, Burne-Jones, Constable, and even an honorary Englishman, the American expat James Whistler. The pride of the collection is J. M. W. Turner, whose paintings and memorabilia fill the Clore Gallery. The gift shop has an excellent selection of books, gifts, and postcards, and the café is top-notch—remember that spending money in either helps support this excellent free art gallery and its sister gallery across the river, the Tate Modern. Take the ferry service across the Thames to get to it.

Tate Modern

Type of Attraction Museum of international modern art

Location Zone 5; 25 Sumner Street, Bankside, SE1; tube: Southwark or Blackfriars

Admission Free, except for special exhibitions, lectures, and films

Hours Sunday–Thursday, 10 a.m.–6 p.m.; Friday–Saturday, 10 a.m.–10 p.m.

Phone (0207) 887-8008

Website www.tate.org.uk

When to Go Anytime

Special Comments Individuals with wheelchairs or strollers should use the north entrance from river walkway or the west entrance on Holland Street. To reserve a parking space or wheelchair, call (0207) 887 8888.

Overall Appeal by Age Group

Pre-school —	Teens ★★★★	Over 30 ★★★★
Grade school ★★	Young Adults ★★★★	Seniors ★★★★

Author's Rating ★★★★

How Much Time to Allow 1–2 hours

Description and Comments Housed in the old Bankside Power Station, the Tate Modern opened in 2000. This national museum's nucleus was formed from the old Tate's (now called the Tate Britain) modern art collection, from 1900 to the present day. The work of Dali, Picasso, Matisse, Duchamp, Warhol, and Rothko are here, among many other names prominent in modern art. This former utility megalith has been put to good use, housing enormous art installations and sculptures, and the views across the Thames are wonderful, taking in the Millennium Bridge and St. Paul's. There are good exhibits here, two cafés and an espresso bar, a large shop in Turbine Hall, and an overall interesting architectural conversion from power station to art gallery. You can take a ferry from the Tate Modern to Tate Britain across the river.

Touring Tips Walk across the Millenium Bridge to St. Paul's for a nice contrast between centuries.

Tower Bridge Experience

Type of Attraction History of the bridge and a walk across the top of it

Location Zone 3; Tower Bridge, SE1; tube: Tower Hill or London Bridge

Admission £6.25 for adults; £4.25 for children ages 5–15; £18.25 for family tickets

Hours April–October, daily, 10 a.m.–6:30 p.m.; November–March, daily, 9:30 a.m.–6 p.m. (last admission is 75 minutes before closing)

Phone (0207) 403-3761

Website www.towerbridge.org.uk

When to Go Early morning or around 4 p.m.

Special Comments Disabled access; call for details and to make plans

Overall Appeal by Age Group

Pre-school ★	Teens ★	Over 30 ★★
Grade school ★	Young Adults ★★	Seniors ★★

Author's Rating ★★

How Much Time to Allow 90 minutes

Description and Comments This is the bridge that everyone thinks is London Bridge, and allegedly what the American investors thought they were getting when they bought London Bridge in the 1970s to put up in the Arizona desert. They must have been quite disappointed to get the real, boring London Bridge! Tower Bridge was built in 1894 and remains a beautiful piece of architecture, as well as a marvel of engineering. It is adequately appreciated from the ground, and I don't really think all that much is gained by waiting in the interminable lines to go in it, but if you can get in without waiting for more than half an hour, it's worth a look. They seem to be straining to provide a tour of some length, with a kind of corny multimedia trip through time to the bridge's inception, but the old films are fun to watch, and the history of how they ended up using this design is interesting, but probably not to small children. However, once you are on the walkway high above the Thames, with views everywhere, you can't help but be glad you visited.

Touring Tips If there's a huge line—one that reaches out onto the bridge—go enjoy the south riverside cafés and stores or go to the Tower of London and return when the line has shortened (to just inside the ticket area), which is, according to the staff, usually around 4:15 p.m.

The Tower of London

Type of Attraction Ancient, history-rich fortress on the banks of the Thames

Location Zone 3; Tower Hill, EC3; tube: Tower Hill

Admission £12 for adults; £8 for children; free for children under age 5; £34 for family tickets

Hours March–October, Monday–Saturday, 9 a.m.–5 p.m., Sunday, 10 a.m.–5 p.m.; November–February, Sunday and Monday, 10 a.m.–4 p.m. and Tuesday–Saturday, 9 a.m.–4 p.m.

Phone (0870) 756-6060

Website www.hrp.org.uk

When to Go The lines get pretty ferocious in the summer; line up early or go later in the day.

Special Comments Lots of difficult stairs and passageways. A limited number of wheelchairs are available; ask at the group ticket office.

Overall Appeal by Age Group

Pre-school ★★★	Teens ★★★★	Over 30 ★★★★★
Grade school ★★★★	Young Adults ★★★★★	Seniors ★★★★★

Author's Rating ★★★★★

How Much Time to Allow 3 hours or more

Description and Comments The first time I entered the Tower of London through the Middle Tower, I literally went weak in the knees. To an American with more than a passing interest in English history, a trip to the tower is a transcendent experience. There has been much written about how tourist-ridden it is, but I never found that to be a mitigating factor in my awe and appreciation of it. Yes, it is usually packed with howling schoolchildren and tourists; yes, there are gift shops and snack bars all over the place; and yes, some of the attempts at historical verisimilitude are corny. But this is still one of the most important sites in all of England and was the scene of dramas beyond counting. Numerous guidebooks will tell you that it's hard to feel the essential grimness of the place with all the happy sightseers around, but I say that with a little imagination and focus, you can sense the ghosts that plague this place of imprisonment, torture, and death.

As anyone who is near there after dark can tell you, the place is lousy with ghosts, and not the happy kind. Macaulay, the nineteenth-century historian, wrote of the small burial ground by the Chapel of St. Peter Ad Vincula: "In truth, there is no sadder spot on earth as this little cemetery. Death is there associated, not, as in Westminster Abbey and St Paul's, with genius and virtue . . . but with whatever is darkest in human nature and in human destiny, with the savage triumph of implacable enemies, with the inconstancy, the ingratitude, the cowardice of friends, with all the miseries of fallen greatness and of blighted fame." It does make you shiver when you hear the roll call of the imprisoned and beheaded: Thomas More, Anne Boleyn, Lady Jane Grey and her husband, Queen Catherine Howard, a host of lords and ladies whose only crime was to end up on the wrong side of the monarch. There were also kings of Scotland and France, William Wallace (alias Braveheart), King Henry VI, the two little princes murdered in their sleep (allegedly by their uncle, Richard III), Sir Walter Raleigh, and countless victims of religious persecutions. It is, for all its present serenity and beauty, a place soaked in centuries of blood.

The tower was started as a simple fortification on the Thames in 1066 by William the Conqueror, and grew over the years to include 13 different towers, numerous houses, walks, armories, barracks, and greens, all surrounded by a moat. The moat was drained in 1843 due to the mephitic stink of it, but there are plans afoot to fill it in again, which would be quite pleasing to the eye. The Yeoman Warders, also known as Beefeaters, have been at the tower since the 1300s and are now an invaluable source of information about the tower. They are happy to answer questions, and you may attach yourself to any group that is being entertained and enlightened by a Beefeater. There are Yeoman Warder talks and free tours every day; the Lanthorn Tower and the Middle Tower have information boards outlining the day's talks, tours, and events. You will see ravens there. They are a very important part of the tower, and have been kept here with wings clipped for over 600 years. The legend is that if the ravens should ever leave, the tower will fall and England will be in great danger. There is one there at present, named Thor, who has somehow been trained to imitate human speech, so any disembodied "Hellos" you hear will not always be the work of the ghosts.

One of the most famous sights at the tower is the Crown Jewels. I was not all that interested in them—the line can be awfully long, and while the crowns and scepters are interesting as historic emblems, they are strangely lifeless. Seeing them was not nearly as gratifying as reading the scratched graffiti—in English and Latin—of the unfortunate prisoners in Beauchamp Tower, or sitting under a tree in one of the greens absorbing the atmosphere. It's a good place to hang around, so take your time. The audio tours are great and can be done at your own pace, and the guidebook is an excellent investment.

Touring Tips There is a security check that slows down the entrance; if possible, leave your knapsack or bag at home when you visit.

Victoria and Albert Museum

Type of Attraction Breathtaking collection of decorative arts and design

Location Zone 11; Cromwell Road (second entrance on Exhibition Road), South Kensington, SW7; tube: South Kensington

Admission Free; charge for special exhibits

Hours Daily, 10 a.m.–5:45 p.m.; Wednesday open until 10 p.m.

Phone (0207) 942-2000

Website www.vam.ac.uk

When to Go Anytime

Special Comments Wheelchair access is from the Exhibition Road entrance; there are ramps over most of the many small sets of steps.

Overall Appeal by Age Group

Pre-school ★★	Teens ★★★★	Over 30 ★★★★★
Grade school ★★★	Young Adults ★★★★★	Seniors ★★★★★

Author's Rating ★★★★★

How Much Time to Allow As much as possible

Description and Comments The Victoria and Albert Museum is the jewel in the South Kensington museumland's crown. It houses the most engaging assortment of treasures, and although it has been criticized for not having a strict enough focus, that is precisely its charm. It could be the enormous attic of some mad uncle, wealthy beyond all measure, indiscriminately collecting anything and everything of interest that might make his home more beautiful. You have an endless choice of things to see: armor, religious artifacts, stained glass, sculptures, wood carvings, jewelry, musical instruments, ironwork, furniture, glasswork, clothing, paintings, photographs, and whatever special exhibit is being held at the time, always very well mounted.

The original V&A was part of Prince Albert's grand scheme to make South Kensington a center for arts, science, and learning. When it opened in 1852, funded by the Great Exhibition of 1851, Prince Albert envisioned the South Kensington Museum, as it was known then, to be a repository of applied arts—items that happily married beauty and utility. Such restrictions were hopeless from the start, as treasures started arriving from all over the empire and thousands of legacies. As you wander around the museum—and I believe that's the best way to go, although many would guide you toward the introductory tours that occur daily—you might bear in mind the fact that there are millions more objets d'art, paintings, photographs, clothing, textiles, and so on stored away in the basement.

By 1899, the old housing for the collection was clearly unfit, and work was begun on the present building, named by Queen Victoria, who never neglected an opportunity to honor her long-departed husband. She didn't live to see it completed ten years later, but she presides over its Cromwell Road entrance like a secular version of the Virgin Mary, who tops the Brompton Oratory Church next door. There has been talk about finding a more appropriately descriptive name for this wonderful museum, but I think that evoking the quintessential couple of that inquisitive, acquisitive nineteenth-century British empire is perfect. The building is a real beauty, inside and out, and any visit to the museum should always include a few moments to appreciate the grace of the main-entrance dome with its fantastic glass chandelier by Dale Chiluly, the Fakes and Forgeries' immense halls and skylights, the Pirelli Courtyard, and especially the areas that, in a less populated age, served as the museum's main eateries: the Poynter, Gamble, and Morris Rooms. These rooms are simply magnificent. The recently renovated British Galleries are a must-see, as are Raphael's cartoons, the Beasts of Dacre, the dress collection, and the stained glass.

Touring Tips On Wednesday (depending on the season, call (0207) 942-2209 to make sure it's on), there's a Late View, with a limited number of galleries open, a lecture in the beautiful old lecture hall past the Silver Galleries, and a gallery talk. The restaurant is open and has candles on the table, and live music is played there as well as in the front hall. It's a wonderful way to pass a Wednesday evening. The weekends feature a Family Cart, with activities for children. It's extremely entertaining and educational for kids of every age.

If you arrive before the doors open, or prefer not to eat in the cafeteria-style dining room downstairs, please go across the street to the wonderful Orsini's Café, a little slice of Italy in South Kensington, for the best cappuccino in London, as well as great toasted sandwiches and pasta.

The Wallace Collection

Type of Attraction Collection of nineteenth-century Anglo-French art

Location Zone 14; Hertford House, Manchester Square, W1; tube: Bond Street

Admission Free

Hours Monday–Saturday, 10 a.m.–5 p.m.; Sunday, noon–5 p.m.

Phone (0207) 935-0687

Website www.the-wallace-collection.org.uk

When to Go Anytime

Special Comments Good disabled access including an outdoor ramp, lifts to the upper floors, and mostly uncluttered rooms in which it is easy to maneuver

Overall Appeal by Age Group

Pre-school ★	Teens ★★	Over 30 ★★★
Grade school ★	Young Adults ★★★	Seniors ★★★

Author's Rating ★★★

How Much Time to Allow 1–3 hours

Description and Comments The Wallace Collection is tucked away in a lovely Georgian square between Regent's and Hyde Parks. The second marquess of Hertford leased the home, now Hertford House, in 1797, for the good duck shooting available in the area. Today, Hertford House holds the combined acquisitions of five generations of marquesses of Hertford. Between 1750 and 1880, this family formed an impressive collection to decorate their impressive home.

The collection is displayed over this French chateau's two main floors, and some areas are worthy of special note. Galleries 2, 3, and 4 contain some fabulous pieces of Louis XIV furniture and art. A remarkable European Renaissance armory is housed in Galleries 8, 9, and 10; and Gallery 11 is devoted to Asian arms, armor, and art. Hertford House's largest room, Gallery 22, offers one of the finest displays of European paintings to be seen anywhere in the world. This impressive gallery, formerly called "The Long Picture Gallery," houses works by such masters as Titian, Fragonard, Poussin, Rembrandt, Rubens, Van Dyck, and Velázquez. Even if the house were empty of treasures, it would still be worth visiting to see the carved mantelpieces and elegant design of this architectural paragon of a bygone era.

Temporary exhibits, new educational facilities, new galleries, and a café, along with certain engineering reconstructions, were part of an intensive Centenary Project in 2000 that cost over £10 million. It was money well and wisely spent, making this good small museum a great small museum.

Touring Tips Free public lectures and tours on various aspects of the collection are given on weekdays and weekends. Tours usually last about 45 minutes and give good insight into the styles and history of the artists and their times. If you are on a tight schedule, call for touring times, or just arrive and wander on your own until a tour begins.

The Wellington Arch

Type of Attraction Architectural- and London-related items in the arch

Location Zone 10; in the middle of Hyde Park Corner roundabout, SW1; tube: Hyde Park Corner

Admission £2.50 for adults; £1.30 for children; £1.90 concessions

Hours April–September, daily, 10 a.m.–6 p.m.; October, daily, 10 a.m.–5 p.m.; November–March, Wednesday–Sunday, 10 a.m.–4 p.m.

Phone (0207) 973-3494

Website www.english-heritage.org.uk

When to Go Anytime

Special Comments The entrance is on the south side inside the arch, a small doorway with no banners or big signs announcing its position. You reach the island either through the subways, or at the street crossing in front of the Lanesborough Hotel.

Overall Appeal by Age Group

Pre-school —		Teens ★		Over 30 ★★
Grade school ★		Young Adults ★		Seniors ★★

Author's Rating ★★

How Much Time to Allow Depending upon your interest, 30 minutes to an hour

Description and Comments This is one of those specialty museums for either architectural historians or London-obsessed cranks. It was designed in the 1820s by Decimus Burton to commemorate England's victory over Napoléon, and was originally located at Buckingham Palace. It's our good fortune that the statue of Wellington that once topped the arch was replaced by the magnificent *Peace Descending on the Quadringa of War,* which gives Hyde Park Corner such a stunning aspect. It's worth a go, as it's relatively inexpensive, and if you combine it with a visit to Apsley House across the way, it will leave you feeling as if you know all there is to know about that corner of London. There are a couple of films running in loops that have wonderful old shots of Hyde Park Corner from the horse-and-cart era to the present; and the molds from the magnificent statue on top of the arch are most inspiring. But the best thing about it is the views to be had from the observation platforms. The look in at the tennis courts in the "backyard" of Buckingham Palace was a first for me; and the views of the London Eye and Westminster are nice, too. A photo display of Londoners' snapshots of their city is riveting.

Touring Tips If you go from Apsley House to the Arch via the tube (follow signs for Green Park), you get the story of the duke of Wellington recapitulated in tile on the walls, as well as an hour-to-hour description of the battle of Waterloo.

Westminster Abbey

Type of Attraction England's historically most important church

Location Zone 9; 20 Dean's Yard, just off of Parliament Square; tube: St. James's Park or Westminster

Admission Free admission for services or to visit the nave and cloisters; royal chapels and tombs: £6 for adults; £3 for students and seniors; £2 for children; £12 for family; Chapter House, Pyx Chamber, and museum: £1 with royal chapels admission or £2.50 for adults, £1.90 for students and seniors, and £1.30 for children

Hours Royal chapels are open Monday–Friday, 9:30 a.m.–3:45 p.m.; Saturday, 9:30 a.m.–1:45 p.m. (Closing times given are for last admission.) Chapter House, Pyx Chamber, and museum hours are Monday–Saturday, 10 a.m.–3:30 p.m. The abbey is closed before special services, on Sunday (except for services), December 24–28, Good Friday, and on Commonwealth Observance Day.

Phone (0207) 222-5152

Website www.westminster-abbey.org

When to Go Early mornings on weekdays, especially during the busy summer months. If you really hate crowds in close spaces, make a quick call to be sure you aren't arriving at the same time as three tour groups.

Special Comments Audio guides are available in seven languages for £2.50, Monday–Friday, 9:30 a.m.–3 p.m. and Saturday, 9:30 a.m.–1 p.m.

Overall Appeal by Age Group

Pre-school ★	Teens ★★★★	Over 30 ★★★★
Grade school ★★★	Young Adults ★★★★	Seniors ★★★★

Author's Rating ★★★★

Additional Tips My favorite way to experience Westminster Abbey is to arrive around 3:30 p.m. and then wander the cloisters (especially the lovely Little Cloister) before returning to the nave to wait for the 5 p.m. evensong. It is worth waiting at the head of the line (which starts to form at about 4:15 p.m.), as the first evensong attendees are seated in the stately choir stalls where the atmosphere and view of the Westminster Boys Choir is the best.

How Much Time to Allow 1½–2 hours for audio guides; evensong is about 45 minutes

Description and Comments Since the 900-year-old Abbey is one of the most popular tourist sights in London, the key here is to avoid touring when it is mobbed. When you are moving in a sluggish single-file line through the chapels, you lose sight of the beauty of the interiors (displaying at least four different eras of architecture), the sheer numbers of people buried here (over 3,000), and the incredible amount of history that this building has seen. Instead, try to start off your day with a visit or end your day with one.

Since 1998, the primary entrance to the abbey has been through the North Transept, which gives a rather disjointed image of the abbey on first glance. I suggest that you immediately head back toward the West Front entrance so that you can see the abbey as it was meant to be viewed. From this perspective you can clearly see the majesty of the tallest nave in England (at 102 feet). In front of you is the Tomb of the Unknown Soldier and to your right is a fourteenth-century portrait of Richard II, the oldest known image of a monarch painted from life. As you head back toward the North Transept, also called Statesmen's Aisle, you pass through Musician's Aisle and end up back near the admissions and information desks. From here you move in a mostly single-file line through the smaller chapels of Elizabeth I and Innocents Corner and head toward the fantastic display of English perpendicular architecture that makes up the Henry VII Chapel. The elaborately carved choir stalls here are dedicated to the Knights of the Order of the Bath, whose banners and helmets decorate the stalls. Among the notable names buried in this chapel alone are Henry VII and his wife; King George II and Queen Caroline; Henry VIII's only son, Edward VI; and James I and his lover, George Villiers, the first nonroyal to be buried in this part of the abbey.

As you head along the south aisle of Henry VII's chapel, you can see the tombs of Mary Queen of Scots; Lady Margaret Beaufort, Henry VII's mother; as well as William and Mary, Queen Anne, and Charles II. Walking back toward the nave, you pass the oak throne dating back to 1300 called the Coronation Chair, which has been used in every royal coronation since then. Just beyond this point, tombs and gatework hide much of the abbey's most famous tomb, the shrine of St. Edward the Confessor. Unfortunately, this tomb, although recently restored, remains closed to the public. The South Transept of Poet's Corner, however, continues to be a favorite of visitors and contains the grave slabs of, among many others, Geoffrey Chaucer, Robert Browning, Alfred Lord Tennyson, Charles Dickens, Rudyard Kipling, and Thomas Hardy, as well as impressive memorials to William Shakespeare and George Frideric Handel. The last person to have been buried here was Sir Laurence Olivier, who died in 1989.

After exploring the abbey's interior, be sure you find your way out to the cloisters, where the monks worked, studied, and lived. Visiting on a cold day gives you insight into the hearty constitution these early scholars must have had. Today, the cloisters contain a small shop and café. English Heritage also runs a small area just off the east cloisters. This includes the Chapter House, which was the original meeting place of the House of Commons until the time of Henry VIII, and the Pyx

Chamber, which served as the sacristy and royal treasury of the earliest church.

Touring Tips Before you enter Westminster Abbey, take the time to enjoy its lesser-known neighbor. Many people head straight for the entrance and fail to even notice St. Margaret's Church, which shares the churchyard. Built in 1523, this tiny church's simple and uncluttered interior will contrast sharply with the abbey's appearance as an overflowing mausoleum.

Photography is not permitted in any part of the abbey at any of the times mentioned above. If you are a camera buff and will not settle for putting postcards in your albums, plan your visit for Wednesday between 6 and 7 p.m. At this special time, admission is half price and amateur photography is permitted, although no tours or audio guides will be available.

Windsor Castle

Type of Attraction The queen's country house, a mighty fine old castle

Location Windsor, Hertsfordshire, outside London; British Rail: Waterloo Station to Windsor Riverside

Admission £11.50 for adults; £6 for children ages 5–16; free for children under age 5

Hours March–October, daily, 9:45 a.m.–5:15 p.m., last admission at 4 p.m.; November–February, daily, 9:45 a.m.–4:15 p.m., last admission at 3 p.m.; St. George's Chapel closed Sunday

Phone (0175) 318-3118

Website www.royalresidences.com

When to Go Always call first! Windsor Castle is subject to regular, annual, and sudden closures due to various royal ceremonies and events. The month of June is particularly susceptible to this sort of thing. Otherwise, go anytime, but show up early before the tour groups.

Special Comments Limited wheelchair access, lots of walking

Overall Appeal by Age Group

Pre-school ★	Teens ★★★	Over 30 ★★★★
Grade school ★★	Young Adults ★★★★	Seniors ★★★★

Author's Rating ★★★★

How Much Time to Allow Half a day, plus time to wander in Windsor

Description and Comments In November 1992, the world saw film footage of Windsor Castle with smoke and flames pouring out from behind its distinctive crenelated keep and foremen running to and fro with priceless paintings and furniture. The fire destroyed over 100 rooms, and it took five years to repair the terrible damage done to the ancient castle. Even if you don't normally like gaping at castles, you might make an exception of Windsor, for the restoration of the gutted and devastated castle—burnt to its medieval stone walls, with roofs collapsed—is a marvel in itself, and the exhibition that describes the process is remarkable.

William the Conqueror, who also built the Tower of London, chose the site in Windsor for a fortress to protect London from Western invaders. The castle has been continually inhabited for the past 900 years, and many additions—and deletions, too, through other fires—have been made over those years.

It is presently a place of overwhelming splendor and tremendous riches, which might be best summed up by the awesome Queen Mary's Dolls' House. This is big luxury on a small scale: Sir Edward Luytens designed the multistory dollhouse in the 1920s, and it took three years and a thousand craftsmen and artists to complete it. It has running water, electric lights, a working elevator, actual miniature books, fine art, gorgeous furniture, and even two tiny thrones with crowns on them.

Another attraction at Windsor is St. George's Chapel, started in 1475; it's a stunning example of great medieval architecture, with stained-glass windows of unparalleled beauty. Ten monarchs are buried within its precincts, and there are some stupendously crafted sarcophagi. The crests and banners of the Knights of the Order of the Garter are all there, and you get a feel for the ritual and pageantry that have propped up the ruling classes of England for centuries. A new garden, the first one planted since 1820, was designed to celebrate the Queen's Golden Jubilee, and features a bandstand on which Her Majesty's various military bands perform.

Touring Tips Be sure to make time to wander around the pleasant town of Windsor.

Green and Pleasant Lands: Parks of London

On the weekends, when the museums and tourist attractions are packed, go to the parks and soak up the gratifying English appreciation for nature tame and wild. Part of London's appeal as a city is its careful conservation of greenery—whether in its many squares or its enormous parks. For more information, contact The Royal Parks Agency at (0207) 298-2000 or go to www.royalparks.gov.uk.

PARKS	DESCRIPTION	ZONE
Green Park	Between Hyde Park and St. James's Park	9
Hampstead Heath	Enormous expanse of country	1
Highgate Cemetery	Atmospheric Victorian graveyard	1
Holland Park	54-acre landscaped park	13
Hyde Park	350-acre people's park	10

Kensington Gardens	Gardens, walkways, fountains, palace	13
Kew Gardens (The Royal Botanic Gardens)	Botanical extravaganza	12
Regent's Park	490-acre elegant park	15
Richmond Park	London's largest park	12
St. James's Park	Oldest royal park in London	9

Green Park

Type of Park Expanse of green lawn and old trees

Location Zone 9; between Piccadilly and Constitution Hill (between Hyde Park and St. James's Park); enter at Hyde Park Corner; tube: Green Park

Admission Free

Hours Daily, 5 a.m.–midnight

When to Go Anytime; don't miss spring bulbs and blazing autumn foliage

Description and Comments Like St. James's Park, Green Park was also reclaimed from the marshy meadows that surrounded the Tyburn River. Originally purchased by Henry VIII for enclosed grazing and hunting, the land was made into a formal park in 1667. It became a favorite place for duels and highwaymen, military parades, ballooning, and people-watching. Green Park was opened to the public in 1826, and since then people have loved strolling along the east end of the park, admiring the fine mansions there, ending up at Buckingham Palace and St. James's Park. There are no flowerbeds in Green Park, but the crocuses in spring more than make up for that lack, and the 950 magnificent plane, oak, poplar, chestnut, and other varieties of trees to be seen there are completely pleasing. You may rent chairs in the spring, summer, and fall, which makes a nice break from shopping or sight-seeing in the Piccadilly area. A refreshment stand is available at the Buckingham Palace end of the park, and toilets can be found by the Green Park tube station.

Hampstead Heath

Type of Park Enormous expanse of country in Greater London area

Location Zone 1; Hampstead; tube: Highgate, then take 210 bus to West Gate

Admission Free

Hours Daily, 8 a.m.–dusk

When to Go Anytime; don't miss the spring blossoms and autumn colors

Description and Comments Though Hampstead Heath is not actually a park per se, it is a most remarkable place, covering a staggering 1,600 acres of undeveloped land and offering stunning views over London. There are hills, lakes, wild woods, and landscaped gardens. Hampstead heath has so much to offer, not the least of which is Kenwood House, a stately home and art museum at the northernmost top of the heath. There are outdoor concerts in the summer on Saturday nights, which are followed by displays of fireworks. People bring blankets and picnic hampers and sit on a hill outside, while those who pay for tickets hunker down a little closer to the music. The Men's and Ladies' Ponds for swimming in the summer are part of a set of lakes along the Highgate border of the heath. There's also a pond for model boats and one for bird-watching. Parliament Hill, across the bicycle track that cuts through the heath, is the best place in London for viewing the Guy Fawkes Day fireworks, and in all seasons has spectacular views of London. You can hardly believe you are even near an urban area in many parts of the heath, where mansions on hills look like castles and conspire to make you feel you are in a storybook. You can get a good lunch at the Kenwood House outdoor café in the summer.

Highgate Cemetery

Type of Park Wildly overgrown Victorian graveyard

Location Zone 1; located on either side of Swains Lane in Highgate, adjacent to Waterlow Park; tube: Archway (Northern line)

Admission West Cemetery (access is as part of guided tours only) £3; East Cemetery £2; £1 photo permit

Hours West Cemetery, April to September: tours are given Monday–Friday at noon, 2 p.m., 3 p.m., and 4 p.m.; Saturday and Sunday, 10 a.m.–4 p.m. October to March: tours are given on weekends only, hourly, 11 a.m.–3 p.m. East Cemetery, April to September: daily, 10 a.m.–5 p.m. October to March: daily, 10 a.m.–4 p.m.

Phone (0208) 340-1834

Website www.highgate-cemetery.org

When to Go Anytime, although they only allow 20 people on each weekend hourly tour, so if you arrive late you may find yourself wandering the East Cemetery for an hour. Also, the cemetery will close for funerals, so call to check before setting out.

Description and Comments Opened in 1839, Highgate Cemetery became "the" place to be buried for London's wealthy Victorian families, intellectuals, and artists. One of seven cemeteries designed and opened during this time of continued population explosion, it remains one of the most elaborate and stirring examples of Victorian statuary excess. Overgrown and badly vandalized, the West Cemetery was closed in 1975 and is now diligently cared for by the Friends of Highgate Cemetery. Lush vegetation fills what was once an open, rolling hillside, and volunteers continue to clear overgrown pathways and graves. This extensive foliage creates eerie shadows; this, combined with the cracked and toppled grave markers everywhere, gives the cemetery its fabulously gothic atmosphere. Tour guides are well versed on the many famous residents of the cemetery, as well as having a number of fascinating anecdotes that explain the elaborate and symbolic Victorian statuary. The cemetery's creepiest section includes the Egyptian Avenue and the Terrace Catacombs. Buried here are Karl Marx, Christina Rossetti, George Eliot, and others, all watched over by magnificent angels of stone.

You can wander on your own in the East Cemetery, but it holds a less eerie charm. Still, it is nice to be able to linger where you will and get up close to the graves, some of which contain the most interesting epitaphs. There is a £1 "camera permit fee" for those interested in capturing the morose views. It's best to go early in the day, hopefully on a day with some sun, as the shadowy effects can create fantastic photographic images.

Holland Park

Type of Park 54-acre landscaped park with a Japanese garden

Location Zone 13; Holland Park, between Kensington and Shepherd's Bush; tube: Holland Park Avenue (then a 10-minute walk to park) or Kensington High Street and take westbound bus 9, 10, 27, 28, 31, or 49

Admission Free

Hours Daily, 7:30 a.m.–dusk

When to Go Anytime; there are camellias, roses, irises, and other blossoms in spring; dahlias in summer; and autumn leaves

Description and Comments Holland Park once housed the magnificent Holland House, more castle than mansion, where the literati of the early nineteenth century flocked to mix with the politicians and aristocrats of the day. The house was bombed during World War II, but what remains are fascinating monuments to the past: the surviving wings of Holland House, one of which houses a youth hostel; the wrought-iron gates that formed the entrance to the estate; the Orangery; the Ice House from the 1770s; the summer ballroom that is now a restaurant; The Belvedere, run by the famous chef Marco Pierre White; the old stables; and the many walks and enclosures that make up Holland Park.

There is a wonderful variety of flora and fauna here, thanks to Lord Holland—a venerable Victorian gentleman—and his great interest in planting and wildlife. He can be seen as styled by sculptor G. F. Watts, surveying his land, occasionally providing a roosting place for some of the 60 wild bird species that have been spotted in the park. One feature he never saw, which was created in 1991, is the Kyoto Garden, a perfect

Japanese garden. The peacocks gather in the Yucca Lawn, along with numerous rabbits. There is an adventure playground in the park that is a must-do for families with young children.

Hyde Park

Type of Park 350-acre park with expansive lawns

Location Zone 10; bordered by Park Lane, Knightsbridge, and Bayswater Road; tube: Hyde Park Corner

Admission Free

Hours Daily, dawn to dusk

When to Go Anytime; there are roses in summer, crocuses and daffodils in spring, fall foliage in autumn, and atmospheric bare trees in winter

Description and Comments During the dissolution of the monasteries in 1536, Henry VIII grabbed a hunk of land from the manor of Hyde and enclosed it for his hunting pleasure. James I opened the park to aristocrats, who took the air daily, a habit that persisted into the early twentieth century with Rotten Row—originally Route du Roi, King's Road—resounding with the beating of hooves and the chatter of the idle classes. Once, Kensington Gardens was part of Hyde Park—and is still separated only by a roadway—but in the mid-1700s, Queen Caroline appropriated 200 acres to make suitable gardens for Kensington Palace.

Hyde Park today is a wonderful escape from the high-decibel traffic noise of Park Lane, Knightsbridge, and Bayswater. One enters the park from any of those streets; and within minutes of walking toward the Serpentine, the watery heart of the park, a delightful quiet descends. There's so much to do in Hyde Park: There are biking and inline skating paths through and around the edge of the park (do not bicycle on any paths not marked with the outline of a bike); there are cricket and soccer pitches; there are tennis courts, paddle- and rowboats; and one can even ride along Rotten Row on horseback. During the warm months, there are numerous places to rent lawn chairs, and you can get a bite to eat at the Lido or the cafeteria at the east end of the Serpentine. The Rose Walk by Hyde Park Corner is magnificent in June, and the Italian Piazza, with fountains and statues, is wonderful at all times. Speaker's Corner, at the northeast end of the park, is hopping on Sunday, often featuring born-again Christians yelling at us to repent, no longer on soapboxes, but on little stepladders or overturned buckets. The queen's guards exercise their horses and rehearse their ceremonies in Hyde Park, on the south by Prince's Gate. It's an astonishing thing to be walking through the park and suddenly be set upon by a regiment of sword-waving, plume-hatted horsemen. Hyde Park in sunlight is the best place to be in London. They have something called the Liberty Drive for the disabled to enjoy a tour through the park. They pick up passengers at clearly marked spots on the park's perimeters. To book, call (046) 749-8096.

If you want to get from South Kensington to Piccadilly, or from Knightsbridge to Marble Arch, do yourself a favor and walk through Hyde Park.

Kensington Gardens

Type of Park Gardens, walkways, fountains, statues, and a palace

Location Zone 13; Kensington Gore; tube: Kensington High Street

Admission Free

Hours Daily, dawn to dusk

When to Go Anytime, especially when Kensington Palace and the Orangery are open. In spring and summer there is the flower walk and great foliage in fall.

Description and Comments Kensington Palace will probably be forever associated with the extraordinary event of public mourning for Princess Diana, when in the days after her death in Paris, people arrived and laid flowers in front of the palace that was her home. By week's end there was a sea of blooms and cellophane in front of the gates, and the trees nearby were festooned with pictures, poems, and flowers, and candles stood burning everywhere. A permanent tribute to the "People's Princess" is the Princess Diana Memorial Playground in the northwest corner of the park, a state-of-the-art playground that is always filled to capacity. A monument to her, in the form of a fountain, is in the works.

By the side of the palace is a lovely sunken garden that can be looked at, but not entered. In front of the Orangery, which is a good place for tea, are topiary trees that recall the Restoration; and the Round Pond on which children have sailed toy boats for generations brings *Mary Poppins* vividly to mind. By the bridge over the Serpentine is a statue of Peter Pan; author J. M. Barrie lived right by the park, and the island in the middle of the lake is clearly the model for the Island of the Lost Boys.

The Broad Walk is good for inline skating, as is the area in front of the Albert Memorial. And if you're in the mood for modern art, the Serpentine Gallery has changing exhibits, a good bookshop, and a café.

Kew Gardens (The Royal Botanic Gardens)

Type of Park Botanical extravaganza with 30,000 species of plants and flowers planted over 300 acres; follies, water features, and conservatories

Location Zone 12; southwest London on the Thames; tube: Kew Gardens

Admission £6.50 for adults; free for children under age 17

Hours Daily, 9:30 a.m.–4:14 p.m. in winter; open later in spring and summer

When to Go Anytime of the year, although summer is the best time to get your money's worth

Description and Comments The Royal Botanical Gardens at Kew were begun in the eighteenth century, when wealthy and royal folks began to move out of smelly, crowded London. The Botanical Gardens, originally developed for the pleasure of the royal family, intersected nicely with the global travels of adventurers such as Captain Cook, who brought home never-before-seen specimens of plant life, such as the geranium. The gardens have gone from strength to strength since then as one of the world's most remarkable and serious centers of botanical research.

The enormous glass Palm House is a treasure trove of exotic tropical plants, with two levels on which to wander through the huge fronds and steamy atmosphere. There's a tropical aquarium in the basement that furthers the impression of being in a foreign clime. The Water Lily House is also interesting, and a testament to the wide-ranging journeys of the English explorers. The Temperate House is an even more impressive structure than the Palm House, twice as large, and containing plants from each and every continent, some of which were planted at Kew in the middle of the nineteenth century.

There are identifying plaques on the trees and signs on the flower beds, so that a visit to Kew can be a real education in botany. Two art galleries, Kew Palace, a Japanese pagoda, and numerous follies and conservatories make Kew an outing at which you can easily spend the whole day. There are a few cafés to choose from, and believe me, you'll need refreshment after a long day at plant-viewing. It's a shame that Kew is right in the path of heathrow—the impression of stepping back in time is continually spoiled by the noise of overhead jets.

Regent's Park

Type of Park Playground of 490 acres with 6,000 trees

Location Zone 15; at end of Baker Street; for south entrance, take the tube to Regent's Park or Baker Street

Admission Free

Hours Daily, 5 a.m.–dusk

When to Go Anytime; there are flower gardens in spring and summer, autumn leaves

Description and Comments Named for George IV, when he was mad King George's understudy monarch, Regent's Park was designed by John Nash as part of the grand plan for a garden city of terraced mansions with countrylike views. Started in 1811, the scheme ultimately failed, with only a portion of the terrace houses sold (and those were said to be of substandard quality). However, in 1835, the park was flourishing and was opened to the public. Although the neighborhood may not have turned out exactly as Nash planned, it's still gorgeous, and few can resist the grace and beauty of the classically inspired white mansions of Cumberland Terrace that look out on the magnificent landscape.

Within the park you will find the home of the American ambassador, donated by the heiress Barbara Hutton and suitably fenced and secured; a boating lake with ornamental bridges and an island; a lake by Queen Mary's Rose Gardens, which are quite extraordinary and include a waterfall and an open-air theater; a number of lodges; a mosque; Regent's Canal; and of course, the London Zoo. In the summer there are concerts on the Bandstand and plays at the theater, bird-watching walks, puppet shows, and outdoor refreshments. The Royal Horse Artillery can be seen occasionally on Cumberland Green. Primrose Hill, north of the zoo, is not officially part of Regent's Park, but can be accessed easily from there, and provides a lovely view of all London.

Richmond Park

Type of Park London's largest park, featuring deer and ancient oak trees

Location Zone 12; southwest London; tube: Richmond Station, then take bus 72, 265, 371, or 415

Admission Free

Hours Daily, 7 a.m.–dusk

When to Go Anytime

Description and Comments Richmond Park is a gargantuan 2,470-acre preserve in which 400 fallow deer and 250 red deer live and graze. It is an extraordinary place, a piece of rolling countryside a stone's thrown (seven miles from Charing Cross) from the center of a major metropolitan city, with wildlife still roaming freely. Richmond had its first royal connections when Henry VII rebuilt a fine old palace on the Thames; his granddaughter Elizabeth I died at the palace. In 1625, surrounding lands were seized and walled to give King Charles I a country asylum from the plague. His wall created much ill will among the neighbors, who had been used to grazing their animals on the land and using the common roads. The king tried to compensate by allowing foot traffic through the park and permitting the local poor to gather deadwood for their hearth fires. After the Civil War, the House of Commons voted to leave the park as undeveloped land, and so it has remained ever since. There were various skirmishes between the royals and the public over right of access, which were put to rest on the death of the last royal ranger, Edward VII in 1910. Today, Richmond Park is a testament to the admirable environmental protectionism of the British and provides for the visitor a wonderfully unchanged picture of a medieval hunting ground.

Be aware that the deer are not completely harmless and can be aggressive if they are bothered while tending young or during rutting season. There are refreshments found in the Pembroke Lodge Cafeteria from April through October, from 10 a.m. to 5:30 p.m. (7 p.m. on weekends). White Lodge houses the Royal Ballet School. There are a number of seasonal events that take place in Richmond Park—check a newspaper or *Time Out* to see when, what, and where. Pembroke Lodge often stages lunchtime concerts. It's a bit of a hike from central London, so you may need to budget a whole day for the outing. It's not fun for unwilling walkers.

St. James's Park

Type of Park Oldest royal park in London

Location Zone 9; east of Buckingham Palace gates; tube: St. James's Park

Admission Free

Hours Daily, 5 a.m.–midnight

When to Go Anytime is excellent, but in summer it is the most floral, and there are concerts on the bandstand between May and August

Description and Comments St. James's is certainly London's most royal of all parks, lying as it does between Buckingham and St. James's Palaces. There is a view from Buckingham Palace and from the bridge in the middle of the lake that is just magical—it looks like our fondest fantasy of an enchanted fairy-tale kingdom, with the turrets and steeples of Whitehall in the distance. St. James's is the place to go see birds; the famous pelicans are there, as well as a huge assortment of unusual feathered friends. The Ornithological Society of London donated some birds in 1837 and started this particular feature of this beautiful park.

A leper hospital, called St. James, was erected here in the 1400s. The Tyburn River flowed through this area, so the land was marshy and unsuitable for much more than hunting until King James I drained and planted the area as a pleasure garden, filling it with pelicans and other rara avis. He also had an exotic menagerie there, with crocodiles and elephants, for his court's entertainment. When Charles II returned from exile in France, he redesigned the park in a more formal, French manner, and opened St. James's Park to the public. It was embraced enthusiastically and began its long life as a favorite spot for Londoners to meet and stroll—although it did have its darker days when people hung laundry there, muggers prowled the bushes, and prostitutes conducted business. Its appeal was upgraded when George IV rebuilt Buckingham House to be a royal palace and had John Nash make the park a more beautiful and natural-looking place.

There is a children's playground on the southwest corner of the park, and The Cake House (open daily from 9:30 a.m. to 5:30 p.m.) is in the east end, north of the lake. There are concerts at the bandstand in summer, and the birds are there all year to be admired. Green-and-white-striped deck chairs can be rented on an hourly basis between April and September.

Greenwich

In 1863, American author Nathaniel Hawthorne described the quiet town of Greenwich as "beautiful,—a spot where the art of man has conspired with Nature." No doubt he was thinking how the rolling hills of Greenwich Park create a glorious backdrop for Christopher Wren's splendid Royal Naval College and Inigo Jones's equally noble Queen's House, while Wren's other Greenwich project, the Royal Observatory, sits serenely on the park's highest hill. Greenwich has undergone a recent renaissance, as rising rents have pushed businesses and Londoners further from the center of the city. Greenwich is also an ideal place for those who work at Canary Wharf. The streets of Greenwich are good for strolling; whether you are wandering down historic Croom's Hill or over past St. Alfrege's near the town center, the area has retained much of its cozy village atmosphere. Weekends bring craft and antiques lovers of all kinds converging on the busy Greenwich Market.

Greenwich is steeped in royal history. The park dates from 1433, and the Palace of Placentia once graced the riverside where the Royal Naval College now stands. Henry VIII and all three of his children, Mary I, Elizabeth I, and Edward IV were born here. In 1616, Jones began building the Queen's House as a Palladian country home at the bottom of the park for Charles II's wife, Henrietta Maria; Wren followed this project with the hilltop Observatory and the Naval College, which elegantly frames the Queen's House today. Just north of the town's center, the colossal Millennium Dome sits in anticipation of its next incarnation as an arena for sports and entertainment.

Getting There

Located only a few miles downriver from London, Greenwich is easy to reach and makes a delightful day trip for visitors. The town center provides a wide variety of book, art, and nautical shops as well as a diverse selection of restaurants from Vietnamese to Mexican to good old English pub food. On weekends, the Greenwich Market is teeming with craft stalls and, combined with the nearby flea market and secondhand book market, can allow for hours of browsing.

To get to Greenwich, catch Docklands Light Railway (DLR), a fully automated and electric overland tram car type of transport that leaves from Bank Street or Tower Hill. The trip takes about 20 minutes from either station and in the summer includes a recording that guides you through the wharfs and docks of London's East End, leaving you at the Greenwich Pier or the *Cutty Sark*. Another, more leisurely travel option is to take a guided riverboat ride along the Thames, past views of St. Paul's Cathedral, Tower Bridge, and Docklands. Boats leave from Westminster, Charing Cross, and Tower Pier for Greenwich approximately every 45 minutes and take 40 minutes to an hour, depending on where you embark. Enquiries can be made by calling (0207) 930-4097 or (0207) 987-1185.

Finally, you can call the Greenwich Tourist Information Center at (0208) 858-6376, write them, or stop by their location at 46 Greenwich Church Street, London SE10 9BL, for information on guided tours in Greenwich, special events, or any additional information you may need.

Part Seven

Children's London

London with Children

London is a wonderful city for children, even jet-lagged ones who can't quite figure out when to go to sleep. Before you go to London, get out some English nursery rhymes or Dickens (depending on the age of your children) and introduce them to the wonders of London in letters. It will make it that much more exciting when you get here. Rent some good London movies for kids: *101 Dalmatians* (not the animated one), *Oliver!*, *Mary Poppins*, *A Little Princess* (Shirley Temple version), *The Prince and the Pauper*, *A Christmas Carol* (the Muppets version is less scary than the old Alistair Syms one), and *The Princess Carabou* are just a few that can get them thinking about and looking at London. There's a brilliant website by the London Tourist Board at **www.londontown.com** that provides a kid's-eye view of London and its attractions. We strongly recommend that grade-school children visit it.

London has an enormous selection of attractions for children of all ages. The museums are getting more interactive and attention-grabbing all the time. Even the staid old Victoria and Albert features a fun cart on weekends to keep the kids busy, entertained, and actually learning something about the wonderful collection. Parents will enjoy the kids' attractions as much as the children will. Just maybe, if you give the kids a chance, they will find something great in the places that cater to a more mature palate, such as the National Portrait Gallery or the Globe Theatre. But don't count on it with the really little ones. They're more into playgrounds and riding on the fun double-decker buses, although there are some museums that can keep their little hands and minds busy.

A "London Book"

A great idea to really get the kids paying attention and having fun is to start a "London book" before you even leave. Pick out a blank book big enough to paste lots of things in, and write down the itinerary; paste in pictures of planes, get the stewardess to sign it, and so on. Then, everywhere you go, you can collect stubs and pamphlets and take plenty of photos. Get film developed at one-hour labs, and spend the evening helping with the scrapbook. Drawings, poems, thoughts, a leaf from Holland Park, a feather from the Serpentine—all these things can make a beautiful scrapbook that children will always love to look through. Get a disposable camera for your child to use to take his or her own photos; you'll be surprised at how much more they'll go in for sight-seeing when it has such a personal purpose.

Planning and Touring Tips

Here are a few ideas to bear in mind when planning a vacation with the little and not-so-little ones:

Age Although the wonderful park playgrounds and certain tourist attractions of London have much to offer toddlers and preschoolers, the bulk of London's attractions are generally oriented to older kids and adults. Children should be a fairly mature 6 years old to get the most out of popular attractions such as the Imperial War Museum, the HMS *Belfast,* possibly even the Tower of London, and a year or two older to enjoy the art museums, cathedrals, and palaces that London has in such grand abundance.

Time of Year to Visit If there is any way to swing it, avoid the crowded summer months. Try to go between late September and November or between early April and mid-June. If you have children of varying ages and your school-age kids are good students, consider taking the older ones out of school so you can visit during the less expensive, less congested off-season. Arrange special study assignments relating to the many educational aspects of London. If your school-age children cannot afford to miss any school, take your vacation as soon as the school year ends in June.

Building Naps and Rest into Your Itinerary London offers more attractions than you can possibly see in a whole week, so don't try to see everything in one day. Tour in the early morning and return to your hotel midday for lunch and possibly a lie-down. Go back and visit more attractions in the late afternoon, or go to a park or to The London Eye, which stays open till dusk in the summer; or take a bus tour that is easier on the legs. Don't pooh-pooh jet lag; children seem to suffer from it less than the adults, but they are definitely thrown off-kilter by the time change. Try to get them adjusted to the time by exposing them to plenty of sunlight and not letting them nap too long during the day.

Where to Stay The best area to stay in when you're carting kids around is near a park—Hyde, Holland, and Kensington Gardens are good. Kids who will complain about tired feet and hunger in a museum will perk up amazingly when they see a swing set, have some room to kick a soccer ball around, or can watch horses ride by. It's important to get small children off the tourist trail for some rest and recuperation. Neglecting to relax and unwind is the best way to get the whole family in a snit and ruin the day.

With small children, you will be glad to have planned ahead. Make sure you get a hotel within a few minutes' walk to a tube station. Naps and relief from the frenetic pace of touring London are indispensable. Even if you do get some good downtime in a park, for the little ones there is no true substitute for returning to the familiarity and security of your own hotel. Children too large to sleep in a stroller will relax and revive better if you get them back to your room.

You may want to choose a hotel that has a swimming pool. A lot of visitors to London assume that, like those in so many American destinations, the big London hotels automatically come with a pool. Nothing could be further from the truth. There are a few expensive ones that do; more to the point, there are many hotels that can steer you to a public pool or that have some arrangement with a health club. Call ahead to find out if there are any age restrictions on swimming. A swimming pool can be a lifesaver for both you and your kids, keeping you all happily busy and healthily exercising in between the sight-seeing.

Getting Around   Getting around can be a bit of a hassle because of traffic congestion, hence decisions about how to get around and how much time to allow need to be made. Probably the most fun way is to take a double-decker bus. Sitting on the top deck of a double-decker is a great way to see London, as there are plenty of sights and weird people for the kids to goggle at. The problem with buses is that you might get stuck in traffic, and the old-fashioned double-decker buses are not stroller-friendly, unlike the newer single-deck buses, which you can usually board without having to collapse your stroller. Fine if you have eight arms to struggle with the bags, baby, and other bits and pieces!

The quicker way to get around is via the tube. However, the system is neither disabled- nor stroller-friendly. Strollers can be negotiated on the escalators, but there are a lot of stairs to deal with. This is fine if there are two or more adults in your group, but if you're alone, you could be left struggling, scooping up the whole stroller with baby inside, to get up and down the stairs. You'd be surprised how many other passengers are quick to push or scurry by, rather than offer a helping hand.

If you are expecting a baby, don't expect people to surrender their seats for you. It is worth noting that there is priority seating on the bus and tube trains clearly indicated for the elderly, the handicapped, or those with small children. So, if no one has offered and you're feeling bold, you have every right to ask someone to move.

For short hops with the kids, a black cab might be the best idea (if walking is not an option, of course). Children love the jump seats. Do be warned, though, that the traffic can be bad in the central areas during the day (Oxford Street, Marble Arch, Piccadilly, Bayswater, Knightsbridge, Chelsea, and Kensington), and taxis are not cheap.

Stay Loose   As every parent has discovered by day three of their first baby's life, flexibility is everything in parenting, and that goes double for sight-seeing with children. Remember that having fun is not necessarily the same as seeing everything. When you and your children start getting tired and irritable, call a time-out and regroup. Trust your instincts. What would really feel best right now? Another museum, a break with some ice cream, or going back to the room for a nap or quiet time? The way to have a great vacation is to put the emphasis on being happy and having a good time, whatever that takes. You do not have to meet a quota for experiencing every museum or attraction, seeing every neighborhood and monument, or following every suggestion in the book. London has been here for a long time, and it's not going anywhere. Your kids' childhood, on the other hand, is a flash of lightning. Make sure their memories of London are happy ones, and they'll want to come back when they're grown up.

All for One and One for All   When you're traveling *en famille,* you are a moving unit made up of many differing tastes, abilities, and interests. Accept that energy levels vary among individuals, and be prepared to respond to small children or other members of your group who poop out. Try not to let your own disappointment hurt the tired one's feelings. Maybe you can take turns with the other grown-up, if there is one with you, in taking the walking wounded back to the hotel, so that one of you can continue sightseeing.

Setting Limits and Making Plans   The best way to avoid arguments and disappointments is to develop a game plan before you go. Establish some general guidelines for each day and try to get everybody excited about the plans. Be sure to include:

1. Wake-up time and breakfast plans.
2. Departure time for the part of London you plan to explore.
3. Necessary items to take.
4. A policy for splitting the group up or for staying together.
5. A plan for what to do if the group gets separated or someone is lost.
6. Estimate of morning touring time and what you want to see, including fallback plans in case an attraction is too crowded or unexpectedly closed.
7. A policy on what you can afford for snacks, lunch, and refreshments. This is very important in this very expensive city.

8. A target time for returning to your hotel for a rest.

9. If you rest, a target time for returning to the touring and for how late you will stay out.

10. Plans for dinner.

11. A policy for shopping and buying souvenirs, including who pays (parents or kids).

Be Flexible   Having a game plan does not mean forgoing spontaneity or sticking rigidly to the itinerary. Once again, listen to your intuition. Alter the plan if the situation warrants. Be prepared to roll with the punches.

Rain, Sunburn, and Dehydration   London's weather is changeable. Although it's not often terribly hot, it can get quite warm in the sun, and you can get a beauty of a sunburn. Carry a small bottle of sunscreen, or smear it on before you go out. Remember a bottle of water to rehydrate the happy campers. Rain is the biggest surprise in London; you never know when it's going to come, but chances are it will, if only for a sprinkle. The best and lightest protection is a plastic rain poncho; you can carry a few and not have as much weight or bulk as with a couple of umbrellas.

Blisters   Blisters and sore feet are common for visitors of all ages, so wear comfortable, well-broken-in shoes. If you or your children are unusually susceptible to blisters, carry some precut moleskin bandages; they offer the best possible protection and won't sweat off. When you feel a hot spot, stop, air out your foot, and place a moleskin over the area before a blister forms. You'll probably find some in London in a pharmacy under a Dr. Scholl's display, but bring some with you just in case. Sometimes small children won't tell their parents about a developing blister until it's too late. Check out your preschooler's feet a couple of times a day—this penny's worth of prevention will be worth many pounds of cure to you and them.

Health and Medical Care   If you have a child who requires medication, pack plenty and bring it on the plane in a carry-on bag. A bottle of liquid Dramamine will come in handy to fight off motion sickness, which can affect kids who are normally fine in a car but may get sick in a plane, train, or boat.

A small first-aid kit, available at most pharmacies, will handle most minor cuts, scrapes, and splinters, and is easy to pack. Grown-up and children's strength aspirin or Tylenol, a thermometer, cough syrup, baby wipes, a plastic spoon, a battery-powered night-light, and pacifiers will round out a small kit of health-related items for people traveling with children or infants.

If You Become Separated   Before venturing out of your hotel room, sit down with your kids and discuss what they should do if they get separated from you while touring a museum or attraction. Tell them to find a uniformed guard and ask for help. Point out that the main entrance of most London attractions has an information desk where they should go if they temporarily get separated.

It's not a bad idea to dress the smaller kids in distinctive colors so you can find them with a quick scanning. It is also considered prudent to sew a label into each child's shirt indicating his or her name, your name, and the name of your hotel. The same thing can be accomplished less elegantly by writing the information on a strip of masking tape. Hotel security professionals suggest that the information be printed in small letters and that the tape be affixed to the outside of the child's shirt five inches or so below the armpit.

Rainy Days   As you know, London is a pretty rainy place—certainly not as bad as its reputation (Rome actually has more inches per year), but it does come down. Museums and galleries are obvious solutions to the rainy-day blues; that old stand-by, the movies, is a good place to kick back, but finding kids' movies is easier said than done. Look in the *Evening Standard* for Imax movies—there are a number of venues. Leisure Box in Queensway has an indoor ice-skating rink and bowling alley, and there are a few paint-your-own-pottery places that kids just love—see "Activities" below for names and numbers. You have to wait a day or two to pick up your finished pieces, so ask ahead how long it will take to fire your kids' work. There's also brass rubbing at St. Martin-in-the-Fields, a cheaper option, and the kids can take their rubbings with them when leaving the church. Look in *Time Out* under children's events; there may be a puppet show or story-time reading where you can stay dry.

The lists below are very general; obviously some kids will be of a more appropriate age to enjoy some attractions than others. We've left out some of the attractions that one can see in any city, such as arcades and amusement parks.

THE TOP 10 MOST POPULAR SIGHTS FOR CHILDREN

1. The British Airways London Eye
2. Science Museum
3. London Aquarium (toddlers and preschoolers are very entertained here; older ones might prefer something more Londonesque)
4. Museum of London
5. Pollock's Toy Museum
6. Victoria and Albert Museum
7. Tower of London
8. London Transport Museum

9. Natural History Museum
10. London Zoo

ALSO SEE

1. Royal Mews
2. Theatre Museum
3. British Museum
4. London Bridge
5. London Dungeon (for gore-loving adolescents)
6. All the military museums for children of that bent: Cabinet War Rooms, Imperial War Museum, Guards Museum, National Army Museum, HMS *Belfast*

THE TOP 10 LEAST POPULAR SIGHTS FOR CHILDREN

1. Queen's Gallery
2. Leighton House
3. Design Museum
4. Saatchi Gallery
5. Dickens House
6. British Library
7. Royal Academy of Arts
8. Florence Nightingale Museum
9. Carlyle's House
10. Sir John Soane's Museum

Services for Families

Rental Equipment and Child Care

Chelsea Baby Hire (phone (0208) 540-8830; www.chelseababy hire.co.uk) and **Nappy Express** (phone (0208) 361-4040; www.nappy express.co.uk) rent cribs, high chairs, double strollers (or buggies, as they're known here), along with toys, household products, and more. For child care, consider **Childminders** (phone (0207) 935-3000; www.babysitter.co.uk). You'll first pay a joining fee of £59 for the service, and then an hourly fee starting at £7. **Universal Aunts** (phone (0207) 386-5900) can deal with any domestic need or crisis, like a good auntie should, including short-term baby-sitting needs. **Hopes and Dreams Montessori Nursery School** (phone (0207) 833-9388; www.hopesand dreams.co.uk) is a baby-sitting and nanny agency, as well as a day nursery for kids, complete with organic food and big fun. Day rates (8 a.m. to 6 p.m.) from £60, plus registration fee. You can register with them on the website. **Pippa Pop-Ins Excursions and Activities** (phone (0207) 385-2458; www.pippapopins.com) is another good day nursery that's been around for years, based in Fulham. Call and check for available space. £75 for full day (8:15 a.m. to 6 p.m.).

Activities

Paint Your Own Pottery

Bridgewater Pottery Café (zone 11; 735 Fulham Road, SW6; phone (0207) 736-2157; www.pottery-cafe.com; Number 14 bus toward Fulham, or tube: Fulham Broadway) They have a good selection of ceramic items to paint and fire, and you can also decorate drinking glasses or glass vases. There is another branch in Richmond.

Colour Me Mine (zone 14; 168–70 Randolph Avenue, W9; phone (0207) 328-5577; www.colourmemine.com; tube: Maida Vale) This studio offers ceramics, mosaics, glass-painting, and even bead-stringing. Drop in with your kids (it entertains them right up to adolescence and even beyond) or bring your tiny child to get a foot or hand impression done.

Brass Rubbings

Brass Rubbing Centre (zone 7; Trafalgar Square, WC2; phone (0207) 930-9306; tube: Leicester Square) in the crypt of St. Martin-in-the-Fields offers a wonderful treat for kids age 6 and up. They can make their own souvenirs by rubbing a waxy color stick over paper to reveal the beautiful carved brasses with medieval motifs such as knights, dragons, crests, etc. **All-Hallows-By-The-Tower** (zone 3; Byward Street, EC3; phone (0207) 481-2928; tube: Tower Hill) is another option. The church, which was built in 675 A.D., has an interesting history. John Quincy Adams, the sixth president of the United States, was married here, and William Penn, founder of Pennsylvania, was baptized here. Check out the museum (with an audio tour available); it's good for kids, because it covers all sorts of exciting historical events, including the Great Fire of London (1666), complete with sound effects. Brass rubbing is done 11 a.m.–4 p.m. but call first to be sure it's open.

Skating

Leisure Box Ice-Skating Rink (zone 14; 17 Queensway, W2; phone (0207) 229-0172; tube: Queensway or Bayswater) is a big rink that is part of a fun complex that also has bowling. The minimum age of skaters allowed is 3 years. (For a full description of sports and exercise venues, see Part 11.)

Bookstores

Call the following to check on storytelling performances: **Books Etc.** (zone 14; Whiteleys Center, W2; phone (0207) 229-3865; tube: Queensway or Bayswater) and **Children's Book Centre** (zone 13; 237 Kensington High Street, W8; phone (0207) 937-749; tube: High Street Kensington). Also see **Daisy & Tom's** under "Shopping for Children" below. They have a huge, wonderful selection of children's books.

Playgrounds

Battersea Park (zone 11; Albert Bridge Road, SW11; tube: Sloane Square, then bus 19 or 137) is all-over fun, plus a zoo (which is threatened with closure, so hurry before it's too late!)

Coram Fields (zone 2; 93 Guildford Street, WC1; phone (0207) 837-6138; tube: Russell Square) is a famous playground that only allows adults with an accompanying child—and they mean it. It was built in 1936 on the site of the old foundling hospital. It's got a wide variety of play equipment to suit all ages. Animals are on view, and it's open 9 a.m. to dusk.

Holland Park (zone 13; tube: Holland Park) has peacocks and an impressive multilevel adventure playground, with an area for kids under age 8.

Hyde Park (zone 13; tube: High Street Kensington) There's a good playground on the south side of the park, near the riding ring where you may see the Queen's Horse Guards exercise their steeds (not to mention the regular traffic of folks on horseback). Weekends there are soccer games for the young footie fan to watch. There are ducks and paddleboats on the Serpentine in summer and Peter Pan's statue all year.

Kensington Gardens (zone 13; tube: High Street Kensington) has the Princess Diana Memorial Playground at the north end of Broad Walk, and remote-control model boats to watch in the Round Pond.

Regent's Park (zone 15; tube: Regent's Park) has three playgrounds and two boating lakes, one of which is expressly for children.

St. James's Park (zone 8; tube: Green Park) has a smallish playground by Birdcage Walk and plenty of pelicans and other birds to watch. The 3 p.m. feeding of pelicans is very popular.

Syon Park & London Butterfly House (tube: Gunnersbury or Kew Bridge rail, then bus 267 or 237) is an estate open daily, 10 a.m. to 5:30 p.m. Older kids might appreciate the Butterfly House, but the younger ones will appreciate the **Aquatic Experience** (phone (0208) 847-4730), which features fish, reptiles, amphibians, and other small animals in their natural habitats. There's also **Snakes & Ladders** (phone (0208) 847-0946), an adventure playground. Check out the miniature steam train in the gardens. Call (0208) 560-0881 for Syon Park information and (0208) 560-0378 for Butterfly House information. Two caveats: This attraction is not easy to get to without a car, and the planes overhead landing or taking off from Heathrow are most annoying. Otherwise it's got enough activities to easily fill a day.

Theaters

Little Angel Theatre (zone2; 14 Dagmar Passage, off Cross Street, N1; phone (0207) 226-1787; www.littleangeltheatre.com; tube: Angel or Highbury & Islington) The city's only permanent puppet theatre, which has been running for 40 years, is a delightful venue with a 100-seat audi-torium. Weekend shows by the resident or visiting puppet companies are offered, as well as shows during Christmas and half-term holidays.

National Film Theatre (zone 5; South Bank, SE1; phone (0207) 928-3535; www.bfi.org.uk; tube: Waterloo or Embankment) runs Movie Magic matinee screenings of perennial movie favorites for kids every week-end day from 3 to 4 p.m., and some weekdays during school holidays.

Polka Theatre for Children (zone 12; 240 The Broadway, SW19; phone (0208) 543-4888; www.polkatheatre.com; tube: Wimbledon or British Rail to South Wimbledon) seats 300 and also has an 80-seat adventure room for children under age 5, a small but unusual play-ground, a café, and a gift shop; excellent disability access.

Puppet Theatre Barge (zone 14; Blomfield Road [opposite #35], W9; phone (0207) 249-6876; www.puppetbarge.com; tube: Warwick Avenue) is a traveling puppet barge featuring wonderful string marionettes. It is moored in Little Venice, Maida Vale, from November to May. Shows run on weekends and during school holidays, beginning at 3 p.m. From July to October, the theater travels on the Thames River, with shows at Henley-on-Thames, Marlow, and Richmond. Call or look on the website to find out where and when. Advance reservations are recommended.

Transportation

Travel is free for children ages 5 years old and under on all buses, tubes, and local trains. Under-16s pay child's fares until 10 p.m., after which they pay adult fares. Because of the difficulty of identifying an adoles-cent's age, 14- and 15-year-olds are required to produce proof of age (a passport or copy of one), or a Child Photocard, which can be obtained from any post office. Bring a passport-size photo and proof of age, and you'll be good to go. Unfortunately, many conductors on buses will not take your word for your teen's age.

Where to Eat

Kids need a bit of entertaining to keep them happy in a restaurant, and they generally require something fried and finger-fed. Most kids will be happy as clams at the outdoor cafés in the parks, or with a picnic of sandwiches from one of the "sarnie" shops such as Pret à Manger (the best quality in take-away sandwiches and they're all over town). The chains of Boots, Waitrose, Sainsbury's, and Starbucks all sell ready-made sandwiches and drinks—buy a bagful, some crisps, drinks and bob's your uncle, as they say here. If you require a sit-down out of the weather, here are some kid-friendly places to eat, none of which are at the top of any serious gourmand's list, but they'll serve your children with a smile:

Big East   (zone 11; 332–334 King's Road, SW3; phone (0207) 352-4071; tube: Sloane Square) is geared up for kids; there's a special menu, plus crayons to keep those hands busy. Kids' prices are £4.95–£8.95 and include unlimited soft drinks and some chocolate gooey thing.

Hard Rock Café   (zone 8; 150 Old Park Lane, W1; phone (0207) 629-0382; www.hardrock.com; tube: Green Park or Hyde Park Center) has lots of loud music and rock memorabilia festooning every available surface. It may not be suitable for very young children, as the music rocks hard, as you would imagine. There is a special kids' menu for £5.95 and crayons to distract them.

Maxwells   (zone 7; 8–9 James Street, WC2; phone (0207) 836-0303; www.maxwells.co.uk; tube: Covent Garden) is in a great location, near the Covent Garden piazza, and has a special kids' menu, crayons, balloons, and more. During some holidays, they decorate the restaurant and provide seasonally festive menus.

Rainforest Café   (zone 7; 20 Shaftsbury Avenue, WC2; phone (0207) 434-3111; www.therainforestcafe.co.uk; tube: Piccadilly Circus), an American import, is a great place for kids, with its children's menu (burgers, ribs, sandwiches) and special treats for parties (face painting, goodie bags, and more), all in a jungle-esque setting with a rumbling faux volcano that erupts intermittently.

Sticky Fingers   (zone 11; 1A Phillimore Gardens, W8; phone (0207) 938-5338; www.stickyfingers.co.uk; tube: High Street Kensington) is owned by Bill Wyman (ex–Rolling Stones member) and offers a kids' menu for £4.95 that includes burgers, ribs, chicken, pasta, and more. Sundays are best, with face painting, balloons, and a generally fun atmosphere.

Smollensky's   (zone 7; 105 The Strand, WC2; phone (0207) 497-2101; www.smollenskys.co.uk; tube: Charing Cross) on The Strand is the perfect place for kids, especially for Saturday and Sunday lunch. There's a play area, a crèche for the really young ones, and endless entertainment, including magicians, clowns, face painting, computer games, and more.

TGI Friday's   (zone 7; 6 Bedford Street, WC2; phone (0207) 379-0585; www.fridays.co.uk; tube: Covent Garden or Charing Cross), another American import that's family friendly, offers balloons, crayons, and children's menus, including a Sesame Street one that comes with a free toy. On weekends, there is face painting and a magician on Sunday. They offer free organic baby food.

Texas Embassy Cantina   (zone 7; 1 Cockspur Street, SW1; phone (0207) 7925-0077; www.texasembassy.com; tube: Charing Cross) This is an authentic Tex-Mex place, situated in the building that housed the embassy of the short-lived nation of Texas. It's near the National Gallery and Trafalgar Square. Lots of room for big parties, plus outdoor seating (watch the buses inch along). Very cool decor that will make an American feel right at home, and children most welcome.

Tootsies (zone 13; 120 Holland Park Avenue, W11; phone (0207) 229-8567; www.tootsiesrestaurant.co.uk; tube: Holland Park) A really great place for upscale diner-type food, with a huge menu that includes burgers of every description, all-day breakfasts, and lots of salads. Very child-friendly and relaxed. There are branches in zone 11, 107 Old Brompton Road, phone (0207) 581-8942, tube: South Kensington; and zone 14, 35 James Street W1, phone (0207) 486-1611, tube Marble Arch or Bond Street.

Shopping for Children

Toys

Daisy & Tom's (zone 11; 81 King's Road, Chelsea, SW3; phone (0207) 352-5000; tube: Sloane Square) is a great kids' store with toys, books, nursery furniture, a carousel, and a very cool hair-cutting salon. **Davenport's Magic Shop** (zone 7; 7 Charing Cross Underground Concourse, Strand, WC2; phone (0207) 836-0408; tube: Charing Cross) is still going strong after 100 years of selling magic. **Hamleys** (zone 8; 188–196 Regent Street, W1; phone (0207) 734-3161; www.hamleys.com; tube: Oxford Street or Piccadilly Circus), with its seven floors, is said to be the largest toy store in the world; and kids instinctively seem to know this, going bonkers with toy-lust. Consider yourself warned. **Harrods** (zone 10; 87 Brompton Road, SW1; phone (0207) 730-1234; www.harrods. com; tube: Knightsbridge) has a remarkable selection of dolls, games, and action toys, but watch that wallet: They also feature miniature automobiles. **Tridias** (zone 11; 25 Bute Street, SW7; phone (0207) 584-2330; tube: South Kensington) sells lots of interesting European toys and small, inexpensive gimcracks.

Clothing

These stores tend to be like kids themselves—here one minute, gone the next. Most of the clothes stores listed in our first edition have gone belly-up, so it's wise to call before you venture to the following stores. Most of the stores listed are included not so much because they represent good deals (the prices can be as breathtaking as the clothes in some of the stores, and unless you're loaded or plan to hand-me-down to a large brood, these are strictly luxury purchases) but because they have interesting and distinctive European selections from Petit Bateau, Petite Ourse, Laura Ashley, and other British or French designers.

Brora (zone 11; 344 King's Road, SW3; phone (0207) 352-3697; www.brora.co.uk; tube: Sloane Square) specializes in cashmere and woolen clothes for newborns and young children, along with their established adult line.

Caramel (zone 11; 291 Brompton Road, SW3; phone (0207) 589-7001; tube: South Kensington) offers lots of cute and trendy gear for children up to approximately 8 years of age. They have a little sale box, which, depending on your luck, can yield a treasure or two.

Clementine (zone 13; 73 Ledbury Road, W11; phone (0207) 243-6331; tube: Notting Hill Gate or Westbourne Park) specializes in French and Italian clothes for children of all ages.

Catimini (zone 8; 52 South Molton Street, W1; phone (0207) 629-8099; www.catimini.fr; tube: Bond Street) has cute clothes with unusual details, such as pockets that resemble dolls' faces and candy-shaped buttons. It carries clothing for children up to approximately 14 years of age.

Daisy & Tom's (zone 11; 181–183 King's Road, SW3; phone (0207) 352-5000; tube: Sloane Square) is a great kids' shop with designer labels such as Petit Bateau, Miniman, and Damask. While you shop, kids can ride the carousel or get a haircut. Clothes are for children up to 10 years old.

Jigsaw Junior (zone 13; 190 Westbourne Grove, W11; phone (0207) 229-8654; www.jigsaw-online.com; tube: Notting Hill) offers simple clothes from the successful Jigsaw chain of fashion stores; for girls only. There are plenty of playthings in the store to keep young shoppers happy. Clothes are for children up to 13 years of age.

Mothercare World (zone 8; 461 Oxford Street, W1; phone (0207) 629-6621; www.mothercare.com; tube: Marble Arch or Bond Street) Although a chain store, this is a great place to snap up affordable home-brand basics and clothing featuring licensed characters such as Barbie, Action Man, and Winnie the Pooh. Additional branches abound. The shop also carries baby products (see "Baby Goods").

Oilily (zone 10; 9 Sloane Street, SW1; phone (0207) 823-2505; www.oilily.nl; tube: Knightsbridge) Oilily is a bright and cheerful collection from a popular Dutch design team. It's very 1960s in a pop-art way, featuring beautiful patterns and well-decorated basics. There are one-of-a-kind knit sweaters and gorgeous baby blankets, cool shoes, affordable hats, and baby bags.

Petit Bateau (zone 11, 103 Kings Road, SW3; phone (0207) 838-0818; tube: Sloane Square) This venerable French company has been dressing European infants in its luxurious cotton onesies and sweet fashions for years, and now the teenagers have rediscovered the label, making the PB T-shirts a must-have fashion.

Please Mum (zone 10; 85 Knightsbridge, SW1; phone (0207) 486-1380; tube: Knightsbridge) specializes in Italian designers, from Moschino to Versace, plus the Please Mum home-brand collection.

Frilly, old-fashioned children's ball gowns are a unique offering. Clothes are for children up to 14 years of age.

Paul Smith for Children   (zone 7; 40–44 Floral Street, WC2; phone (0207) 379-7133; www.paulsmith.co.uk; tube: Covent Garden) features this world-famous designer's funky collection, including bold duck, helicopter, and airplane prints, which really do look cool. Shoes are also available. Clothes are for children up to 16 years of age.

Tartine et Chocolat   (zone 8; 66 South Molton Street, W1; phone (0207) 629-7233; tube: Bond Street) is the place to go if you're looking for more conservative outfits. You'll find double-breasted coats, velvet dresses, lots of blues for baby boys, and lots of pinks for baby girls at this Parisian boutique.

Shoes

Buckle My Shoe   (zone 8; 19 St. Christophers Place, W1; phone (0207) 935-5589; www.bucklemyshoe.com; tube: Bond Street) has more cute delights for those tiny feet—funky animal-print slippers, glittery sandals. Not cheap, but so cute!

Instep   (zone 14; 45 St. John's Wood High Street, NW8; phone (0207) 722-7634; tube: St John's Wood) They design their own shoes here and have them made in Italy. They have very cool decorative footwear for those babies who have yet to put a foot down, good learning-to-walk shoes, and plenty for older kids to choose from.

Look Who's Walking   (zone 1, 78 Heath Street, NW3; phone (0207) 433-3855; tube: Hampstead) Love the name, love the store. Very small store with very big taste: Dolce & Gabbana, Pom d'Api, Naturino make beautiful shoes for kids to quickly grow out of. Plus the store has designer clothes for up to age 12.

Baby Goods

Mothercare World is always heaving with expectant and established parents, stocking up on cribs, bedding, strollers, high chairs, bottles, diapers, toys, and more. Particularly handy are the bathroom stalls (big enough to push strollers into), a feeding area with bottle warmers, and a special room for nursing mothers complete with rocking chairs and a water dispenser. (See the entry in the "Clothing" section, above, for location information.)

   Nursery Window (zone 11; 83 Walton Street, SW3; phone (0207) 581-3358; www.nurserywindow.co.uk; tube: South Kensington), which is not too pricey, specializes in nursery furnishings: cribs, bedding, curtains, and even wallpaper. All fabrics are designed and printed in the United Kingdom. There's also a mail-order service.

Part Eight

Dining in London

Ten years ago, if you had said you were going to London for the food, your friends would have advised a long period of rest and perhaps a visit to your doctor. The idea simply seemed crazy. Food in London, and in all of the United Kingdom, was famous for its brutally unyielding awfulness.

To say that things have changed is to make a gross understatement. London now boasts two restaurants with three Michelin stars (the highest accolade restaurateurs can receive) and has been described as one of the gastronomic capitals of the world. Well, you can argue that kind of point endlessly, and making comparisons with other cities is an academic exercise. But there's no denying that you can now eat better in London than at any time since the Romans arrived.

Asian and South Asian cuisines have always been a strong point in London, and they remain so—but they're even better now, especially Indian cooking. There's a bigger range than ever before, with more regional variety and a general emphasis on fresh ingredients cooked to order. The same can be said of Chinese food, another traditional area of strength. It's true also of French and Italian cooking. Even old-fashioned British food is taken with the greatest seriousness, again at every price level.

But if there's anything special about London's food at the moment, it's a phenomenon that's called modern British, or (the term used here) modern European cooking. Nearly everyone who pays attention to gastronomic trends will use some version of this term. Defining it precisely . . . well, that's another matter. But here's a rough working definition: classic European techniques (especially French and Italian) applied to top-quality ingredients that may—but don't necessarily—come from any corner of the globe.

London is well suited to the development of this kind of eclecticism in cooking. The ingredients are there because of the city's location within Europe and its long-time connections with Asia. In addition, a widely traveled customer base provides a serious demand for good cooking.

Some of the best chefs exploit these elements with amazing results. Some borrow widely from Asia and the Americas, with the results bordering on so-called fusion cooking. Some remain deliberately French and Italian in orientation, whereas others emphasize the British source of ingredients and inspirations. Modern European is the most interesting food being cooked in London now, and restaurants of this type feature prominently in these listings.

If eating out in London is better than ever, you should also be warned of the downside: It's often bruisingly expensive—even for Londoners, and especially for traveling Americans, with the dollar weak against the pound sterling. It is nearly impossible to find a good three-course meal with a bottle of wine for under £30 a head outside Asian restaurants, and even fairly basic restaurants have an annoying tendency to cost twice that amount if you drink more than the house wine. We wish it weren't so, but there's nothing to be done unless exchange rates and pricing policies change.

In the meantime, those who seek high quality at low prices should pay special attention to the list of gastropubs in the "More Recommendations" section. These are old-fashioned pubs, refurbished in a simple style, that place the greatest emphasis on good food rather than beer and crisps (potato chips). The top gastropubs are usually off the beaten track (one reason they can charge lower prices), but you should seek them out if you don't mind a bit of extra traveling. They are some of London's best bets for budget eating in totally relaxed surroundings.

At the other restaurants, there are ways to cut costs. Lunch is likely to be considerably cheaper than dinner, and some places have pre- or post-theater offers with limited choice and lower prices. With drinks making up a large part of many bills, look for house wines or order by the glass if that's all you want. And don't feel obliged to order a bottle of water (almost always marked up heavily) if tap water will please you just as well. If you're traveling with children but don't see a children's menu, ask if a child-size portion can be prepared, as many good restaurants will oblige.

The other big complaint about London restaurants is the quality of service, and there's a lot of merit in the complaint. Cooking skills have zoomed up, but there is a perennial shortage of well-trained, conscientious waiters. At expensive restaurants this should not (in theory) be a problem, but in others—well, you may be lucky and you may not. Complain if you feel it's warranted. You'll be doing the restaurant a favor. And if you get poor service at high prices, complain even more vociferously. It shouldn't happen, but it does.

One final word is in order here. There's almost nonstop change in the London restaurant world. Restaurants accept reservations one day and announce their closure the next. Chefs move around at an unprecedented rate. Menus are changed fundamentally. New management moves in on well-established operations. The pace of change from week to week makes it inevitable that further change will have occurred by the time you hold this book in your hands—some months after the section was written. Needless to say, this is out of our control.

The Restaurants

Rating Our Favorite London Restaurants

We have developed detailed profiles for the best and most interesting (in our opinion) restaurants in town. Each profile features an easily scanned heading that allows you, in just a second, to check out the restaurant's name, cuisine, star rating, cost, quality rating, and value rating.

Cuisine   This is actually less straightforward than it sounds. A couple of years ago, for example, "pan-Asian" restaurants in Washington, D.C., were serving what was then generally described as "fusion" food—Asian ingredients with European techniques, or vice versa. Since then, there has been a pan-Asian explosion, but nearly all specialize in what would be street food back home: noodles, skewers, dumplings, and soups. Once-general categories have become subdivided—French into bistro fare and even Provençal, "new continental" into regional American and "eclectic"— while others have broadened and fused: Middle Eastern and Provençal into Mediterranean, Spanish and South American into nuevo Latino, and so on. In some cases, we have used the broader terms (e.g., "French") but added descriptions to give a clearer idea of the fare. Again, though, experimentation and "fusion" are ever more common, so don't hold us, or the chefs, to too strict a style.

Overall Rating   The overall rating is a rating that encompasses the entire dining experience, including style, service, and ambience, in addition to the taste, presentation, and quality of the food. Five stars is the highest rating possible and connotes the best of everything. Four-star restaurants are exceptional, and three-star restaurants are well above average. Two-star restaurants are good. One star is used to indicate an average restaurant that demonstrates an unusual capability in some area of specialization—for example, an otherwise unmemorable place that has great barbecued chicken.

Cost   Our expense description provides a comparative sense of how much a complete meal will cost. A complete meal for our purposes consists of an appetizer, entree, and dessert. Drinks and tips are excluded.

Inexpensive	Less than £20 per person
Moderate	£20–£50 per person
Expensive	More than £50 per person

Quality Rating   The food quality is rated on a scale of one to five stars, five being the best rating attainable. The quality rating is based expressly on the taste, freshness of ingredients, preparation, presentation, and creativity of food served. There is no consideration of price. If you are a person who wants the best food available and cost is not an issue, you need look no further than the quality ratings.

Value Rating   If, on the other hand, you are looking for both quality and value, then you should check the value rating. The value ratings are defined as follows:

★★★★★	Exceptional value; a real bargain
★★★★	Good value
★★★	Fair value; you get exactly what you pay for
★★	Somewhat overpriced
★	Significantly overpriced

Locating the Restaurant   At the end of the heading is a designation for geographic zone. This zone description will give you a general idea of where the restaurant described is located. We've divided London into the following 15 geographic zones (see pages xx–xxix for detailed zone maps).

Zone 1	North London—Hampstead, Highgate
Zone 2	Bloomsbury and Holborn
Zone 3	The City, Clerkenwell, Barbican
Zone 4	East End—Spitalfields, White Chapel, Bethnal Green
Zone 5	South London—South Bank, Lambeth, Brixton
Zone 6	Greenwich and Docklands
Zone 7	Soho and the West End
Zone 8	Mayfair and Piccadilly
Zone 9	Victoria and Westminster
Zone 10	Knightsbridge and Belgravia
Zone 11	Chelsea and South Kensington
Zone 12	West London—Hammersmith, Chiswick, Richmond, Kew
Zone 13	Kensington, Holland Park, Notting Hill
Zone 14	Bayswater, Marylebone, Little Venice, St. John's Wood
Zone 15	Regent's Park and Camden Town

Payment   We've listed the type of payment accepted at each restaurant using the following codes: AMEX equals American Express (Optima), CB equals Carte Blanche, D equals Discover, DC equals Diners Club, JCB equals Japan Credit Bureau, MC equals MasterCard, and VISA is self-explanatory.

Who's Included   Restaurants in London open and close at an alarming rate. So, for the most part, we have tried to confine our list to establishments with a proven track record over a fairly long period of time. The exceptions here are the newer offspring of the demigods of the culinary world—these places are destined to last, at least until our next update. Also, the list is highly selective. Noninclusion of a particular place does not necessarily indicate that the restaurant is not good, only that we did not feel it ranked among the best in its genre. Detailed profiles of individual restaurants follow in alphabetical order at the end of this chapter.

LONDON RESTAURANTS BY CUISINE				
Restaurant	Overall Rating	Price	Quality	Value
American				
Cactus Blue	★★½	Mod	★★½	★★★½
Joe Allen	★★½	Inexp/Mod	★★½	★★½
Arkansas Café	★★	Inexp	★★★	★★★★
Asian				
Wagamama	★	Inexp	★★	★★★★
Belgian				
Belgo	★	Inexp/Mod	★	★★★
British				
Richard Corrigan at Lindsay House	★★★★	Mod/Exp	★★★★½	★★½
Rules	★★★	Mod/Exp	★★★	★★★
Boisdale of Belgravia	★★½	Mod	★★★	★★★
Caribbean				
Mango Room	★★½	Inexp	★★★½	★★★★
Chinese				
Mr. Kong	★★★½	Inexp/Mod	★★★½	★★★★
Royal China	★★★	Inexp	★★★	★★★★
Chuen Cheng Ku	★★	Inexp/Mod	★★★	★★★★
French				
Deca	★★★★½	Mod/Exp	★★★★½	★★★★
Le Gavroche	★★★★½	Exp	★★★★½	★★★
Angela Hartnett at Connaught	★★★★	Exp	★★★★	★★★½
Chez Gérard	★★	Inexp/Mod	★★★	★★★
Fusion				
Providores	★★★★	Mod/Exp	★★★★½	★★★★
Indian				
Café Spice Namaste	★★★★	Mod	★★★★	★★★★
Rasa	★★★½	Mod	★★★½	★★★★
Tamarind	★★★½	Mod	★★★½	★★★

LONDON RESTAURANTS BY CUISINE *(continued)*

Restaurant	Overall Rating	Price	Quality	Value
Indian (continued)				
Zaika	★★★½	Exp	★★★½	★★★
Veeraswamy	★★★	Mod	★★★	★★★½
Masala Zone	★★	Inexp/Mod	★★★½	★★★★
Italian				
Orsini's Café	★★★½	Mod	★★★★	★★★
Strada	★★★½	Inexp	★★★	★★★★
Café Carluccio's	★★★	Mod	★★★	★★★★
Pollo	★	Inexp	★★	★★★★★
Japanese				
Nobu	★★★★	Exp	★★★★	★★
Matsuri	★★★½	Mod/Exp	★★★½	★★
Modern European				
Orrery	★★★★½	Exp	★★★★½	★★★
Pied à Terre	★★★★½	Exp	★★★★½	★★★
Clarke's	★★★★	Mod/Exp	★★★★	★★★
The Ivy	★★★★	Mod	★★★★	★★★
Bibendum	★★★★	Exp	★★★★	★★
Heartstone	★★★½	Inexp/Mod	★★★½	★★★★★
Prospect Grill	★★★½	Inexp/Mod	★★★½	★★★★★
Blue Print Café	★★★	Mod	★★★★½	★★★
Bank	★★★	Mod	★★★½	★★★
Le Caprice	★★½	Mod	★★★½	★★★
Cantina Vinopolis	★★½	Mod	★★½	★★★★
Mash	★★	Inexp/Mod	★★★½	★★★
Corney & Barrow	★★	Mod	★★★	★★★
Pizza				
Pizza Express	★	Inexp	★★	★★★★
Polish				
Baltic	★★½	Mod	★★★	★★★
Sandwiches				
Pret à Manger	★	Inexp	★★	★★★★
Seafood				
Livebait	★★★	Inexp/Mod	★★★	★★★
fish!	★★	Inexp/Mod	★★½	★★★½

LONDON RESTAURANTS BY CUISINE (continued)

Restaurant	Overall Rating	Price	Quality	Value
Seafood (continued)				
North Sea Fish Restaurant	★½	Inexp	★★½	★★★★★
Spanish				
Moro	★★★★	Mod	★★★★	★★★★
Cambio de Tercio	★★★	Mod	★★★½	★★★★

LONDON RESTAURANTS BY ZONE

Zone 1: North London

Pizza Express

Zone 2: Bloomsbury and Holborn

Bank	North Sea Fish Restaurant	Wagamama

Zone 3: The City, Clerkenwell, and Barbican

Moro	Pret à Manger	St. John

Zone 4: East End

Arkansas Café	Café Spice Namaste	Corney & Barrow

Zone 5: South London

Baltic	Cantina Vinopolis	Livebait
Blue Print Café		

Zone 7: Soho and the West End

Belgo	Joe Allen	Prospect Grill
Caffé Carluccio's	Livebait	Richard Corrigan at Lindsay House
Chez Gérard	Masala Zone	
Chuen Cheng Ku	Mash	Rules
Deca	Metro Club	Salsa!
fish!	Mr. Kong	Veeraswamy
The Ivy	Pollo	Wagamama

Zone 8: Mayfair and Piccadilly

Angela Hartnett at the Connaught	Nobu	Tamarind
Le Gavroche	Rasa	Strada

Zone 9: Victoria and Westminster

Le Caprice	Matsuri

LONDON RESTAURANTS BY ZONE *(continued)*		
Zone 10: Knightsbridge and Belgravia		
Boisdale of Belgravia		
Zone 11: Chelsea and South Kensington		
Bibendum	Cambio de Tercio	Cactus Blue
Orsini's Café		
Zone 13: Kensington, Holland Park, Notting Hill		
Clarke's	Zaika	
Zone 14: Bayswater, Marylebone, Little Venice, St. John's Wood		
Orrery	Pied à Terre	Providores
Royal China		
Zone 15: Regent's Park and Camden Town		
Heartstone	Mango Room	

More Recommendations

Chinese

Fung Shing   (zone 7, tube Piccadilly, 15 Lisle Street, WC2; (0207) 437-1539) features cooking similar in ambition to Mr. Kong (see page 299) and is capable of producing memorable dishes.

Harbour City   (zone 7, tube Piccadilly, 46 Gerrard Street, WC2; (0207) 439-7120) serves superb dim sum and is good in the evenings as well. This place is very popular with the local Chinese community.

Hunan   (zone 10, tube Sloane Square, 51 Pimlico Road, SW1; (0207) 730-5712) is one of London's few Hunan specialists and is essential for devotees of that spicy cuisine.

Mandarin Kitchen   (zone 14, tube Queensway, 14–16 Queensway, W2; (0207) 721-7946) is just across the street from Royal China (see page 308). It's dreary in decor but offers wonderful dim sum and special dishes.

Indian

Benares   (zone 8, tube Green Park, 12 Berkeley Square, W1; (0207) 629-8886) is the creation of Atul Kochhar, formerly of Tamarind (see page 311) and universally regarded as one of London's greatest Indian chefs; swanky setting and location that serves staggeringly good food.

Fish, and Fish and Chips

Back to Basics   (zone 7, tube Goodge Street, 21A Foley Street, W1; (0207) 436-2181) is a small, buzzy place that has been packing in locals for sensationally good, and sometimes very innovative, fish cooking; very reasonable prices, too.

Geales   (zone 13, tube Notting Hill, 2 Farmer Street, W8; (0207) 727-7969) is long established and consistently good. This popular spot in fashionable Notting Hill is almost always crowded.

French

Mon Plaisir   (zone 7, tube Covent Garden, 21 Monmouth Street, WC2; (0207) 836-7243) ranks among London's longest-established French restaurants. This is simple bistro fare, centering on steak and frites (French fries); decent prices and generally very sound quality.

Racine   (zone 10, tube Knightsbridge, 239 Brompton Road, SW3; (0207) 584-4477) is a lovely place serving bistro food of the highest quality, and at very fair prices. The chef is Henry Harris, who formerly worked at Bibendum (see page 281).

1 Lombard Street   (zone 3, tube Bank, 1 Lombard Street, EC3; (0207) 929-6611) is a big brasserie and a smaller, pricier dining room in a building that began life as a bank; the cooking can be sensational, and the location is good if you're exploring the City (London's financial district).

Gordon Ramsay   (zone 11, tube Sloane Square, 68–69 Royal Hospital Road, SW3; (0207) 352-4441) boasts three Michelin stars, an extraordinarily talented chef, and a small space that means tables are hard to come by: You have to reserve tables a month in advance. But it's probably the best restaurant in London, so if the dizzying prices (outside the set lunch) don't scare you, it's worth a last-minute call to see if they've had a cancellation.

The Square   (zone 8, tube Green Park or Bond Street, 6–10 Bruton Street, W1; (0207) 495-7100) Some people consider the modern European cooking here among the best in London, and their views are legitimate. Only the pricey wine list and occasional wobbles of service excluded it from the main entries, but it should be a top choice for a special, expensive meal.

Gastropubs and Wine Bars

Cork & Bottle Wine Bar   (zone 7, tube Leicester Square, 44–46 Cranbourn Street, WC2; (0207) 734-7807). The food is nothing special, but the wine list is amazing, and the Leicester Square location is as central as you can get. This is why the cramped basement rooms are always packed. It's good for a light bite and a drink before or after a movie or play.

The Cow   (zone 13, tube Ladbroke Grove, 89 Westbourne Park Road, W11; (0207) 221-0021). Prices are not especially low, but quality is especially high at this popular place near Notting Hill.

The Eagle   (zone 3, tube Farringdon, 159 Farringdon Road, EC1; (0207) 837-1353) is the first of the gastropubs and still one of the best, though its immense popularity means space is hard to come by; if you're nearby, pop in for classy Italian/French cooking.

The Havelock Tavern (zone 13, tube Shepherds Bush, 57 Masbro Road, W14; (0207) 603-5374) is a popular local pub in a nice residential area of Shepherd's Bush; it has great atmosphere and great food.

Greek

Café Corfu (zone 15, tube Camden Town, 7–9 Pratt Street, NW1; (0207) 267-8088). London was once famous for its Greek restaurants, but most are a shadow of their former glory. This is one of the exceptions, featuring innovative cooking in a trendy Camden Town setting.

Italian and Pizza

Condotti (zone 8, tube Green Park, 4 Mill Street, W1; (0207) 499-1308) In an expensive area (Mayfair), this is a cheap source of good pizza in an attractive space; the proprietor was one of the founders of Pizza Express (see page 304).

Locanda Locatelli (zone 14, tube Marble Arch, 8 Seymour Street, Wl; (0207) 935-9088) is one of London's very best Italian restaurants. Fairly pricey, and incredibly difficult to get a table, but it's worth a try if you want spectacular cooking in attractive surroundings.

Riva (zone 12, tube Hammersmith, 169 Church Road, SW13; (0208) 748-0434) is way, way out in quasi-suburban Barnes, but if you really love the finest Italian food and feel like a walk around one of London's loveliest neighborhoods, consider it a top destination.

Japanese

Kulu Kulu (zone 14, tube Regent's Park, 76 Brewer Street, W1; (0207) 734-7316) is the first and best of London's kaiten sushi restaurants— where dishes are circulated on a conveyor belt and you pick what you want as it goes around. Some of the best sushi in town, and cheap, too.

Misato (zone 7, tube Piccadilly, 11 Wardour Street, W1; (0207) 734-0808) is a small, simple place in Chinatown for a quick meal; don't expect anything astounding, but quality is good and prices are low.

Itsu (zone 7, tube Piccadilly, 103 Wardour Street, W1; (0207) 479-4790) Another kaiten sushi restaurant, this one with a European spin on the sushi dishes; trendy, attractive, and very popular with local office workers.

Middle Eastern and Turkish

Al Hamra (zone 8, tube Green Park, 31–33 Shepherd Market, W1; (0207) 493-1954) is popular with tourists and locals alike. This Middle Eastern restaurant specializes in meze (assorted small dishes); it sometimes disappoints, but when it's good, it's very good.

Patogh   (zone 14, tube Marble Arch or Edgeware Road, 8 Crawford Place, W1; (0207) 262-4015). Simple in decor but with exceptionally fine cooking, Patogh is one of the better Middle Eastern restaurants in an area that's crowded with them. There's no license to serve alcohol but you can bring your own.

Ranoush Juice Bar   (zone 14, tube Edgware Road, 43 Edgware Road, W2; (0207) 723-5929). This is London's first juice bar and still a source of excellent sandwiches, kebabs, and cakes, as well as a lovely range of delicious fruity drinks; great budget food.

Sofra Bistro   (zone 8, tube Green Park, 18 Shepherd Market, W1; (0207) 499-3320) is a chain specializing in reasonably priced Turkish food. Service doesn't always achieve the high standards set by the food, but this branch is better than most—and the others are worth considering if you want something cheap and tasty.

Thai

Nahm   (zone 10, tube Hyde Park Corner, The Halkin Hotel, Halkin Street, SW1; (0207) 333-1234) is easily London's best Thai restaurant—and its most expensive by a long shot. Lunch is the affordable time to go; dinner is only for people who really love Thai cooking and are willing to pay around £50 a head before drinks.

Patara   (zone 10, tube Knightsbridge, 9 Beauchamp Place, SW3; (0207) 581-8820) has been one of the best Thai places in London and with prices that aren't too painful considering the ritzy area (Knightsbridge). Despite some inconsistency in the cooking, it's a useful place in this part of town.

Sri Siam   (zone 7, tube Piccadilly, 16 Old Compton Street, W1; (0207) 434-3544). This old warhorse is very central, very popular, and still capable of doing good things when everything's working well; the £5.95 set lunch is a bargain.

Restaurant Profiles

Angela Hartnett at the Connaught   ★ ★ ★ ★

FRENCH AND ITALIAN (HAUTE CUISINE) | MODERATE/EXPENSIVE | QUALITY ★ ★ ★ ★ |
VALUE ★ ★ ★ ½ | ZONE **8**

Carlos Place, W1; (0207) 592-1222 ; tube: Green Park; www.savoy-group.co.uk/connaught/restaurants-and-bars.html

Customers Hotel guests, tourists, and locals **Reservations** Essential **When to go** Lunch or dinner **Entree range** Lunch menu £25 for 3 courses, dinner £45 for 3 courses (Menu and the Grill); £12–£18 (The Terrace) **Payment** VISA, MC, AMEX, D, DC, CB **Service rating** ★ ★ ★ ★ **Friendliness rating**

★★★★½ **Bar** Yes **Wine selection** Excellent **Dress** Smart casual **Disabled access** Limited

Lunch Monday–Friday, noon–3 p.m.; Saturday and Sunday, noon–3:30 p.m.

Dinner Monday–Saturday, 5:45–11 p.m.; Sunday, 6–10:30 p.m.

Setting & atmosphere Grand, old-fashioned room with modern touches in lighting, decoration, and furniture; formal but not intimidating.

Summary & comments In 2003, when it was announced that the venerable restaurants at the Connaught hotel were being closed down and taken over by Gordon Ramsay (see page 275), there were anguished wails of horror from all over London. The hotel dates back to 1897 and is accustomed to catering for royalty—the old menu had a special symbol for dishes created by long-serving chef Michel Bourdin for the queen's silver jubilee (1977). Ramsay announced his intention of sweeping away the old restaurant and installing one of his best protegées, Angela Hartnett, to run the restaurants instead with an Italian-oriented menu. You could hear the wailing rise in decibel count. But Hartnett and her team created a restaurant of fitting excellence: very fine cooking (much of it French rather than Italian), good service, and a much livelier atmosphere, it has to be admitted, than the old regime. There are two principal restaurants, Menu and the Grill, but serving the same food. The Terrace, opened in July 2003, offers simple dishes including snacks—and with a good view. The old place was one of a kind not just in London but in the world. Its successor is not unique, but it is very good—if expensive, as you would expect in these surroundings.

Arkansas Café ★★

AMERICAN | INEXPENSIVE | QUALITY ★★★ | VALUE ★★★★ | ZONE 4

Spitalfields Market, E1; (0207) 377-6999; tube: Liverpool Street

Customers Locals and American business community **Reservations** Not necessary **When to go** Lunch **Entree range** £3.50–£13.50 **Payment** VISA, MC **Service rating** ★★★ **Friendliness rating** ★★★★½ **Bar** Yes **Wine selection** Minimal but inexpensive **Dress** Shirt and shoes mandatory **Disabled access** Main dining room only

Lunch Monday–Friday, noon–2:30 p.m.; Sunday, noon–4 p.m.

Setting & atmosphere Roadhouse barbecue joint.

House specialties Barbecued ribs, brisket, sliced pork, chicken, burgers.

Entertainment & amenities Two-man rockabilly band, on occasion.

Summary & comments If you are suffering withdrawal symptoms for top-quality American barbecue, come to the Arkansas. The proprietor is a prizewinning barbecue chef from Maryland, and his specially imported pit barbecues turn out what is, by a margin of several hundred miles, the best ribs in town. As a matter of fact, there's no competition: If you don't believe us, ask the U.S. ambassador, who gets the Arkansas to cater parties at the embassy. Much of the meat comes from the United States, and the rest of it is from impeccably chosen sources (English, Irish, French). The totally laid-back atmosphere will make you feel at home. Vegetarians won't have much fun; everyone else will have loads of it.

Baltic ★★½

POLISH | MODERATE | QUALITY ★★★ | VALUE ★★★ | ZONE 5

74 Blackfriars Road, SE1; (0207) 928-1111; tube: Southwark or Waterloo

Customers Diverse, mostly young locals **Reservations** Recommended **When to go** Lunch or dinner **Entree range** £10.90–£13.90 **Payment** VISA, MC, AMEX, DC **Service rating** ★★★ **Friendliness rating** ★★★★½ **Bar** Yes **Wine selection** Small but good and very reasonable **Dress** Casual **Disabled access** Yes

Lunch Monday–Friday, 12:30–2:30 p.m.

Dinner Every day, 7–11:15 p.m.

Setting & atmosphere Small rooms and plain decor; popular at both lunch and dinner, and very welcoming.

House specialties Traditional Polish dishes such as blinis, dumplings, and herring; extensive vodka list.

Other recommendations Vodka.

Entertainment & amenities Jazz Sunday evenings, 7–11 p.m.

Summary & comments London has a long tradition of hosting emigrés from Eastern and Central Europe, who have brought with them the richness of their national cuisines. Baltic is part of that tradition, but it is not a traditional restaurant: The setting is very contemporary, and so is the food, despite paying due respect to classic Polish fare. This gives a meal at Baltic a welcome element of surprise, and it also means you can eat more lightly here than at many restaurants serving this type of cuisine. For many customers, however, Baltic is preeminently a vodka bar: Aficionados can choose from around 30, including vodkas flavored on the premises (such as vanilla or pear). There's a good wine list, however, and beers as well. For interesting, flexible eating with a different twist, Baltic is a great spot—and justly popular.

Bank ★★★

MODERN EUROPEAN | MODERATE | QUALITY ★★★½ | VALUE ★★★ | ZONE 2

1 Kingsway, WC2; (0207) 379-9797; tube: Covent Garden or Holborn; www.bankrestaurants.com/westminster

Customers Mostly locals **Reservations** Recommended **When to go** Lunch or dinner **Entree range** £8.95–£19.50 **Payment** VISA, MC, AMEX, D, DC, CB

Service rating ★★★½ **Friendliness rating** ★★★½ **Bar** Yes **Wine selection** Good **Dress** No code **Disabled access** Yes

Breakfast Every day, 7–10:30 a.m.

Brunch Saturday and Sunday, 11:30 a.m.–3 p.m.

Lunch Monday–Friday, noon–2:45 p.m.; Saturday and Sunday, 11:30 a.m.–3 p.m.

Dinner Monday–Saturday, 5:30–11 p.m.; Sunday, 5–9:30 p.m.

Setting & atmosphere The big, ultramodern room is almost always packed in the evening, both at the bar and in the restaurant.

House specialties Baltic herring, new potatoes, and Swedish mustard dressing; peppered foie gras parfait, apple and pear chutney, toasted brioche; shellfish (lobster, crab, oysters); fish and chips; pan-roasted venison; beet marmalade; and sautéed potato Lyonnaise.

Other recommendations Pretheater prix fixe menu, breakfast, steak and chips, desserts.

Summary & comments Bank is one of London's big restaurants, occupying a huge site that was formerly a branch of one of the national banks. Despite its size, it manages to wear a human face, and its central location and extensive opening hours make it a very useful place to know about. Though the chef is French, the food takes on Italian, Asian, and ultratraditional British cooking—what's more, everything is done with consistent skill. Due to its size, Bank is not necessarily a place to linger, though you can if you want to. The low-cost prix fixe menu (available at lunch and in the evening until 7 p.m.) offers two courses for just £12.50 and three for £15. The wine list offers ample choices under £20, service is friendly, and the bar would not be out of place in any big American city. If you like buzz and bustle, chances are you'll like Bank.

Belgo ★

BELGIAN | INEXPENSIVE/MODERATE | QUALITY ★★ | VALUE ★★★ | ZONE 7, 15

50 Earlham Street, WC2; (0207) 813-2233; tube: Covent Garden;
72 Chalk Farm Road, NW1; (0207) 267-0718; tube: Chalk Farm or Camden Town; www.belgo-restaurants.com

Customers Locals and tourists **Reservations** Recommended **When to go** Lunch or dinner **Entree range** £8.75–£17.95 **Payment** VISA, MC, AMEX, D, DC, CB **Service rating** ★★ **Friendliness rating** ★★½ **Bar** No **Wine selection** Adequate; beers are outstanding **Dress** Casual **Disabled access** Yes

Meals served Monday–Thursday, noon–11 p.m.; Friday and Saturday, noon–11:30 p.m.; Sunday, noon–10 p.m.

Setting & atmosphere Big, high-ceilinged subterranean room with a view of the kitchen and a deliberately encouraged air of conviviality.

House specialties Croquettes de fromage; salade Liègoise; tomato crevettes; Belgian braised meats; mussels in all guises; Belgian crêpes and waffles.

Other recommendations The beer list.

Summary & comments Belgo is an incredible success story with a new location opening in New York. The formula is simple: Sell Belgian food and drink at low prices—with a helpful array of special offers to keep them even lower—and get the waiters to dress in monks' robes. Not everyone's a fan, and the food (especially more complicated dishes) can be of variable quality. But the simpler mussel dishes are usually just fine. What's more, you can wash them down with a truly stunning array of the great beers of Belgium, one of the world's great beer producers. Belgo is not the great bargain it once was, and the novelty value has long since worn off; moreover, the business has had its ups and downs, with the closing of its venture in New York City. But these two original branches continue to offer reasonable food at fairly reasonable prices, and should not be overlooked in their respective locations.

Bibendum	★★★★

MODERN | EXPENSIVE | QUALITY ★★★★ | VALUE ★★ | ZONE 11

Michelin House, 81 Fulham Road, SW3; (0207) 581-5817; tube: South Kensington; www.bibendum.co.uk

Customers Locals, tourists, and gastronomes **Reservations** Recommended **When to go** Lunch for the cheapest option and lovely view; dinner for that special occasion **Entree range** Lunch £19–£26.50 **Payment** VISA, MC, AMEX, D, DC Service rating ★★★★ Friendliness rating ★★★★ **Bar** No **Wine selection** Excellent but expensive **Dress** Smart casual **Disabled access** Yes

Lunch Monday–Friday, noon–2:30 p.m.; Saturday and Sunday, 12:30–3 p.m.

Dinner Monday–Saturday, 7–11:30 p.m.; Sunday, 7–10:30 p.m.

Setting & atmosphere A large, wonderfully high-ceilinged art deco room in what was formerly the headquarters of the Michelin Tire Company. The decor is simple and contemporary, but the setting is dominated by the huge stained-glass windows, which let in a shower of light by day and offer a fine view.

House specialties Escargots de Bourgogne; sauté foie gras with turnip fondant; warm smoked eel with Jersey Royals and quail eggs; poisson de soupe; fish and chips; roast Bresse pigeon with lettuce, peas, and sauté foie gras; poulet de Bresse à l'estragon.

Other recommendations Set lunch (£28.50 for three courses), French and Italian desserts.

Summary & comments Bibendum was the first restaurant in Sir Terence Conran's soon-to-be empire, and it remains one of the best exponents of modern cooking in London despite the departure of two first-rate chefs (founding chef Simon Hopkinson and his successor, Henry Harris, now at Racine, page 275). You can come here for lunch or dinner knowing that you'll get superbly cooked food from ingredients of the highest quality, served with consummate professionalism that still manages to be friendly. As you can see from the dishes listed above, the orientation is French and classic, but Asian influences appear as well, as does solid Britishness (the fish and chips may be the best in London). This is what has brought London food fanatics back to Bibendum for years. There are sometimes complaints about service, though not enough to keep the place from being enduringly popular. The real complaint: cost. They're not ripping anyone off with the food prices (attention to detail is expensive, especially when success depends heavily on top-quality ingredients), but wine is marked up without mercy, making an evening meal here a very costly exercise. Is it worth it? Yes, for a rare and very special treat in exquisite surroundings—or for the much more affordable set lunch. There is also a small oyster bar and a separate café (both downstairs) where you can eat quickly and lightly.

Blue Print Café ★★★

MODERN EUROPEAN | MODERATE | QUALITY ★★★★½ | VALUE ★★★ | ZONE 5

28 Shad Thames, SE1; (0207) 378-7031; tube: London Bridge or Tower Bridge; www.blueprintcafé.co.uk

Customers Mostly locals **Reservations** Recommended **When to go** Lunch or dinner **Entree range** £11–£18.50; set lunch: 2 courses £19.50, 3 courses £22.50 **Payment** VISA, MC, AMEX, D, DC, JCB **Service rating** ★★★ **Friendliness rating** ★★★★ **Bar** Yes **Wine selection** Very good **Dress** Informal **Disabled access** Yes

Lunch Every day, noon–3 p.m.

Dinner Monday–Saturday, 6–11 p.m.

Setting & atmosphere This attractive, modern room with big windows overlooking the Thames hosts a trendy clientele.

Summary & comments The Blue Print is one of many restaurants in the Shad Thames area, and one of several in the empire of Sir Terence Conran (see Bibendum, page 281). It is also one of several with a sweeping view of the Thames, and for this reason alone it is worth a visit. But it's also cheaper than much of the local competition. And the food is more or less consistently good, year after year: modern in style and with heavy emphasis on the Mediterranean, especially Italy. The seasons and the market are king here, so the menu changes twice daily to reflect what's available. Fish, pasta, and home-curing are strong points. The wine list is not huge but is carefully chosen and easily accommodates diners on a budget. In warm weather, beg for a table on the terrace.

Boisdale of Belgravia ★★½

BRITISH | MODERATE | QUALITY ★★★ | VALUE ★★★ | ZONE 10

15 Eccleston Street, SW1; (0207) 730-6922; tube: Victoria; www.boisdale.co.uk

Customers Tourists and usually affluent locals **Reservations** Recommended **When to go** Lunch or dinner Entree Range £15–£25 **Payment** VISA, MC, AMEX, D, DC, CB **Service rating** ★★★½ **Friendliness rating** ★★★½ **Bar** Yes **Wine selection** Good **Dress** Smart casual **Disabled access** No

Lunch Monday–Friday, noon–2:30 p.m.

Dinner Monday–Saturday, 7–10:30 p.m.

Setting & atmosphere Dark wood and red paneling, clublike ambience, garden at rear open in warm weather.

House specialties Anything with a Scottish element, such as smoked salmon, smoked grouse, venison, Highland lamb, Aberdeen Angus beef.

Other recommendations Set menus.

Entertainment & amenities Late jazz bar, live music.

Summary & comments Boisdale has established itself as London's most serious champion of the food and drink of Scotland. The emphasis is on getting great ingredients, whether raw or cured, and presenting them to their best advantage. You can go for the simplicity of an Aberdeen Angus steak, grilled and served with béarnaise sauce, or venture into more modern territory if you're feeling adventurous. The kitchen does well with both approaches, and the cozy atmosphere makes a warmly attractive setting. If you're game enough to try haggis, one of Scotland's national dishes, this is probably the place to do it. Whiskey lovers should note that Boisdale's Back Bar, open throughout the day, has London's largest selection of single-malt scotch; the selection of cigars is also notable.

Cactus Blue ★★½

AMERICAN/MODERN EUROPEAN | MODERATE | QUALITY ★★½ | VALUE ★★★½ | ZONE 11

86 Fulham Road, SW3; (0207) 823-7858; tube: South Kensington

Customers Mostly locals **Reservations** Recommended **When to go** Dinner is best **Entree range** £9.95–£18.95 **Payment** VISA, MC, AMEX, D, DC **Service rating** ★★★ **Friendliness rating** ★★★★½ **Bar** Yes **Wine selection** Small but good **Dress** Smart casual **Disabled access** Yes

Open Monday–Friday, 5:30 p.m.–midnight; Saturday, noon–midnight; Sunday, noon–11 p.m.

Setting & atmosphere Nicely decorated with wrought iron and South-western U.S. artifacts, this restaurant has an affluent, mostly young local crowd.

Entertainment & amenities Live funk/jazz Sunday brunch and Tuesday and Wednesday evenings.

Summary & comments Cactus Blue has lovely decor, good food, great drinks, and unusually low prices for this chichi part of town. The menu is modern Southwestern plus a smattering of modern European, with appetizers and small plates followed by a short group of quesadillas and a longer list of main courses. And though the format may not be out of the ordinary, the cooking is adventurous and innovative, all very modern and executed with skill. Sunday brunch is a popular event among local residents, but evenings are better if you want a drink with your meal. They make some of London's best margaritas and have a good range of premium tequila by the shot. And the mostly American wine list is reasonably priced.

Café Spice Namaste   ★★★★

INDIAN | MODERATE | QUALITY ★★★★ | VALUE ★★★★ | ZONE 4

16 Prescot Street, E1; (0207) 488-9242; tube: Aldgate, Aldgate East, Tower Hill
247 Lavender Hill; (0207) 738-1717

Customers Mostly locals, especially businesspeople and aficionados
Reservations Recommended **When to go** Lunch or dinner **Entree range**
£9.95–£15.95; set meals £25–£35 **Payment** VISA, MC, AMEX, D, DC, CB, JCB
Service rating ★★★ **Friendliness rating** ★★★★ **Bar** Yes **Wine selection**
Good **Dress** Casual **Disabled access** Yes

Lunch Monday–Friday, noon–3 p.m.

Dinner Monday–Saturday, 6:30–10:30 p.m.

Setting & atmosphere A nicely redecorated, high-ceilinged room in a nineteenth-century building.

House specialties Unusual curries from various Indian regions; tandoori dishes; breads; vegetarian dishes.

Other recommendations Weekly changing specialty menus.

Summary & comments Since 1995, chef Cyrus Todiwala has made Café Spice Namaste one of London's best places to find really serious Indian food. Indeed, he is one of the prime "modernizers" of this favorite British cuisine, raising standards in every aspect over the nondescript "curry houses" of the bad old days. The dishes on the regular menu cover nearly every area of the Indian subcontinent and are distinguished for their subtle, complex spicing and relative rarity on British menus. There is a weekly specialty menu as well, featuring a particular region, and the wine list is notable for its serious attention to matching every style of food on the menu. There are only two minor negative points to bear in mind.

One is the out-of-the-way location. The other is an occasional problem with rowdy (affluent) clients, given the restaurant's proximity to London's financial center. Apart from that, there's no way to recommend Café Spice Namaste too highly.

Caffè Carluccio's ★★★

ITALIAN | MODERATE | QUALITY ★★★ | VALUE ★★★★ | ZONE 7

St. Christopher's Place, W1; (0207) 935-5927; tube: Bond Street
12 West Smithfield, EC1; (0207) 329-5903; tube: Farringdon

Customers Locals **Reservations** Recommended **When to go** Lunch or dinner **Entree range** £4.95–£10.50 **Payment** VISA, MC, AMEX **Service rating** ★★★½ **Friendliness rating** ★★★★½ **Bar** No **Wine selection** Small and inexpensive **Dress** Casual **Disabled access** No

Meals served Monday–Friday, 8 a.m.–11 p.m.; Saturday, 10 a.m.–11 p.m.; Sunday, 11 a.m.–10 p.m.

Setting & atmosphere Simply decorated deli-style rooms, bustling all hours of the day, friendly and informal.

House specialties Breads, antipasti, pasta, salad, simple meat and fish dishes.

Summary & comments The 11 branches of this incredibly—and justly—successful chain are nearly always full to bursting. The reason is simple and obvious: This is top-quality, mostly very simple food served in pleasant (if somewhat noisy) surroundings and with an absolute minimum of fuss. Cheerful waiting staff may want to place you at one of the long, cafeteria-style tables, and if there's nothing else available you won't mind a bit. Pasta is a particularly strong point, as you would expect, and you can eat lightly on just an antipasto such as bruschetta served with roasted or grilled vegetables (£3.95). Being open all day is another major attraction, especially because the baked goods and the coffee are of exceptional quality. There is also a deli counter where you can get takeout. And if you're eating in, try to leave some room for delicious desserts; a real star of the current catering scene.

Cambio de Tercio ★★★

SPANISH | MODERATE | QUALITY ★★★½ | VALUE ★★★★ | ZONE 11

163 Old Brompton Road, SW5; (0207) 244-8970; tube: Gloucester Road

Customers Locals **Reservations** Recommended **When to go** Lunch or dinner **Entree range** Lunch £13.50–£15.50 **Payment** VISA, MC, AMEX **Service rating** ★★★★ **Friendliness rating** ★★★★ **Bar** No **Wine selection** Excellent, mostly Spanish **Dress** Casual **Disabled access** Restaurant only **Lunch** Every day, 12:30–2:30 p.m.

Dinner Monday–Saturday, 7–11:30 p.m.; Sunday, 7–11 p.m.

Setting & atmosphere A cozy, comfortable basement room decorated with bullfighting motifs.

House specialties Oxtail, hake, suckling pig, tapas.

Summary & comments Cambio is one of London's best Spanish restaurants. The kitchen is equally adept at staple dishes, using the best and most authentic imported ingredients, and at reinterpreting classics with a modern slant. Lovers of tapas, the "little dishes" with which Spanish people love to begin an evening's festivities, should note that the selection and quality here are excellent—and the choice of sherries, the perfect partner for this kind of eating, is similarly broad. There have been a few personnel changes in the kitchen in recent years, but standards seem to have remained high. And though there have been grumbles about service from some quarters, they are neither numerous nor serious enough to keep Cambio off your list of possibilities. Dessert lovers should note that while Spain does not always excel in that department, Cambio de Tercio almost always does.

Cantina Vinopolis ★★½

MODERN EUROPEAN | MODERATE | QUALITY ★★½ | VALUE ★★★★ | ZONE 5

1 Bank End, SE1; (0207) 940-8333; tube: London Bridge; www.vinopolis.co.uk

Customers Mostly locals **When to go** Lunch or dinner **Entree range** £9.50–£15.50 **Payment** VISA, MC, AMEX, DC **Service rating** ★★★ **Friendliness rating** ★★★★ **Bar** Yes **Wine selection** Enormous **Dress** Casual **Disabled access** Yes

Lunch Monday–Saturday, noon–2:45 p.m.; Sunday, noon–3:45 p.m.

Dinner Monday–Saturday, 6–10:15 p.m.

Setting & atmosphere Plain but comfortable decor in a converted industrial space with high, vaulted ceilings.

Summary & comments Vinopolis is London's "wine museum," and this is part of it (though run by an outside company). The museum has had a hard time commercially, but its catering side is a great success. Unsurprisingly, the wine list is huge—and all are sold by the glass. That would be reason enough to come here, since the location is good for the ever-increasing attractions of the Bankside area. The food supplies the rest of the reason for coming along: It can be really excellent with good ingredients treated with care, flair, and respect. French and Italian dominate, but there are a lot of New World features as well, and the prices are exceptionally reasonable. You can't easily spend more than £25–£30 before drinks. And with all those wines by the glass, this can be one of the most reasonable high-quality meals in the area. One thing not to expect, however, is atmosphere: This is a big, bustling place with few frills.

Le Caprice ★★½

MODERN | MODERATE | QUALITY ★★★½ | VALUE ★★★ | ZONE 9

Arlington Street, SW1; (0207) 629-2239; tube: Green Park

Customers Celebrities, affluent locals **Reservations** Recommended **When to go** Dinner or Sunday brunch **Entree range** £9.75–£21.75 **Payment** VISA, MC, AMEX, D, DC **Service rating** ★★★ **Friendliness rating** ★★★ **Bar** Yes **Wine selection** Short but good **Dress** No code **Disabled access** Yes, but not to toilets

Lunch Monday–Saturday, noon–3 p.m.; Sunday, noon–3:15 p.m.

Dinner Monday–Saturday, 5:30 p.m.–midnight; Sunday, 6 p.m.–midnight

Setting & atmosphere Lively but low-key, modern room that is pleasant but of no great distinction.

House specialties Nearly everything on the menu; especially simple dishes such as fish and chips, salmon cakes, and eggs Benedict.

Summary & comments Le Caprice has a well-deserved reputation for serving food that reaches a high standard pretty consistently. But that is not the main reason that Londoners come here, even if it helps. Le Caprice is a supremely fashionable restaurant in a low-key, understated kind of way. It's the kind of place where no one raises an eyebrow if the next table is occupied by a princess, two movie stars, and a Nobel Prize–winning novelist—well, anyway, not in a way that you would notice. This is surely one of the reasons why the rich, fashionable, and celebrated love the place so much, just as they love its sister restaurant, The Ivy (see page 293). For us mortals, the possibility of stargazing might be a bonus. But I have paid three visits with not a star in sight and have loved the place anyway. It is comfortable and well run, and the food can be outstanding. And when it isn't outstanding, it's still very good. Dinners are buzzy, while Sunday brunch is more laid-back.

Chez Gérard ★★

FRENCH (BISTRO) | INEXPENSIVE/MODERATE | QUALITY ★★★ | VALUE ★★★ | ZONE 7

The Market, The Piazza, WC2; (0207) 379-0666; tube: Covent Garden; www.chezgerard.com

Customers Locals and tourists **Reservations** Recommended **When to go** Lunch or dinner (restaurant), anytime (bar) **Entree range** Lunch £8.25–£15.85 **Payment** VISA, MC, AMEX, D, DC, CB **Service rating** ★★½ **Friendliness rating** ★★★½ **Bar** Yes **Wine selection** Good **Dress** Casual **Disabled access** No

Lunch Monday–Saturday, noon–3 p.m.; Sunday, noon–3:30 p.m.

Dinner Monday–Saturday, 5:30–11:30 p.m.; Sunday, 5:30–10:30 p.m.

Setting & atmosphere Conservatory overlooking Covent Garden market with an open-air terrace in warm weather.

House specialties Steak, especially Châteaubriand and onglet (hanger steak), served with pommes frites.

Other recommendations Simple bistro-style dishes such as oysters, fish soup, snails, and Bayonne ham with pickles.

Summary & comments Groupe Chez Gérard, which has seven other branches in addition to this one, has a very simple formula: French-style steak, French-style pommes frites (better known as French fries), and French-style service. They usually do it very well, though there are variations from branch to branch, and prices are kept low enough to keep most people happy even if they run into occasional problems with cooking or service. Fisheaters will always find at least one dish aimed at them, as will vegetarians, but these are the most variable options in terms of quality, and they are not—let's be frank—what Chez Gérard is about. Set menus can offer exceptionally good value: £15.95 for three courses at lunch or in the evening. Don't come here expecting the meal of a lifetime, but if you're a steak lover this will be your home away from home.

Chuen Cheng Ku ★★

CHINESE | INEXPENSIVE/MODERATE | QUALITY ★★★ | VALUE ★★★★ | ZONE 7

17 Wardour Street, W1; (0207) 734-3281; tube: Leicester Square or Piccadilly Circus

Customers Locals and tourists **Reservations** Not necessary **When to go** Lunch is best **Entree range** £5.50–£12.50 **Payment** VISA, MC, AMEX, DC, CB **Service rating** ★★½ **Friendliness rating** ★★½ **Bar** No **Wine selection** Adequate **Dress** Casual **Disabled access** Restaurant only

Open Every day, 11 a.m.–midnight

Setting & atmosphere This huge establishment is very busy at lunch (especially weekends) and mostly quieter in the evening.

House specialties Dim sum, rice and noodles, fish, and shellfish.

Other recommendations Standard Cantonese dishes.

Summary & comments Chuen Cheng Ku has been packing happy eaters into its capacious rooms for a couple of decades now and shows no sign of flagging in popularity. The best thing here, without a doubt, is the dim sum: Served daily until 5:45 p.m., it comes around on trolleys and offers a huge selection with quite consistent quality. Weekends are the busiest time. You can expect a line of 1–20 parties, but the crowd is well managed and waits rarely exceed 20 minutes. The large numbers of Chinese families show that the place is appreciated by those who know quality when they see it. Dinner is usually less busy and of solid rather than exciting quality—but certainly good enough to make CCK a top choice when you're in the area, as you're sure to be, at some point. If there are six or more of you eating, the nine-dish set menus offer excellent value and a simplified choice.

Clarke's ★★★★

MODERN EUROPEAN | MODERATE/EXPENSIVE | QUALITY ★★★★ | VALUE ★★★ |
ZONE 13

124 Kensington Church Street, W8; (0207) 221-9225; tube: Notting Hill Gate

Customers Mostly locals **Reservations** Essential **When to go** Lunch or dinner **Entree range** Lunch £14; dinner set menu £44 for 4 courses **Payment** VISA, MC, AMEX, D, DC **Service rating** ★★★★½ **Friendliness rating** ★★★★½ **Bar** No **Wine selection** Outstanding **Dress** Casual **Disabled access** Restaurant yes, toilets no

Lunch Monday–Friday, 12:30–2 p.m.

Dinner Monday–Friday, 7–10 p.m.

Setting & atmosphere Upstairs room is tiny and intimate; downstairs is big and bustling, with a view of the kitchen.

House specialties Menu changes daily.

Summary & comments No one in Britain understands Californian cooking better than Sally Clarke, who worked there years ago (at Chez Panisse and elsewhere) before moving back to London and opening her own place. She bases her cooking on the seasons and on what's available in the market on a given day. Thus, menus change every day, with a short carte at lunchtime and fixed menus (following the example of Chez Panisse) at dinner. The cooking is strong in baking (including some of the best bread in London), roasting, and char-grilling. Combinations are often simple, but they never fail to impress, partly because the execution is so skilled and especially because the ingredients are as good as money can buy. The lack of choice at dinner may be somewhat irritating. Phone in advance to find out what's on the menu; however, given enough warning they will happily provide alternatives if possible. The wine list is superb and not especially high priced. Clarke's is not cheap, but at its price level it is one of the best restaurants in London.

Corney & Barrow ★★

MODERN EUROPEAN | MODERATE | QUALITY ★★★ | VALUE ★★★ | ZONES 3 & 4

19 Broadgate Circle, EC2; (0207) 628-1251; tube, Liverpool Street, 3 Fleet Place, EC4; (0207) 329-3141; tube: Mansion House; www.corneybarrow.co.uk

Customers Mostly locals, especially businesspeople **Reservations** Not necessary **When to go** Lunch or dinner **Entree range** £7–£10 (lunch), £5–£9 (evening) **Payment** VISA, MC, AMEX, DC, CB **Service rating** ★★½

Friendliness rating ★★★ **Bar** Yes **Wine selection** Excellent **Dress** Casual
Disabled access No

Open Monday–Friday, 7.30 a.m.–11 p.m.

Setting & atmosphere Three separate bar areas, some open-air seating under heated canopies, comfortable and lively contemporary feel.

Summary & comments Corney & Barrow has established itself as a high-class group of wine bars, mostly now concentrated in the EC postal codes and especially popular with a young, local office-based crowd. The group is backed up by a retail and wholesale wine merchant of great distinction, so the wine list is predictably strong: plenty of choices under £20, a rarity for London, and interesting bottles from all over. But the food is taken seriously, too, and being open all day it allows you to eat and drink—whether a snack or a full meal—whenever you want. Note: each bar has its own menu, and there are 12 other branches in addition to the 2 listed above, mostly in zone 3. Worth bearing in mind when you're doing the sights in the City.

Deca ★★★★½

FRENCH | MODERATE/EXPENSIVE | QUALITY ★★★★½ | VALUE ★★★★ | ZONE 7

23 Conduit Street, W1; (0207) 493-7070; tube: Oxford Circus

Customers Office workers, tourists, locals **When to go** Lunch or dinner
Entree range £12.50–£18.50 **Payment** VISA, MC, AMEX, D, DC **Bar** No **Wine selection** Excellent and fairly priced **Dress** Smart casual **Disabled access** Yes, but not to rest rooms

Lunch Monday–Saturday, noon–3 p.m.

Dinner Monday–Saturday, 5:30–11:30 p.m.

Setting & atmosphere Elegant contemporary decor, quiet but lively.

House specialties Warm escalope of foie gras with orange and brioche, truffle risotto, roast red peppers with feta, breast of duck with honey and peppercorns, corn-fed breast of chicken with wild mushrooms and ravioli of foie gras, sea bass with citrus fruits and fennel, pineapple with kirsch and coconut ice cream, apple tart with vanilla ice cream, lemon tart with raspberry coulis.

Other recommendations Set lunch.

Summary & comments Deca is the latest venture from Nico Ladenis, one of the great figures in the London restaurant world, and some would say it's his best restaurant yet. The dishes are often those that he and his numerous teams have been cooking for years, and that long experience shows through in well-nigh flawless execution. What's more, the prices here are cheaper than they've been in several of Ladenis's other places.

This is not cheap, exactly, except at lunchtime, but certainly not expensive by London standards at this exalted level of cooking. Ladenis loves clarity, simplicity, and bold flavors on the plate. He doesn't make elaborate combinations of long lists of ingredients, preferring to use just a few components but make each one taste as good as it can possibly taste. His meals are always memorable. If your budget is limited, the set-price lunch at £12.50 is possibly the greatest bargain in London: three courses with two choices for each course, and the cooking is every bit as good as on the more expensive carte. One of London's best.

fish! ★★

FISH AND SHELLFISH | INEXP/MODERATE | QUALITY ★★½ | VALUE ★★★½ | ZONE 7

3B Belvedere Road, SE1; (0207) 234-3333 Cathedral Street, London Bridge, SE1; (0207) 234-3333; tube: Westminster; www.fishdiner.co.uk

Customers Locals and tourists, many families **Reservations** Call (0207) 234-3333 for all branches **When to go** Lunch or dinner **Entree range** £8.50–£16.95 **Payment** VISA, MC, AMEX, D, DC, JCB **Service rating** ★★★ **Friendliness rating** ★★★½ **Bar** In some branches, but designed for customers waiting for tables **Wine selection** Small, adequate, inexpensive **Dress** Smart casual **Disabled access** Yes

Open Monday–Saturday, 11:30 a.m–11 p.m.; Sunday, noon–10:30 p.m.

Setting & atmosphere Informal, modern dining rooms with a view of the kitchen.

House specialties Fresh fish, plainly cooked.

Entertainment & amenities Watching the chefs at work.

Summary & comments There were six fish! restaurants in London and four more in other towns and cities a while ago; the empire has shrunk considerably, so now there are just two. Quality and consistency have suffered somewhat as the group's troubles bit, but this is still a useful place to know about. The emphasis is on buying top-quality fish, offering it steamed or grilled, and allowing customers to choose the sauce (e.g., salsa, hollandaise, herb and garlic butter, and so on). There are a few appetizers, too, along the lines of rock oysters, prawn (shrimp) cocktail, and smoked salmon; and there are a few concessions to meat lovers among the main courses, as well as a few slightly more complicated fishy main courses. But the core concept is by far the best way to be sure of success. The restaurants are specifically designed with children in mind, and they make it possible to eat quickly if that's what you're after—the spartan decor won't make you want to linger endlessly, though of course no one will kick you out. These are just good, reliable restaurants that won't break the bank. Though it should be noted that bills can rise quickly if you eat a full meal with extra options such as side orders.

Le Gavroche ★★★★½

FRENCH (HAUTE CUISINE) | EXPENSIVE | QUALITY ★★★★½ | VALUE ★★★ | ZONE 8

43 Upper Brook Street, W1; (0207) 408-0881; tube: Marble Arch

Customers Locals and tourists **Reservations** Essential **When to go** Lunch or dinner **Entree range** £26.80–£38.80 **Payment** VISA, MC, AMEX, DC, CB **Service rating** ★★★★★ **Friendliness rating** ★★★★½ **Bar** Yes, for diners only **Wine selection** Excellent **Dress** Formal **Disabled access** No

Lunch Monday–Friday, noon–2 p.m.

Dinner Monday–Friday, 7–11 p.m.

Setting & atmosphere This downstairs room offers intimate comfort at both lunch and dinner; it's indisputably grand, but with the kind of ultraprofessional service that pampers without being intimidating.

House specialties Soufflé Suissesse; Foie gras chaud et pastilla de canard à la canelle; Rable de lapin et galette au Parmesan; Le Palet de chocolat amer et praline croustillant.

Other recommendations Set lunch.

Summary & comments Le Gavroche is one of London's most famous and most expensive restaurants. It is classic in every sense, even though the menu has been "modernized" in recent years. The service is among the best in London, priding itself on knowing what customers want before they themselves know they want it, and the care taken with every detail is astonishing. All this comes at a truly frightening price outside the set lunch, which at £40 per person includes three courses, half a bottle of wine, water and coffee, and service. Sure, that's pretty expensive, too. But with main courses alone costing £30 on average, lunch is the only way most people can afford Le Gavroche. It's worth that one splash-out, because this is a great restaurant of the old-fashioned, perfectionist kind. Bread, ice creams and sorbets, premeal tidbits—they're all outstanding. And the all-French cheese board is probably the best in London. Come here if you want to treat yourself.

Heartstone ★★★½

MODERN EUROPEAN | INEXPENSIVE/MODERATE | QUALITY ★★★½ |
VALUE ★★★★★ | ZONE 15

106 Parkway, NW1; (0207) 485-7744; tube: Camden Town

Customers Mostly locals **Reservations** Advisable for dinner **When to go** Anytime **Entree range** £8.50–£15 **Payment** VISA, MC **Service rating**

★★★★½ **Friendliness rating** ★★★★★ **Bar** No **Wine selection** BYO **Dress** Casual **Disabled access** Yes

Open Tuesday–Saturday, 9 a.m.–9 p.m.; Sunday, 10 a.m.–4 p.m.

Setting & atmosphere Simple but very attractive lilac-painted room with a skylight.

Entertainment & amenities Massage/aromatherapy/nutritional consulting in the basement.

Summary & comments No place in London remotely resembles Heartstone. Its operation is based on the desire to promote healthy living and eating, but it serves a far more diverse menu—and far better food—than you'll find in most places that share the same aim. They don't serve alcohol, though they're happy to see you bring your own, and there's a no-smoking policy— a rarity in London. Instead, on the drinks front, there's unlimited filtered water and juice combos fresh from the juicer. The whole place is serene; it makes you feel peaceful just to be there. But none of this would count for anything without the excellent food, good ingredients (often organic) expertly cooked (often on the grill) in the open-plan kitchen. Some of the offerings would be classified as whole foods, but you can also get an awesome steak or rack of lamb. In short, Heartstone does not sermonize. It simply aims to present the best of everything in a way that satisfies both principles and the need for profit. And it succeeds. Note: There is a good place to buy wine a few doors down, and an even better one (Oddbins, Camden High Street) just five minutes away; corkage is £2.

The Ivy   ★★★★

MODERN EUROPEAN | MODERATE | QUALITY ★★★★ | VALUE ★★★ | ZONE 7

1 West Street, WC2; (0207) 836-4751; tube: Leicester Square

Customers Mostly locals **Reservations** Essential **When to go** Lunch or dinner **Entree range** £8.75–£21.50 **Payment** VISA, MC, AMEX, D, DC, JCB **Service rating** ★★★★ **Friendliness rating** ★★★ **Bar** For diners only **Wine selection** Good **Dress** No dress code **Disabled access** Restaurant only

Lunch Monday–Saturday, noon–3 p.m.; Sunday, noon–3:30 p.m.

Dinner Every day, 5:30 p.m.–midnight

Setting & atmosphere Exceptionally comfortable wood-paneled room with stained-glass windows, discreet and refined.

House specialties Simple classics such as steak tartare, calf's liver, smoked salmon with scrambled eggs, shepherd's pie, eggs Benedict, grilled or fried fish.

Other recommendations Salads, desserts, Asian dishes; set lunch (Saturday and Sunday), £17.50 for 3 courses.

Summary & comments Let's get the bad news out of the way first. Getting a table at The Ivy is famously difficult. If you're planning a trip and are dying to eat here, it's advisable to reserve at least a month in advance. Why should this be? Here's the good news: The Ivy is a supremely wonderful place. The food is mostly simple but always executed with skill. Service is professional and efficient, though there are sometimes complaints about off-handedness. But The Ivy isn't just a place to eat and drink. It is also, for most people, a spot to do a bit of stargazing. The rich and famous love it, and chances are reasonable that you'll spot a familiar face while enjoying your eggs Benedict or fish and chips. But don't stare, please. That wouldn't be in keeping with Ivy etiquette.

Joe Allen   ★★½

AMERICAN | INEXPENSIVE/MODERATE | QUALITY ★★½ | VALUE ★★½ | ZONE 7

13 Exeter Street, WC2; (0207) 836-0651; tube: Covent Garden

Customers Varied, locals and tourists **Reservations** Recommended **When to go** Anytime **Entree range** Lunch £7.50–£14.50 **Payment** VISA, MC, AMEX **Service rating** ★★★½ **Friendliness rating** ★★★★ **Bar** Yes **Wine selection** Small but good **Dress** Casual **Disabled access** No

Open Monday–Friday, noon–1 a.m.; Saturday, 11:30 a.m.–1 a.m.; Sunday, 11:30 a.m.–midnight

Setting & atmosphere Think of your favorite local bar/restaurant—the kind of place you go for a cheerful, noisy night out with friends—and you have it.

House specialties Black-bean soup; chopped chicken liver; Caesar salad; eggs Benedict or eggs Joe Allen; grilled sirloin steak with steak fries; brownies; cheesecake.

Other recommendations Anything cooked simply (which means just about everything on the menu), especially hamburgers, sandwiches, and salads.

Entertainment & amenities Piano player Monday–Saturday, 9 p.m.–1 a.m.; jazz Sunday, 8 p.m.–1 a.m.

Summary & comments Like its two other branches in Paris and New York, the London Joe Allen is a place to go for unpretentious, American-style food in a lively atmosphere. It's set in the heart of theaterland, and its theatrical connections are firmly cemented in the cheap precurtain menus (£12 for two courses, £14 for three courses) and the late opening hour. Actors come in from the nearby theaters after their performance, and if you're lucky you may find yourself eating Caesar salad next to someone you watched on stage an hour earlier. It's the spirited buzz that brings Londoners in rather than any fancy fireworks in the food; and there are sometimes complaints about brusque and unhelpful service. But the food itself is solid, rarely disappointing those who like simple classics done well, and the drinks list, though short, is enticing at every level.

Livebait ★★★

SEAFOOD | INEXPENSIVE/MODERATE | QUALITY ★★★ | VALUE ★★★ | ZONES 5 & 7

43 The Cut, SE1; (0207) 928-7211; tube: Waterloo, 21 Wellington Street, WC2; (0207) 836-7161; tube: Covent Garden; www.livebaitrestaurants.co.uk

Customers Locals and tourists **Reservations** Recommended **When to go** Lunch or dinner **Entree range** £8.95–£28.50 **Payment** VISA, MC, AMEX, D, DC, CB **Service rating** ★★½ **Friendliness rating** ★★★½ **Bar** Yes **Wine selection** Good **Dress** Casual **Disabled access** No

Lunch Monday–Saturday, noon–3 p.m.

Dinner Monday–Saturday, 5:30–11:30 p.m.

Setting & atmosphere Black and white tiles, minimal decor, brash and fun and noisy.

House specialties Ever-changing selection of fish dishes and shellfish platters.

Summary & comments The original Livebait, in SE1, took London by storm when it opened in 1997. It has since been taken over by Groupe Chez Gérard, but standards have remained consistently high. The Covent Garden branch is centrally located and duplicates the formula— a simple setting with fairly elaborate cooking—very successfully. The secret lies in wonderfully fresh fish, some from exotic sources and some local to the United Kingdom, which you will find cooked in exceptionally innovative ways and in classic presentations such as sumptuous shellfish platters of oysters, clams, crevettes, cockles, winkles, whelks, prawns, and crab. Service can slow down as the kitchen gets busy (especially in the evening), but it never fails in the friendliness department. Prices à la carte are not exactly cheap, but it's worth noting the set menu (from £15.50) available at lunch and both pre- and post-theater.

Mango Room ★★½

CARIBBEAN | INEXPENSIVE | QUALITY ★★★½ | VALUE ★★★★ | ZONE 15

10 Kentish Town Road, NW1; (0207) 482-5065; tube: Camden Town

Customers Fairly young locals **Reservations** Recommended **When to go** Dinner is livelier **Entree range** £8.50–£11 **Payment** VISA, MC, CB **Service rating** ★★★ **Friendliness rating** ★★★★★ **Bar** Yes **Wine selection** Minimal **Dress** As you wish **Disabled access** Yes

Lunch Tuesday–Saturday, noon–3 p.m.; Sunday, meals served 11 a.m.–midnight

Dinner Every day, 6 p.m.–midnight

Setting & atmosphere Colorful decor with a handmade look; mostly young, trendy crowd.

House specialties Ebony chicken wings, marinated in chile, pepper, garlic, and soya; curry goat with hot pepper, scallions, garlic, pimiento, and spices; mango and banana brûlée.

Other recommendations Steamed green-lip mussels with ginger, scallions, garlic, and coconut; ackee and avocado with spinach, plantains, tomatoes, and olives; grilled barracuda with courgettes and coconut sauce.

Entertainment & amenities Great ska, reggae, and "jazz Jamaica" background music.

Summary & comments Camden Town is one of London's hip, casual areas. With the popular Camden Lock market nearby and Regent's Park not much farther away, it gets incredibly crowded, especially on weekends. A host of establishments cater to the crowds, but few match Mango Room for quality. Being here is just a pleasure: The music is wonderful, the staff is really friendly, and the food is good, filling, and cheap. Based in Caribbean cooking, Mango Room offers both traditional classics and modern variations in the spirit of gastronomic globalism. There's a bar next door with comfortable chairs and sofas. If you're in the area, Mango Room is a great place to eat or drink after sight-seeing and shopping. Consider beer or a fruit punch rather than wine from the short list and get set to enjoy yourself in laid-back surroundings.

Masala Zone ★★

INDIAN | INEXPENSIVE/MODERATE | QUALITY ★★★½ | VALUE ★★★★ | ZONE 7

9 Marshall Street, W1; (0207) 287-9966; tube: Oxford Circus

Customers Locals, mostly office workers at lunch **Reservations** Not accepted **When to go** Anytime **Entree range** £5–£9.50, thalis £7.75–£11 **Payment** VISA, MC **Service rating** ★★★ **Friendliness rating** ★★★★ **Bar** No **Wine selection** Cheap and good **Dress** Casual **Disabled access** Yes

Lunch Monday–Friday, noon–2:45 p.m.; Saturday, 12:30–3 p.m.; reduced menu, 3–5 p.m.

Dinner Monday–Friday, 5:30–11 p.m.; Saturday, 5–11 p.m., Sunday, 6–10:30 p.m.

Setting & atmosphere Open-plan cafeteria-style, modern and light decor.

House specialties Thalis, snacks.

Summary & comments Masala Zone is part of the group that owns Veeraswamy (see page 312), and it opened in 2001 with a very novel approach: high-quality, adventurous, and sometimes unorthodox Indian-style food at very low prices. It has gone from strength to strength, never wavering in its commitment to quality, freshness, and precise, friendly service. One of the best things about it is the flexibility of the food: You can have a full meal or a "light bite" if your appetite is small. There's a grilled club sandwich—chicken, bacon, egg, cheese, and mayo—if that's all you want, and filling noodle bowls for a heartier meal. Because of the no-reservations policy you may have trouble getting a table—and sometimes there's a long line both at lunch and dinner. But sometimes there is no wait at all. If you like Indian food, and don't want to spend a fortune for it, Masala Zone is well worth seeking out. And its central location, close to theaterland, makes it all the more attractive.

Mash   ★★

MODERN EUROPEAN | INEXP/MODERATE | QUALITY ★★★½ | VALUE ★★★ | ZONE 7

19–21 Great Portland Street, W1; (0207) 637-5555
26B Albemarle Street, W1; (0207) 495-5999; tube: Oxford Circus

Customers Mostly young locals **When to go** Lunch or dinner, weekend brunch, late night **Entree range** £7–£14.50 **Payment** VISA, MC, AMEX, D, DC **Service rating** ★★½ **Friendliness rating** ★★★½ **Bar** Yes **Wine selection** Very good **Dress** Smart casual but relaxed **Disabled access** Ground floor only

Lunch Monday–Friday, 7:30 a.m.–2 a.m.; Saturday, noon–2 a.m.

Food served Monday–Friday, 7:30 a.m.–11 p.m.; Monday–Saturday, noon–11 p.m.

Bar Monday–Saturday, 11 a.m.–1 a.m.

Setting & atmosphere Futuristic, modern decor with high ceilings and a microbrewery in the ground-floor bar; fairly noisy when crowded.

House specialties Fresh fruit drinks, microbrewed beer.

Entertainment & amenities DJ Thursday through Saturday nights.

Summary & comments Mash is lively, boisterous, ultracool, and very popular with a mostly young clientele, who crowd into the ground-floor bar and upstairs restaurant by day and night. Some come for the excellent beers brewed on premises, and you can join a lunchtime tour on Saturday (12:30 p.m.) for a tour, tasting, and two-course lunch. Or you can just come in to eat and drink without the educational angle. Grilling over wood and pizzas baked in a wood oven are strong points of the hip, usually well-judged cooking, from a short menu that does pretty well by vegetarians. The bar is a good place for a quick lunch, and there's also a deli counter where you can get meals to take out. Noise-phobics should avoid the restaurant in the evening, but everyone else will enjoy the good buzz and decent food.

Matsuri ★★★½

JAPANESE | MODERATE/EXPENSIVE | QUALITY ★★★½ | VALUE ★★ | ZONE 9

15 Bury Street, SW1; (0207) 839-1101; tube: Green Park;
www.matsuri-restaurant.com

Customers Locals and tourists **Reservations** Recommended **When to go**
Lunch or dinner **Entree range Lunch** £13–£30 **Payment** VISA, MC, AMEX,
DC, CB **Service rating** ★★★½ **Friendliness rating** ★★★½ **Bar** Yes **Wine
selection** Adequate; beer and sake better **Dress** Casual **Disabled access** Yes,
for diners only

Lunch Monday–Saturday, noon–2:30 p.m.

Dinner Monday–Saturday, 6–10:30 p.m.

Setting & atmosphere Big, spacious main dining room and smaller sushi
bar; elegant but relaxed.

House specialties Sushi and teppanyaki.

Summary & comments London has its full share of big Japanese restaurants catering to businesspeople with expense accounts as big as the
Grand Canyon. You'll find a few of them in the "More Recommendations" section, along with some smaller places at significantly lower
prices. This is a big place, but the prices are relatively reasonable (starting
at £6.50 for a set lunch, though climbing steeply) and the quality is high.
Sushi and sashimi are expertly prepared and can be ordered either à la
carte at the bar or in various permutations of a set meal. Most of the
space is given over to teppanyaki tables, where your choice of fish, meat,
and vegetables is prepared and cooked for you on a sizzling hot plate;
very theatrical, but also good food. There's even a nod toward fusion
cooking, in the form of tuna tartare, foie gras "Japanese," and little dishes
such as deep-fried chicken. The list of specialty brand sakes is intriguing,
though not cheap. But, then, top-quality Japanese never comes cheap.

Moro ★★★★

SPANISH/MIDDLE EASTERN | MODERATE | QUALITY ★★★★ | VALUE ★★★★ | ZONE 3

34–36 Exmouth Market, EC1; (0207) 833-8336; tube: Farringdon or Angel

Customers Locals, both young and old **Reservations** Recommended
When to go Anytime **Entree range** £11–£15.50 **Payment** VISA, MC, AMEX, D
Service rating ★★★ **Friendliness rating** ★★★½ **Bar** Yes, with tapas menu
Wine selection Very good **Dress** Casual **Disabled access** Yes

Lunch Monday–Friday, 12:30–2:30 p.m.

Dinner Monday–Saturday, 7–10:30 p.m.

Drinks and tapas Monday–Friday, 12:30–10:30 p.m.; Saturday,
6:30–10:30 p.m.

Setting & atmosphere Casual and lively; high-ceilinged room with simple decor.

House specialties Everything cooked in the wood-fired oven, such as cod with saffron rice, caramelized onions, and tahini; charcoal-grilled dishes like lamb kebab with egg and mint salad and bulgur; homemade breads and yogurt; tarts and other desserts.

Other recommendations Vegetarian dishes, well-chosen Spanish cheeses, braised dishes.

Summary & comments Since opening in 1998, Moro has become one of the hottest, coolest, and most popular restaurants in London. The area is off the beaten track as far as sight-seeing is concerned, apart from Sadler's Wells Theatre, but the area is also increasingly trendy in a nicely bohemian way. Moro has played a part in this. It is popular because the food is really outstanding: If anyone has ever had a bad time there, we haven't heard about it. The prices are very reasonable for cooking of this quality. Based on the cuisine and culture of Moorish Spain, when the country was under Islamic rule, the food has big, bold flavors and generous spicing. You can never tell what you'll find at Moro, because the menu changes weekly. But it doesn't matter: Everything's delicious. This is not a place for a quiet evening, but definitely a place for a memorable meal in a bustling restaurant that shows why people enthuse about London's gastronomic renaissance.

Mr. Kong ★★★½

CHINESE | INEXPENSIVE/MODERATE | QUALITY ★★★½ | VALUE ★★★★ | ZONE 7

21 Lisle Street, WC2; (0207) 437-7341; tube: Leicester Square

Customers Mostly locals **Reservations** Recommended **When to go** Lunch or dinner **Entree range Lunch** £6–£26 **Payment** VISA, MC, AMEX, D, DC, CB **Service rating** ★★★ **Friendliness rating** ★★½ **Bar** No **Wine selection** Adequate **Dress** Casual **Disabled access** Restaurant

Open Every day, noon–2:45 a.m.

Setting & atmosphere Unexceptional if well-appointed Chinese decor; usually very busy.

House specialties Chef's specials, especially shellfish and hot-pot dishes.

Other recommendations Standard Cantonese dishes.

Summary & comments In an area crowded with Chinese restaurants, Mr. Kong stands out by virtue of its interesting and innovative cooking. The menu is long, but you don't need to look any further than the Chef's Special page—over 50 dishes, some of them found nowhere else. They seldom climb beyond the £12 mark, and there's enough to keep you happy and interested for a good half-dozen mealtimes. Adventurous eaters can sample baked frogs' legs, fish maw, or pig's intestines; seafood fans should have soft-shell crabs (an occasional special), clams in various guises, or steamed crab with rice wine. Even if you stick with more conventional dishes, you will be well fed. Though Mr. Kong is somewhat more expensive than most restaurants in the area, it's worth the money.

Nobu ★★★★

"NEW-STYLE" JAPANESE | EXPENSIVE | QUALITY ★★★★ | VALUE ★★ | ZONE 8

19 Old Park Lane, W1; (0207) 447-4747; tube: Hyde Park Corner

Customers Businesspeople, tourists, the occasional celebrity **Reservations** Essential **When to go** Lunch or dinner **Entree range** £5–£27.50 **Payment** VISA, MC, AMEX, DC, CB **Service rating** ★★★½ **Friendliness rating** ★★★ **Bar** Yes **Wine selection** Very good **Dress** Fashionable **Disabled access** Yes

Lunch Monday–Friday, noon–2:15 p.m.

Dinner Monday–Friday, 6–10:15 p.m.; Saturday, 6–11 p.m.; Sunday, 6–9:30 p.m.

Setting & atmosphere Ultraminimalist decor for an ultrachic clientele.

House specialties Special appetizers such as yellowtail sashimi with jalapeño and tomato rock shrimp seviche; all traditional sushi and sashimi.

Other recommendations Special dishes such as black cod with miso and Inaniwa pasta salad with lobster.

Summary & comments Nobu is a one-of-a-kind restaurant, with two branches in New York City and Beverly Hills. If you know about those outlets for Matsuhisu Nobuyuki's extraordinary reworking of Japanese cuisine, then you know what to expect here. There are three things that come to mind, and the most important is startling innovation that almost invariably sends diners into raptures. This is like no other Japanese food, taking in influences from every corner of the globe, especially South America. But it's innovation that works, which is what counts. The second thing is chic: Nobu attracts entertainment people, and you may get to see one or two when you eat here. The third thing is the daunting expense. If you order a full meal, it's hard to come away without spending £50 or more on food alone, and that won't even fill you up. This means Nobu doesn't rate well for value. And there have been complaints about service. But it is an amazing place, and everyone should visit once: Consider going for a sushi lunch, which shouldn't set you back more than £20 a head as long as you avoid alcohol. And one encouraging point: Prices have not risen in three years!

North Sea Fish Restaurant   ★½

FISH AND CHIPS | INEXPENSIVE | QUALITY ★★½ | VALUE ★★★★★ | ZONE 2

7–8 Leigh Street, WC1; (0207) 387-5892; tube: Holborn or King's Cross

Customers Mostly locals **Reservations** Not necessary **When to go** Lunch or dinner **Entree range** £7.90–£16.95 **Payment** VISA, MC, AMEX, DC **Service rating** ★★★ **Friendliness rating** ★★★★ **Bar** Yes **Wine selection** Adequate **Dress** Casual **Disabled access** Limited

Lunch Monday–Saturday, noon–2:30 p.m.

Dinner Monday–Saturday, 6–10:30 p.m.

Setting & atmosphere Charmingly old-fashioned room with wooden beams and a lively buzz.

House specialties Fish and chips, avocado prawn, seafood platter, scampi, salmon, Dover sole.

Other recommendations Traditional desserts.

Summary & comments Everyone visiting London should eat fish and chips at least once. And if you eat it here, you'll see why it's one of the national dishes. To succeed, a cook needs top-quality fish and potatoes, good batter and oil, and an intimate knowledge of the art of deep-frying. At North Sea, they have all the requirements. You can have your choice of fish either fried in batter or matzo meal, or plainly grilled. Don't be put off by the fear of frying (even if it's supposedly "bad for you"). Batter-fried cod at the North Sea is absolutely delicious, not leaden or greasy like some fried foods. If you want to be authentic, have a side order of pickled onion to go with it. Service is decorous and efficient, the wine list is short but good, and the homemade desserts are wonderful. If you have room for them, that is.

Orrery   ★★★★½

MODERN EUROPEAN | EXPENSIVE | QUALITY ★★★★½ | VALUE ★★★ | ZONE 14

55 Marylebone High Street, W1; (0207) 616-8000; tube: Baker Street;
www.conran.com/eat

Customers Affluent locals from all over London **When to go** Lunch or dinner **Entree range** £14.50–£24 **Payment** VISA, MC, AMEX, D, DC, JCB **Service rating** ★★★★★ **Friendliness rating** ★★★★★ **Bar** Yes **Wine selection** Outstanding but expensive **Dress** Smart **Disabled access** Yes

Lunch Monday–Saturday, noon–3 p.m.; Sunday, noon–2:30 p.m.

Dinner Monday–Saturday, 7–11 p.m.; Sunday, 7–10:30 p.m.

Setting & atmosphere Long, narrow second-floor room with skylight; small adjacent bar; open-air terrace in good weather.

House specialties Pot-roast foie gras and baby vegetables; terrine of foie gras, Sauternes gelée, pain Poilane; seared scallops, pork belly, and cauliflower; Scottish Highland spring lamb–braised shank with baby vegetables, roast saddle, aubergine, red pepper jus; tranche of wild salmon confit tomato, wild asparagus and langoustines; tagine of pigeon, saffron couscous, pastilla and harissa jus; apple tatin and crème fraîche; brochette of pineapple and mango with lemon thyme.

Other recommendations Light dinner menu on the terrace, weather permitting (summer only); set lunch and Sunday set dinner menus; menu gourmand (£50).

Summary & comments Orrery is part of the large Conran group and is universally regarded as the best of its restaurants for those seeking high-quality cooking in more intimate surroundings. The restaurant is small by Conran standards; the emphasis here is on the food rather than the buzz. And the kitchen consistently meets the high standards it sets itself: The cooking here is among the best in London, and sometimes reaches dazzling heights in inventiveness, seasoning, and presentation. It has a Michelin star, but probably deserves two. On the other hand, the prices are as dazzling as the food. It is alarmingly easy to spend £75 a head for a full meal with wine, and if you take on the five-star reaches of the fine but costly wine list, you can go a lot higher than that. But they also have many wines by the glass, and the set lunch (£23.50 for three courses) and set Sunday dinner (£30) are a bargain by anyone's standards. With service that combines military precision with a genuinely warm welcome, this is one of London's top stars.

Orsini's Café

ITALIAN CAFÉ | MODERATE | QUALITY ★★★★ | VALUE ★★★ | ZONE 11

8A Thurloe Place, SW7; (0207) 581-5553; tube South Kensington

Customers Locals and museum-goers **Reservations** No **When to Go** Breakfast, lunch or afternoon coffee **Entree range** Lunch £4–£9 **Payment** MC, AMEX, D, DC, JCB **Service rating** ★★ **Friendliness rating** ★★★★★ **Bar** Basic mixed drinks, Italian liquors, beer, and wine **Wine selection** Italian table red or white, specials weekly **Dress** No dress code **Disabled access** For downstairs nonsmoking area or outdoor tables only

Breakfast/Lunch Tuesday–Sunday, 9 a.m.–7 p.m. (closed Monday)

Dinner Early dinner only

Setting & atmosphere Rotating art exhibits decorate the walls; wooden tables and chairs on two floors. Casual, very Italian.

House specialties Daily pasta specials using fresh, organic products, such as mozzarella and aubergine fettuccini; homemade soups, panini, breaded chicken cutlets with salad; great cappuccino, fresh-squeezed orange juice.

Other recommendations Homemade desserts, Italian pastries, cookies.

Summary & comments Located across the street from the Victoria and Albert Museum on a leafy stretch of road, Orsini's Café is a family-run eatery that features good, homemade food and the authenticity of a café in Naples. It's a favorite with the locals, museum goers, and visitors staying at the nearby Rembrandt Hotel. The friendly service, provided by good-looking young Europeans, could be a bit less laid-back, but the sense of Mediterranean relaxation is part of the charm. In the best tradition of Italy, children are more than welcome, and the owners' toddler is often seen on-site being adorable. The daily specials are uniformly good: The chef relies on the best of the early morning markets, such as porcino mushrooms or baby artichokes, to create unique pasta dishes. The chicken cutlets are fabulous, the ravioli is deliciously homemade, and any of the creative pasta sauces are excellent. Breakfast is strictly continental, with baguette, toast, or ciabatta. The prices reflect the high rents of the area, but it's still a good value, and no one raises an eyebrow if you linger over an espresso for hours. There's a smoking section upstairs, which leaves the nonsmokers run of a fume-free ground floor.

Pied à Terre ★★★★½

MODERN BRITISH/FRENCH | EXPENSIVE | QUALITY ★★★★½ | VALUE ★★★ | ZONE 14

34 Charlotte Street, W1; (0207) 636-1178; tube: Goodge Street; www.pied.a.terre.co.uk

Customers Locals, tourists, business community **When to go** Lunch or ndinner **Entree range** Lunch, £19.50 for 2 courses; dinner, £39 for 2 courses **Payment** VISA, MC, AMEX, D, DC, JCB **Service rating** ★★★★★ **Friendliness rating** ★★★½ **Bar** No **Wine selection** Exceptional **Dress** Smart casual

Lunch Monday–Friday, 12:15–2:30 p.m.

Dinner Monday–Saturday, 7–11 p.m.

Setting & atmosphere Small, quiet room with simple decor.

House specialties Spaetzli with soft poached egg, trompette de la mort, hazelnut emulsion with black truffle; seared and poached foie gras in a sauternes consommé; fillet of sea bass with parsnip purée, tagliatelle of English asparagus and parsnip foam; roasted best end (rack) of Pyrenees lamb with cumin-scented aubergine purée and red pepper sauce; roasted baby banana with praline mousse and butterscotch ice cream; bittersweet chocolate tart with stout ice cream; tasting menu at £59.50 (eight courses) with optional wines by the glass to match each course (£45).

Summary & comments Pied à Terre is one of the most distinguished restaurants in London, and a survivor of numerous chef changes over recent years. While the chefs have changed, the food has remained remarkably consistent both in quality and style: The aim is for big, bold flavors with complex assemblies.. But the effect is always harmonious and carefully thought out. Menus change, so it's impossible to say what will be offered when you come. Here are a few more dishes to give the idea: lime-marinated scallop seviche with avocado and crème fraîche and sesame filo; red mullet with a terrine of confit tomatoes, sardine mousse and gazpacho foam; roasted halibut with smoked bacon risotto, pea and ham sauce. This is modern cooking at its most sophisticated and expert; matching wine with food is taken very seriously. The room has been redecorated in the last few years and is now a much warmer, cozier place than when it was just white walls and rather lacking in personality. One of London's best for people who really love food.

Pizza Express ★

PIZZA | INEXPENSIVE | QUALITY ★★ | VALUE ★★★★ | ZONE 1

70 Heath Street, NW3; (0207) 433-1600; tube: Hampstead;
www.pizzaexpress.co.uk

Customers Locals and tourists **Reservations** Not necessary **When to go** Anytime **Entree range** £4.95–£7.75 **Payment** VISA, MC, AMEX, DC **Service rating** ★★ **Friendliness rating** ★★★½ **Bar** No **Wine selection** Minimal **Dress** Casual **Disabled access** Yes

Open Every day, 11 a.m.–midnight

Setting & atmosphere Relaxed, unpretentious, and notably child-friendly.

Summary & comments This branch is just one of dozens: There are over 200 branches nationwide. Its formula is very simple. There are 16 types of pizza, a couple of baked pasta dishes and salads, and a few side dishes. The thin-crust pizzas are smallish by American standards but good; the pasta dishes are acceptable if not exciting; main-course salads are so-so. In short, not a place to come for a special meal but when you want something cheap and fast. It is especially good for children, who are always made welcome. Art lovers should note that they contribute 25p to the Veneziana Fund, formerly Venice in Peril, whenever they order a Veneziana pizza (onions, capers, olives, pine nuts, sultanas, mozzarella, tomato, £5.30). Pizza Express is listed here because of its ubiquity and decent quality; for something better in the pizza field, see Strada (page 310).

Pollo ★

ITALIAN | INEXPENSIVE | QUALITY ★★ | VALUE ★★★★★ | ZONE 7

20 Old Compton Street, W1; (0207) 734-5917; tube: Leicester Square or Tottenham Court Road

Customers Locals **Reservations** Not necessary **When to go** Lunch or dinner **Entree range** £3.50–£6.70 **Payment** Cash or sterling, traveler's checks

Service rating ★★ Friendliness rating ★★★★ Bar No **Wine selection** Minimal **Dress** Casual **Disabled access** No

Open Every day, noon–midnight

Setting & atmosphere Old-fashioned 1950s decor, charmingly rundown, very lively at all hours.

House specialties Pasta.

Summary & comments The reasons for including Pollo in this book can be summed up in three words: pasta, price, and character. The prices are so low they're almost surreal, especially in a city where nothing comes cheap. The pasta is consistently pretty good, whether sauced or baked— but good as in hearty and filling, not as in adventurous and thrilling. And the character is just great, made equally by the cheerful staff and the customers who pile in for cheap eats any time of day. It's a glimpse of a London that has nearly disappeared from most areas frequented by tourists, and it's worth a visit for that reason alone. If you think of it as an Anglo-Italian diner, you'll have the right idea. Avoid appetizers and desserts; stick to pasta. One of a kind, and useful for budget-watchers.

Pret à Manger

SANDWICHES, ETC. | INEXPENSIVE | QUALITY ★★ | VALUE ★★★★ | ZONE 3

The Tower of London, EC3; tube: Tower Hill; www.pret.com/flash

Customers Locals and tourists **Reservations** Not necessary **When to go** Breakfast, lunch, or snack **Entree range** 99p–£4.75 **Payment** VISA, MC, AMEX, D, DC, CB **Service rating ★★★ Friendliness rating ★★★½ Bar** No **Wine selection** None **Dress** Casual **Disabled access** Yes

Open Every day, 8:30 a.m.–6 p.m.

Setting & atmosphere Sandwich shop.

Summary & comments Pret à Manger isn't a restaurant but an outlet for fast food, mostly sandwiches, and part of a chain of over 100 in the capital (and many more outside London and overseas). Sandwiches range from ultrasimple egg salad (called "egg mayonnaise" in Britain) to wraps filled with hummus and red pepper salad and even vegetarian sushi or deluxe sushi. Cakes and desserts are decent; coffee is of high quality. Pret is good, it's cheap, it's quick, and it's everywhere. If you just want a light, quick refueling session, this is one place to get it.

Prospect Grill

MODERN EUROPEAN/AMERICAN | INEXPENSIVE/MODERATE | QUALITY ★★★½ | VALUE ★★★★★ | ZONE 7

4–6 Garrick Street, WC1; (0207) 379-0412; tube: Leicester Square

Customers Varied **Reservations** Advisable **When to go** Lunch or dinner **Entree range** £9.95–£15.95 **Payment** VISA, MC, AMEX, DC, **Service rating**

★★★★ **Friendliness rating** ★★★★★ **Bar** No **Wine selection** Small but good **Dress** Casual **Disabled access** Restaurant only, not rest rooms

Open Monday–Saturday, 11:45 a.m.–3:30 p.m. and 5:45–11:45 p.m.

Setting & atmosphere Small, intimate front room with booths and plush decor; simpler side room with tables only.

Summary & comments The Prospect has been a great success ever since it opened in 1999, and it's easy to understand why. Few neighborhoods have such an appealing, welcoming cheapish restaurant where the cooking is this good, and in the West End it's as rare as a snowman in August. The food is simple, specializing (as you'll guess from the name) in grilled meat, fish, and vegetables. Steaks and burgers are made with organic beef and cooked just as you order with great fries on the side. But roast dishes are also good, and desserts are of the stick-to-your-hips variety. It's worth phoning well ahead to get a table in the front room, with its red walls and superbly comfortable seating. The other room is fine, but this is the one that most makes you think you're in an American steak house of ancient pedigree. Diners on a budget should note that the set lunch and pretheater menus (£14.95 for two courses, £16.95 for three) are terrific bargains.

Providores and Tapa Room   ★★★★

FUSION | MODERATE/EXPENSIVE | QUALITY ★★★★½ | VALUE ★★★★ | ZONE 14

109 Marylebone High Street, W1; (0207) 935-6175; tube: Bond Street

Customers Mostly locals **Reservations** Essential **When to go** Lunch or dinner **Entree range** Tapa Room, £5.10–£9.80; Providores, £15.30–£19.30 **Payment** VISA, MC, AMEX **Service rating** ★★★★½ **Friendliness rating** ★★★★★ **Bar** "People can come and just drink but they cannot sit or stand at the bar." **Wine selection** Excellent **Dress** Smart casual **Disabled access** Yes

Open Tapa Room, Monday–Friday, 9 a.m.–11:30 p.m.; Saturday, 10 a.m.–10:30 p.m.; Sunday, 10 a.m.–10 p.m.; Providores, daily, lunch/brunch noon–3 p.m.; dinner, Monday–Friday, 6–10:30 p.m.; Saturday and Sunday, 6–10 p.m.

Setting & atmosphere Beautiful modern decor, minimal with a New Zealand theme.

House specialities Deep-fried egg with chile, coriander, mint, and crispy shallots; smoky coconut and tamarind and coconut laksa with green tea noodles; chicken and hijack dumpling, white turmeric and coriander; roast Appleton pork belly with truffled flageolet purée and grilled raddichio; grilled Scottish scallops on a plantain fritter with sweet chile sauce and salted coconut milk; roasted organic salmon on salsify; samphire and morning glory with green papaya; and mango and Avruga caviar salad and vanilla and Szechuan pepper dressing.

Summary & comments Just looking at the list of specialties may tell you you're on unfamiliar territory. But while the dishes sound strange, the genius of chefs Peter Gordon and Anna Hansen ensures that even the strangest-sounding combinations work beautifully on the plate. They really know their stuff, regardless of where the ingredients and methods come from. Asian influences are effortlessly and expertly absorbed into their own highly individualist cooking. And one of the nicest things here is the plentiful plateful of dining possibilities. You can go in for breakfast, brunch, a light snack in the Tapa Room, or a full meal in the main restaurant. Prices are not ultra-low except in the Tapa Room, but they are not out of line for restaurants of this quality. And the quality—even while challenging every known rule of modern cooking—is truly exceptional. If you have a sense of culinary adventure, head straight for Providores.

Rasa ★★★½

INDIAN | MODERATE | QUALITY ★★★½ | VALUE ★★★★ | ZONE 8

6 Dering Street, W1; (0207) 629-1346; tube: Oxford Circus
55 Stoke Newington Church Street, N16; (0207) 249-0344; tube: Manor House

Customers Locals and aficionados **Reservations** Recommended **When to go** Lunch or dinner **Entree range** £6.50–£11.95 **Payment** VISA, MC, AMEX, D, DC, CB **Service rating** ★★★½ **Friendliness rating** ★★★ **Bar** Yes **Wine selection** Small but good **Dress** Casual **Disabled access** Restaurant only

Lunch Monday–Saturday, noon–3 p.m.

Dinner Monday–Saturday, 6–11 p.m.

Setting & atmosphere Pleasant modern interior, simply decorated, friendly and informal.

House specialties Southern Indian vegetarian dishes.

Other recommendations Breads, pickles, and chutneys.

Summary & comments The original Rasa, in out-of-the-way Stoke Newington, has educated thousands of Londoners about the beauties of Keralan (Southern Indian) vegetarian cuisine. The second branch, in W1, more centrally located, deserves a visit if you have the slightest interest in Indian food. You can ask them to put together a Kerala feast, which will give a good balance and range of dishes featuring different flavors and textures. Or choose for yourself among the dosas (filled pancakes), curries, and side dishes of rice, vegetables, and exquisite bread. The food is filling but not stodgy, and no one who eats it comes away unimpressed. If you like the idea but don't like vegetarian meals, there's a branch called Rasa Samudra (tube: Goodge Street; 5 Charlotte Street, W1; (0207) 637 0222) specializing in Southern Indian fish and shellfish. The Stoke Newington restaurant has humbler decor, far lower prices, and a huge local fan club that can cause a long wait for tables.

Richard Corrigan at Lindsay House ★★★★

BRITISH | MODERATE/EXPENSIVE | QUALITY ★★★★½ | VALUE ★★½ | ZONE 7

---

21 Romilly Street, W1; (0207) 439-0450; tube: Leicester Square or Piccadilly Circus; www.lindsayhouse.co.uk

Customers Mostly locals **Reservations** Recommended **When to go** Lunch or dinner **Entree range** Lunch only, £20–£25; set menus £23 (lunch), £48 (dinner) **Payment** VISA, MC, AMEX, D, CB, JCB **Service rating** ★★★★ **Friendliness rating** ★★★★ **Bar** No **Wine selection** Excellent but expensive **Dress** Smart casual **Disabled access** No

Lunch Monday–Friday, noon–2:30 p.m.

Dinner Monday–Saturday, 6–11 p.m.

Setting & atmosphere Two stories of a town house decorated with quiet elegance; cozy and subdued but not stuffy.

House specialties Roasted pigeon, sweet corn and cured foie gras; warm English asparagus with hen's egg and caviar; saddle of rabbit, black pudding, polenta and garlic confit; butter-poached haddock, braised haricots blancs, potato cream; raspberry soufflé with lavender ice cream; warm spice cake, fig jam, lemon cream, grapefruit, and dates.

Summary & comments Richard Corrigan, the chef at Lindsay House, has long had devoted followers for his robust, sophisticated approach to modern cooking. After moving around a slew of London restaurants, he seems to have settled in here, giving his fans the kind of hearty food that they've come to expect from him. Corrigan is Irish, and his native tradition shows in a love of pork, offal, and Irish ingredients such as black pudding. But his cooking is also based in French classicism, and it is both refined and adventurous. And it is now equally assured in its handling of fish. Desserts are a strong point. Prices are not low on the menu or (especially) the wine list; this is a restaurant for a special occasion. And a few grumbles have been heard about lax service. But if you like hearty cooking raised to the level of culinary art, chances are you'll love the Lindsay House. They'll cook specially for vegetarians if asked.

Royal China ★★★

CHINESE | INEXPENSIVE | QUALITY ★★★ | VALUE ★★★★ | ZONE 14

---

13 Queensway, W2; (0207) 221-2535; tube: Bayswater or Queensway

Customers Locals and tourists, many Chinese **Reservations** Not necessary **When to go** Weekend lunch or dinner **Entree range** £6–£40 **Payment** VISA, MC, AMEX, D **Service rating** ★★ **Friendliness rating** ★★½ **Bar** Yes **Wine selection** Excellent for a Chinese restaurant **Dress** Casual **Disabled access** Restaurant only

Open Monday–Thursday, noon–11 p.m.; Friday and Saturday, noon–11:30 p.m.; Sunday, 11 a.m.–10 p.m.

Setting & atmosphere Plush Chinese decor with lots of black lacquer and gold, comfortable seating; can be quite hectic when there's a crowd.

House specialties All shellfish, especially lobster (cooked in six different ways), scallops, and prawns; dim sum.

Other recommendations Chicken with cashews; sautéed chicken with black beans and chili; fillet steak with black pepper; hot and spicy veal; Royal China Dover sole; Royal China lotus leaf rice; chilled mango pudding.

Summary & comments Probably the best restaurant in this Chinese restaurant–crowded street, Royal China is also a cut above in comfort, and care has been taken with the decor, even if it is not to everyone's taste. But the food is to everyone's taste, as you'll see if you go along for dim sum. There are the usual dumplings and rolls, as well as special dishes rarely found elsewhere, and the quality is exceptional. The only problem is the crowds, which on weekends (especially Sunday) can lead to enormous lines outside. Go during the week for a more leisurely affair, and for dinner as well as lunch. Seafood is exquisite, and even the set meals (normally a no-go area) are good. Service can be a little abrupt but it is better than at many comparable places. And the wine list is a surprise, as good as some upper-echelon European restaurants—and much cheaper!

Rules ★★★

BRITISH | MODERATE/EXPENSIVE | QUALITY ★★★ | VALUE ★★★ | ZONE 7

35 Maiden Lane, WC2; (0207) 836-5314; tube: Covent Garden or Charing Cross; www.rules.co.uk

Customers More tourists than locals **Reservations** Recommended **When to go** Dinner is best **Entree range** £14.95–£19.95 **Payment** VISA, MC, AMEX, D, DC, JCB **Service rating** ★★★ **Friendliness rating** ★★★ **Bar** No **Wine selection** Small but good **Dress** Casual **Disabled access** Yes

Open Monday–Saturday, noon–11:30 p.m.; Sunday, noon–10:30 p.m.

Setting & atmosphere Ornate old-fashioned decor with prints and statues, but modern lively bustle at busy times.

House specialties Game dishes, Aberdeen Angus beef.

Other recommendations Morecambe Bay potted shrimps; rabbit and foie gras terrine; steak and kidney pie or pudding; smoked haddock fish cake with spinach, hollandaise, and chip; roast rack of lamb with dauphinoise potatoes; grilled Dover sole, lemon butter, spinach, and chips; raspberry trifle syllabub; dark chocolate pudding soufflé with chocolate sauce and cream.

Summary & comments Rules has been serving food from this location since 1798. That by itself is not a reason to recommend it, and for years the restaurant served indifferent food to tourists seeking a taste of tradition. But for some years now it has had a highly trained French-trained chef who combines classic game and meat cookery with up-to-the-minute modern touches. The menu doesn't stand still, which is a good sign. There is less unusual experimentation than before, and fish lovers will find more choice. But many will choose the appetizing selection of meat and game. The selection of "feathered and furred game" (some from their estate in Scotland, which also occasionally supplies beef and pork) is as good as you'll find anywhere in London. Vegetarians should probably go elsewhere. If you want to try a classic, old-fashioned rib of beef, or steak and kidney pie (with or without oysters), Rules is one of your best bets.

Strada ★★★½

ITALIAN | INEXPENSIVE | QUALITY ★★★½ | VALUE ★★★★½ | ZONE 8

15-16 New Burlington Street, W1; (0207) 287-5967; tube: Oxford Circus; www.strada.co.uk

Customers Local office workers, families, tourists **When to go** Lunch or dinner **Entree range** £7.50–£12.95 **Payment** VISA, MC, AMEX **Bar** No **Wine selection** Adequate **Dress** Casual **Disabled access** Yes

Lunch Monday–Friday, noon–2:30 p.m.; Sunday, noon–2:45 p.m.

Dinner Monday–Saturday, 6:30–10:45 p.m.

Setting & atmosphere Casual, informal Italian.

House specialties Pasta and pizza.

Other recommendations Salads, soups, simple appetizers, risotto.

Summary & comments Pizza Express (see page 304) may have more branches and a higher public profile, but everyone in the know will assure you that Strada is the better bet. Their menus feature a range of dishes, with good choice at every course. The level of cooking is generally very sound. But most people who come to Strada come for pizza or pasta, served in friendly, lively surroundings by a young (usually) Italian waitstaff. Prices are low by London standards and ingredients really taste of Italy. Moreover, they positively adore children in true Italian fashion. Don't expect fireworks, but do expect to be well fed and well looked after. And note that there are 11 other locations at the time of writing.

St. John ★★★★

MODERN BRITISH | MODERATE | QUALITY ★★★★½ | VALUE ★★★★ | ZONE 3

26 St. John Street, EC1; (0207) 251-0848; tube: Farringdon; www.stjohnrestaurant.co.uk

Customers Mostly locals **When to go** Lunch or dinner **Entree range** £10–£23.50 **Payment** VISA, MC, AMEX, DC **Service rating** ★★★★ **Friendliness rating** ★★★★★ **Bar** Yes, with full menu available **Wine selection** Very good **Dress** Casual

Lunch Monday–Friday, noon–3 p.m.

Dinner Monday–Saturday, 6–11 p.m.

Setting & atmosphere Big, minimally decorated rooms in a converted industrial building; almost always crowded.

House specialties Radishes and butter; cockle and white cabbage salad; smoked eel and horseradish; roast bone marrow and parsley salad; chitterlings and dandelion; pigeon; roast sirloin, green beans and anchovy; ox tongue and beetroot; Welsh rarebit; Eccles cake and Lancashire cheese; chocolate terrine and crème fraîche.

Summary & comments You can learn a great deal about St. John from reading the list of specialties; then again, the list might tell you very little if you're not already familiar with the selections. Perhaps a better way of understanding it is through the restaurant's motto, now famous in London: "Nose to tail eating." This is a place for people who love meat and fish, but especially meat. And not just meat but the bits of meat (pork especially) that fancy restaurants sometimes throw away—but which "peasant" cooks have always known and loved. Everything is described in few words, because the emphasis is on top-notch ingredients (many of them organic) prepared and cooked very simply. This is a style of cooking that St. John pioneered in London, and which has been much imitated. Prices are not high for cooking at this level—please note that most main courses are £10–£16. The commitment to quality is unyielding and passionate. If your idea of great cooking means taking the best products available and treating them with simple respect, St. John may be your idea of heaven. Note: It's not a place for vegetarians, and the adventurous eater is better served than the squeamish.

Tamarind   ★★★½

INDIAN | MODERATE | QUALITY ★★★½ | VALUE ★★★ | ZONE 8

20 Queen Street, W1; (0207) 629-3561; tube: Green Park;
www.tamarindrestaurant.com

Customers Locals and tourists **Reservations** Recommended **When to go** Lunch or dinner **Entree range** £13.50–£28 **Payment** VISA, MC, AMEX, D, DC, CB **Service rating** ★★★ **Friendliness rating** ★★★ **Bar** Yes **Wine selection** Very good **Dress** Smart **Disabled access** No

Lunch Sunday–Friday, noon–3 p.m.

Dinner Monday–Saturday, 6–11:30 p.m.; Sunday, 6–10:30 p.m.

Setting & atmosphere Chic, stylish decor sets the tone.

Summary & comments Tamarind's immensely gifted founding chef, Atul Kochhar, left the restaurant in 2003 to set up his own Benares (see page 274). But things have remained steady here, despite the new competition. Tamarind has always produced excellence in every department, from chutneys and pickles (available for sale) to breads and rice, and on to the meat, fish, and vegetable dishes that make this one of the best Indian eateries in London. (Vegetarians could do very well just ordering rice, bread, and a selection of side dishes.) Mind you, it's also one of the most expensive. A three-course meal with all the right side dishes can easily cost £40 before drinks. Part of that is paying for the setting, for a large and polished team of waiters, and for rent in one of London's most exclusive areas. But it's also paying for the best ingredients, cooked with exceptional skill and attention. If you want to find out how good Indian restaurant cooking can be and don't mind paying "European" prices for the pleasure, this is one of the three or four best places to do it. The Group Menus, a large selection of dishes to be ordered family style by diners at a table, are a good value at £34, £38, or £45 a head.

Veeraswamy ★★★

INDIAN | MODERATE | QUALITY ★★★ | VALUE ★★★½ | ZONE 7

Mezzanine Floor, Victory House, 99 Regent Street, W1; (0207) 734-1401; tube: Piccadilly Circus
Chutney Mary, 535 King's Road, SW10; (0207) 351-3113; tube: Fulham Broadway; www.veeraswamy.com

Customers Mostly locals **Reservations** Recommended **When to go** Lunch or dinner **Entree range** £9–£13.50 **Payment** VISA, MC, AMEX, DC, CB **Service rating** ★★★★ **Friendliness rating** ★★★★ **Bar** No **Wine selection** Very good **Dress** No dress code **Disabled access** Restaurant only, not rest rooms

Lunch Monday–Friday, noon–2:30 p.m.; Saturday and Sunday, 12:30–3 p.m.

Dinner Monday–Saturday, 5:30–11:30 p.m.; Sunday, 5:30–10:30 p.m.

Setting & atmosphere Stylish, colorful room overlooking Regent Street; mostly young, fashionable crowd.

House specialties Mussels in coconut and ginger sauce; supreme of chicken with sesame; Malabar lobster curry with fresh turmeric and raw mango; white lamb curry from Kerala; tandoori chicken tikka sautéed in a sauce of tomato and onion; green chili and cheese naan.

Other recommendations Breads, condiments, set lunch Monday–Saturday (£11 for 2 courses), all-you-can-eat Sunday lunch (£15 for 3 courses).

Summary & comments Veeraswamy, Britain's first Indian restaurant, has been on this site for decades, but the quality-conscious Chutney Mary group took over and revamped it in 1998. They modernized everything from decor to menu to wine list, and the result is one of London's better Indian restaurants. The unusually attractive room has contrasting pale wood with deep, well-chosen color. Service is from a young, multiethnic crew, and the kitchen specialists prepare dishes of their own region. This means that each dish is likely authentic, whatever part of India it represents. Vegetable and fish/meat/chicken dishes are given equal prominence and cooked with equal care, making Veeraswamy a particularly good place to come with a mixed group of vegetarians and meat eaters. Prices are fair, compared with other Indian restaurants at this level, and set-price offerings make them even better. If your time is limited and you can eat only at one Indian place, this is a good candidate.

Wagamama   ★

ASIAN | INEXPENSIVE | QUALITY ★★ | VALUE ★★★★ | ZONES 2 & 7

4A Streatham Street, WC1; (0207) 323-9223; tube: Tottenham Court Road
10A Lexington Street, W1; (0207) 292-0990; tube: Oxford Circus or Piccadilly
Circus; www.wagamama.com

Customers Mostly locals **Reservations** Not accepted **When to go** Anytime
Entree range £5.25–£8.50 **Payment** VISA, MC, AMEX, D, DC, JCB **Service rating** ★ **Friendliness rating** ★★ **Bar** No **Wine selection** Minimal **Dress** Casual **Disabled access** No, but see below

Open Monday–Saturday, noon–11 p.m.; Sunday, 12:30–10:30 p.m.

Setting & atmosphere Spartan room with seating at long tables.

House specialties Soup noodles, fried noodles, dumplings.

Summary & comments This is the original branch of Wagamama; there are 11 others, and several outside London as well. The expansion tells the story of a phenomenal success based on a simple idea. Produce a menu that focuses on just a few things, make them consistently well, and cut out all the frills so you can sell them cheap. The focus is on noodles, mostly Japanese varieties such as ramen and udon. The frills that disappear are personal space (you sit at long tables with other diners) and flexibility. You're in a machine at Wagamama, and it's not a place to dawdle. But the meals are cheap, well made and filling, and you can be in and out very quickly when you're on the go. Complaints almost always deal with service, which has little to do with personalized attention and much more with keeping the machine working smoothly. The places can't be ignored for their quality and speed; just don't expect to feel pampered. *Note:* The other branches have disabled access.

Zaika ★★★½

MODERN INDIAN | EXPENSIVE | QUALITY ★★★½ | VALUE ★★★ | ZONE 13

1 Kensington High Street, W8; (0207) 795-6533; tube: South Kensington;
www.zaika-restaurant.co.uk

Customers Tourists and affluent locals **When to go** Lunch is best **Entree range** £12.50–£31.50 **Payment** VISA, MC, AMEX, D, DC, JCB **Bar** No **Wine selection** Good **Dress** Smart casual **Disabled access** Yes, but not to rest rooms

Lunch Monday–Friday, noon–2:30 p.m.; Sunday, noon–2:45 p.m.

Dinner Monday–Saturday, 6–10:45 p.m.; Sunday, 6:30–9:45 p.m.

Setting & atmosphere Swanky, elegant Indian.

House specialties Dhungar machli tikka (tandoori smoked salmon); kala murg (grilled spiced chicken); zaika platter; tikhe machli (spice marinated sea bass); samundri khazana (Hawaiian soft-shell crab and seared spiced scallops with Indian risotto); lal mirch murg (spicy chicken masala); gilafi dum biryani (crusted lamb biryani).

Other recommendations Desserts.

Summary & comments This genuinely innovative Indian restaurant won rave reviews on opening in 1999, and in 2001 became one of London's first Indian possessors of a Michelin star. It's easy to see why Michelin liked them: Chef Vineet Bhatia's food is less authentic Indian than a sophisticated, contemporary interpretation bringing in elements and ideas from outside the subcontinent. It pays careful attention to presentation and presents some interesting desserts (not an Indian strong point) to finish off the meal. And everything about the place reflects the ambition: decor, wine list, and some of the highest prices of any Indian restaurant in London. Lovers of traditional Indian food sometimes object to the liberties taken here, but if you're not a stickler for authenticity, you're likely to be very impressed—if quite a bit poorer.

Part Nine

Entertainment and Nightlife

The London Scene

No other metropolis can rival London for the overall quality and quantity of its theaters, opera, ballet, concert halls, jazz venues, art galleries, antiques fairs, auctions, exhibitions, cinemas, cabarets, comedy clubs, television, historic buildings, historic walks, private clubs, nightclubs, pubs, shops, restaurants, and publishing houses. An enormous number of books and magazine titles are published in the United Kingdom, and Londoners enjoy four quality national newspapers and numerous tabloids, as well as a bumper crop of pointless celeb-worshipping mags (*Heat, Now, Closer, Hello, OK,* to name a few).

Although London remains English in character, it has, since World War II, become a microcosm of the defunct British Empire with one person in five now hailing from an ethnic minority. The Indian, Asian, and Afro-Caribbean influences on the London scene have helped make it as vibrantly international as New York.

As any James Bond expert is aware, gambling has long been legal in Britain. Along with the high-class and the seedy casinos, most high streets (the main shopping street of an area) have an easily recognizable Ladbrokes betting shop, where one might place a wager on the horses, cricket results, snow at Christmas, or even on who will win the latest series of reality/humiliation TV contests, which England has so taken to heart.

Soho, in zone 7, is the epicenter of London's nightlife. Here's where you'll find the theaters, cinemas, pubs, clubs, and restaurants that have made London famous. But London's culture and night fun is not limited to this neighborhood by any means. Pick up copies of *Time Out, What's On,* or the Thursday supplement of *The Evening Standard, Metro Life,* to see what's going on where and when. (Before you arrive, check www.timeout.com.)

Theater

London theater comes in three categories: the West End, London's equivalent to New York City's Broadway; off–West End, ditto; and fringe, which equals New York's off-Broadway.

The West End

Although "the West End" refers to an area of central London, it also indicates cultural status and encompasses the **National Theatre,** which is located south of the Thames. West End theaters are famous for their musicals and mainstream productions, but drama in the West End is of variable quality, ranging from the sublime to the overtly commercial.

However, the theaters of London's West End enjoy such renown that Hollywood actors able to command millions of dollars per film clamor to appear in the theaters for a relative pittance and, more often than not, to mixed reviews. Nicole Kidman, Daryl Hannah, Jerry Hall, Kevin Spacey, Madonna, Matthew Perry, and Ellen Burstyn are just a few of the Yankee stars who have lit up the West End recently.

Try www.officiallondontheatre.co.uk for a listing of current plays, plus reviews, phone numbers, and tips. Choose the production venue, and you can even have a seating plan of the theater faxed to you.

When purchasing tickets for the theater, it is helpful to remember to never buy a ticket from a tout (essentially, a scalper type), because he or she will charge an astronomical sum for it. Instead, you should queue up in front of the discount ticket booth, called tkts, a little house located on the south side of the grassy part of Leicester Square (tube: Leicester Square). It is a tan building with a clock on top of it. You can also identify it by the lines forming on either side of it. The west side is for night performances; the east side sells matinee tickets. They charge £2.50 per ticket for a service fee, they accept cash or credit cards (no traveler's checks), and limit each customer to four tickets. The booth is open Monday through Saturday from 10 a.m. to 7 p.m., Sunday from noon to 3:30 p.m. (for matinees only). Be sure you go to this booth only and not one of the many shop fronts around Leicester Square that call themselves discount or half price, but actually offer no deals at all.

Tickets for the big West End shows are expensive, ranging in price from £15 to £50 (and even beyond) and can also be elusive, especially for the big musicals or star-turn limited-run plays. In plays that tend to be sold out, you may be forced to obtain advance tickets through **Ticketmaster** (phone (0207) 344-4444 or visit www.ticketmaster.co.uk) and **Firstcall** (phone (0207) 420-0000 or visit www.firstcalltickets.com) or call the box office directly. However, booking fees add around 10% (and can soar to a punishing 20% in some cases) to the price of a ticket, and many theaters charge a telephone booking fee. The least expensive way to acquire a ticket is to turn up at the box office in person, hoping that the show's not sold out.

Many theaters offer half-price tickets on Mondays and for dress rehearsals. Some also grant concessions to students and seniors. Queuing for return tickets (or standby tickets) before a performance can also sometimes yield a discount. London recognizes the need to make cultural events affordable: In 2003 the National Theatre, with the financial sponsorship of Travelex, launched a £10 a ticket scheme that will fill the seats and please the pockets. The London Symphony Orchestra has also reduced prices, and has introduced a £5 concert ticket. West End/Broadway impresario Cameron Mackintosh has even reduced some of the ticket prices for the massive musicals he produces (although you can still get skinned for as much as £50 for a good seat on a Saturday night). So some things actually do go down in price in London—and it all seemed to start with the handful of big museums eliminating entrance fees in December 2001. Interestingly, these adjustments have nothing to do with getting more government subsidies, which in fact continue to drop shamefully.

The National Theatre (zone 5; South Bank, SE1; box office (0207) 452-3000; information (0207) 452-3400; www.nationaltheatre.org.uk; tube: Waterloo) has three theaters (Cottesloe, Lyttelton, Olivier) presenting plays in repertory, as well as special events with live music or dance DJs. In 2003 Trevor Nunn yielded his position as director to Nicholas Hytner, whose first change was to drop the superfluous "royal" from the theater's title to the approbation of many. The quality of the theatrical presentations continues from strength to strength, encompassing classical as well as new and neglected plays from the whole of world drama. On the lighter side, the National also offers musicals and even productions for children, six days a week throughout the year. The box office is open Monday through Saturday, 10 a.m.–8 p.m. Prices range from £10–£35. Go for the standby tickets a half hour before the performance.

Royal Court (zone 11; Sloane Square, SW1; (0207) 565-5000; www.royalcourttheatre.com; tube: Sloane Square) re-opened in 2001 after an extensive and expensive refurbishment. The Royal Court is considered the most important venue for new writers in Britain and therefore deserves a big mention. There are two theaters: the Downstairs main theater and the Upstairs studio. Performances are held Monday–Saturday at 7:30 p.m., and the Saturday matinee is held at 3:30 p.m. Tickets are £5–£26. This is a great alternative to the West End theaters, and it's cheaper, too.

The authentic re-creation of **Shakespeare's Globe Theatre** (zone 5; New Globe Walk, SE1; (0207) 401-9919; www.shakespeares-globe.org; tube: Blackfriars), close to its original site, is the achievement of American expat actor Sam Wannamaker. Sadly, Wannamaker died shortly before the completion of the Globe's restoration. It is an amazing accomplishment and as fascinating to the student of historical architecture as it is to Bard buffs. Although its basement remains open throughout the year to provide the world's largest exhibition devoted to the life and work of Shakespeare and the theater of his time, the roofless Globe's theatrical season is limited to April through October. The box office is open Tuesday–Saturday, 10 a.m.–6 p.m. Matinees are Saturday at 2 p.m. and Sunday at 1 p.m. or 6:30 p.m. (times alternate each week). Tickets are £5–£29.

Restaurants in the vicinity of the larger theaters often offer preshow menus at reduced prices, as do some of the theaters themselves; the three theaters above have decent restaurants with preshow dinners.

Off–West End

Off–West End theaters often provide the most outstanding productions in terms of creativity because they offer writers, directors, and actors an artistic freedom that can sometimes be lacking in the more commercially motivated organizations. With emphasis firmly on the modern and avant-garde, the recently renovated **Almeida** (near zone 3; Almeida Street, N1; (0207) 359-4404; www.almeida.co.uk; tube: Angel) features cerebral drama from top writers and actors, and came under the direction of former Royal Shakespeare Company head Michael Attenborough when it re-opened in spring 2003. Tickets are £5–£30. The intimate 105-seat **Bush Theatre** (west of zone 13; Shepherd's Bush Green, W12; (0207) 610-4224; www.bushtheatre.co.uk; tube: Shepherd's Bush or Goldhawk Road) is considered the next most important spot (after the Royal Court theater) for productions by new writers, many of whom have gone on to greater successes. Tickets are £8–£14. The **Donmar Warehouse** (zone 7; 41 Earlham Street, WC2; (0207) 369-1732; www.donmar-warehouse.com; tube: Covent Garden) became an exciting venue in the late 1990s under the artistic direction of Sam Mendes, who was followed in early 2003 by Michael Grandage, who continues to provide provocative drama. Tickets are £12-29. Home to gay and lesbian productions, the **Drill Hall** (zone 7; 16 Chenies Street, WC1; (0207) 307-5060; www.drillhall.co.uk; tube: Goodge Street) welcomes everyone. The atmosphere of this intimate theater is brilliant. Monday evenings are for women only. Tickets are £7–£16. A small theater located above a pub, **The Gate** (zone 13; at The Prince Albert, 11 Pembridge Road, W11; (0207) 229-0706; tube: Notting Hill Gate) has a fine reputation for its low-budget yet high-quality drama from all over the world. Budding actors and directors relish the opportunity to work here and will happily do so for free, so great are the kudos. Performances run Monday through Saturday. Tickets are £6–£12. **The King's Head** (zone 15; 115 Upper Street, N1; (0207) 226-1916; tube: Angel) is London's most venerable pub theater, frequently putting on top-quality, small-scale plays, revues, and musicals. It's a fine pub as well. Tickets are £5–£18.

Regent's Park Open Air Theatre (zone 14; Regent's Park, NW1; (0207) 486-2431; www.open-air-theatre.org.uk; tube: Baker Street) provides for those who like their theater alfresco. Set in the middle of the eponymous park and furnished with a bar and snacking facilities, this charming summer theater is an ideal venue in which to see the company's vastly entertaining version of *A Midsummer Night's Dream.* The season kicks off on June 4, and tickets are £9–£26. Be prepared, however, for the vagaries of British weather. Performances will be canceled in torrential rain, but the show must go on in the usual drizzle; bring a rain poncho.

Riverside Studios (zone 12; Crisp Road, W6; (0208) 237-1111; www.riversidestudios.co.uk; tube: Hammersmith) overlooks the river Thames near Hammersmith Bridge. There are three studio spaces: One seats 400, another seats 150, and the third is in permanent use for a TV show. In addition to the theatrical and dance productions, there is also a repertory cinema, a gallery, and a café overlooking the river. The **Soho Theatre** (zone 7, 21 Dean Street, Soho, W1; (0207) 478 0100; www.sohotheatre.com; tube: Tottenham Court Road) has been happily at home in this modern and well-appointed space for the last few years, producing topical new plays, as well as occasional stand-up comedy, and book readings by authors. Standing in the shadows of the Old Vic theater, **YoungVic** (zone 5; 66 The Cut, SE1; (0207) 928-6363; www.youngvic.org; tube: Southwark) has become a successful venue, attracting big-name actors and touring companies such as the Royal Shakespeare Company. Shows run Monday through Saturday. Tickets are £9–£25.

Fringe

Fringe theater can be found throughout London, but like British weather, is variable and generally of patchy quality. Still, the following theaters do provide the occasional ray of histrionic sunshine:

The small **Chelsea Theatre** (zone 11; King's Road, SW10; (0207) 352-1967; www.theatrezone.org; tube: Sloane Square, then bus 211, 319, 19, 22; or South Kensington, then bus 49, 45) focuses on exciting new plays, which run seven to eight weeks at a time. Performances are held Monday–Saturday, at 8 p.m. Tickets are £7–£11. **The Finborough** (zone 10 at Finborough Arms, Finborough Road, SW10; (0207) 373-3842; www.finboroughtheatre.itgo.com, tube Earl's Court) is a small pub venue that hosts new writers, some of whom have ended up in the West End or on Broadway. Performances are Tuesday–Saturday, at 7:30 p.m.; Sunday matinees occur at 3:30 p.m. Tickets are £10. For Tuesday performances, all seats are £8. Credit cards are *not* accepted. Being so close to Piccadilly, **Jermyn Street Theatre** (zone 7; 16b Jermyn Street, SW1; (0207) 287-2875; www.jermynstreettheatre.co.uk; tube: Piccadilly Circus) is a great alternative to a big West End production. This intimate 70-seater venue hosts a mixture of shows, but musicals are the main feature. Performances are daily at 7:30 p.m.; Sunday matinees are at 3 p.m. Tickets are £10–£15.

The **New End Theatre** (zone 1; 27 New End, NW3; (0207) 794-0022; tube: Hampstead) is a venue with reliably interesting productions, situated in lovely Hampstead. Those with an ear for a good tune might investigate the musicals staged at **The Bridewell** (zone 3; Bride Lane, off Fleet Street, EC4; (0207) 936-3456; tube: Blackfriars). New writing and a thriving bar can be found in plentiful supply at the legendary **Old Red Lion** (zone 15; 416 St. John Street, EC1; (0207) 837-7816; tube: Angel).

Although a tuxedo is no longer requisite attire when attending the theater, the British middle class still appears to dress with care for certain events, and black tie remains mandatory for any gala charity night where royals may be present. Certainly suits and smart dresses are often seen in West End and off–West End theaters, but you will not feel out of place in the egalitarian sneakers, baseball cap, and jeans.

Laughs in London

The British frequently congratulate themselves on their ironic sense of humor, and justly so; surely no other country has produced so many comic novelists of the caliber of Henry Fielding, William Makepeace Thackeray, Jane Austen, E. F. Benson, George Meredith, Anthony Trollope, Jerome K. Jerome, Evelyn Waugh, Tom Sharpe, Kingsley Amis, and, of course, the divine P. G. Wodehouse, to name only a few.

British humor extends even to politicians, some of whom are given to entertaining quips (intentional and not) that would soon see them hounded out of office in less tolerant societies. Winston Churchill was undoubtedly the wittiest of leaders and is eminently quotable; no prime minister has since lived up to his standards.

Although British sitcoms are currently in the doldrums, the BBC has an unrivaled roster of past triumphs. If you are staying in one evening, try renting videos of *Fawlty Towers, Black Adder, Yes Prime Minister, Jeeves and Wooster, Drop the Dead Donkey, Alan Partridge, Rising Damp, Only Fools and Horses, French and Saunders, The Comic Strip, The Fast Show, Slap the Pony, Absolutely Fabulous,* and *The Office.* They are all very funny shows, although it is hard to gauge how well they travel—some foreigners are mystified by them, as comedy tends to be culture specific.

London has more comedy outlets than most cosmopolitan cities. The humor on display varies in quality and includes traditional improvisation and physical, surreal, and observational comedy. Most venues provide food and drink, both of which help if the acts are dreadful. There's a London Comedy Festival in May (call (0870) 011-9611; www.london comedyfestival.com) that chuckle aficionados will like.

Amused Moose Soho (zone 7; at Barcode, 3–4 Archer Street, W1; (0208) 341-1341; www.amusedmoose.co.uk; tube: Piccadilly Circus)

Shows are at 8:30 p.m. on Monday, Wednesday, and Thursday; and 8 p.m. on Saturday and Sunday. They boast that their comedians are "first date friendly," which presumably means you won't be hounded or humiliated as part of the act.

Comedy Café (zone 3; 66 Rivington Street, EC2; (0207) 739-5706; tube: Old Street) is one of the handful of clubs in London devoted entirely to comedy and takes the generous precaution of granting free admission on Wednesday, when new acts make their debuts. Comedy Café is open Wednesday through Sunday.

Comedy Store, at Haymarket House (zone 7; 1A Oxedon Street, SW1; (0207) 344-0234; www.thecomedystore.co.uk; tube: Piccadilly Circus), is the venue from which alternative comedy exploded onto British television screens. Such stars as Jennifer Saunders (of *French and Saunders,* and *Absolutely Fabulous*) Keith Alan, Ben Elton, and Ric Mayall began their careers here. It's still the best club on the circuit; open Tuesday through Sunday.

Jongleurs (zone 11; The Cornet, 49 Lavender Gardens, SW11; (0207) 564-2500; www.jongleurs.com; tube: Clapham Junction) is as popular as the Comedy Store, with an impressive line-up of performances that aren't all stand-up comedy. Shows are on Friday at 8:45 p.m., followed by a disco and late bar until 1 a.m. Saturday performances start at 7:15 p.m. with a late show at 11:15 p.m. There's another branch in North London, **Jongleurs Camden Lock** (zone 15; Dingwalls, Middle Yard, Camden Lock Camden High Street, NW1; (0207) 564-2500; www.jongleurs. com; tube: Camden Town or Chalk Farm) which is comfortable and busy, so book in advance. Shows on Friday start at 8:45 p.m., followed by a disco; on Saturday, performances start at 7:15 p.m. and 11:15 p.m. Tickets are £11–£14 on Friday and £9–£12 on Saturday.

Classical Music

London, arguably the music capital of the world, is endowed with four highly regarded orchestras, two internationally renowned arts establishments, numerous ensembles, and a correspondingly wide range of concerts.

Although the Barbican's London Symphony Orchestra remains the capital's leading ensemble, with the London Philharmonic only just behind, the South Bank Centre's London Philharmonic Orchestra has been gaining in strength. Then, too, the Royal Philharmonic Orchestra enjoys a distinguished history, despite having to get by without public funding. Many of the world's leading musicians flock to London stages, often for the city's frequent music festivals, especially the Henry Wood Promenade Concerts (more affectionately known as The Proms), held each year from July to September at the **Royal Albert Hall** (zone 13; Kensington Gore, SW7; (0207) 589-3203 or 589-8212; www.royal alberthall.com; tube: Gloucester Road or South Kensington). The Albert is a prodigious Victorian building that hosts pop gigs, opera, ballet, the *Cirque du Soleil,* and even wrestling bouts. Tickets are from £4 right up to £70. The closer the better—the Victorians were more about the eye than the ear when it came to creating auditoriums.

The refurbished **Royal Opera House** (zone 7; Covent Garden, WC2; recorded information (0207) 304-4000 or box office (0207) 240-1200; www.royalopera.org; tube: Covent Garden) is worth a visit just to see the beautiful building, and in fact they do offer tours of the House. They have classical productions of operas and ballets, and the price of the tickets is wonderfully varied: from £3 to £175.

Wigmore Hall (zone 8 at 36 Wigmore Street, W1; (0207) 935-2141; www.wigmore-hall.org.uk; tube: Bond Street) is the best place in town to hear piano recitals and chamber groups. Although the hall was revamped not long ago, Wigmore continues to serve up a largely traditional fare. Tickets are £5–£35.

You might care to attend a lunchtime concert held every second Thursday in the converted church of **St. John's Smith Square** (zone 9; Smith Square, SW1; (0207) 222-1061; www.sjss.org.uk; tube: Westminster). St. John's, near the Houses of Parliament, is nestled in an area of antique civility, and the church is possessed of a magical ambience.

It is easy to lose one's way down the labyrinthine corridors of that monster of modernism, the **Barbican Centre** (zone 3; Silk Street; (0207) 638-8891 or (0207) 638-4141; www.barbican.org.uk; tube: Barbican). Still, the fact that the Barbican has superb acoustics, is home to the London Symphony Orchestra, and hosts the "Great Orchestras of the World" makes it worth a music lover's effort. Other great orchestras that perform a wide range of classical music at the Barbican are the BBC Symphony Orchestra, the City of London Simfonia, and the English Chamber Orchestra.

Perched just above the Thames next to Waterloo Bridge is the **South Bank Centre** (zone 5 at Belvedere Road, South Bank, SE1, box office (0207) 960-4242; recorded information (0207) 633-0932; www.sbc.org.uk; tube: Waterloo). Its Royal Festival Hall (RFH1) is the main auditorium for symphony concerts; the smaller Queen Elizabeth Hall (RFH2) puts on semi-stage operas and chamber groups; and recitals as well as ensembles are performed in the intimate setting of the adjacent Purcell Room (RFH3). The South Bank Centre comes complete with restaurants, cafés, bars, and book and record shops. Ticket prices vary from £5 to £75.

Weather permitting, there is nothing more English or delicious than listening to classical music outdoors in the summer air, beside a great castle or on the grounds of a fragrant park. The **Hampton Court Palace Festival** (outside zones; Hampton Court, East Molesey, Surrey; (0207) 344-4444; www.hamptoncourtfestival.com) is held in June. British Rails, Hampton Court riverboat from Westminster, or Richmond to Hampton

Court Pier (April–October). The impressive historic palace lawns beside the Thames make a perfect picnic ground. Tickets are £15–£85.

The Holland Park Theatre (zone 13; Holland Park, Kensington High Street, W8; box office (0207) 602-7856; information (0207) 603-1123; www.operahollandpark.com; tube: High Street Kensington or Holland Park) stages an array of music, theater, and dance performances in one of London's loveliest parks. Guests are sheltered from the harmful effects of storm and sun by an enveloping canopy. The Holland Park Theatre is open June–August. Tickets are £26–£29.

Kenwood Lakeside Concerts (zone 1; Kenwood House, Hampstead Lane, NW3; (0208) 233-7435; www.picnicconcerts.com; tube: Golders Green or East Finchley to courtesy bus on concert nights) are best enjoyed on the nights when they punctuate the concert with fireworks. Held during July and August on the grounds of Kenwood House in Hampstead Heath, this is one of London's most delightful events.

Dance and Ballet

When one thinks of dance in London, a flood of terpsichorean images come pirouetting to mind: *The Red Shoes,* Fontaine and Nureyev, Fred and Adele Astaire, Sadler's Wells, The Royal Ballet, Covent Garden, and the wonderful movie *Billy Elliot.*

Dance grew steadily in popularity throughout the 1990s, abetted by several festivals. **Dance Umbrella** (phone (0208) 741-5881; www.dance umbrella.co.uk) features contemporary dance from all over the world and normally runs during September and October for six weeks. The events are hosted at various venues across London. **The Place Theatre** (zone 15; 17 Duke's Road WC1; (0207) 387-0031; www.theplace.org.uk; tube: Euston, Euston Square, or British Rail: Euston) hosts over 32 dance events annually, featuring British and international contemporary dance companies, with a platform for new and emerging choreographers. The 300-seat theater also features a special children's season.

Two of the largest and most active dance venues are the **Barbican Centre** and the **South Bank Centre** (see "Classical Music," above, for contact information).

The **Royal Ballet** hosts productions in the main theater of the **Royal Opera House** (see entries for the venue in the "Classical Music" and "Opera" sections). One can expect to see performances of such classics as *Don Quixote, The Nutcracker, La Bayadere, Giselle, and Romeo and Juliet.* Tickets are £3–£155.

The refurbishment of **Sadler's Wells** (zone 2; Rosebury Avenue, EC1; (0207) 863-8000; tube: Chancery Lane) has been completed at last, and the more intimate and central **Peacock Theatre** (zone 2; Portugal Street, off Kingsway, WC2; (0207) 314-8800; www.sadlers-wells.com; tube:

Holborn), which served as the interim house during the refurbishment, is now a permanent branch of Sadler's Wells. The revamped Sadler's Wells has extensive bars, state-of-the-art flying and lighting equipment, an ultraflexible stage—twice its original size—and an 80-seat orchestra pit, among other attractions. Tickets are £7–£35. Please note that the Peacock and Sadler's Wells tend to feature more contemporary ballet performances. Vast in scale, yet graceful in outline, the **London Coliseum** (zone 7; St. Martin's Lane, WC2; (0207) 632-8300; www.eno.org; tube: Charing Cross) is the home of the **English National Opera** (ENO) for most of the year, and also presents such leading dance companies as the English National Ballet and The Royal Ballet during its Christmas and summer seasons. Christmastime will feature *The Nutcracker*. See separate listing in "Opera" below.

Opera

The **Royal Opera House**'s (see "Classical Music," above, for contact information) main theater is home to the **Royal Ballet,** but within the Royal Opera House there are two more intimate venues for opera and dance: the **Linbury Studio Theater** with 420 seats, and the **Clore Studios,** a 200-seater space, which is ideal for workshops and performances. At these smaller theaters one can see opera stripped to its essentials and for a more affordable price than the great productions in the main theater. Disability access has also improved. There is also the enticing Amphitheatre Bar and Restaurant, whose terrace overlooks Covent Garden. Ticket prices range from £4 for lunchtime performances and some severely restricted views of evening performances to £155 for the best seats. Go to www.royalopera.org for the latest information.

Home to the English National Opera, the **London Coliseum** (zone 7; St. Martin's Lane, WC2; (0207) 632-8300, www.eno.org; tube: Charing Cross) is a grand venue that tries to promote a populist image—with affordable ticket prices and challenging productions. While restoration work will continue until 2004, the building will not be closed, and every effort is being made to keep disruption to a minimum. Here, the operas are sung in English. Please note that the English Ballet takes over the Coliseum mid-December through mid-January. Tickets run from £3 to £55.

Live Jazz, Pop, and Rock

London is a matrix of performing talent, and on any given Saturday night there will be well over 100 gigs being played throughout the city. Tickets vary in price from a fiver or less for pop gigs, to more than £100 for a top pop attraction.

Again, as with the theater, you must never buy tickets from scalpers, because the practice is illegal and their merchandise is probably forged. It is always best to purchase tickets from the concert venue itself. You will usually not be charged a booking fee if you pay with cash.

The thriving London jazz scene has, over the years, given the world such international luminaries as John McLauglin, George Shearing, and Dave Holland, which is indicative of the talent found here. Numerous restaurants, bars, pubs, and cafés continue to pleasantly enhance their atmosphere with live jazz music; see *Time Out* and the *Evening Standard's Metro Life* magazine for details. Among the leading jazz venues for largely local talent (all of which are profiled in the following club section) are **Ronnie Scott's, The 606 Club, Jazz Café,** and **Pizza Express.**

The Barbican and South Bank Centre often present top international stars, and two big jazz festivals are held in the autumn: the **Soho Jazz Festival** and the **Oris London Jazz Festival.**

The **Notting Hill Carnival,** held in late August, is Europe's largest street festival and features huge sound systems pumping out reggae, rap, and drum bass. Be warned, though: This event is not for the agoraphobic or timid—there are entirely too many muggers, pickpockets, and deranged people pumped full of alcohol for it to suit every sensibility.

Gargantuan rock structures include the dreadful 11,000-seat **Wembley Arena** (outside zones; Empire Way, Wembley, Middlesex; (0208) 902-8833 or (0870) 739-0739; www.wembley.co.uk/venues; tube: Wembley Park); the 20,000-seat **Earl's Court Exhibition Centre** (zone 11; Warwick Road, SW5; (0207) 385-1200, www.eco.co.uk; tube: Earl's Court); and the 12,000-capacity **London Arena** (zone 6; Limeharbour, Isle of Dogs, E14; (0207) 538-1212; www.londonarena.co.uk; tube: take Jubilee to Canary Wharf, change to Docklands Light Rail south to Crossharbour & London Arena). Of course, the sheer vastness of these coliseums tends to undermine the sonic and visual aspects of performance, and refreshments are overpriced. Still, if you want to catch the gargantuas of rock and pop, you'll probably have to go to these places.

Smaller-scale venues are preferable in every way. The midsize **Shepherd's Bush Empire** (near zone 12; Shepherd's Bush Green; W12; (0207) 771-2000; www.shepherds-bush-empire.co.uk; tube: Shepherd's Bush) had previously been the BBC Television Theatre before developing into a top popular music spot with an excellent sound system. The Empire has a three-tiered seating arrangement, and the first balcony has better views than the ground floor. Expect to pay £5–£30 for tickets.

The **Brixton Academy** (zone 5; 211 Stockwell Road, SW9; (0207) 924-9999; www.brixton-academy.co.uk; tube: Brixton) has a 4,300-person capacity with a seated balcony and standing room at ground level. Many popular bands perform here, and the place has a good atmosphere. However, it does lie within one of London's more dodgy areas, so use common sense and don't go wandering around after the gig.

Dance Clubs

London has a huge range of nightclubs, offering everything from hard-core techno to smooth jazz to tabletop dancers. London's clubs generally provide excellent quality. However, select clubs may sometimes refuse to admit you on the basis of a doorman's arbitrary decision.

Therefore, it may be a good idea not to set your heart on one club when there are so many to choose from. Only do make an early start—before 11 p.m.—then, should the doorman prove intractable, you have the option—indeed, satisfaction—of repairing to a rival club.

Many clubs offer reduced admission rates before 10:30 p.m., and it is easier to gain admittance at that hour. A club that is quiet at 11 p.m. can often be packed to the rafters by midnight.

Some clubs in London start late and carry on until 6 a.m., with their busiest period between 11:30 p.m. and 2 a.m. If you intend to dine at the club, we recommend you book a table for 10 p.m., after which you will be permitted to stay on for the dancing. Not all clubs serve dinner; call the club and ask for information.

The following clubs (all profiled in the following section) are reliably fun, and have managed to withstand the violent winds of change that constantly blow through the club scene: **Embargo, Hanover Grand, Ministry of Sound,** and **Café de Paris.** Most venues have a rotation of club nights, with musical themes such as techno, blues, ska, trance, house and garage, rhumba, salsa, or disco. Some have school-night parties where you have to wear a school uniform to get in. Best to check in *Time Out, What's On,* or Thursday's *Metro Life* magazine section of the *Evening Standard* newspaper to see what is offered at which club so you aren't turned away for not wearing your old school tie or skirt.

Bars and Pubs

The British are, generally speaking, formidable drinkers, with the pub having stood since time immemorial as the central institution in the British experience. Sadly, pubs have been closing in droves in the last decade, victims of high rents, gentrification, and changing fashions. What used to be a quiet neighborhood place for the local working man to get quietly inebriated with his friends has had to change with the times by offering entertainment, upgrading its menu (there are more than a few Thai-food pubs in London), charging extortionate prices for a pint, or coming up with some hook to get the punters in. A favorite tradition of some bars and pubs is the Quiz/Trivia Night, which provides great entertainment—and education—while you drink.

Keeping pace with the British as they effortlessly knock back pint after pint is not an easy task for the uninitiated. Still, accomplished boozers, after putting in an appropriate amount of time and practice, should be able to hold up their end of the proceedings. If, however, you have inadvertently permeated the wall of British reserve to strike up an acquaintance with some friendly natives in a pub, and it is your turn to spring for a round but you haven't finished your pint, it is better to swallow one's pride, rather than keep everyone waiting, and head over to the bar, cash in hand.

It's no surprise that the British lead the world at the sport of drinking pints of beer. Their superb beer comes in a variety of appealing guises, including lager (light continental beer), bitter (rightly named Anglo-Saxon ale), mild (concocted with chocolate malt), cider (fermented apple juice), and shandy (half lager, half lemonade). Best of all are real ales, the boozy equivalent of organic whole-meal bread.

Pub food also can be surprisingly good, depending on the overall quality of the pub itself. Most pubs are strongly historical in ambience, with walls festooned with attractive eighteenth- and nineteenth-century bric-a-brac. In winter, many pubs have a roaring fire, and in summer, a beer garden.

Although bars with a special-hours certificate may remain open until 3 a.m., pubs tend to close at 11 p.m. on weekdays and at midnight on weekends. Britain, however, is forging ever closer ties with Europe, and British licensing laws are expected to soon be extended to match those of other EU member states.

If you wish to include a visit to an archetypal olde-worlde inn on your agenda, you could not do better than the **Prospect of Whitby** (zone 4; 57 Wapping Wall, E1; (0207) 481-1095; tube: Wapping). Whitby dates back to 1520 and is mentioned in Pepys's diary. The pub is renowned for its Elizabethan pewter bar, flagstone floors, cast-iron hearths, and small round windows. It is open daily, 11:30 a.m.–3 p.m. and 5:30–11 p.m.

A haven for journalists and scribblers of all types since before 1666, when it was singed by the Great Fire, **Ye Old Cheshire Cheese** (zone 2; 145 Fleet Street, EC4; (0207) 353-6170; tube: Blackfriars) is a storybook tavern replete with blazing fires, nooks and crannies, wooden floors, and sundry bars and dining sections. During your visit to Old Cheesy, you may as well raise a glass to previous regulars Thackeray, Johnson, Voltaire, Pope, and Tennyson. It's open noon–11 p.m. daily.

By contrast, **The Saint** (zone 7; 8 Great Newport Street, WC2; (0207) 240-1551; www.thebreakfastgroup.co.uk; tube: Leicester Square) is ultramodern, with its patronizing door staff; chic, spotlit decor; and attractive cocktails and cuisine. It is open 5 p.m.–2 a.m. on weekdays and 5 p.m.–3 a.m. on weekends.

One venue worth visiting, with three great individual bars under one roof, is the **Hilton Hotel** (zone 8; Park Lane, W1; (0207) 493-8000; www.hilton.com; tube: Hyde Park Corner or Green Park). If Britain's inclement weather causes you to yearn for sunnier climes, you might like to go to the hotel's **Trader Vic's** (phone (0207) 208-4113) for an ersatz night on a South Pacific island. Home of the Mai Tai cocktail and delicious food, Vic's is something of a mood lagoon. It's open Monday–Saturday, 5 p.m.–12:45 a.m. and Sunday, 5–10:30 p.m. Alternately, you could venture up to the 28th floor to the chichi and romantic **Windows Bar and Restaurant** (phone (0207) 208-4021), which offers a great view of London. Please note smart/casual dress code (no jeans or sneakers) and you will need to make reservations if you wish to dine. Windows' hours are Monday–Friday, 12:30–2:30 p.m. and 5:30 p.m.–2 a.m.; Saturday, 5:30 p.m.–3 a.m. Finally, the latest addition to the Hilton bar scene is the Zen-trendy **Zeta Bar** (it has a separate entrance on Hertford Street; (0207) 208-4067). Cocktails are the specialty here—either nonalcoholic, delicious, health-inducing "liquid lunches," or the more lethal, alcoholic variety. Good bar food is also available. As the night wears on, a stricter door code is operated—but as long as you look affluent or trendy, you'll have no problem getting in. Zeta Bar is open Monday–Tuesday, noon–1 a.m.; Wednesday–Friday, noon–3 a.m.; Saturday, 5 p.m.–3 a.m.; and Sunday, 5–10:30 p.m.

A Sexy City

The oldest profession has long flourished in London, with some of its more accomplished practitioners establishing links with the greatest names in England. Indeed, many noble lines were started by the illegitimate progeny of a royal sire and his concubine—an argument the Labour Party used in its abolishment of the right of hereditary peers to sit in the House of Lords.

Although prostitution is not as endemic as it was during its Victorian heyday (when even Tory Prime Minister Gladstone used to prowl the streets, in quest of fallen women in need of reforming), one cannot enter a telephone box in the central London of today without noticing the numerous salacious cards deposited within.

Soho is the sex center of London, and the area around Old Compton Street hosts quite a few sex shops and strip clubs. Beware of unlicensed venues, though, for they are, quite literally, tourist traps. A common practice of these establishments is to plant a siren-like hostess at the door who lures her victim inside for a drink and a show. The hapless fellow subsequently discovers that the bill for her orange juice and his beer comes to some astronomically unreasonable figure—and there are always a number of belligerent security staff on hand to ensure that customers pay up.

If you don't fancy the Soho scene, which is frankly still a bit sleazy, despite local clean-up campaigns, the next safest bet would be the erotic shows held at the following venues. These are mainly "saucy" cabaret shows or lap-dance clubs.

For Your Eyes Only (zone 8; 11 White Horse Street, W1 (0808) 100-8899; tube: Green Park; and 28 Abbey Road, Park Royal, NW10; (0208)

965-7699; www.fyeo.co.uk; tube: Park Royal) is the place to go if you want your dancers to go the "full monty." It's open Monday–Wednesday, 7:30 p.m.–2:30 a.m.; Thursday–Saturday, 7:30 p.m.–3 a.m.

Stringfellow's (zone 7; 16 Upper St. Martin's Lane, Covent Garden, WC2; (0207) 240-5534; www.stringfellows.com; tube: Leicester Square) Peter Stringfellow's club pays host to the mass-market sort of celebrity: soap stars, footballers, and AWMs (actress/model/whatevers). The place is rife with 1980s glamour and pleasant enough in its way, particularly since Stringfellow's came into possession of a table-dancing license. It's open Monday–Saturday, 7:30 p.m.–3 a.m.

Sophisticats at Voltane (zone 8; 1 Marylebone Lane, W1; (0208) 201-8804 or 201-8968; tube: Bond Street) is presided over by the amiable Catman, David Simones, and was recently the subject of a seven-part television documentary; it features ballerinas and showgirls from all over the world. Indeed, Sophisticats has a distinctly Parisian decadence about it; in addition to the twice-nightly Catgirl cabaret, the club also provides table dancing, caviar girls, and cocktail waitresses. It is recommended, since it is a private club, that you call first to see if you can get a reservation. It's open Monday–Friday, 8:30 p.m.–3 a.m.

Gaming in the United Kingdom

The gaming industry in Great Britain is one of the most carefully regulated in the world. All casinos across England, Scotland, and Wales are licensed under the Gaming Act of 1968, which stipulates that unless already a member or the guest of a member, a player must register at the casino 24 hours before entering to play. The Gaming Act is designed to protect the public purse from the perils of compulsive gambling. Or, in the strictest legalese: it is a legal requirement that the membership application form is signed on the premises of the casino. A passport, driver's license, or other suitable identification is required. Authorization of all new memberships takes 24 hours. The casinos of London Clubs International begin with the magnificent **50 St. James** (zone 7; 50 St. James Street, SW1; (0207) 491-4678; tube: Piccadilly), which opened as London's first club built for the purpose of gaming, in 1828, and is, along with the legendary **Les Ambassadeurs Club** (zone 8; 5 Hamilton Place, W1; (0207) 495-5555; www.clublci.com; tube: Hyde Park), at the top end of the market. These exclusive and lavishly appointed clubs are frequented by royalty, the aristocracy, and celebrated figures from the world of entertainment. Both clubs are open daily, 2 p.m.–4 a.m. The dress code prohibits jeans, and men are expected to wear coats and ties in the evenings.

Midmarket venues include the **Rendezvous Casino** (zone 8; 14 Old Park Lane, W1; (0207) 491-8586; www.clublci.com; tube: Hyde Park), with its spacious gaming floor, French-influenced bistro, and relaxed sports bar; and **The Sportsman Casino** (zone 8; 40 Bryanston Street, W1; (0207) 414-0061; www.clublci.com; tube: Hyde Park), designed in the style of a Mississippi riverboat. As well as offering roulette, blackjack, and baccarat, the Sportsman boasts a dice game that has proven to be particularly popular with American visitors. Both clubs are open from about noon until 6 a.m.; gaming begins at 2 p.m. The dress code is smart/casual; no jeans are allowed. Coats and ties are required for men in the evening.

The mass-market **Golden Nugget Casino** (zone 7; 22 Shaftesbury Avenue, W1; (0207) 439-0099; www.clublci.com; tube: Piccadilly) is the largest and busiest casino in the London Clubs group. It offers a fast-moving environment and fast food to go with it. The atmosphere of this casino is both friendly and informal. Games include roulette, baccarat, blackjack, and stud poker; it is open daily, 2 p.m.–6 a.m.

Freeloader's Forum

Visitors to London rapidly discover the disparity in prices between goods and services purchased in England and pretty much anywhere else in the world. British merchandise is far more expensive due to, among other things, the legalized swindle called the Recommended Retail Price Index, whereby prices are fixed at scandalously high levels by agreement between manufacturers and retail outlets.

But please do not complain about Britain's rip-off prices to those working on the shop floor, because although company bosses are raking it in, the poor worker at the checkout counter makes considerably less than he or she would in America. Yet the British can also be generous, as evidenced by the bonanza of free activities taking place throughout London.

Free Music

Many churches in central London, such as **St. John's** (zone 7; Waterloo Road; tube: Waterloo), **St. Martin-in-the-Fields** (zone 7; St. Martin's Place; tube: Leicester Square or Charing Cross), and **St. Pancras Church** (zone 15; Euston Road; tube: Euston) offer free lunchtime classical concerts and recitals, as do music schools such as the **Royal College of Music** (zone 13; Prince Consort Road, SW7; (0207) 591-4314; www.rcm.ac.uk; tube: Gloucester Road or High Street Kensington) and the **Royal Academy of Music** (zone 14; Marylebone Road; (0207) 873-7300; www.ram.ac.uk; tube: Marylebone or Baker Street). Performances at the Royal College of Music are held Monday–Thursday at 1:05 p.m., and during term time they are held evenings at 7 p.m. Performances at the Royal Academy of Music are held daily at 1:05 and 5:05 p.m.

You can also hear a mixture of musical delights at the aptly named **Freestage at the Barbican** (zone 3; Silk Street, EC2; (0207) 638-8891; www.barbican.org.uk; tube: Barbican) and at the **South Bank's National**

Theatre (zone 5; South Bank, SE1; (0207) 452-3000; www.national theatre.org.uk; tube: Waterloo or Westminster) and **Royal Festival Hall** (zone 5; South Bank, SE1; (0207) 960-4242; www.sbc.org.uk, tube; Westminster or Waterloo). Performances at the Barbican are held daily at 1 p.m.; the National Theatre features music in the foyer area daily at 6 p.m. Performances in the foyer of the Royal Festival Hall run from 12:30 to 2:30 p.m. every day; they also feature jazz on Friday evenings at 7 p.m.

The **100 Club** (zone 8; 100 Oxford Street, W1; (0207) 636-0933; tube: Oxford Street) presents a well-liked series of swing and traditional gigs during Friday lunchtimes. Some bookshops also present free music. Try **Border's Books & Music** (zone 8; 197 Oxford Street, W1; (0207) 292-1600; tube: Oxford Circus) every Friday night, upstairs, at 6:30 p.m.; **Helter Skelter Music Bookshop** (zone 7; 4 Denmark Street, WC2; (0207) 836-1151; tube: Tottenham Court Road); and **Filthy MacNasty's Whiskey Café** (zone 2; 68 Amwell Street, EC1; (0207) 837-6067; www.philkav@globalnet.co.uk; tube: Angel) for a DJ on Friday nights and live music on Saturday evenings and Sunday afternoons.

Free Friday can be found at the **Cock Tavern** (zone 15; Phoenix Road, NW1; (0207) 387-1884; tube: Euston), where you can enjoy a variety of music and pints and alco-pops (frozen liquor on a stick) costing only £3, which is as cheap as can be found in London. Numerous bars, restaurants, and pubs also supply the customer with free music. Check *Time Out, What's On,* and *Metro Life* for listings.

Free Comedy

Since the practice of adding canned laughter to television soundtracks was universally condemned, the BBC now requires a constant supply of jolly spectators willing to be audience members for their comedy productions. For free tickets—just imagine the fun you'll have telling everyone back home that you appeared on British TV—contact the BBC Ticket Unit at Room 30, Design Building, BBC TV Centre, Wood Lane, W12 7RJ; (0208) 576-1227.

LONDON NIGHTCLUBS		
Name	**Description**	**Zone**
Bagleys	Gigantic disco and bar	15
Browns	Glamorous disco	7
Café de Paris	London's most renowned club	7
Dover Street Restaurant	Large jazz restaurant and bar	8
Down Mexico Way	Mexican fiesta of food, fun, and salsa	8
Embargo	Chelsea dance club	11
Emporium	High-tech, ultramodern dance club	7

LONDON NIGHTCLUBS *(continued)*		
Name	**Description**	**Zone**
The Fridge Bar	Brixton's most celebrated disco	5
The Glasshouse	Nightclub in a theater in the city	3
Hanover Grand	Popular discotheque	8
Heaven	Gay dance club	7
Hippodrome	Tourist trap dance club	7
Jazz Café	Modern jazz club	15
Metro Club	Venerable live rock 'n' roll dive	8
Ministry of Sound	U.K.'s most famous disco	5
Pizza Express	Intimate jazz club and restaurant	7
Ronnie Scott's	London's premier jazz club	7
606 Club	Jazz club and restaurant	11
Turnmills	Late-night disco	3
Zoo Bar	Bar and dance club	7

Nightclub Profiles

Bagleys

GIGANTIC DISCO AND BAR

Who Goes There Youthful dancers and soaks

Zone 15 King's Cross Depot, York Way, N1; (0207) 278-2777; www.bagleys.net; tube: King's Cross

Cover Friday, £6–£20; Saturday, £14 **Prices** Cheap by club standards **Dress** Smart/casual **Food available** Snacks

Hours Friday, 10:30 p.m.–6:30 a.m.; Saturday, 10:30 p.m.–7:30 a.m.

What goes on Sweat rises like smoke off the dance floor. Different fun on different nights. Thursday is disco roller skating from 7 to 10:30 p.m.

Setting & atmosphere Bagleys is colossal, with five dance floors, six bars, and something different going on in every room.

If you go You will be part of a heaving, throbbing mob of young movers in one of the many rooms.

Browns

GLAMOROUS DISCO

Who Goes There Browns has been an oasis to the stars for years and continues to be so. Although ostensibly a private members' club, the public is permitted entrance on Friday and Saturday nights.

Zone 7 4 Great Queen Street, WC2; (0207) 831-0802; tube: Covent Garden

Cover £15 **Prices** Expensive **Dress** Fashionable **Food available** Catering available for large parties

Hours Friday and Saturday, 10:30 p.m.–4 a.m.

What goes on The club has a three-tiered social system: The downstairs dance floor is Midgard; the second floor is the Rainbow Bridge; and the VIP members' bar on the third floor is Asgard, home of the gods.

Setting & atmosphere Loud, glamorous, and urgent.

If you go Call to get on guest list.

Café de Paris

LONDON'S MOST RENOWNED CLUB

Who Goes There Everyone who is anyone in London

Zone 7 3–4 Coventry Street, W1; (0207) 734-7700; www.cafedeparis.com; tube: Piccadilly Circus

Cover £15 **Prices** Somewhat pricey **Dress** Elegant **Food available** French cuisine, of course

Hours Closes at 3 a.m.

What goes on Live jazz music accompanies dinner, after which a DJ spins records for the more athletically inclined. The café is furnished with numerous bars.

Setting & atmosphere Since its launch in the 1920s, Café de Paris has been synonymous with high society—even the queen has given a party there. Such luminous performers as Marlene Dietrich, Maurice Chevalier, Fred Astaire, Noël Coward, Frank Sinatra, Edith Piaf, and your humble correspondent have graced its stage. Plush, opulent, and elegant, the Café's art deco design was influenced by the operas *Don Giovanni* and *La Bohème*. A 50-foot bar encompasses the oval ballroom, and the restaurant is highly regarded.

If you go You will be dining, drinking, and dancing in style. You may, however, need to know the right people to get in. Therefore we suggest that you circumvent all of the nonsense at the door by booking a table for dinner. Please do not turn up in your baseball cap and sneakers.

Dover Street Restaurant & Bar

A LARGE AND JUSTLY POPULAR JAZZ RESTAURANT AND BAR

Who Goes There Numerous personalities from the worlds of stage, film, television, and sport mingle with white-collar workers

Zone 8 8–10 Dover Street, W1; (0207) 491-7509; www.doverst.co.uk; tube: Green Park

Cover £7–£15 **Prices** Reasonable **Dress** Smart/casual; jeans and sneakers are not permitted **Food available** Lunch menu offers a good deal; French and Mediterranean cuisine served until 2 a.m.

Hours Monday–Friday, 5:30 p.m.–3 a.m.; Saturday, 7 p.m.–3 a.m.

What goes on Fine dining, live music, dancing, and DJs.

Setting & atmosphere Dover Street has been established as one of London's most atmospheric restaurants and jazz, blues, and R&B venues for over 25 years and has recently been refurbished to become the largest venue of its kind in the capital. This place swings.

If you go Remember to adhere to the dress code.

Down Mexico Way

THREE FLOORS OF FOOD, FUN, AND FIESTA, MEXICAN-STYLE

Who Goes There Twentysomethings, salsa fiends, boisterous parties

Zone 8   25 Swallow Street, W1; (0207) 437-9895; tube: Piccadilly Circus

Cover No **Prices** Not too bad, for London **Dress** Casual **Food available** Full Mexican menu

Hours Daily lunch to 3 a.m.

What goes on Although it's not actually run by Mexicans, the food is close enough to authentic and there's a distinctly Southern vibe here, with no cover charge, no velvet rope, and lots of fun. Salsa lessons prepare you for the late night revelries, as do the excellent margaritas.

Setting & atmosphere Truly gorgeous decor of hand-painted tiles that are rumored to have been nicked from the King of Portugal a hundred years ago.

If you go Try the nachos, do tequila shots, and try to salsa.

Embargo

CHELSEA'S ALWAYS-IN-VOGUE DESIGNER DANCE CLUB

Who Goes There The young single Chelsea set

Zone 11   533B King's Road, SW10; (0207) 351-5038; tube: Sloane Square

Cover £10 **Prices** Slightly pricey **Dress** Stylish **Food available** A modern European restaurant serves dinner

Hours Daily, 9:30 p.m.–2 a.m.

What goes on Despite the occasionally sadistic doorkeepers, Embargo still draws a trendy crowd that dances the night away to thunderous house DJs. **Setting & atmosphere** A modern designer club with clean, hard surfaces and mirrors, Embargo is often attended by beautiful young women.

If you go Don't disturb the beautiful young people.

Emporium

MOST DISCOS WOULD LOVE TO HAVE THE DESIGN AND SOUND OF THIS PLACE

Who Goes There Sports stars and soap stars

Zone 7 62 Kingly Street, W1; (0207) 734-3190; tube: Tottenham Court Road

Cover £10–£15 **Prices** Expensive **Dress** Smart—no sneakers or jeans **Food available** An expensive restaurant

Hours Closes on Saturday at 4 a.m.

What goes on The pop celebrities discuss show biz and football over deafening DJs while waiters dance attendance on them.

Setting & atmosphere A high-tech and ultramodern club glistening with the sheen of success.

If you go Browse through a few tabloids beforehand so that you'll be able to recognize the subjects of the latest scandals.

The Fridge Bar

BRIXTON'S MOST CELEBRATED DISCO

Who Goes There The clientele varies according to what is on during any given night, but the Fridge has been playing host to the gay and lesbian market for some time now.

Zone 5 Town Hall Parade, Brixton Hill, SW2; (0207) 326-5100; www.fridge.co.uk; tube: Brixton

Cover Friday, £5–£12 **Prices** Average **Dress** Casual **Food available** Fast

Hours Daily, 10 p.m.–6 a.m.

What goes on Dancing and trancing out to techno.

Setting & atmosphere With a vast dance floor, a huge bar, capacious balconies, and plenty of variety in the theme nights, the Fridge is a place to really let it all hang out. Highly recommended for the open-minded. Renowned DJs spinning every night. Call for special-event information. Some nights only those over 22 or 23 are admitted.

If you go Call a respectable minicab company to get home.

The Glasshouse

COOL CLUB IN THE CITY SET WITHIN THE MERMAID THEATRE

Who Goes There Fewer city-boys than you'd think, given its location within the Square Mile; depends on what kind of club night is being promoted, but you can bet on plenty of young, hip-hopping dance freaks

Zone 3 The Mermaid Theatre Building, Puddle Dock, EC4 Blackfriars; (0207) 248-5444; www.glasshouse-club.com, tube: Blackfriars

Cover £5–£15 **Prices** Low to moderate **Dress** Smart/casual **Food available** bar snacks

Hours Daily, 10 p.m.–5 a.m.

What goes on This is popular for promoters, who host a variety of special treats for the patrons: There are smartie-parties, school-night discos, gay raves, you name it. Check the website.

Setting & atmosphere Good-looking and appealing decor throughout the three themed rooms.

If you go Eat first—the low-priced alco-pops and brews are sure to go to your head.

Hanover Grand

A POPULAR DISCOTHEQUE

Who Goes There Fashionistas during the week, while the house set attends on Friday and Saturday

Zone 8 6 Hanover Street, W1; (0207) 499-7977; www.hanovergrand.com; tube: Oxford Circus

Cover £8–£15 **Prices** Uppish **Dress** Smart/casual **Food available** No

Hours Daily, 10:30 p.m.–5 a.m.

What goes on Different evenings include Fresh 'n' Funky on Wednesday, schooldisco.com on Friday, carwash on Saturday and plenty of good dancing any day of the week.

Setting & atmosphere The club has a capacity for 800 people, with two dance floors and five bars on three levels.

If you go Don't dress down on the weeknights.

Heaven

GAY PARADISE

Who Goes There Party animals of both hetero- and homosexual persuasion

Zone 7 The Arches, Villiers Street, WC2; (0207) 930-2020; www.heaven-london.com; tube: Embankment or Charing Cross

Cover £12 **Prices** Average **Dress** Flamboyant **Food available** Coffee bar–type sandwiches and munchies

Hours Daily, 10:30 p.m.–3 a.m.; Friday and Saturday, 10 p.m.–6 a.m.

What goes on Originally a gay club, London quickly twigged that the fun quotient was sky-high here, and now everyone is dying to get into Heaven. Check website for special nights.

Setting & atmosphere The crowded rooms pulsate to techno music.

If you go Arrive before 10:30 p.m. Heaven is notorious for the length of its queues.

Hippodrome

TOURIST TRAP

Who Goes There Unwary tourists

Zone 7 Leicester Square, W1; (0207) 437-4311; www.londonhippodrome.com; tube: Leicester Square

Cover £12 **Prices** Slightly pricey **Dress** Smart **Food available** Bar snacks

Hours Tuesday–Saturday, 9 p.m.–3 a.m.

What goes on Drinking, dancing, and flirting to top 40.

Setting & atmosphere Opened in 1900 as a circus, it's still got that vibe. A gigantic lighting rig, black mirrors, a large neon sign over the entrance, and a superb sound system playing chart toppers. Take advantage of the Saturday-night drink specials—buy one get one free.

If you go Don't admit it.

Jazz Café

MODERN CLUB GEARED TOWARD RAP, SOUL, FUNK, AND JAZZ

Who Goes There 20–55-year-olds, depending on whether jazz or rap is featured

Zone 15 5 Parkway, N1, Camden Town; (0207) 916-6060; www.jazzcafe.co.uk; tube Camden Town

Cover £5–£30 according to the popularity of the act **Prices** Average **Dress** Anything goes **Food available** Dinner is offered via a modern European menu

Hours The Jazz Café remains open until 2 a.m. on Friday and Saturday.

What goes on This club's name is something of a misnomer, as is the radio station Jazz FM's. Both entities attempt to confer the superior artistic status of jazz on lesser forms of music. Thus the Jazz Café, on any given night, may have rap, soul, or funk bands performing rather than jazz groups. I therefore suggest that you consult the listings pages of *Time Out* or *Metro Life* magazine before going.

Setting & atmosphere The bar leads onto the dance floor, where there are some seats available. The restaurant is situated on the balcony overlooking the stage, and projectors transmit arty neon images onto the awnings.

If you go Tell the soul band that is performing that you thought you were coming to a jazz club and then ask them to attempt a rendition of John Coltrane's "Giant Steps."

Metro Club

AUTHENTIC HEADBANGER DIVE WITH IMPRESSIVE ROCK 'N' ROLL HISTORY

Who Goes There Live music lovers who aren't particular about fashion or decor

Zone 8 19 Oxford Street, W1; (0207) 437-0964; tube: Oxford Circus

Cover Depends on who's playing **Prices** Cheap **Dress** Very casual **Food available** none

Hours Depends on who's playing; closes at 4 a.m.

What goes on This is a good old Soho rock and roller, where Queen and Black Sabbath played in the early days, and where you just might catch the next big act. After 11, a DJ spins punk, metal, and rock till the wee hours.

Setting & atmosphere It's not going to win any design awards, but you can drink cheaply here, and you can hear some new artists and possibly some great music.

If you go Make sure you're up for the live act that's playing.

Ministry of Sound

THE UNITED KINGDOM'S MOST FAMOUS DISCO

Who Goes There Regulars who've been coming for years, as well as newcomers

Zone 5   103 Gaunt Street, SE1, Elephant and Castle; (0207) 378-6562; www.ministry ofsound.com; tube: Elephant and Castle

Cover Friday, £12; Saturday, £15 **Prices** Slightly expensive **Dress** Glamorous **Food available** None

Hours Friday, 10:30 p.m.–6 a.m.; Saturday, midnight–8 a.m.

What goes on Young to youngish clubbers bopping to monotonously loud and repetitious drum 'n' bass grooves.

Setting & atmosphere Ministry of Sound is a vast converted warehouse located in the not exactly salubrious boondocks of Elephant and Castle, so you must be sure to take a cab both there and back. You will need plenty of energy because this place will blow your head off. Check the listings pages of the press for the nights on which American DJs are imported to show the locals how it is done. You will find yourself dancing to everything from U.K. garage to R&B hits. Get ready for a fun time!

If you go Wear your dancing shoes.

Pizza Express

AN INTIMATE JAZZ CLUB AND RESTAURANT

Who Goes There Pizza and jazz lovers of both the tourist and local variety

Zone 7   10 Dean Street, W1; (0207) 439-8722; tube: Tottenham Court Road

Cover £10–£20, depending on the band **Prices** Average **Dress** Casual **Food available** Pizza, pasta, lasagna, salad Niçoise, and so on

Hours Opens at 7:45 p.m., with shows beginning at 9 p.m., and closes at midnight.

What goes on Eighty percent of the bands booked are celebrated Americans of the status of Tal Farlow, Art Farmer, Kenny Garret, and Roy

Haynes. Pizza Express also books top British talent such as Martin Taylor and Guy Barker.

Setting & atmosphere Pizza Express is an intimate basement club equipped with modern stage lighting and sound. The environment is friendly, sophisticated, and relaxed.

If you go Order pizza—it's what they do best.

Ronnie Scott's

LONDON'S PREMIER JAZZ CLUB

Who Goes There Yuppies, buppies, musicians, and arty types come to hear the world's best jazz musicians in the downstairs club, while the younger set tends to congregate around the upstairs dance floor.

Zone 7 47 Frith Street, W1; (0121) 643-4525; tube: Tottenham Court Road

Cover Varies. Free if you belong to the musician's union; £20 is normal for a Saturday **Prices** A little lower than average **Dress** Smart **Food available** A full menu of modern European cuisine and a la carte as well

Hours Daily, 8 p.m.–3 a.m.

What goes on Affluent diners and drinkers are serenaded by famous musicians downstairs while others choose to attend the upstairs disco. Doors open at 8 p.m. and the live shows start at 9:30 p.m.

Setting & atmosphere Ronnie's is pushing 40 now and is as close as London will ever get to the classic sort of jazz club you have seen in films.

If you go Prepare for an enjoyable evening.

606 Club

A HIGHLY REGARDED JAZZ CLUB AND RESTAURANT OPEN FOR OVER 25 YEARS

Who Goes There Yuppies, buppies, and bohemians, young and old

Zone 11 90 Lots Road, SW10; (0207) 352-5953; www.606.co.uk; tube Sloane Square

Cover There is no cover per se, but there is a music charge of £4.75 per person Sunday–Thursday, and £6 on Friday and Saturday, which is added onto the bill at the end of the night **Prices** Modest to reasonable **Dress** Casual **Food available** An extensive European-based menu, featuring a wide selection of meat, fresh fish, and vegetarian meals. The cuisine at the 606 has been praised by the *Sunday Times* and TV's *The Restaurant Show,* among others.

Hours Friday and Saturday, 8 p.m.–2 a.m.; Sunday, 8 p.m.–midnight; Monday–Wednesday, 7:30 p.m.–midnight; Thursday, 8 p.m.–1:30 a.m.

What goes on There are two jazz groups on each night from Monday through Wednesday playing from 7:30 p.m. until midnight. One band is featured, playing from around 8 p.m. until 11 p.m. The groups are selected from a variety of up-and-coming players and more established musicians. The music ranges from traditional to contemporary, with an emphasis on the modern.

Setting & atmosphere A basement club with a relaxed atmosphere, the 606 is a great place to take a date for a late supper and a bottle of wine.

If you go Don't ask any of the bands to play "Tie a Yellow Ribbon."

Turnmills

THE DISCO WHERE ALL NIGHTCLUBBERS END UP

Who Goes There Hard-core club hoppers; Turnmills also hosts Trade, Britain's top gay night

Zone 3 63B Clerkenwell Road, EC1; (0207) 250-3409; tube: Farringdon

Cover £10 on Saturday only **Prices** Lowish **Dress** Casual **Food available** Yes, bar food

Hours Friday, 10:30 p.m.–7:30 a.m.; Saturday, 10 p.m.–5 a.m.

What goes on In addition to the mandatory drinking and dancing, this club provides a few pinball machines.

Setting & atmosphere Candlelit tables and an Electronica bar area provide a refreshing contrast to the throbbing chaos of the dance floor.

If you go Take a taxi both there and back—if you last until 7 a.m. you will be in no condition to find your way home.

Zoo Bar

BAR AND DANCE CLUB

Who Goes There Eclectic range of regulars, from laborers to lawyers, and plenty of young tourists. Over 21 only.

Zone 7 13–17 Bear Street, Leicester Square, WC2; (0207) 839-4188; tube: Leicester Square

Cover Monday–Wednesday after 9 p.m., £3; Thursday, £4; Friday and Saturday after 9 p.m., £5, after 11 p.m., £8 **Prices** Average; about £3 a drink and less at happy hour **Dress** Trendy **Food available** Snacks

Hours Daily, 4 p.m.–3 a.m.

What goes on A mixed bag, very laid-back. Everyone is there to have a great time. There are happy hours every night, and good dance music, too.

Setting & atmosphere Two floors of fun. On the first floor, there is a bar area in which to mingle and meet friends. The basement floor has a huge dance floor surrounded by a few smaller bars to ease traffic flow.

If you go Beware of the throngs of Leiscester Square on the weekends—it's a zoo, so hold on to your valuables.

Part Ten

Shopping in London

It's safe to say that everything is cheaper outside of London, especially in the United States. It's common for any Londoner going abroad, from taxi drivers to investment bankers, to take an empty suitcase to load up with the comparatively low-priced clothing and household goods found in Anytown, USA; Australia; New Zealand; or Canada. Even prices in Paris are better than in London, which is the most expensive city in the European Union. This has something to do with the fact that England is an island without much manufacturing, and goods must be delivered. And the sky-high rents that central London shops must pay don't help prices either.

So as not to completely dash your shopping dreams, let me hasten to emphasize that London has a vibrant shopping scene, with stores, stalls, and shops as far as the eye can see and some goods that are difficult to find elsewhere. Some of these things, like the hundreds of items with the Harrods name and logo plastered on them, you wouldn't necessarily want to find anywhere else, but others, like Liberty scarves, bespoke shirts from Harvie & Hudson, and bath products from Lush, are a must for the worldly shopper. If you come during the big sales, the best being during the month of January (there's also one in August), you just might be able to pay fair-to-good prices for stuff you can't readily get at home. These January and August sales are a retail tradition to make way for the next season of goods, but you can also expect some closing-down sales, minor spur-of-the-moment sales, or just plain desperate-to-sell sales in any given month.

Wise Buys in London

The following items are worth buying in London because of their high quality or their unavailability in the United States. See our "Where to Find" section later in this chapter for information on shops that sell these items.

Antiques

If you're an early bird and can get up before dawn to get to the early-morning Bermonsey Market, or check out the Camden Passage on Wednesdays, you'll find a huge selection in London at decent prices. At one time you did not have to pay VAT on antiques, but alas, those days are over. You can bargain around the VAT by paying cash at some places. There are also Antique Centers, wonderful warrens of individual stalls selling everything from military artifacts to charms for bracelets.

Aromatic Body Stuff

Bath oils, salts, soaps, and scents abound in London, made by Culpepper the Herbalist, Neal's Yard Remedies, Floris, Lush, Crabtree & Evelyn, and Penhaligon; and there are always some less well-known products making a name for themselves in stores such as Space.NK or Harvey Nichols.

Bone China

Look in the stalls on Portobello Road in Notting Hill on Saturday market day, or at the Reject China Shops (phone (0207) 434-2502) for patterns you can't find at home. Even Harrods can provide some deals at sale times, and their stock is enormous. Crystal goods, too, can be cheaper than in other countries.

Books

London is a city of readers, and there are thousands of bookstores that cater to readers with all possible interests. You can get books here that are only published in England, antiquarian volumes in gorgeous sets, and crates full of secondhand books. The Harry Potter or Lord of the Rings books published here are more attractive to the serious fan because of the unedited English spelling, punctuation, vocabulary and idioms (the first Harry Potter book, for example, is entitled *Harry Potter and the Philosopher's Stone,* rather than the less historically precise *Sorcerer's Stone,* as it is called in America).

Children's Clothing

Some children's clothing may be, if not cheaper, of better quality and value than in the States. English smock dresses and French baby clothes are beautiful, and you don't have to pay VAT. There is a new trend of designers (Dior, Jigsaw, Paul Smith, to name a few) making children's clothing, which well-heeled Londoners have taken to enthusiastically.

Designer Clothing

Secondhand, that is. There are tons of resale shops in which you can get "preowned" Chanel, Voyage, Prada, Dolce & Gabbana, Gucci, Matthew Williamson, Westwood, Armani, you name it, for (relatively) reasonable prices. A lot of ladies seem to have worn these clothes twice and moved on to the next big thing. There are outlets in which you might find semi-good deals on brand new English and French designer clothes, but it's an iffy business, dependent on exchange rates and the size of the VAT refund.

Fabrics

England has long been known for its gorgeous fabrics; try John Lewis or Peter Jones for the best deals on locally made material and things like elaborate trim and curtain swags. Antique fabrics are also available at specialty shops or for auction.

Souvenirs of London

Yes, cheaper here than anywhere, naturally. The best buys are on the street in stalls; Oxford Street, Leicester Square, Soho (Tottenham Court Road), and Piccadilly Circus are the places to look. For more quirky or upscale souvenirs of London, you must see the gift shops of Westminster Abbey, British Museum, Queen's Gallery, Hampton Court Palace, Victoria and Albert Museum, and the Tower of London.

Stationery

Filofax, the personal organizer so well loved by professionals in the States, is an indigenous English product and much cheaper here than anywhere else, especially at sale time. Which is not to say it's all that affordable.

Time to Shop

Stores in central London open late and close early. The usual times are 10 a.m. to 6 p.m., with a few opening at 9 a.m. (but closing at 5 p.m.), and a very few, like Waterstone's Bookstores, staying open until 9:30 p.m. (the Piccadilly branch stays open until 11:30 p.m.). Some places, such as those in Covent Garden and some fashionable stores, don't open until 10:30 or 11 a.m.

There is a "late" night for shopping. Stores stay open until 7 or 8 p.m. on Thursdays on Oxford Street, Regent Street, and the West End. Just to keep you on your toes, Knightsbridge's and Chelsea's late night is Wednesday. Sunday is finally starting to join the rest of the week as a shopping day, with most stores (except for the big department stores and the mom-and-pop stores) opening for at least a half day, from noon to 5 or 6 p.m. Shockingly, Harrods has broken with tradition to open on Sundays during the weeks leading up to Christmas (can't imagine why). Street markets follow their own muse as far as opening hours and days go.

Paying Up

All the major credit cards are taken at most shops. Some stores will take traveler's checks in British sterling, but they don't even want to hear about

U.S. dollar traveler's checks. If they are kind enough to cash them, it may not be at a rate favorable to you. (Bring a passport to cash traveler's checks.) A good exchange rate is available at Harrods and at Marks and Spencer.

The credit card is a mixed blessing. On the plus side, you'll have a record of your purchases and the exchange rate will be fair. The rate used will be that on the day the credit purchase clears the credit card company or bank. Be careful about which card you use: Some credit cards have recently started adding from 1–2% on each purchase made in a foreign currency— "conversion costs." This is a real rip-off and can run into a huge amount of money between hotel costs, restaurants, and shopping trips. One way to avoid this is to put lots of money in your bank account and use your bank card to get cash to pay for the bulk of your purchases. At some small shops, paying cash can get you a bit of a discount—give it a try.

As for VAT

Value-added tax is the mind-boggling 17.5% the British government adds on to the cost of all goods and services except for books, food, and children's clothing. Most goods will have the VAT already figured into the price on the tags, but other items, especially those sold at fancy knickknack stores and other high-priced shops, try to prevent total sticker shock by placing a discreet "+VAT" after all those zeros. If you have your goods shipped directly from the store, the VAT will be deducted from the price, but you'd have to be paying a lot of money to balance the cost of shipping. There's also the added cost of duty on expensive imported goods when you arrive in the United States. You are allowed $400 per person of goods duty free, and families may combine this allowance, so that a family of five is allowed $2,000 worth of goods. The next $1,000 worth of goods gets charged a flat 10%—after that it will vary according to what type of import you're bringing.

Yes, you may be able to get a refund of some of the VAT you've paid, but it requires a little footwork. I'll let Her Majesty's Customs and Excise Department explain it all, but first, let me get this off my chest: It's true that VAT is expensive, and if you're buying a £1,000 watch or £600 silver salt-and-pepper shakers, go ahead, fill out the form, stand in the line, and get the refund. However, I see so many visitors spending £50 or £100 in a museum souvenir shop and then spending valuable vacation time trying to get a refund that won't really amount to much. Consider that visitors use the public transport, walk on the sidewalks, enjoy the magnificent parks, take pictures of the changing of the guard—basically, they are taking advantage of all the fruits of the National Trust's hard work to make England worth visiting—and they think they are such savvy travelers for getting back less than £10 on every £100 they spend. I don't get it. OK, I feel better. Here's how the VAT-refund process works.

Value-Added Tax Refunds: The Official Story

Here are the highlights from a pamphlet entitled "Guide to Tax Free Shopping—the VAT Refund Scheme" (VAT/704/3/93), produced by Her Majesty's Ministry of Customs and Excise and published here by her kind permission.

What is the retail-export scheme?   When you visit the United Kingdom, you pay value-added tax (VAT) on most things you buy. The retail-export scheme allows you to obtain a refund of the tax on certain goods you intend to export from the European Community (EC).

Can I buy goods under this scheme?   Yes, if you are an overseas visitor who:

- has not been in the EC for more than 365 days in the two years before the date you buy the goods; and
- you intend to leave the EC with all the goods in your personal luggage, within 3three months of the date you bought them.

How do I know which shops operate the scheme?   The shops that operate the scheme usually have a sign in the window advertising the scheme as "tax-free shopping." If in doubt, ask for the "tax-free" sales assistant.

What must I do to obtain a VAT refund?

- ask the shop to complete a VAT or tax-free shopping form (this is very important, as without the form from the shop, you cannot get a refund);
- obtain an EC certification stamp when you leave the EC;
- mail or hand in your stamped forms to obtain your VAT refund.

Do I get all the tax back?   Most shops charge a small administrative fee which will be deducted from the tax refunded to you.

What export documents will I be given?   The shop will give you one of the following VAT-refund documents:

- the customs form VAT 407(1993); or
- a shop's or refund company's tax-free shopping form; or
- a retail-export scheme sales invoice.

These documents are available only from shops operating the scheme, and the shop from which you purchase the goods on which you intend to claim a refund must fill out a portion of the form it provides.

When must I export the goods?   You must permanently export the goods from the EC within three months of purchase.

Do I have to carry all the goods bought under the scheme in my hand baggage?   You should always carry items of high value, including jewelry, furs, cameras, watches, silverware, and small antiques, in your hand baggage. However, if the goods are too large to carry on board an aircraft you may pack them in your hold baggage. If you do this, you must contact the British Customs export officer before you check in. The airline will tell you how to do this.

Do I get the VAT-refund document back? You must give the document and show the goods to Customs at the port or airport when you finally leave the EC. The Customs export officer will certify the document and return it to you so that you can get a refund. These procedures may take some time, so please arrive at least two hours before you are due to depart. (Author's note: I would make that three-and-a-half hours in summer.)

What if I leave the EC on a through (transit) flight via another member state? There are special rules for goods being carried on through flights that leave the EC via another member state.

Hand baggage: Goods carried on as hand baggage and VAT-refund documents must be produced to Customs in the member state of final transfer before leaving the EC. You would process your VAT goods in the United Kingdom, but keep the goods and documents handy for inspection when leaving the EC. The same applies for check-in luggage.

Hold baggage: If you will be leaving the United Kingdom on such a flight and intend carrying large or heavy goods in hold baggage, you should ask the shopkeeper for a separate VAT-refund document for those goods. The goods and VAT-refund document must be produced to U.K. Customs before departure from the United Kingdom.

How do I get a refund? There are several methods to try for getting a refund. You may:

- mail the certified document back to the shopkeeper; or
- mail the certified document to a VAT-refunding company; or
- hand the certified document to a cash-refund booth at the point of departure, if the shopkeeper has authorized you to do so (a charge may be made for this service).

Important Reminder If you do not produce the goods and VAT-refund document to the Customs export officer when you finally leave the EC, you will not get a refund of VAT.

The Unofficial Version

Only those who are NOT British subjects or citizens of other EU countries qualify for VAT refund, and they have to leave the country with their goods within six months.

You will not get the entire 17.5% back—it's more like 10–15% (plus an additional fee that you pay for the processing of the papers) and can actually be as little as 4% with some refund companies.

Ask what is the minimum you must spend in a given shop to qualify for the papers being filled out—it can vary, although the law puts the minimum at £50. Some shops will refuse outright, and some will charge at least £5 for issuing the papers.

You must have the refund form filled out at the place of purchase! You cannot get it done anywhere else by anyone else. Bring your passport to the store.

There are refund companies that handle the VAT refund, and they have set the refund at different rates. The clerk can tell you which company the shop uses and help you decide whether it's worth your while or not.

You must show your VAT-refund purchases at the airport Customs, usually (and most easily) in carry-on luggage. Factor the size of the item against the amount of the refund, times the degree of hassle you're willing to go through.

Go to the Customs official to get the VAT papers before you check in your luggage.

Allow time for all the forms to be filled out—about five minutes for each one.

After you go through passport control, line up at the VAT desk to show them what you've bought and the papers that go with them.

You then get the papers back, mail them to the shop, or take them to the Tax-Free Europe desk. Tax-Free Europe is a tax-refund company that many stores are starting to use to expedite the VAT returns. They give you a cash refund at the airport, but a lot of your money stays in their hands. There's also VatBack, which will do a credit-card refund by mail; this takes about three months, but you'll get a bigger percentage back. They also give immediate cash back, at £8.60 for over £100 of goods or £18.50 for over £500 of goods.

If your VAT-refund items are too big to carry on, budget an extra hour at the airport, as you will need to have a security guard watch you go through passport control and then return the items to your airline for checking.

In the summer and after sales, there are often long lines at the VAT-refund desk at Heathrow, and this is getting worse all the time as people have started working the VAT-refund scheme in earnest.

There is also the possibility of getting the VAT refund from a hotel or holiday apartment, or from a car-rental agency; ask the concierge or the person with whom you book your travel arrangements for the forms and the information.

Salespeople's Attitudes and Behavior

Salespeople in London are (although one hates to make a generalization about such things) among the most laid-back in the world. It's not that they don't want to make a sale; it's just that they don't want to be perceived as pushing anyone to buy something. Except in a few upscale stores, where the staff is rigorously trained to look like they give a damn, the salespeople in London will surprise and perhaps bewilder you with their laissez-faire attitudes. Personally, I find it a relief from the kind of sales style in which you are forced to engage in banter (read: pressured to buy) with salespeople when all you want to do is have a look, but if you are in need of assistance, you will have to get used to approaching them.

There's nothing malicious or lackadaisical about them; it's just that this is not a culture in which overeager selling is admired. Even the famous funny East End sales patter at the markets is more a tradition of being quick and clever than it is of making a sale. The correct response is to be equally laid-back and not get demanding and rude—London salespeople are masters of the cold dismissal, and you won't win.

The Big Shopping Neighborhoods

Beauchamp Place and Walton Street   Located in zone 10 (take the tube to Knightsbridge), Beauchamp (pronounced "Beecham") Place is a swiftly changing street these days, due to the punishingly high rents and an ever-changing economy. The **Reject China Shop** dominates the entrance to Beauchamp Place at Brompton Road, with two floors of china plates and accessories. As you make your way up the street, you'll find jewelry **(Dower & Hall, The Watch Department, Hamilton & Inches),** shoes and purses **(Sergio Rossi, Franchetti Bond, Anello & Davide),** hats **(John Boyd),** secondhand and clearance designer clothes **(Bertie Golightly, Pamela's),** deluxe underwear **(Janet Reger),** and, of course, designers **(Bruce Oldfield, Isabel Kristiansen, Caroline Charles, Paddy Campbell,** and others). This is also the street on which to see fashionable women push food around on their plates at the restaurants **Floriana's** and **San Lorenzo.**

At the end of Beauchamp, make a right into Walton Street and get ready to really spend some money. There are jewelers, a slew of interior decorators' shops full of wonderful curiosities, and a couple of decent restaurants. Try **Patrizia Wigan Designs** for Alice-in-Wonderland smocked dresses and other classic children's clothing. There's **Stephanie Hopper,** who features old portraits whose faces have been erased and replaced with dog faces—very strange, and very popular with Americans apparently. **Chelsea Textiles Ltd.** has fiercely expensive and awesomely beautiful hand-embroidered reproductions of seventeenth- and eighteenth-century linens; **Tappisserie,** for industrious craftspersons, has hand-painted needlepoint designs that are stunning. Reasonably priced monogrammed linens and unreasonably expensive Porthault sheets are at the **Monogrammed Linen Shop.** See also the extraordinary display of glass and crystal work by contemporary British artists at **The Room. Louise Bradley** and **The Wedding List Company** have everything a bride could want, and you can find jewelry for yourself at **Cox & Power.** Don't miss the slice of Italy at the **Farmacia Santa Maria Novella** (expertly hidden at 117) for creams, candles, and soaps. Everyone on the street is happy to ship their products to America, so if you want to buy new or antique children's furniture at **Dragons of Walton Street,** or fine Aubusson reproduction carpets at **Orientalist Carpets,** it's no problem to send them directly home.

Fulham Road and Brompton Cross This area is found in zone 11; take the tube to South Kensington. The area, which is at the end of Walton Street and the beginning of Fulham Road, marked by the old Michelin Building that houses **Conrans** (housewares, fabrics, furniture, stationery, children's stuff, and books) and the restaurants **Bibendum** and its sister, **Oyster Bar,** is known as the **Brompton Cross.** Here you will find **Chanel, Jimmy Choo Shoes,** designers **Jean Paul Gaultier, Betsy Johnson, Joseph, Ralph Lauren, Jigsaw,** and other smaller haut monde stores: **Whistles, Paul & Joe, Tokio, The Library,** and **Space.NK Cosmetics.** From the Bromptom Cross to Edith Grove, Fulham Road features a stretch of shops whose goods cover the gamut, from the height of fashion, antiques, and housewares, to the best used treasures, at the **Notting Hill Charity Shop. Ralph Lauren** recently opened a beautiful three-story shop there, crammed with goods from first-edition books (with very New York–centric topics and costing a bundle) to an English saddle. And of course, clothes. Moving west on Fulham you pass **Agnes B,** and **Jigsaw** and **Jigsaw Junior** for women's and children's fashions. **Butler & Wilson** is an antique clothes and jewelry store that has a ton of tiaras, including a huge one on the top of the building. The jeweler **Theo Fanell,** the delightful **Wedding Shop** with secondhand dresses, and the upscale stationery store **Papyrus** all precede the block devoted to expensive antiques. There's a good bookstore, **Pan Books,** past the **UGC Cinema**, that stays open to 9:30 p.m., as does the best Italian deli in the world, **Luigi's.**

New and Old Bond Streets (Zone 8, tube: Bond Street) Wow, what a stretch of real estate these streets are! Starting from Oxford Street, New Bond Street begins with a battery of designer shops and clothing boutiques, such as **Warehouse, Cecil Gee, Next, Guess, Emma Somerset, Armani, Cerruti 1881, Versace, Herbie Frogg** (this one's the so-called Sale Shop—the really expensive one is down the way on Old Bond), **Calvin Klein, Hermés, Joseph, Tommy Hilfiger, Miu Miu (Prada), Lanvin, Guy LaRouch, Thierry Mugler, Donna Karan, Burberry, Yves Saint Laurent, Ermenegildo Zegna, Chanel, Ralph Lauren, Valentino, Nicole Farhi**—the list goes on and on. Suffice it to say they're all here. Not to mention designer shoes, fine art, jewelry (**Tiffany** and **Cartier,** natch), Hermès scarves, and so on. **Smythson of Bond Street** is a stationery store that begs your jaw to drop with its £25 pigskin mini Post-it note holder, or the blank writing book for £59. There's a bench on the great divide (a pedestrian walkway) between New and Old Bond Streets, on which you will see two very realistic statues of Winston Churchill and Franklin Roosevelt. Old Bond is more of the same: exactly the same, in fact, in the cases of Donna Karan, Chanel, Joseph, Ralph Lauren, Armani, Versace, and others. Old Bond is also home to **Tiffany, Cartier, Prada, Ferragamo, Dolce & Gabbana, Gucci.** Recently opened shops in this area, also known as the "Golden T," include **Stella**

McCartney, Voyage, Gibo, and **Alexander McQueen.** Check out the bodyguards and limos lurking around these stores; you might even get to see some shop-aholic celebs in a spending trance.

Kensington Church Street (Zone 11, tube: High Street Kensington) This is the street of antiques, with shops stretching from Kensington High Street all the way to Notting Hill Gate. It's a great place to window-shop and cruise in and out of the stores that have displays that strike your fancy. As with all antiques stores, the inventory is always changing, but there are a few places that specialize in certain periods and styles. The **Pruskin Gallery** is known for its art nouveau, art deco, and 1940s objets d'art and furniture; **Patrick Sandberg** has eighteenth- and early-nineteenth-century furniture and decorations; Meissen porcelain can be found at **Davies Antiques;** there's **Berwald Oriental Art;** and antique clocks and scientific instruments are sold at both **Raffety & Walwyn** and **Roderick Antique Clocks.** Neil Phillips opened a new stained-glass window shop here, with fewer (but more valuable) pieces than in the longstanding Portobello shop. There are also wonderful mirror stores and a great crystal chandelier place. The prices can be quite high on this street, but it's fun to look, and you never know when you'll find something you really love. **Kensington Place Restaurant** has excellent food and is a popular eating spot on this street.

King's Road Located in zone 11 and accessible via the Sloane Square tube stop, this was the place to be in the 1960s and 1970s, when Mary Quant set up shop to sell her revolutionary miniskirts, and Vivienne Westwood kept changing the name of her and Malcolm McLaren's punk chic boutique. The Mary Quant place is now a coffee and snack shop, but the Vivienne Westwood store still has the fast-moving backward clock outside, and the floor inside still slants dangerously. King's Road is long and full of quickly changing boutiques and trendy stores, but there are some places that will, one can only hope, always be there. Starting at the Vivienne Westwood end (the western part near World's End) and heading to Sloane Square, you'll find thrift shops; **Oxfam, Trinity Hospice,** and **Imperial Cancer Fund** will have the occasional great buys. Some fabric stores along the way include **Anna French, Thomas Dave, Osbourn & Little,** and the **Designer's Guild. Wilde Ones** will take care of all your New Age needs. **Lello Bracio, Johnny Moke,** and the **Natural Shoe Store** offer the latest in shoes, both comfortable and stylish. **Old Church Galleries** has wonderful old and rare prints, and there are some good antiques and reproduction places along the way, including **Antiquarius**, a market housing many stalls with lots of goods. Check out **Steinberg** and **Tolkien** and be sure to go downstairs—they have the most amazing selection of vintage clothes in London, though it's more like a museum than a store, with prices to match. Other stores include

Marks and Spencer, Lush, Daisy & Tom's Children's Store, lots of clothing and shoe boutiques. **The Duke of York Square** opened in 2003, and continues to fill its mall space with upscale stores. **The London Furniture Store** is at the moment the largest emporium on the complex, with reasonably priced and interesting house decor. There's also a **Patisserie Valeries** for cappuccino, **Yves Delorme** for luscious sheets and towels, and a large **Joseph** boutique. At the end of King's Road, at Sloane Square, is **Peter Jones,** the stolid department store. Good restaurants are plentiful, and there are two **Starbucks.**

Sloane Street   This is a street (zone 10; tube: Knightsbridge) running between Brompton Road in Knightsbridge and Sloane Square that is shockingly chock-full of every hot designer you can think of. It's like a mini Bond Street: **Chanel, Dior, Dolce & Gabbana, Valentino, Prada, Lacroix, Tomasz Starzewski, Max Mara, Katharine Hamnett, Fendi, Yves Saint Laurent, Gianfranco Ferre, Armani, Oilily, Alberta Ferretti, Tommy Hilfiger, Hermès,** and **Gucci.** If you don't find the designer store you need, there's always **Harvey Nichols** right at the end of the street on Brompton Road. The street smells of money and lots of perfume (the fabulous scents of **Jo Malone**).

Oxford and Regent Streets   (zone 7; tube: Oxford Circus) These streets are a bit boring, with lots of chain stores. However, **Selfridges** is pretty fantastic, inside and out, and getting better all the time. **John Lewis, Marks and Spencer, Dixons Electronics, Debenhams, The Body Shop, The Gap, Virgin Megastores**—these are not places that a visitor to London would really need to go (except maybe Marks and Spencer for their famous underwear. Turn at Oxford Circus down Regent Street, and you will probably enjoy stopping in at **Liberty,** the Tudor-style department store that has fascinating architecture and some interesting goods. **Fenwicks** is an august department store that has been trying (successfully) to update its genteel reputation. **Hamley's,** the big toy store, is worth a look for toys and books specific to England. Avoid the **Disney Store,** but drop by the **British Air Travel Store** for its wonderful selection of travel goods and London books. **Burberry's, Jaeger,** and **Aquascutum** offer some high-class and high-priced clothing. Another good place to turn off Oxford Street is at St. Christopher's Place, a pedestrian alley full of fun shops and restaurants. The famous **Carnaby Street** is still worth a look-in (it's off Regent Street) but the old days of groovy independent designers and head shops are long gone; now it's got **Puma, O'Neill, Diesel, Soccerscene, Rugby Scene,** and young street wear labels in **High Jinks** and **Mambo.** Take a teen.

Covent Garden   (zone 7, tube: Covent Garden or Leicester Square) has also been taken over by branches of high street shops, but it is always a joy to visit whether you shop or not. There is usually a remarkable busker somewhere around the piazza entertaining with music, song, or daredevilry, and lots of places to sit and take in the urban energy. **Gap, Monsoon, Kookai, Hamleys,** and **Whistles** are some of the stores with branches here. The big **Dr. Martens Department Store** is just off the piazza, by the church. Downstairs at the piazza is the fabulous **London Doll House Co.** with extraordinary furnishings fit for a doll castle. Nearby **Neal Street** and **Neal's Yard** is a fun shopping area as well, with plenty of hip little shops, such as the makeup store **Pout,** which is an amusement park for young beauties; hippy shoes to be had at both **Birkenstock** and **The Natural Shoe Store; Equinox** will do your horoscope in five minutes; all your crystal and New Age needs will be met in **Mysteries** on Monmouth Street (cool retro clothes stores on that street, too). There are plenty of clothing and shoe stores for the urban cool cat, and **Filofax** for the busy professional.

Markets

Markets cover a fair amount of space, so rather than addresses, we've given the tube stop, from where signs will direct you most efficiently.

Apple Market   (zone 7; tube: Covent Garden) Open daily from 9 a.m. to 5 p.m., this is a permanent market on the south side of the piazza. The market is set up in stalls and includes everything from crafts to woolens, with a juice bar and other food stalls thrown in. The brick structure that once housed the fruit, vegetable, and flower sellers is now given over to clothing, silverware, old photos and prints, handcrafts, jewelry, and whatever else the wind blows in that day. A variety of craftspeople set up stalls depending on the day, and at Christmas even more stalls are set up around the piazza.

Bermondsey Market   (zone 5; Bermondsey Square; tube: London Bridge and Borough) Open only Friday from 4 a.m. to 2 p.m., this market, also known as the **New Caledonian,** gives preference to the early bird, and that means arriving in pitch darkness to vie with the dealers buying antiques of every description and value, including clothing and jewelry. It's a serious place, and supposedly the "really good" stuff is gone before 9 a.m., but if you're not a dealer that shouldn't bother you. No credit cards are taken here; bring plenty of cash.

Brick Lane Market   (zone 3; Brick Lane; tube: Aldgate East, Shoreditch, or Liverpool Street) This East End market is open only on Sundays from 8 a.m. to 1 p.m. It is still kind of basic, without much of the sexy stuff, but it does have its fans. As the East End becomes more fashionable, the market shares in the gentrification, with hip, young designer gear vying with chipped crockery for your attention. Check it out on your way to the more predictable Spitalfields Sunday market.

Camden Market (zone 15; Camden Town; tube: Camden Town) A word of warning about this market: It is now one of London's biggest tourist attractions, which means huge crowds of people. An absolute must for teens and twentysomethings, this market has cheap and trendy clothing, jewelry, records, and lots of curious-looking young people to watch. Camden is sort of a latter-day Haight-Ashbury, complete with head shops, local crafts, incense, and Indian fabrics. There are plenty of good food stalls and cafés in the area and lots of outdoor seating in warm weather. Be sure to stop in at the **Victorian Market Hall,** which is open daily and has three floors of shops and stalls of everything from London souvenirs to antiques to books—something for everyone. Camden Market is open Thursday and Friday from 9 a.m. to 5 p.m. and weekends from 10 a.m. to 6 p.m.

Follow Chalk Farm Road to **The Stables Yard,** a weekend market of antiques and secondhand goods.

Camden Passage Market (zone 3; Camden Passage, off Upper Street; tube: Angel) Not to be confused with the above Camden Market, this market offers an interesting array of antiques and collectibles in outdoor stalls. It's open Wednesday from 10 a.m. to 2 p.m. and Saturday from 10 a.m. to 5 p.m., but the Passage itself has permanent antiques stores open all week. You can visit www.antiquescamdenpassage.co.uk.

Greenwich Markets (zone 5; take Greenwich Docklands Light Rail (DCR) or Cutty Sark DLR from Tower Tube) There are a number of markets in Greenwich that are open on Saturday and Sunday from 9 a.m. to 6 p.m. You should have no trouble finding them, because the town is small and you just can't miss them. There's the crafts market in the center of town; the Bosun's Yard market, which also sells crafts and such; the Canopy Antiques Market, which is really a flea market with plenty of interesting junk; and the Greenwich Antiques Market, which has many stalls of vintage clothes, as well as a variety of collectibles and antiques.

Leather Lane Market (zone 2; tube: Chancery Lane) There has been a market on this site at Leather Lane for more than 300 years. As you may guess, it does have leather goods, and they're not too expensive either. Besides the clothing, the other stuff probably won't get your attention; it's mostly electrical and household items, CDs, and so on, but the market itself has an interesting atmosphere. It's open Monday through Friday from 10:30 a.m. to 2 p.m.

Petticoat Lane Market (zone 3; Middlesex Street and environs; tube: Liverpool Street) Open only on Sunday from 9 a.m. to 2 p.m., Petticoat Lane Market used to be located on a street of that name until the Victorian sensibilities became too delicate to handle the reference to ladies' unmentionables. Now there are tons of stalls—selling clothing, shoes, household goods, crafts, you name it—that line a number of streets in the area.

Portobello Market (zone 3; tube: Notting Hill Gate) Located on Portobello Road, from the Notting Hill end to the Ladbroke Grove end, this market is really several markets in one. The antiques market is held on Saturday from 7 a.m. to 6 p.m.; the general market is open Monday through Wednesday from 9 a.m. to 5 p.m.; the organic market takes place Thursday from 11 a.m. to 6 p.m.; and clothing and knickknacks are for sale on Friday from 7 a.m. to 4 p.m., Saturday from 8 a.m. to 5 p.m., and Sunday from 9 a.m. to 4 p.m. On Saturday, at the Notting Hill end, in addition to the stalls galore of antiques, the stores that are often closed on weekdays are open for business. It's a major scene, so come early. As you head toward Ladbroke Grove, clothing takes over, and at the end of the street, you turn left on Westbourne Grove Road and walk through densely packed stalls of secondhand clothes, head shop–type paraphernalia, vintage shoes, food, and loud music.

St. Martin-in-the-Fields Market (zone 7; St. Martin's Lane; tube: Charing Cross) Have a look around when you're in the Trafalgar Square area, as this market is in the same zone. It's mostly clothing and teenage items, although one might find some nice and inexpensive secondhand velvet jackets from the 1970s. Lots of neo-hippie gear. While you're at it, go see the gift shops in the crypt of St. Martin-in-the-Fields Church and make a brass rubbing of one of the many Celtic and other designs.

Spitalfields Market (zone 3; Commercial Street between Lam and Brushfield; tube: Liverpool Street) Sunday is the best time for Spitalfields—both the general and organic markets are open, starting at 9 a.m. (The general market is also open Monday through Friday from 11 a.m. to 3 p.m., and the organic on Friday from 11 a.m. to 3 p.m.) Combine your trip to Spitalfields with one to the Petticoat Lane and/or Brick Lane Markets. Spitalfields has the most extensive offering of delicious organic foods, as well as lots of fast meals, including Indian and other international cuisine. It's a good place to find inexpensive gifts.

Walthamstow (zone 5; Walthamstow High Street; tube: Walthamstow Central) Open Monday through Saturday from 8 a.m. to 6 p.m., Walthamstow is billed as Europe's longest daily street market, with 450 stalls and 300 shops. It's mostly ordinary consumer goods for a bargain, including food, clothes, electrical equipment, and the like, but it is fun to see. It also offers lots of stalls serving delicious food and, in the summer, live entertainment.

Department Stores

These are most like the American stores we know so well, although they're more expensive. John Lewis and Peter Jones (different names, same company) have everything you might need in life, and they claim to beat all other department store prices. Harrods pretends to have every-thing under the sun but really doesn't and charges at least a few quid more than John Lewis. Marks and Spencer has clothes and food and a limited selection of grocery items. Selfridges, Debenhams, and Harvey Nichols are somewhat similar to each other, all with lots of fashions, cos-metics, and a café or two.

Debenhams (zone 14; 334–338 Oxford Street, W1; (0207) 580-3000; www.debenhams.com; tube: Bond Street) It has the usual fashion, cos-metics, and a few designers. The store has numerous locations.

Fortnum & Mason (zone 9; 181 Piccadilly, W1; (0207) 734-8040; www.fortnumandmason.co.uk; tube: Green Park) You might not think of this as anything other than a food emporium, but in fact F&M has floors that carry clothing, clocks, and gifts above its ground floor stocked with jellies and jams. The interior is beautiful, and the cream tea is clas-sic. Make sure you see the mechanical clock outside striking the hour.

Harrods (zone 10; 87 Brompton Road, SW1; (0207) 730-1234; www.harrods.com; tube: Knightsbridge) Harrods made its reputation in the mid–nineteenth century as a goods emporium unparalleled in the Empire, capable of satisfying every possible whim: It once famously delivered a camel to a customer. It still has an impressive array of stock, but in my opinion, it takes itself too seriously with its dress code and £1 charge for use of the ground floor rest room (use the ones on the upper floors). The food halls are quite wonderful, with restaurants on the perimeters of the produce and prepared-foods stalls. Prices are high, except at its much ballyhooed sales.

Harvey Nichols (zone 10; 109–125 Knightsbridge, SW1; (0207) 235-5000; www.harveynichols.com; tube: Knightsbridge) Beloved by fash-ionistas, Harvey Nichols offers floors of designer clothes, plus a good restaurant on the fifth-floor flood hall.

John Lewis/Peter Jones (John Lewis is in zone 14; 278–306 Oxford Street, W1; (0207) 629-7711; www.johnlewis.co.uk; tube: Oxford Cir-cus. Peter Jones is in zone 11; Sloane Square, SW1; (0207) 730-3434; tube: Sloane Square.) There's nothing fancy or trendy here, but they actu-ally do carry everything at good prices, from picture hooks to computers.

Liberty (zone 7; 210–220 Regent Street, W1; (0207) 734-1234; www.liberty-of-london.co.uk; tube: Oxford Circus) A wonderful store in the Tudor style that perks up the Georgian cool of Regent Street, Liberty is full of interesting items and home to the famous Liberty fabrics and to antiques.

Marks and Spencer (main branch in zone 14; 458 Oxford Street, W1; (0207) 935-7954; www.marks-and-spencer.co.uk; tube: Bond Street) M&S, or Marks and Sparks as it's known, carries a lot of good stuff. With its own St. Michel name brand, it provides food and fashion. Apparently, their underwear is worn by 70% of all Londoners, and I can vouch for its comfort and design. I know of a few Americans who stock up whenever they're in town. Solid if unimaginative clothing is offered in every possible size. Branches are everywhere.

Selfridges (zone 14; 400 Oxford Street, W1; (0870) 837-7377; www.selfridges.co.uk; tube: Marble Arch) Thanks to a £100 million facelift in 1999 and the reorganizing efforts of a new director, Selfridges has regained a grip on its identity and now thoroughly lives up to the grand promise of its extravagant facade. Designer wear, silver, beauty products, furniture, as well as restaurants and a very comprehensive food hall, make this a satisfying shopping experience. In 2003, Selfridges gave new meaning to cutting-edge trendiness by opening its very own tattoo parlor.

Where to Find . . .

Antiques

There are so many antiques stores in London, from White Chapel to Hammersmith, that an entire book could be devoted to listing them. What we will point you toward are the antiques arcades that are plentiful here, and let you wander through the great variety of antiques to be had among the stalls, including jewelry, books, clothing, furniture, clocks, silver, decorative arts, knickknacks, and more. See pages 354–356 for information about the larger markets that include antiques—Bermondsey, Camden Passage, and Portobello. Other antiques markets include:

Alfie's Antique Market (zone 14; 13–5 Church Street, NW8; (0207) 723-6066; tube: Edgeware Road) is open Tuesday–Saturday, 10 a.m.–6 p.m.

Antiquarius (zone 11; 131–141 King's Road, SW3; (0207) 351-5353; tube: Sloane Square) is open Monday–Saturday, 10 a.m.–6 p.m.

Bourbon-Hanby Antiques Centre (zone 11; 151 Sydney Street, SW3, on the corner of King's Road; (0207) 352-2106; www.antiques.co.uk/bourbon-hanby; tube: Sloane Square) is open Monday–Saturday, 10 a.m.–6 p.m. and Sunday, 11 a.m.–5 p.m.

Gray's Antiques Market and **Gray's Mews Market** (zone 8; off Oxford Street at 58 Davies Street, W1; (0207) 629-7034; www.graysantiques.com; tube: Bond Street) is open Monday–Friday, 10 a.m.–6 p.m.

London hosts a lot of antique fairs over the course of the year. Check out the following websites for more information.

- www.antiques-london.com
- www.portobelloroad.co.uk
- www.bada.org
- www.antiquesweb.co.uk
- www.lapada.co.uk

Auction Houses

These can be a lot of fun, and you can also get some amazing items, as the treasures of the empire continue to pass through acquisitive hands. Bargains are not to be had by the likes of common folk, because the dealers know what they're doing and how to do it, but you can give it a go. Call to find out what is being sold and when, and go take a look at the catalogs to familiarize yourself with the prices. These are the four most prestigious auction houses in London, not to mention in the world: **Bonhams** took over Phillips, and now has two London auction houses: the one in Knightsbridge (zone 10; Montpelier Street, SW7; (0207) 629-1602, www.bonhams.com; tube: Knightsbridge) and the head office in Mayfair (zone 8; 101 New Bond Street, W1; (0207) 629-6602; tube: Bond Street); **Christie's** (zone 11; 85 Old Brompton Road, SW7; (0207) 581-7611; www.christies.com; tube: South Kensington); and **Sotheby's** (zone 8; 34–35 New Bond Street, W1; (0207) 293-5000; www.sothebys. com; tube: Bond Street; and Sotheby's Olympia, Hammersmith Road, W14; (0207) 293-5555; tube: Olympia Kensington).

   How it's done: For each of the hundreds of auctions these houses hold, there is an exhibition of the goods to be sold. These exhibitions are open to one and all for free. They will be listed on the websites, and they are worth a visit even if you aren't in the market for treasure. A catalog is produced for the goods, and is available at the auction house (for a small to middling cost) or for free (and sometimes without illustrations) online. This is where you can get a handle on provenance, price, and possibility of purchase. You can buy without attending the auction through the absentee bidding service or by telephone. Going in person to the auction is the most fun, however, whether you buy or not. When you arrive at the auction, you must register and receive your numbered bidding paddle (these have eliminated the old slapstick humor of a person with a chronic nervous tic unwittingly buying a million-dollar spittoon). Lots are brought out in numerical order; the auctioneer will describe the item and start the bidding at about two-thirds of the estimated price in the catalog. Raise your paddle to bid and the auctioneer will acknowledge it and continue asking for higher bids. Bids increase in approximately 10% increments. When no more bids are accepted, the hammer comes down and the auctioneer pronounces the item "sold" and names the number of the winning paddle. If you have won, you go to the cashier and pay for your new toy with credit card, cash, bank transfer, or an approved personal check. The total cost is your bid, plus tax, plus a buyers' premium (a percentage of the cost paid to the auction house). The auction house will deliver your goods for a fee; some things may be brought home that very day, but it usually takes a few weeks to take possession of your purchase.

Beauty and Bath Stores

Culpepper the Herbalist (zone 7; 8 The Market, Covent Garden Piazza, WC2; (0207) 379-6698 (hang on, it switches from fax to telephone); tube: Covent Garden) sells bath salts, oils, teas, spices, essential oils—they've got it all here. A branch is located at zone 7, 21 Bruton Street, W1; (0207) 629-4559. **Shu Uemura** (zone 7; 55 Neal Street, WC2, (0207) 240-7635; tube: Covent Garden) just opened its flagship store here; and it has everything the international beauty wants, from cosmetics to massages. **Lush** (zone 7; 7 & 11 The Market, Covent Garden Piazza, WC; (0207) 240-4570; www.lush.co.uk; tube: Covent Garden) is a wonderful place for chocolate massage bars, soaps by the hunk, fizzy bath bombs, and homemade oatmeal masks. The design is witty and ecologically sound: It looks like a delicatessen, with wheels of soap resembling cheeses, and minimal packaging; great gifts here. There are more and more branches opening all the time. **MAC Cosmetics** (zone 11; 109 King's Road, SW3; (0207) 534-9222; www.maccosmetics.com; tube: Sloane Square) is a Canadian company that offers trendy makeup that doesn't cost the world. **Neal's Yard Remedies** (zone 7; 15 Neal's Yard, WC2; (0207) 379-7222; tube: Covent Garden) is a great place for homeopathic remedies, fresh herbs, essential oils, soaps, and hair-care products, all in beautiful blue glass bottles. Other branches are too numerous to mention, so call for information. **Space.NK Apothecary** (zone 7; 37 Earlham Street, WC2; (0207) 379-7030; tube: Covent Garden) offers the latest and greatest in cosmetics and beauty products at its popular store. The apothecary also has many branches, so call for additional locations. For **Dr. Hauschka** products, stop into **The Life Centre** (zone 13; 15 Edge Street, W8; (0207) 221-4602; www.thelifecentre.org; tube: Notting Hill), a yoga studio that pretty much stocks the full range of the all-natural lotions and cosmetics at close to European prices.

Bookstores

There are many chain bookstores in London, which have branches everywhere. Call to find the one nearest you: **Books Etc.** (phone (0207) 404-0261; www.booksetc.co.uk); **Borders Books & Music** (phone (0207) 379-6838; www.borders.com); **WH Smith** (phone (0207) 261-1708; www.whsmith.co.uk); and **Waterstones** (phone (0207) 434-4291; www.waterstones.co.uk).

Then there are the more unusual stores: **Atlantis Bookshop** (zone 2; 49A Museum Street, WC1; (0207) 405-2120; www.atlantisbookshop. demon.co.uk; tube: Tottenham Court Road) caters to a clientele interested in psychic research, witchcraft, and supernatural phenomena. Incredible deals are found in **Book Thrift** (zone 11; 22 Thurloe Street, SW7; (0207) 589-2916; tube: South Kensington), which specializes in fine-arts books for a fraction of the original cost. Buy immediately:

When the stock is gone, it's gone for good. **European Bookshop** (zone 7; 5 Warwick Street, W1; (0207) 734-5259; tube: Piccadilly Circus) sells books and mags in most European languages. **Grant & Cutler** (zone 8; 55–57 Great Marlborough Street, W1; (0207) 734-2012; www.grantc. demon.co.uk; tube: Oxford Street) has books, videos, cassettes, and more. About 200 languages are represented, so you're certain to find something you can understand.

Henry Sotheran (zone 8; on the ground floor at 2 Sackville Street, W1; (0207) 629-6517; tube: Green Park) is the place to look for real antiquarian books. Within Henry Sotheran is **The Folio Society Gallery,** where reproductions of fine antiquarian books are available. The books are magnificent, well bound, and illustrated like in the old days, and the titles available are classics of every kind. The only catch is you have to join the society with the obligation to buy four books as the price of membership (the difficulty is limiting yourself to only four). The society, at the same address as Henry Sotheran, can be reached by phone at (0207) 439-6151 or on the Internet at www.sotherans.co.uk.

Forbidden Planet (zone 2; 71–75 New Oxford Street, WC1; (0207) 836-4179; tube: Tottenham Court Road), billed as The Science Fiction Entertainment Store, has got it all, from toys to videos to every kind of printed matter you can imagine. **French's Theatre Bookshop** (52 Fitzroy Street, W1; (0207) 387-9373; www.samuelfrench-london.co.uk; tube: Warren Street) has play scripts beyond compare and is a must for the theater student or aficionado.

Hatchard's (zone 8; 187 Piccadilly, W1; (0207) 439-9921; www.hatchards.co.uk; tube: Piccadilly Circus) is London's oldest bookstore, with a very fine selection and a great atmosphere. **Helter Skelter** (zone 2; 4 Denmark Street, WC2; (0207) 836-1151; www.skelter. demon.co.uk; tube: Tottenham Court Road) is a music bookshop with sheet music, mags, music-related art, and all possible fiction and nonfiction about the subject. **Librairie La Page French Booksellers** has everything for the French student, young and old (zone 11; 7 Harrington Road, SW7; (0207) 589-5991; tube: South Kensington). **Pan Bookstore** (zone 11; 158 Fulham Road, SW10; (0207) 373-4997; tube: South Kensington, then bus 14 toward Fulham) has lots of signed editions of recently published books. **Daunt Books** (zone 14; 83 Marylebone High Street, W1, (0207) 224-2295: tube Baker Street) is a beautiful store to browse in and to find good travel books.

Politico's (zone 9; 8 Artillery Row, SW1; (0207) 828-0010; www.politicos,co.uk; tube: St. James's Park) has great political paraphernalia, plus a fine selection of books on biography, reference, and history. **Stanford's** (zone 7; 12–14 Long Acre, WC2; (0207) 836-1321; www.stanfords.co.uk; tube: Leicester Square) has the biggest collection of maps, globes, and travel books you'll ever see. **Talking Bookshop** (zone 14; 11 Wigmore

Street, W1; (0207) 491-4117; www.talkingbooks.co.uk; tube: Bond Street) has the best selection of books on tape—a huge wall of unabridged fiction from classics to this year's best-sellers—as well as books on CD. Theirs are not cheaper than those sold in the United States, but they offer an extraordinary range. **Dover Bookshop** (zone 7: 18 Earlham Street, WC2, (0207) 836-2111; www.thedoverbooks.co.uk; tube: Covent Garden) is a fabulous resource for arcane books of old and interesting copyright-free illustrations, with CD-ROMs included with many of them.

Antiquarian and Secondhand Books

Let us not forget the antiquarian and secondhand books. It would behoove anyone interested in browsing to take a walk down Charing Cross Road or around Soho to look in the many secondhand bookstores. The prices are generally good, and you could get your hands on some very fine antique books for a couple of quid. Many of the secondhand bookstores listed below also have antiquarian books in locked glass cabinets. (Antiques neighborhoods, markets, and arcades, as listed in this book, will also have many shops and stalls featuring old and beautiful books.) Visit:

Any Amount of Books (zone 7; 62 Charing Cross Road, WC2; (0207) 240-8140; www.anyamountofbooks.com; tube: Leicester Square); **Gloucester Road Bookshop** (zone 11; 123 Gloucester Road, SW; (0207) 370-3503; www.gloucesterbooks.co.uk; tube: Gloucester Road); **Skoob Books** (zone 2; 15 Sicilian Avenue, WC1; (0207) 404-3063; www.skoob. com; tube: Holborn); and **Unsworths Booksellers** (zone 2; 15 Blooms-bury Street, WC1; (0207) 436-9836; www.unsworths. com; tube: Totten-ham Court Road).

Decorative Home Accessories

Architectural Components (zone 11; 8 Exhibition Road, SW7; (0207) 581-2401; tube: South Kensington) has brass fittings for every possible household use with an emphasis on the bathroom. **The Conran Shop** (zone 11; Michelin House, 81 Fulham Road, SW3; (0207) 589-7401; tube: South Kensington) has a lot of interesting, though expensive, modern items for bed, bath, kitchen, and nursery. Very traditionally English in style are the wares at **General Trading Company** (zone 11; 144 Sloane Street, SW1; (0207) 730-0411; www.general-trading.co.uk; tube: Sloane Square), which offers everything you can imagine wanting for the home or tabletop. **India Jane** (zone 11; 140 Sloane Street, SW1; (0207) 730-1070; tube: Sloane Square) has some good buys in the way of Indian silver and picture frames.

The London Silver Vaults (zone 2; 53–64 Chancery Lane, WC2; (0207) 242-3844; tube: Chancery Lane) is actually 40 shops selling silver, old and new, and for every budget.

The Reject China Shop (zone 10; 183 Brompton Road, SW3; (0207) 581-0739; www.chinacraft.co.uk; tube: Knightsbridge) is a great place to replace missing Spode or Wedgwood plates or to pick up a cow creamer. It has numerous branches. Finally, don't miss **Thomas Goode** (zone 8; 19 South Audley Street, W1; (0207) 499-2823; tube: Green Park) for a genuine English shopping experience, with major china, silver, and crystal as well as knickknacks. Have a spot of tea there, too.

Designer Clothes

Below is a list of some of London's homegrown designers. They are certainly London's best-known designers, and not all sell their clothes in other countries. Some have their own boutiques, but unless you just want to see what they have to offer, you're better off buying in the department stores and boutiques that carry their clothes. If it's an internationally known designer, you're better off buying in the United States, if possible.

Antoni & Alison, Blaak, Boudicca, Hussein Chalayan, Caroline Charles, Jasper Conran, Emma Cook, English Eccentrics, John Galliano, Ghost, Joseph, Katherine Hamnett, Justin Oh, Nicole Farhi, Bella Freud, Betty Jackson, Sophia Kokosalaki, Markus Lupfer, Stella McCartney, Julian MacDonald, Alexander McQueen, Hamish Morrow, Bruce Oldfield, Red or Dead, Pierce Fionda, Lainey Keogh, Zandra Rhodes, Paul Smith, Tomasz Starzewski, Phillip Treacy (hats only), Catherine Walker, Amanda Wakeley, Vivienne Westwood, and Matthew Williamson have stores here or can be found in Selfridges, Harvey Nichols, Harrods, or smaller designer boutiques (see below). Check the phone book for locations and phone numbers.

Designer Boutiques

Harvey Nichols, Harrods, Selfridges, and Liberty will likely carry some or all of the above designers' clothes (see the section "Department Stores," (pages 356–358). Here are a few smaller boutiques that carry many of England's designers:

Browns (zone 7; 23–27 South Molton Street, W1; (0207) 491-7833; tube: Bond Street) has a huge selection of all the big names. Other stores are: **A La Mode** (zone 10; 36 Hans Cresents, SW1; (0207) 584-2133; tube: Knightsbridge); **Feathers** (zone 10; 40 Hans Crescent, SW1; (0207) 589-0356; tube: Knightsbridge); **Joanna's Tent** (zone 11; 289B King's Road, SW3; (0207) 352-1151; tube: Sloane Square); **Koh Samui** (zone 7; 50 Monmouth Street, WC2; (0207) 240-4280; tube: Covent Garden); **Question Air** (zone 7; 38 Floral Street, WC2; (0207) 836-8220; tube: Covent Garden); **Tokio** (zone 11; 309 Brompton Road, SW3; (0207) 823-7310; tube: South Kensington); and **Whistles** (zone 14; 12 St. Christopher's Place, W1; (0207) 487-4484; tube: Bond Street).

Designer Resale Shops

Such a good idea, these shops. It's hit or miss, but you can get your hands on some very expensive designer threads and shoes for a fraction of what they'd cost new. Unfortunately, there tend to be more size 4s than 14s, but shoes and purses will work for anyone. Some good places to try are: **Bang Bang** (zone 14; 21 Goodge Street, W1; (0207) 631-4191; tube: Goodge Street); **Bertie Golightly** (zone 10; 48 Beauchamp Place, SW3; (0207) 584-7270; tube: Knightsbridge); **Catwalk** (zone 14; 52 Blandford Street, W1; (0207) 935-1052; tube: Baker Street); **Designer Bargains** (zone 14; 29 Kensington Church Street, W8; (0207) 795-6777; tube: Kensington High Street); **The Dresser** (zone 14; 10 Porchester Place, W2; (0207) 724-7212; tube: Marble Arch); **L'Homme Designer Exchange** (zone 14; 50 Blandford Street, W1; (0207) 224-3266; tube: Baker Street). For men's fashions (not exclusively), visit **The Loft** (zone 7; 35 Monmouth Street, WC2; (0207) 240-3807; tube: Covent Garden); W11 and **Sign of the Times** (zone 11; 17 Elystan Street, SW3; (0207) 589-4774; tube: Sloane Square). When visiting **Pandora** (zone 10; 16–22 Cheval Place, SW7; (0207) 589-5289; tube: Knightsbridge), see also, along this same street, **The Dress Box** (8 Cheval Place; (0207) 589-2240) and **Salou** (6 Cheval Place; (0207) 581-2380).

Fabrics

Anna French (zone 11; 343 King's Road, SW3; (0207) 351-1126; tube: Sloane Square, then bus 11 or 22) sells children's room fabrics, as well as sheer, lacy, and flowery textiles. **Beaumont & Fletcher** (zone 11; 261 Fulham Road, SW3; (0207) 352-5594; tube: South Kensington, then bus 14) offers period (eighteenth- and nineteenth-century) and reproduction fabrics of a very high standard. **Colefax & Fowler** is one of the greats in traditional English decoration (zone 11; 110 Fulham Road, SW3; (0207) 244-7427; tube: South Kensington, then bus 14). The **Decorative Fabrics Gallery** (zone 11; 278–280 Brompton Road, SW3; (0207) 589-4778; www.decorativefabrics.com; tube: South Kensington) has a wide range of traditional and upscale fabrics, with good export service. **Osbourne & Little** (zone 11; 304–308 King's Road, SW3; (0207) 352-1456; www.osbourneandlittle.com; tube: Sloane Square) sells traditional and modern designs, all of high quality. **VV Rouleaux** (zone 11; 54 Sloane Square (Cliveden Place), SW1; (0207) 730-3125; tube: Sloane Square) has the best collection of ribbons, trimmings, and braids in London.

Linens

Irish Linen Company (zone 8; 35–36 Burlington Arcade, W1; (0207) 493-8949; tube: Piccadilly Circus) sells Irish linen and Egyptian cotton sheets and table clothes. **The Linen Merchant** (zone 10; 11 Montpelier

Street, SW7; (0207) 584-3654; tube: Knightsbridge) sells bathrobes as well as bed linens. **Monogrammed Linen Shop** (zone 11; 168 Walton Street, SW3; (0207) 589-4033; tube: South Kensington) has a good stock of expensive, beautiful linen that can be monogrammed to order. **The White House** (zone 8; 40–41 Conduit Street, W1; (0207) 629-3521; tube: Bond Street) sells unbelievably lovely bedclothes at unthinkably extravagant prices. Ditto the French sheet designer **Yves Delorme** (zone11: 54 Duke of York Square, King's Road, SW3; (0207) 730-3435; www.yvesdelorme.com; tube: Sloane Square), where elegant patterns are combined with rich, practically edible, cotton.

Museum Shops

My favorite stores in London are the gift shops at museums. The **British Museum's** shop offers good gifts for old and young—reproductions of museum treasures such as the Lewis chess pieces and Roman coins or jewelry. **Hampton Palace's** shop has the best all-around selection of housewares, books, food, and decorative arts. **Museum of London's** shop has the best books on London. The **National Gallery** and **National Portrait Gallery** shops have the best postcards, calendars, and art books. The **Natural History Museum** shop has the best nature selection for kids, including tons of plastic and stuffed animals. The **Queen's Gallery** shop and the **Buckingham Palace** shop (open only in August and September) have the best royal-related items. The **Royal Academy** has art books and cool T-shirts. The **Science Museum** has great gifts for children. Both **Tate Museums** have shops with good art books and postcards. The **Victoria and Albert Museum** has the best reproduction jewelry, decorative arts, and books on design and interior decoration. The **Tower of London** has a number of gift shops featuring everything from kid's costumes to reproductions of the royal jewels. **Westminster Abbey** has a quirky shop full of cheap tourist stuff as well as genuinely interesting souvenirs. All the gift shops in England have excellent chocolate in whimsical packaging.

Perfumeries

One of the great things about London is its proximity to France, home of a thousand scents. The interest in aromas has wafted across the English Channel, and you can find some of the best perfumes in the world at the following stores. **L'Artisan Parfumeur** (zone 11; 17 Cale Street, SW3; (0207) 352-4196; tube: South Kensington) has scents for men, women, and children(!); candles, too. **Crown Perfumery** (zone 8; 51 Burlington Arcade, W1; (0207) 493-1717; tube: Green Park), now also known by the name **Pure,** is a must-go place, where scents made specially for the likes of Queen Victoria, the duke and duchess of Windsor, Oscar Wilde, and Isadora Duncan can be sniffed. **Floris** (zone 8; 89 Jermyn Street, SW1;

(0207) 930-2885; tube: Piccadilly Circus) is the classic English fragrance and soap maker, in business since 1730. Also offered are potpourri and candles. **Jo Malone** (zone 11; 150 Sloane Street, SW1; (0207) 730-2100; www.jomalone.co.uk; tube: Sloane Square) is a wildly popular store with remarkable, imaginative scents and creams. **Penhaligons** (zone 7; 41 Wellington Street, WC2; (0207) 836-2150; tube: Covent Garden) has been a lovely place with lovely smells since 1870. It's great for gifts and has numerous branches. **Les Senteurs** (zone 9; 71 Elizabeth Street, SW1; (0207) 730-2322; tube: Victoria or Sloane Square) has very unusual fragrances, straight from France, as well as fine skin-care products.

Shoes

Birkenstock (zone 7; 37 Neal Street, W2; (0207) 240-2783; www.birkenstock.co.uk; tube: Covent Garden), the hippy shoe from the 1960s, has never been so popular or mainstream. The real thing costs a bundle in the United States, but here you can get such styles as the Vegan, which contains no animal parts, or the Classic for slightly, and in some cases much, less. **Dr. Marten's Department Store** (zone 7; 1–4 King Street, WC2; (0207) 497-1460; www.drmartens.com; tube: Covent Garden) is five floors of Doc Marten shoes at prices that may be competitive with those in the States. Sale time is really the only time to find a bargain. **Emma Hope** (zone 11; 53 Sloane Square, SW1; (0207) 259-9566; tube: Sloane Square) offers amazingly elegant shoes, as does the less expensive shop of the young English designer **L.K. Bennett** (zone 7; 130 Long Acre, WC2; (0207) 379-1710; www.lkbennett.com, tube: Covent Garden). **Jimmy Choo** (zone 11; 169 Draycott Avenue; (0207) 584-6111; tube: South Kensington) is a very au courant shoemaker, beloved of the stylish young women of London and, increasingly, the world. The red-soled pumps of **Christian Louboutin** (23 Motcomb Street, SW1X; (0207) 823-2234; tube: Knightsbridge) have become the must-have of the deep-pocketed diva set. And while we're at it, how about **Manolo Blahnik** (zone 11, 49–51 Old Church Street, SW3; (0207) 352-3863; tube: Sloane Square) whose shoes were described by a devotee as "better than sex"? Apparently, he is one cobbler who can combine glamour with comfort, which goes to explain the eye-popping prices. The newest shoe master on the block is **Georgina Goodman** (zone 8; 12–14 Shepherd Street, W1; (0207) 499-8599; tube: Green Park), whose Mayfair shop is a fabulous space in which to admire the artful, individual handmade shoes, created to last a lifetime. **John Lobb** (zone 9; 9 St. James Street, SW1; (0207) 930-3664; tube: Green Park) is the oldest, grandest, and most expensive of the bespoke shoemakers; one of these classic pairs of English leather shoes will set you back about £1,500, and it will take months to get them, but they say it's well worth it. **Natural Shoe Store** (zone 11; 325 King's Road, SW3; (0207) 351-

3721; www.naturesko.com; tube: Sloane Square) has the best in comfort shoes: Ecco, Birkenstock, Arche, Krone Clogs, and American brands such as Bass, Dexter, and Rockport. Don't even think of getting the American brands, but check the prices on the Europeans. And finally, the last word in shoe fetishism: paint-your-own-shoes. Designer **Olivia Morris** (by appointment (0208) 962-0353) created this very original concept for her very well-made and elegant shoes, which come with a paint set. Cool gift for artsy types.

Vintage Clothing

Steinberg and Tolkien (zone 11; 193 King's Road, SW3; (0207) 376-3660; tube: Sloane Square) has an astonishing, wonderful range of vintage clothing, from the Victorian period to that worn during the 1970s, and from Worth to Balmain to Schiaparelli to Biba to Halston. It's the place where costume designers from films come to dress their actors, where actors come to play, and where designers come for inspiration. Go for the fun of seeing the largest vintage clothing collection in London, and be sure to go downstairs. **The Antique Clothing Store** (zone 13; 282 Portobello Road, W10; (0208) 964-4830; tube: Ladbroke Grove) also has a large selection; you may even find antique christening gowns. **Virginia** (zone 13 98 Portland Road, W11; (0207) 727-9908; tube: Holland Park) is a visually and atmospherically gorgeous shop, with amazing clothes and accessories from the late Victorian period, which means that unless you've got a corset and a very deep pocket, you'll just want to look.

Wool and Cashmere

Wool and cashmere in London are from Scotland or Ireland and are more expensive and of better quality than the Chinese kind. The best time to buy is during sale times. Many of the wool stores will have sales during the summer to move the goods and take advantage of the influx of tourists, many of whom aren't prepared for the chilly London summer and will need woolens. Liberty, Harrods, Marks and Spencer, Debenhams, and other big stores have good wool departments (see "Department Stores," [xref]).

Shi Cashmere (zone 11; 30 Lowndes Street; (0207) 235-3829; www.shicashmere.com; tube: Knightsbridge) has an elegant selection of cashmeres, wools, and silks, and if you don't see it, you can order it from the Scottish factory. **Westaway & Westaway** (zone 2; 64–65 Great Russell Street, WC1; (0207) 405-4479, tube: Russell Square) is overflowing with sweaters in every color and size possible, at the best prices possible.

Miscellaneous Personal Favorite Shops

Phillips Stained Glass (zone 13; 99 Portobello Road, W11; (0207) 229-2113; www.edgarsglass.com; tube: Notting Hill) This shop is a must-visit for anyone with an interest in stained glass and old architectural features. A family-owned business for over 40 years, it has recently come under the management of stained-glass window restorer Edgar Phillips, while his brother Neil now focuses on his new shop in Kensington Church Street (www.neilphillips.co.uk). Small and portable pieces can be found here at a good price; and massive beauties will be shipped to wherever you want. **Ganesha** (zone 11; 6 Park Walk, SW10; (0207) 352-8972, tube; Earl's Court or South Kensington) Filled with wonderful semi-precious jewels and artifacts of India, this is a great place to browse and to buy gifts. With silk pajamas, silver jewelry, artifacts from the days of the Raj, incense, and house decor, this is a well-filled small shop. **Summer-hill and Bishop** (zone 13; 100 Portland Road, W11; (0207) 221-4566; tube: Holland Park) has kitchen goods from France, as well as unusual gifts such as candles spelling "amour" and "angel." A fun place to browse and a must for domestic goddesses. Cross the street from here to pop into **The Cross** (zone 13, 141 Portland Road, W11 (0207) 727-6760; tube: Holland Park). This place can get expensive, but it's a groove for browsing. Sourced from all over the world, there are kids' clothes and toys, beautifully embroidered silk and cotton clothing, shoes, candles, quilts, and labels from delicately hip designers. **Calmia** (zone 14; 52–54 Marylebone High Street, W1; (0207) 224-3585; www.calmia.com; tube: Baker Street) As its name promises, it is calming just to walk into this shrine to the hip urban yoga lifestyle—just don't look at the prices on the clothes, or your heart rate will soar dangerously. A wonderful place for natural cosmetics, soothing CDs, incense, and beauty/health treatments. Great neighborhood, too. **Fake Landscapes** (zone 14; 164 Old Brompton Road, SW5, (0207) 835-1500; www.fake.com; tube: South Kensington) Only a silk flower shop supremely convinced of its superiority would dare to give itself such a name; the gamble works, as the riot of flowers and plants in this shop looks anything but fake. Not cheap, but if you amortize the cost of real flowers, a pretty good deal. And you'll end up absentmindedly watering the flowering plants, I promise. **Jane Asher Party Cakes & Sugarcraft** (zone 11; 22–4 Cale Street, SW3, (0207) 584-6177; www.jane-asher.co.uk; tube: Sloane Square) This shop in charming Chelsea Green is a favorite of amateur bakers: It has the best cake mixes going, plus an amazing array of unusually shaped pans (such as number pans), adorable sugar or marzipan, as well as nonedible cake decorations, and very sophisticated baking gear. Browsing or buying, you get a sugar high just being here. Any of the **Notting Hill Charity Shops, Oxfams, Sue Ryder Shops,** and other secondhand thrift shops, especially in the upscale neighborhoods, are a blast to breeze through. You never know what you'll find.

Part Eleven

Exercise and Recreation

Spectator Sports

Baseball and basketball are played in the U.K,, but they do not have the same kind of ardent support that they have in other countries—England is about football more than anything, even rugby. But if you simply have to take in a baseball game, call (0207) 453-7055, or visit www.baseball softball.com. If you can't live without basketball, the season runs from September to May, and you can call the British Basketball League (BBL) at (0121) 749-1355, or visit www.bbl.org.uk. Now let's get to the footie.

Football

Soccer, or football as the English call it, is more than a national obsession— it is a religion with serious devotees. The days when rival fans would do bloody battle in the streets are mostly gone due to CCTV, hi-tech detective work, well-organized policing at games, and reconstruction of the grounds themselves. However, the fever burns as strong as ever. There is huge money in football these days and the top teams, which belong to the Premiership league, are all locked into cable TV deals that have the exclusives on their matches. Consequently, tickets for these games are expensive (£20–£60), whereas tickets for the teams further down the league are cheaper (£10–£18). It is well worth a visit to a Premiership game, as the class (and price) of players these days is phenomenal. The spectators themselves are also worthy of close attention. Listen to their songs and chants and their sometimes venomous derision of the visiting team.

The football season runs from August to May. Games are 90 minutes long, with injury time and extra time if it is important that there be a winner (as in, for a cup final). Most of the clubs will take credit-card bookings over the phone, which is crucial for Premiership games. They take place on Saturday afternoons and in the evenings on weekdays.

Wrap up warmly, and if the conclusion of the game is obvious ten minutes before the final whistle, leave early to avoid the crush and possible trouble. Avoid the standing seats at the clubs further down the league, as this is where trouble, if it breaks out, is more likely to occur. Premiership teams include:

Arsenal at Arsenal Stadium   (zone 15, Avenall Road, N5; phone (0207) 704-4000, or visit www.arsenal.co.uk) Take the tube to Arsenal. Tickets are £24–£44; children are full price.

Charlton Athletic at The Valley   (outside zones, Floyd Road, SE7; phone (0208) 333-4010, or visit www.cafc.co.uk) Take British Rail to Charlton. Tickets are £15-£30 for adults and £10 for children.

Chelsea at Stamford Bridge   (zone 11, Fulham Road, SW6; phone (0207) 386-7799, or visit www.chelseafc.co.uk) Take the tube to Fulham Broadway. Tickets are £28–£40 for adults and £13 for children.

Tottenham Hotspurs   (at White Hart Lane, High Road, N17; phone (0870) 011-2222, or visit www.spurs.co.uk). Take British Rail to White Hart Lane. Tickets are £27–£46 for adults and children.

West Ham United (at Boleyn Ground (outside zones), Green Street, E13 phone (0208) 548-2700, or visit www.westhamunited.co.uk) Take the tube to Upton Park. Adult tickets are £26–£46; children's tickets begin at £15.50.

All these teams, except Chelsea, play outside our designated London zones.

Cricket

Despite the fact that it is a truly international sport (at which the Brits have not excelled for years), there is something quintessentially English about the game of cricket. It is sedate, difficult to understand, and full of quaint language. For example, a "maiden over" is a series of six balls, bowled in a swinging overarm motion, during which no runs are scored. The games sometimes last for days, interrupted frequently by rain and tea. It is considered vulgar to thrash one's opponent by too many runs; when it is clear the losing team cannot win, the winning side "declares" and gives the other team a chance to recover some of their dignity. You can see this game played by men in white clothing on many a village green during the season, which runs from mid-April to early September, but there are two main venues in London, Lords and the Oval:

Lords at St. John's Wood Road   (zone 14, NW8; phone (0207) 432-1000, or visit www.lords.org.uk) Take the tube to St. John's Wood. This is the home of the Marylebone Cricket Club (MCC) and is often considered the home of cricket. Tickets range £20–£50; children's tickets are half price.

AMPOval (at Kennington Oval, outside zones, SE11; phone (0207) 582-6660, or visit www.surreyccc.co.uk) Take the tube to Oval. International cricket is often played here; tickets range £30–£50. Tickets for county matches are less expensive.

Tickets for international games need to be booked well in advance, but the league games, played between counties, are much easier to see.

Rugby

This is a brutal and violent game similar to American football but without the padding. Again, the rules are characteristically British: The ball, shaped like an American football, is passed backward or sideways, never forward; during the scrum, the players crouch with their faces or shoulders between the thighs and against the buttocks of the player in front and push against a similarly tightly packed huddle of the opposition. The ball is thrown into this mass of steaming, muddy flesh, from which it is booted out. Whoever catches it then dashes along the field to score a try (touchdown), which is then converted by kicking it over the goalposts for extra points. Like cricket, it is a quintessentially British sport at which the natives no longer truly excel. The New Zealanders, French, South Africans, and Fijians are marvelous rugby players, but tickets for international games are hard to get. The season runs from September to May, and the game is enjoying something of a resurgence in popularity due to the amount of money it now attracts.

Rugby League is the professional form of rugby football. This is a fast-moving collision game with lots of open running, big hits, and tackles (the closest thing to American football). There are 13 players on a team.

Rugby Union is traditionally the amateur form of rugby football with the characteristic scrums, time-outs, and touchdowns, and 15 players per team. However, it now boasts a professional status, with the Allied Dunbar Premiership and the Jewson National League, which draw major crowds. The season runs from August to May. Watch out for the Harlequins, London Irish, Saracens, and the Wasps. Wrap up warmly if you go. The primary rugby venues are:

Athletic Ground at Kew Foot Road in zone 12, Richmond, Surrey (phone (0208) 940-0397; tube: Richmond). These amateur games are free.

Rosslyn Park on Upper Richmond Road in zone 12, Priory Lane, Roehampton, SW15 (phone (0208) 876-6044). Take British Rail to Barnes. Tickets are £10 for adults, £5 for seniors, and £3 for children.

Twickenham Rugby House at 21 Rugby Road (outside zones), Twickenham Middlesex (phone (0208) 892-2000, or visit www.rfu.com). Tickets vary in price depending on the game. Tickets for the Six Nations series held here are almost impossible to get and are distributed to the faithful via the various clubs. You can see cup finals for the leagues here, too, for which tickets range between £15 and £35.

Clubs

Blackheath at Rectory Field (outside zones, Charlton Road, SE3; phone (0208) 293-0853, or visit www.blackheathrugby.co.uk)

N.E.C.Harlequins at Stoop Memorial Ground Langhorn Drive, Twickenham, Middlesex, phone (0208) 410-6000, or visit www.quins.co.uk)

London Welsh at Old Deer Park zone 12, Kew Road, Richmond, Surrey phone (0208) 940-2368)

Saracens at Vicarage Road (outside zones, Watford, phone (0192) 347-5222, or visit www.saracens.com)

London Wasps (outside zones, at Loftus Road Stadium, South Africa Road, W12 phone (0208) 740-2545, or visit www.wasps.co.uk)

Modejski Stadium on Junction 11 (off M4, outside zones; phone (0193) 278-3034, or visit www.londonirish.com)

Boxing

Big fights happen in big venues, like Wembley Arena, Royal Albert Hall, London Arena, and Earl's Court. Publicity will be large scale, and tickets are always expensive. There are smaller venues for amateur or semiprofessional fights, and these will be advertised in local papers, *Time Out,* or on posters. You can catch a good pro or amateur fight at York Hall, Old Ford Road, E2 (phone (0208) 980-4171). This place has a serious East End vibe and has hosted amateur matches since 1929. Tickets are £10. Tickets for pro fights are priced by the promoters. Call Boxing News at (0207) 882-1040 for details on what's on, where, and when.

Tennis

In the build-up to the world-famous Wimbledon championships, the smaller but equally popular Stella Artois tournament takes place in mid-June at Queens Club, Palliser Road, W14. Call (0207) 385-3421 and take the tube to Barons Court. Tickets range from £25 to £60. Book early.

Wimbledon fortnight starts the last week in June, and demand for tickets always far exceeds the supply. Tickets must be applied for well in advance and are awarded by ballot. To get tickets for Centre Court or Number One Court you have to write, enclosing a self-addressed envelope, for an application form, between September 1 and December 31: The All England Tennis Club, P.O. Box 98, Church Road, London, SW19. Phone (0208) 946-2244, or visit www.wimbledon.com. Tickets range £26–£66 for Centre Court and £24–£47 for Number One Court. You can usually get in by showing up on the day of the event and waiting to buy tickets for the outer courts; you can also buy returned tickets for the next day at a good price. Take the tube to Wimbledon (District line). Bring a hat or umbrella and plenty of sunblock.

Racing

Horse racing is very popular in Britain. You can see it almost every day on television, and every high street has at least one betting shop, or "turf accountant," as the Brits like to call them. Gambling is legal in Britain, and bookies will give odds on almost anything, from the gender of the next royal birth to whether it will snow on Christmas Day. A day at the races is as popular with the upper classes (members of which own the horses and can be seen at Ascot wearing hilarious hats that are never worn anywhere else) as it is with the working classes.

The flat season runs from April to September, and the jumps or steeplechase runs from October to April. As well as branches of the major corporate bookies like William Hill and Coral, there are many trackside bookies with whom it is much more fun to bet. They usually take win-only bets, with a minimum stake of £5. Watch the extraordinary ballet of arm swinging and hand signaling as they establish the odds. More complicated bets (exactas, trifectas, accumulators, and so on) can be made at the corporate bookies, or tote, as mentioned before.

All the tracks are just outside London and are well serviced by rail. Take a coat and umbrella, just in case. Most tracks have bars and restaurants, which serve notoriously bad food, so be warned. A day at the races is exactly that; be prepared for a longish haul. Racing venues include:

Ascot Race Course   High Street, Ascot, Berks (outside zones). Phone (0134) 462-2211 or visit www.ascot.co.uk. Take British Rail to Ascot rail. Admission is £7–£52, depending on whether you sit in the grandstand or the silver ring. (The royal enclosure is closed to commoners!) You can catch Her Majesty in June having a punt. Good competitive racing can always be seen here. One of the highlights of the year is the Royal Meeting with Ladies Day on the Thursday of that week.

Epsom   Epsom Downs, Epsom, Surrey (outside zones). Phone (0137) 247-0047 or visit www.epsomderby.co.uk. Take British Rail to Epsom Downs. Admission is £5–£20. This is where the Oaks and the Derby (pronounced "Darby") are held in June. Derby Day is a big betting day in England and is something of a national mood lifter. The winner is always part of the headline news, and most people have a bet. Tickets in the Queen's Stand and Derby Day cost up to £95. Don't forget your top hat and tails.

Kempton Park   Staines Road East (outside zones). Phone (0137) 247-0047 or visit www.kempton.co.uk. Take British Rail to Sunbury on Thames or to Kempton Park. Admission is £12–£16. This course hosts the King George VI stakes on Boxing Day, and has events all year. The summer evenings are particularly fun, with themes such as James Bond,

Irish music, or fireworks. You can bet on and watch the race from the new restaurant.

Sandown Park   The Racecourse, Portsmouth Road, Esher, Surrey (outside zones). Phone (0137) 247-0047 or visit www.sandown.co.uk. Take British Rail to Esher. Admission is £12–£18. This excellent track hosts the Whitbread Gold cup in April and the Coral Eclipse Stakes in July.

Windsor Maidenhead Road   Windsor, Berks (outside zones). Phone (0175) 349-8400 or visit www.windsor-racecourse.co.uk. Take British Rail to Windsor and Eton Riverside. Admission is £5–£18. This is a pretty part of England and worth a visit in its own right. The castle (still very much in use by Her Majesty) can be visited and overlooks the course. The Thames is green and beautiful out here, and you can take a boat to and from the racetrack from the town, making a grand day out.

Greyhound Racing

These sleek animals tear round the track after a wooden hare on a rail. They run amazingly fast, and the race is over in a minute or less. The same deal with the horse-racing corporate and trackside bookies applies, as do the warnings about food. There is a lot of beer drinking at the dog races, and they make for a very entertaining evening out, featuring lots of characters and florid language. Again, all tracks are well serviced by public transport but are far from the center of London. Greyhound-racing venues include:

Catford Stadium   Adenmore Road, SE6 (outside zones). Phone (0208) 690-8000. Take British Rail to Catford or Catford Bridge. Admission is £4.50 for adults, £2 for children. Races start at 7:20 p.m. on Mondays, Thursdays, and Saturdays.

Romford Stadium   London Road, Romford, Essex (outside zones). Phone (0170) 876-2345 or visit www.coraleurobet.co.uk. Take British Rail to Romford. Admission is £1.50–£6 and free on the popular side of the stadium on Thursday afternoon and Saturday morning. All races start at 7:30 p.m. and are held Mondays, Wednesdays, Fridays, and Saturdays. There are afternoon races on Thursday.

Walthamstow Stadium   Chingford Road, E4 (outside zones). Phone (0208) 531-4255 or visit www.wsgreyhound.co.uk. Take the tube to Walthamstow Central and then a minicab from there. Admission is £3–£6, and races are held at 7:30 p.m. on Tuesdays, Thursdays, and Saturdays. Afternoon races are also held on Mondays and Fridays, with free admission.

Wimbledon Stadium   Plough Lane, SW17, in zone 12. Phone (0208) 946-8000 or visit www.wimbledonstadium.co.uk. Take the tube to Wimbledon. Admission is £3–£5.50, and races start at 7:30 p.m. on Tuesdays and Thursdays through Saturdays.

Participation Sports

Gyms and Leisure Centers

Working out and staying in shape are as popular in Britain as in the United States, and gym culture flourishes. There are plenty of expensive and trendy gyms to work out or go posing at, but unless you have membership they can be expensive for a daily visit (£25–£50). There are far too many to list here, so look in the Yellow Pages under Leisure Centres to find one nearest you, or speak to your concierge. Many hotels, even the budget ones, have access to a gym or sports facility. Among the most popular is a chain of gyms called Holmes Place. These boast the usual extras like juice bars, saunas, steam rooms, Jacuzzis, and so on. Many hotels have their own facilities. What follows is a small list of sport and leisure in central London (please note that most of the leisure centers will expect you to do an "induction" to the gym (at a cost); and some of the busier centers have had to limit the gym facilities to members only):

Chelsea Sports Center (zone 11, Chelsea Manor Street, SW3, phone (0207) 352-6985; www.cclprovide.co.uk; tube: Sloane Square) Offers a 25-meter pool and aerobics classes, but you have to be a member to use the gym. They charge £3 to swim, £5 for yoga classes, and aerobics classes cost £4.

Jubilee Hall Leisure Center (zone 7 at 30 The Piazza, Covent Garden, WC2; phone (0207) 836-4835; www.jubileehallculbs.co.uk; tube: Covent Garden) This fully equipped gym (called the Gym at Covent Garden) has been refurbished with a new cardio theater, free weights, and resistance machines, and is in an excellent location. There are also yoga and various exercise classes. The cost is £8 for a day visit.

London Central YMCA (zone 2, 112 Great Russell St., WC1; phone (0207) 343-1700; tube: Tottenham Court Road). This is also very central, and totally comprehensive, with lots of classes. The cost is £15 per day and requires a photo ID.

Queen Mother Sports Center (zone 9 at 223 Vauxhall Bridge Rd., SW1; phone (0207) 630-5522; tube: Victoria) Very central, this center has been modernized to the tune of over £1 million and has a complete range of facilities, equipment, and classes; £7 gym, £4 class, and £2.50 pool.

Porchester Center in Queensway (zone 14, WZ; phone: (0207) 792-2919; www.courtneys.co.uk; tube: Queensway or Bayswater) Facilities include a 30-meter pool, gym, classes, and a wonderful health spa (Russian steam room, Turkish hot room, sauna, Jacuzzi, and plunge pool). The gym, pool, and spa are open daily; £7 gym, £2.65 pool, £4.75 class.

Seymour Leisure Center (zone 14 at Seymour Place, W1; phone (0207) 723-8019; tube: Marble Arch) This center has an Olympic-sized pool, steam rooms, cardiovascular machines, and exercise classes. Fees are £2.25 pool, £9.10 sauna/steam rooms, £7.15 gym, and £4.55 class.

Bicycling

You take your life into your hands bicycling around the streets of London, but there are parks to bike in that are wonderful. You can rent bikes near the golf driving range in Richmond Park; call (0208) 948-3209 for information. The London Bicycle Tour Company runs guided tours and also rents out bikes; call (0207) 928-6838 or visit www.londonbicycle.com.

Inline Skating

Rollerblades are popular in London, with plenty of good paths throughout Hyde Park and Battersea Park. There are hotdoggers with ramps and cones, as well as serious hockey players alongside the Albert Memorial in Hyde Park, which makes for good spectator sport. You can rent roller skates/blades at a number of sports stores; try **Queens Skate Shop**, 35 Queensway, W2; (0207) 727-4669, zone 14; tube Queensway or Bayswater; or **Snow & Rock,** 188 Kensington High Street, W8; (0207) 937-0872, zone 11; tube Kensington High Street. Both stores are conveniently located near Hyde Park. Prices are from £12 per day, £18 for a weekend, and £35 per week. They stock the newest models.

Horseback Riding

Though not exactly the sport of choice of the masses, there are beautiful places to ride in London. Hyde Park is an old favorite, with well-trodden riding paths like Rotten Row. Do not assume that riding in Hyde Park is without danger. You have to traverse a few streets and cross a busy main road to get into the park. The beasts are mostly of the warhorse variety, but you can occasionally get a bolter, and there's one place where they all want to canter. You can make arrangements to ride at the following:

Ross Nye Stables in zone 14 at 8 Bathurst Mews, W2; phone (0207) 262-3791; tube: Lancaster Gate or Paddington. The price is £35 per hour for a ride around Hyde Park (closed Monday); and £45 for individual lessons (Tuesday through Friday only). They won't take anyone under age 6 or anyone who weighs over 200 pounds. The stables are closed for a couple of months in the summer. Beginners and experienced riders are allowed, and children are encouraged. The horses here are gorgeous and well cared for, and they have plenty of ponies.

Hyde Park Stables in zone 14, 63 Bathurst Mews, W2; phone (0207) 723-2813; www.hydeparkstables.com; tube: Lancaster Gate or Paddington. Closed Mondays. The cost is £39 for group riding in the park, and £59 for a solo ride. I'm not crazy about this outfit, but it's the only option in summer and Easter holidays, when Ross Nye closes.

Wimbledon Village Stables in zone 12 at 24 High Street, Wimbledon, SW19, phone (0208) 946-8579; www.wvstables.com; tube: Wimbledon. The price is £30 per hour during the week, £38 on weekends. Expect to pay £15 extra for an individual lesson. This is outside London but worth a trip if you want to avoid automobile traffic. They have small classes for beginners, and you will be taken on a rugged ride through Wimbledon Common, Putney Heath, and Richmond Park, all of which are semiwild expanses. Look out for deer. This is a much more beautiful experience than Hyde Park, though less convenient.

Ice Skating

Considering the fact that it never really gets cold enough for any of the natural bodies of water to freeze over, there is a surprising number of proficient skaters in London, some of whom can be seen whizzing around at breakneck speeds on London's many ice rinks. Admission and skate rental are cheap, and skating can be a fun night out. During December and January there is a wonderful skating venue in the courtyard of the grand old Somerset House on the Strand (phone (0207) 845-4600; www.somerset-house.org.uk).

Broadgate Ice Rink (zone 3, Broadgate Circus, Eldon Street, EC2.; phone (0207) 505-4068; tube: Liverpool Street) Admission plus skate rental is £7 adult, £4 child. This tiny outdoor rink in the middle of London, among the glass castles of the financial district, is open late October through April. There's plenty of room to watch if you don't skate.

Leisure Box (zone 14, 17 Queensway, W2; phone (0207) 229-0172; tube: Bayswater or Queensway) Admission is £6.50, including skate hire. Friday and Saturday nights are disco nights. Good Chinese and Indian restaurants are in the immediate neighborhood for après skate. For those that find falling over again and again too painful, there is bowling at the same venue (see separate entry).

Swimming

Most of the leisure centers listed earlier have pools, but it is worth noting that almost every borough of London has at least one municipally run pool, some of which are more salubrious than others. To find your nearest pool, consult the Yellow Pages. Bearing in mind that no one comes to London for the great swimming, here's a list of some of the better dipping holes, and they're worth checking out when it's hot, although they do get crowded:

Hampstead Heath Ponds (zone 1, Millfield Lane, NW3; phone (0207) 485-3873; tube: Hampstead or Hampstead Heath or British Rail: Gospel Oak) Admission is free. These are three ponds in picturesque surroundings: one for men, one for women, and one for both. The segregated ponds are open all year. The mixed pond opens April through September only. There are no facilities except a basic changing area, so bring refreshments/picnics. The ponds are popular hangouts for gays.

The Lido (zone 1, Hampstead Heath at Gordon House Road, NW3; phone (0207) 485-3873; British Rail to Gospel Oak) Admission is £3.50, £1.50 for concessions. This is London's biggest outdoor pool and is only really worth going to on a hot day; it's open daily, April through September.

The Oasis (zone 7, 32 Endell Street, WC2; phone (0207) 831-1804; tube: Covent Garden or Holborn) Admission is £2.90 for adults, £1.10 for children over age 5, and free for children under age 5. There is an indoor pool, an outdoor pool, and a bathing deck for basking on those rare summer days.

Richmond Pools in the Park (zone 12 at Old Deer Park, Twickenham Road, Richmond, Surrey; phone (0208) 940-0561; www.springhealth leisure.com; tube: Richmond) Admission is £3 for adults, £2.40 for children, and free for kids under age 5. There is an indoor pool, an outdoor pool, and a lush grassy area for flopping on when it's hot.

Serpentine Lido (zone 14, Hyde Park; phone (0207) 706-3422 or Hyde Park at (0207) 298-2100; tube: Hyde Park Corner, Lancaster Gate, or Marble Arch) The Lido is open July through September only, from 10 a.m. to 6 p.m. daily. Admission is £2.70 for adults and 60p for children. Beware of geese excrement.

Karting

A very popular form of high-thrills entertainment, go-karting is catching on among laddish groups of young men. It's not cheap, but definitely exhilarating. The karts don't go all that fast, but it feels like they do. Venues are:

Daytona Raceway (outside zones, Atlas Road, NW10; phone (0500) 145–155; www.daytona.co.uk; tube: Nolt Acron or Willesden Junction) You can race for one hour for £50 or have a practice session of 15 minutes for £20. You'll need to prebook.

Playscape Pro Racing Streatham Kart Raceway (outside zones, 390 Streatham High Road, SW16; phone (0208) 677-8677; www.playscape. co.uk/karting; take British Rail to Streatham, make right out of station and walk for two minutes). The cost is £42.50 for two hours. Special rates available for children on request. It's open daily.

Teamworks Karting (zone 3, 82 The London Fruit Exchange, Brushfield Street, E1; phone (0870) 900-3020; www.teamworkskarting.com) Call Teamworks to be booked into one of the many indoor and outdoor tracks they use in the metropolitan area. Prices vary, and they offer a wide variety of options, from "arrive and drive" sessions to children's parties.

Bungee Jumping

If you just can't get enough thrills with any of the above sports, you could try jumping off a crane with the UK Bungee Club. The itinerant UK Bungee Club is based in Leeds but roams the country, setting up its cranes and making special appearances at major events. Phone (0700) 028-6433 to find out when they will next visit a site near London, or visit www.ukbungee.com. A regular jump from 170 feet above water costs £50. Tandem jumps and cage rides are also available, and for an extra £13 they will video the ordeal. Enjoy!

Yoga

In the past decade yoga has become as popular and mainstream as aerobics was in the 1980s, with new centers springing up, each cooler and more serene than the last. The added attraction could be that you may easily park your yoga mat next to a famous rock star or actor. The following is a list of the main yoga centers, although many leisure centers offer classes, too. If you want a good yoga teacher to come to your hotel for a class, for £40 you can call the excellent, Sivananda-trained Shakti Catherine Nelson at (0798) 417-7505, or Justine Bonner at (0778) 943-2112 (she's also a gifted massage therapist).

Innergy Yoga Center (zone 13, Acorn Hall, Kensal Road, W10; phone (0208) 968-1178; www.innergy-yoga.com; tube: Ladbroke Grove) This place is so cool that they didn't want to give me any information, and even their website resolutely avoids going into too much detail. All I can tell you is that it's seriously trendy, that classes are predominantly Hatha yoga, and that Madonna once did a class here and caused a great frisson of excitement amongst the locals. Classes are £8–£10.

Iyengar Yoga Institute (zone 14, 223A Randolph Avenue, Maida Vale, W9; phone (0207) 624-3080; www.iyi.org.uk; tube: Maida Vale) Classes here are devoted exclusively to the Iyengar practice—precise and slow yoga, which aims at perfecting the postures. There are over 50 classes each week—from beginners to advanced, as well as those for pregnant women, seniors, and teenagers. The Institute is open daily from 9 a.m. to 9 p.m. A membership fee (£35 for a year, £12 for three months) is payable if you attend more than twice. Classes for nonmembers range from £6 to £10.50.

The **Life Centre** (zone 13, 15 Edge Street, W8; phone (0207) 221-4602; www.thelifecentre.org; tube: Notting Hill Gate) A 60-minute class costs £9, a 90-minute class costs £11. The Life Centre offers classes in Sivananda, Ashtanga, and Iyengar yoga, but Ashtanga classes predominate; tai chi and Pilates are also available. Here you can get massages, too, as well as a number of other alternative therapies. Check the website for a schedule of visiting luminaries from the world of yoga.

Sivananda Yoga Vedanta Centre (zone 12, 51 Felsham Road, SW15; phone (0208) 780-0160; www.sivanandayoga.org; tube: Putney Bridge or East Putney then the #14 bus) Daily yoga classes are offered for all levels; open classes are £8 or less; some are free. Satsang and lectures are offered.

Triyoga (zone 1, 6 Erskine Road, Primrose Hill, NW3; phone (0207) 483-3344; www.triyoga.com; tube: Chalk Farm) A very serene spot in the heart of Primrose Hill, Triyoga runs a plethora of classes: Ashtanga, Iyengar, and Okido (a Japanese-style yoga, which focuses on energy balancing and adopts different postures from those more widely practiced by Westerners). Tai Chi, Pilates, post- and prenatal yoga classes are also offered. The center opens at 6:30 a.m., and the last classes are at 8 p.m. The cost is £9 for a one-hour class and £12 for a two-hour class. There are also treatment rooms offering a range of different massages, reflexology, facials, homeopathic treatments, and more.

Water Sports

For those who enjoy messing about on the river, there is plenty to do on the Thames and in the surrounding reservoirs and docklands. Thanks to insurance problems, many of the old watersports clubs no longer offer drop-in fun. But there is still one place that is full-service:

Docklands Sailing and Watersports Centre (zone 5 235A Westferry Road, E14; phone (0207) 537-2626; British Rail: Crossharbour or London Arena DLR) offers sailing, Dragon-boat racing, power boating, rowing, and canoeing. Day membership costs £15, and it's open daily.

Golf

The English Golf Union is an excellent resource for all golf information and can be reached at (0152) 635-4500. It would be worth the trip to the following courses based outside London if golf-withdrawal symptoms get bad! Courses outside the city include:

Richmond Park (zone 12, Roehampton Gate, Richmond Park, SW15; phone (0208) 876-3205; British Rail to Barnes) There are two 18-hole courses that cost £15 on weekdays and £18 on weekends. The price drops for games played late in the day.

Royal Mid-Surrey Golf Club (zone 12, Old Deer Park, Twickenham Road, Richmond, Surrey; phone (0208) 940-1894; British Rail or the tube to Richmond) There are two 18-hole courses here, and although it is a private club, visitors are welcome. Admission is £68 for the day, £45 after 1 p.m., and £28 after 4:30 p.m.

In central London you can get lessons or do a bit of teeing off at the following spots:

Dukes Meadows Golf Club (zone 12, Dukes Meadows, Great Chart-say Road, Chiswick, W4; phone (0208) 994-3314; www.golflessons.co.uk; tube: Hammersmith, then bus 190) The club is open daily 9 a.m. to 10 p.m. There is something for everyone here: a nine-hole course, a 50-bay driving range, a six-hole academy course (child-friendly), and a full teaching center. Golf-club hire is available. Wind down afterward in the restaurant and bar. The cost to play the nine-hole course is £8.50 on weekdays, £10 on weekends. On the driving range, you'll pay £4 for a bucket of balls.

Regents Park Golf School (zone 14, Outer Circle, Regents Park, NW1; phone (0207) 724-0643; www.rpgts.co.uk; tube: Baker Street) There is a driving range, a chipping and a bunker area, and lessons given by professionals. Membership is £75, although nonmembers are welcome. There is limited access to the facilities for nonmembers. Half-hour lessons are £30.

Tennis

Almost all London parks have tennis courts, which cost very little to play on. Bring your own racket and balls. There is usually a grass court or two and a few asphalt ones. It's very informal; just turn up on any weekday and you will almost certainly be able to play. The serious player should call the Lawn Tennis Association at the Queens Club in West Kensington (phone (0207) 381-7000). They will provide you with a booklet called "Where to Play Tennis in London."

Tenpin Bowling

Leisure Box (zone 14, 17 Queensway, W2; phone (0207) 229-0172; tube: Queensway or Bayswater) It's open 10 a.m. to 10 p.m., and the cost for adults is £5.50; you'll pay £4.50 for children before 6 p.m. and £5.50 thereafter. Soft-shoe rental costs £2. There are 12 lanes.

Streatham Mega Bowl (outside zones, 142 Streatham Hill, SW2; phone (0208) 671-5021; www.megabowl.co.uk; British Rail to Streatham Hill) This alley has 36 lanes and is open Tuesday through Saturday, 10 to 1:30 a.m. and Sunday through Monday, 10 a.m. to 11:30 p.m.

Hotel Index

Note: Page numbers in bold face type indicate hotel profiles.

Restaurant Index

Note: Page numbers in bold face type indicate restaurant profiles.

Subject Index

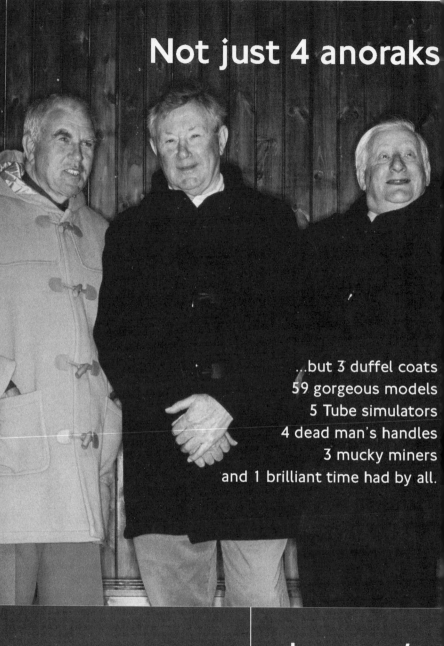

Unofficial Guide to London **Reader Survey**

If you would like to express your opinion about London or this guide-book, complete the following survey and mail it to:

> *Unofficial Guide* Reader Survey
> PO Box 43673
> Birmingham, AL 35243   USA

Inclusive dates of your visit: _____

Members of your party:	Person 1	Person 2	Person 3	Person 4	Person 5
Gender:	M F	M F	M F	M F	M F
Age:					

Have you ever been to Europe before? _____

Was this your first trip to London? _____

On your most recent trip, where did you stay? _____

Concerning your accommodations, on a scale of 100 as best and 0 as worst, how would you rate:

The quality of your room?   The value of your room?
The quietness of your room?   The reservation process?
Staff's relations with foreigners?   Overall hotel satisfaction?

Did you use public transportation?   What kind?

Concerning public transportation, on a scale of 100 as best and 0 as worst, how would you rate:

Ease of use?   Value vs. rental cars?
Cleanliness?   Hours and areas serviced?
Airport shuttle efficiency?

Concerning your dining experiences:

Estimate the number of meals eaten in restaurants per day. _____

Approximately how much did your party spend on meals per day? _____

Favorite restaurants in London: _____

_____

Did you buy this guide before leaving?   while on your trip?

How did you hear about this guide? (check all that apply)

Loaned or recommended by a friend   Radio or TV
Newspaper or magazine   Bookstore salesperson
Just picked it out on my own   Library
Internet

Unofficial Guide to London **Reader Survey (continued)**

What other guidebooks did you use on this trip? _____

_____

_____

On a scale of 100 as best and 0 as worst, how would you rate them?

_____

_____

Using the same scale, how would you rate *The Unofficial Guide(s)?*

_____

Are *Unofficial Guides* readily available at bookstores in your area? _____

Have you used other *Unofficial Guides?* _____

Which one(s)? _____

_____

_____

_____

_____

Comments about your London trip or *The Unofficial Guide(s):*

_____

_____

_____

_____

_____

_____

_____

_____

_____

_____

_____

_____